**THIS IS THE SHOCKING TRUE STORY
OF TWO BUDDIES AND HONORED NYPD
PARTNERS...**

LOUIS EPPOLITO
*Son of Ralph "Fat the Gangster" Eppolito;
joined the NYPD in 1969. Part-time actor.
Credits include* Goodfellas *and* Bullets Over Broadway

STEPHEN CARACAPPA
*Decorated Vietnam War veteran; joined the NYPD in 1969.
A commended undercover narcotics officer.
Created New York's organized-crime homicide unit.*

... WHO HAD A DIRTY LITTLE SECRET.

"It was the worst betrayal of the badge in the NYPD's history."
—John Marzulli, *New York Daily News*

"One of the most shocking examples of criminal activity I've ever witnessed."
—Brooklyn District Attorney Charles Hynes

"One of the most sensational police corruption cases in the city's history."
—CourtTV

"Probably the most heinous crimes ever tried in this courthouse."
—Brooklyn Federal Judge Jack B. Weinstein

**Praise for Greg Smith's
*MADE MEN***

"Smith writes... with great knowledge of his subject. [A] wonderful account."
—Jimmy Breslin

P9-CFY-886

MOB COPS

The Shocking Rise and Fall of New York's "Mafia Cops"

GREG B. SMITH

BERKLEY BOOKS, NEW YORK

THE BERKLEY PUBLISHING GROUP
Published by the Penguin Group
Penguin Group (USA) Inc.
375 Hudson Street, New York, New York 10014, USA
Penguin Group (Canada), 90 Eglinton Avenue East, Suite 700, Toronto, Ontario M4P 2Y3, Canada
(a division of Pearson Penguin Canada Inc.)
Penguin Books Ltd., 80 Strand, London WC2R 0RL, England
Penguin Group Ireland, 25 St. Stephen's Green, Dublin 2, Ireland (a division of Penguin Books Ltd.)
Penguin Group (Australia), 250 Camberwell Road, Camberwell, Victoria 3124, Australia
(a division of Pearson Australia Group Pty. Ltd.)
Penguin Books India Pvt. Ltd., 11 Community Centre, Panchsheel Park, New Delhi—110 017, India
Penguin Group (NZ), Cnr. Airborne and Rosedale Roads, Albany, Rosebank, Auckland 1310, New Zealand
(a division of Pearson New Zealand Ltd.)
Penguin Books (South Africa) (Pty.) Ltd., 24 Sturdee Avenue, Rosebank, Johannesburg 2196, South Africa

Penguin Books Ltd., Registered Offices: 80 Strand, London WC2R 0RL, England

MOB COPS

A Berkley Book / published by arrangement with the author

PRINTING HISTORY
Berkley mass-market edition / December 2006

Copyright © 2006 by Greg B. Smith
Cover design by Rita Frangie
Front cover photos: Louis Eppolito by Bryan Smith / Daily News Pix; Stephen Caracappa by Linda
Rosier / Daily News Pix; Detective badge © William Whitehurst / Corbis
Book design by Kristin del Rosario

ISBN: 0-425-21572-5

BERKLEY®
Berkley Books are published by The Berkley Publishing Group,
a division of Penguin Group (USA) Inc.,
375 Hudson Street, New York, New York 10014.
BERKLEY is a registered trademark of Penguin Group (USA) Inc.
The "B" design is a trademark belonging to Penguin Group (USA) Inc.

PRINTED IN THE UNITED STATES OF AMERICA

10 9 8 7 6 5 4 3 2 1

As always,
to Lizzie, Damon and Brendan.

ACKNOWLEDGMENTS

There are far too many to thank in this small space, so I'll do my best. Thanks first to attorney Ed Hayes, whose assistance, legal insight, and sartorial advice was crucial. Also much praise goes to Dave Giordano and Jack Ryan, tireless private investigators who swam the dark seas longer than most. Also much praise goes to attorneys Rae Koshetz and Bettina Schein for their attention to detail. This case would not have existed without John Peluso and Mark Manko of the United States Drug Enforcement Administration, two men whose insistent pursuit of every lead gave some comfort to the families of those who are gone. Also much credit goes to Assistant U.S. Attorney Robert Henoch, who helped transform all the notes into a symphony. To Greg O'Connell, one of the first to hear the tale, thanks for the history lesson. Thanks also to Leah Greenwald and her attorneys, Ben Brafman and Jennifer Liang, and to George Arzt and David Bookstaver for their help in bringing a difficult truth to light. And as always, much appreciation goes to my editor, Tom Colgan, and my agent, Jane Dystel.

ONE

The guy in the trunk made no sound. It was past midnight on a lonely highway headed out of New York and into the frigid darkness of New England. Inside the car the man at the wheel was all by himself, driving this highway in the middle of the night, the green light of the dashboard illuminating the underside of his face. He was a young man, about twenty-five years old, with a gaunt, tired face and thick eyeglasses. This was the middle of the winter, and cold pressed on the car's windows, increasing the young man's isolation. It was just the young man and the guy in the trunk.

The young man with the eyeglasses did not know the name of the guy in the trunk or precisely why he was there. He had been told to pick up the car and drive it to a spot off the highway somewhere in godforsaken Connecticut where there was a hole waiting, freshly dug. It was a simple plan. He was the delivery guy. That was it. He didn't actually kill the guy and he didn't see who did, so he couldn't say anything about that if he got pulled over by a state trooper for a busted taillight or something out here in the middle of nowhere. Still it would be an awkward moment. The more he thought about it, the more the young man concluded that the guy in the trunk was a very complex matter indeed.

"I drove myself and it made me very uncomfortable," the young man would say later. "I trembled all the way up to Connecticut in the car by myself. I was scared to death."

The way the young man explained the situation to himself was that he had no choice. He was a degenerate gambler. This was the phrase he himself used when describing his choices in life. If he drove around with a body in the trunk, it was all because he was a degenerate gambler. In this particular circumstance, he had borrowed a lot of money from an ex-cop named Wes Daley, and now Wes needed a favor.

"I felt that if I had said no, I would have had some type of problem with Wes over the money I owed," the young man said.

The year he received his bar mitzvah was the year the young man first began to gamble.

"I don't think I was very good," he often said. "I never won."

He had started out with much promise. He got into a high school called Brooklyn Tech, a prestigious school that required a rigorous devotion to academic excellence. He was not up to the task. Sometimes his father would take him to the track. For some young men, this was not a big deal. They bet on a trifecta and walked back into the world of homework and sports and friends and that was it. But not for this young man. When he gambled and lost, he only wanted to gamble and win. In his sophomore year, he was gambling and losing and so he had to leave Brooklyn Tech. He transferred to the far less demanding Manual Training High School and managed to graduate. He continued to gamble.

This was odd because the young man was aware of the vulnerabilities inherent in gamblers. Gambling was at odds with one of the guiding principles of his neighborhood in Brooklyn. This was the guiding principle that dictated under no circumstances do you become a rat. He would put it this way:

"In my background, when you gamble, then you become a liar, and then you become a stool pigeon."

It was possible the young man could have risen above all this. He had survived and prospered in the U.S. Navy. When the Korean conflict broke out he signed up and got a job as a full-time participant in the Cold War with a top security clearance. He served in Japan and Washington, D.C., where he was a radio operator assigned to copy Russian transmissions. This information was considered so vital to national security that he had to swear his allegiance to the president. He promised to fight to the death against every member of the Communist Party he came across, even aunts and uncles. He got so good at it, the National Security Agency tried to recruit him, but in 1956 he had done his time and returned to his old neighborhood in Brooklyn.

He got married to a beautiful girl from the neighborhood. She was kind and good and her father was a cop in the New York City Police Department. He was surrounded by good people and making a decent paycheck. His father, an electrician, had opened an appliance store and hired him when he returned from the navy. The job gave him a working knowledge of electrical appliances such as washing machines and dryers and air conditioners, and soon he began to install air conditioners all over Brooklyn. He was married and was even a father. His only child was born in October 1960.

For a while, the young man was a taxpaying citizen of Brooklyn with a family and a job and a car and a house, which for many would have been good enough. But for this young man, it was not. He decided he could handle a little gambling here and there. He did not know that a little gambling here and there usually turns into a lot of money owed.

"I first started borrowing from the loan sharks in 1958, two years out of the navy," he said.

When he gambled and lost, he had to pay. When he hadn't installed enough air conditioners to pay, he borrowed more. First he went to banks, but they stopped opening the door because he wasn't paying them back. Then he went to high-interest commercial lenders, but even they wouldn't help him after a number of months with no checks. Then he did what tens of thousands of guys had done before him—he turned to the neighborhood shylock.

He turned to quite a few. One was called Charlie P. The way it worked was he would make weekly payments toward the interest without ever paying off the principal. The only way to do that was to pay the entire amount borrowed all at once. That way Charlie P. would be collecting for a long time. The young man started off paying on time but soon he couldn't keep up. The young man was told that he would have his knees broken. When his wife learned of this, she asked her father the cop for help. Her father was a clean cop, but he knew certain people in the neighborhood, including a man named Christy "Tic" Furnari, an old-school Mafiosi who was a respected soldier in the organized crime group named after Gaetano Tommy "Two-Fingers Brown" Lucchese. Christy Tic was either a man of honor or a racketeer, depending on who you asked. The young man's father-in-law asked Christy Tic for help as a favor, and Christy Tic agreed to help out.

Because he was who he was, Christy Tic was able to find a way to make everyone happy. He arranged for the young man to pay only principal to Charlie (no interest), but to pay the money directly to Christy Tic. Charlie P. the shylock had no choice. The young man was intelligent and not the type of degenerate gambler Christy Tic usually encountered, so he took a liking to him.

Christy Tic could not help with the young man's Wes Daley problem. Daley was a retired New York City cop who had serious difficulties locating the thin blue line that separates the civilian world from the underworld. Daley collected a police pension at the same time he was a loan shark. The young man was into Wes up to his neck. This was why he drove the car on a frigid night, following directions to a lonesome spot off the highway in the cold hours before dawn.

When he arrived at the appointed spot, the young man was met by an associate of Wes Daley. He did not know the associate's name and he did not ask. Immediately there was a problem. The ground was frozen as solid as the rink at Rockefeller Center. Nothing would penetrate. There was now a guy in the trunk and no hole to put him in. The young man and the associate had to figure things out because there was nothing they could do about the sun coming up in a few hours. They did not want that guy in the trunk during daylight hours.

A lot of guys in their mid-twenties worry about car payments, their career, how they're going to pay for their kids' college. This young man had to worry about these things, plus figure out what to do about a guy in the trunk. He decided to drive down to Long Island Sound.

There he and his associate opened the trunk and pulled out the body. They walked it to the black water and tossed the guy in. They did what they were supposed to do, and they did it without knowing anything at all about the guy now sinking to the bottom of Long Island Sound. For the young man, not knowing the guy's name or whether he had a wife and kids was a good thing. Knowing about that guy would mean thinking about the unsettling thing he had just done.

The young man's name was Burt Kaplan. One day when he thought about it, he would say, "As I look at my life in retrospect, I did a lot of unsettling things."

1944

The day the only Mob boss ever put to death by the state was electrocuted at Sing Sing, Burt Kaplan was ten years old. He was small and skinny with glasses, a kid from the neighborhood who lived in a three-story walkup on Vanderbilt Avenue in Bedford-Stuyvesant, almost the exact center of Brooklyn, New York. Burt was one of two sons of a self-taught electrician who toiled for his nation in the Brooklyn Navy Yard. He moved to Vanderbilt Avenue when he was five years old and this was all he knew. It was four years into the war. Winchell railed at the *Mirror*, the Fifth Army marched toward Rome, Anne Baxter and Thomas Mitchell starred in *The Fighting Sullivans*. Dodgers fans in Brooklyn had to live with the Yankees winning yet another World Series the previous season with a pitcher named Spud. This was the kid's world.

Burt was handy with numbers. Now that he was ten he was just beginning his Hebrew studies for his bar mitzvah. He was the kind of kid who did what he was told. He rinsed and flattened cans for the war effort, saved newspapers, and he was allowed to curse Hitler and the Japs. He had his heroes.

At the top of the list was his father, Ralph, a man who pulled his family through the Depression when everything looked like it was all going to hell. When the war came he got work at the Navy Yard in Brooklyn and saved enough to buy a three-story walk-up on Vanderbilt Avenue. It was the Kaplan family home.

The ten-year-old also had other heroes. The Fighting Sullivans. General Eisenhower. Anybody who was putting it to those Nazi bastards. And there was always Dem Bums, the unforgettable underdogs of all time, the Brooklyn Dodgers. When you were ten years old, how could you not love a guy like Pistol Pete Reiser? He crashed into outfield walls and stole more bases for the Dodgers than Jimmy Cagney stole scenes in *The Public Enemy*. Now, that was a hero.

For ten-year-old boys on Vanderbilt Avenue, heroes mostly lived in comics. *Military Comics* had Blackhawk. *All-American Comics* had Green Lantern. *Detective Comics* had Batman. The Justice Society of America did battle with gangsters and hoodlums and thugs and Nazis and Japs and all the other forces of evil in the twentieth century. All of the comics offered simple stuff. Black and white. Right and wrong. Not a whole lot of gray. For gray, you turned to the newspapers.

In New York in 1944, there was a lot of gray. The *Times*, the *Journal-American*, the *Herald Tribune*, the *World-Telegram*, the *Mirror*, the *Daily News*, the *Post*, the *Sun*, the *Brooklyn Eagle*. On the sports pages were mostly black and white. In the rest of the newspaper you got your fix of gray. On this Sunday morning, March 5, 1944, the front page of the *New York Times* was filled with gray:

LEPKE IS PUT TO DEATH, DENIES GUILT TO LAST; MAKES NO REVELATION

If you were from certain neighborhoods in Brooklyn, you might have another kind of hero. His name might be Louis "Lepke" Buchalter. "Lepkelen," his mother, Rose, called him. "Little Louie." He'd grown up on the Lower East Side, his father a failing hardware store owner with eleven children to feed and clothe. Growing up, Lepke was a small, skinny Jewish kid, handy with the numbers, just like Burt. By the time Burt Kaplan was memorizing baseball statistics, Lepke Buchalter was neither a war hero nor a baseball star. He was, instead, running one of the most powerful and violent under-world empires ever created in the history of the United States.

By the morning of March 5, 1944, Lepke was not as well known as Meyer Lansky or Dutch Schultz or Benny Siegel, probably the most famous of the Jewish gangsters. His exploits had not filled nearly as many pages as those of the Italian gangsters, Frank Costello or Charlie "Lucky" Luciano or Vito Genovese or Tommy "Two-Fingers Brown" Lucchese. But in many ways, he was the most successful of all of them.

Lepke, like most criminals, started out crude. He burglarized lofts and got caught. He acquired aliases—Louis Buckhouse, Louis Kawar, Louis Cohen. He stayed small-time until he replaced his boss, Augie Orgen, by having the man and his bodyguard, Jack "Legs" Diamond, shot repeatedly. Lepke and his childhood accomplice, Jacob "Gurrah Jake" Shapiro, were the most likely suspects, but there were no witnesses and so neither received any form of career inhibition. Instead, they filled the corner office themselves and took over what Augie had started.

A key element to Lepke's success was to maintain the silence of those who participated in his schemes. Silence meant freedom; informants meant prison. Thus was born Murder, Incorporated. Lepke himself never used the term. It was, like so much else in the underworld, an invention of the newspapers. But it was certainly apt in its description. All homicides committed were a matter of business.

Lepke was obsessed with silence, so he hired the best. His team included Albert Anastasia, whom the papers had dubbed the Lord High Executioner, as if he were a character from *Camelot* and not a sociopath from Brownsville. He had Abe "Kid Twist" Reles, who saw that the ice pick in the ear was the most efficient method, from his point of view. Sixty, seventy, eighty murders. This went on for years. He rose up from the Lower East Side tenements to wear tailored suits, learned to play golf, and married the daughter of a barber from London, Beatrice Wasserman. Mostly nothing of consequence could be tied to Lepke. Then came the candy man from Brooklyn, Rosen.

Rosen had owned a trucking company that Lepke's thugs had attached themselves to like lampreys. He had been forced out of that business, and taken up the sale of candy in Brooklyn. But he was upset about this, and soon Lepke had heard Rosen was talking with the most ambitious man in America, Special Rackets Prosecutor Thomas E. Dewey. "Rosen's shooting his mouth off that he's going down to Dewey," Lepke said, and Lepke hated informants. Rosen was shot down in the street near his candy store. At that moment, he became known forever after in the papers as "the Brooklyn candy man."

In the Sunday paper were all the details. At 4:45 P.M., Buchalter's pretty wife, Betty, and his twenty-two-year-old adoptive son, Harold, appeared in the gangster's cell to beg him to cooperate with the U.S. attorney and reveal what they described as "a widespread coalition between crime and politics."

"He'll listen to you, Lou," she begged. "God knows you can tell him enough to save you."

"Look," he said, "suppose I did talk to him. Suppose he asks for a reprieve. What's the best I can expect? I'll tell you, they'll give me another six to eight months, at best a year. No, Betty; if that's the case, I'd rather go tonight."

The papers that had for years called him the "overlord of the underworld" now noted that he entered the death chamber "a beaten, frightened little man." They noted that he came after his two codefendants, Mendy Weiss and Louis Capone. Capone said nothing; Weiss made some incoherent declarations about "I am here on a framed-up case and Governor Dewey knows it."

Then came Lepke. He said nothing as he was escorted into the room and was able to sit himself down in the chair without assistance. He was a tough guy to the end. The electrical current was applied at 11:13 P.M., Saturday night. At 11:16 P.M., the prison physician placed a stethoscope on Lepke's chest and declared, "I pronounce this man legally dead."

That was it. That was the end of the "overlord of the underworld," the only boss of organized crime who would ever be put to death by the state. The *New York Times* wrote, "Lepke, the man who, it was rumored, had something, had everything to say, who was going to make sensational revelations involving high public officials and nationally known labor leaders, had not a word to say."

This was the lesson for the ten-year-old Burt Kaplan growing up on Vanderbilt Avenue—there is something worse than death: being a rat.

The kids in Brooklyn all understood this. No rat was Lepke. There was nothing worse than a rat. You could be the overlord of the underworld. You could be implicated in up to eighty murders. You could have ordered your best friend killed, as Lepke had done. You could make money off working people by adding a mob tax to the clothing they buy. You could make a mockery of the unions that were supposed to bring a bit of dignity to an otherwise dreary existence. You could pay other men to keep your empire intact by sticking ice picks in ears. All of this you could do, and none of it was as bad as being a rat. The worse thing anyone could do was tattletale.

So Burt Kaplan was ten years old when the old Jewish gangster sat in the chair and said nothing. There was more of a lesson in that than in anything he could pick up in school. Knowing that he would be sitting down in the chair, feeling those straps go around his wrists and ankles, feeling that metal crown encircle his skull, Lepke stayed true to the neighborhood. Here was a man who had committed innumerable atrocities. Here was a man for whom the prospect of the afterlife, if he chose to believe in it, might seem foreboding. If there was a heaven and a hell and all the rest, and if Lepke cared, he surely knew where he was headed. But Lepke knew the rule of the neighborhood:

Hell is better than being a rat.

With gambling, there is no such thing as enough money. There is never enough to win, never enough to lose, never enough to borrow. For Burt Kaplan, the quest for money was never-ending.

He worked installing air conditioners, which paid him not enough. He also got involved in the interstate shipment of stolen goods. In the 1960s and early 1970s, this was a popular method for making money in certain neighborhoods. Burt was a kind of broker. He would hear about something being stolen, buy some of the stolen goods, and then resell them at a profit. This was a form of basic capitalism that existed on the edge of the world, and Burt did well enough with it to sometimes pay off his gambling debts to Christy Tic and Wes Daley and everyone else.

The problem with dealing in stolen anything is sometimes you get caught. In June 1961, his only daughter, Deborah, was four months from her first birthday. At this time, Burt got himself arrested by the New York City Police Department on charges of possessing stolen goods. In three weeks he was acquitted. He went right back to larceny. In January 1966, when his daughter was five years old, he got caught trying to sell stolen flashcubes. This time it was a federal case. While he was waiting for that case to unspool, he was charged by the city cops with possessing stolen hair dryers. Within three months, the hair dryer case was dismissed and Burt got two years' probation on the federal flashcubes case.

On September 7, 1972, when his daughter was almost twelve years old, his record of walking away from bad choices ended. He had tried to sell pants stolen from an overseas shipment, and this time they had Burt with a boatload of pants and the prior stolen flashcubes case. He appeared before Judge Jack Weinstein in federal court in Brooklyn. Weinstein had a reputation as a man who would listen to what a defendant had to say.

On December 8, 1972, Burt Kaplan stood before Weinstein and said, "This arrest taught me a lesson. I started spending all my nights home. I went to work and I became successful at my job and I became successful at my marriage and I'm home every night at seven o'clock and I spend all my spare time with my family." He insisted that he had stopped going to the track and had turned his life around.

"I think I have a good future in this business, Your Honor," he said. "I'm not doing anything criminal."

Judge Weinstein could see Burt's daughter, Deborah, and his wife, Eleanor, in the court, but he sent Burt to prison for four years. He gave him a few weeks to get ready, which meant that Burt entered a federal prison for the first time in his life on February 9, 1973. He was held at the Metropolitan

Correctional Center in lower Manhattan for six days, than sent off to Lewisburg Penitentiary to serve a four-year term.

In a few months Kaplan wrote a letter to Judge Weinstein, asking him to write to prison officials to give him a shot at early release.

"I have never been involved in any violence in any form, physical or verbal in my life. I detest it and all it stands for," he said, forgetting to mention the trip to Connecticut with the guy in the trunk. "I promise you that the name of Burton Kaplan will never again come before you or the court or any court again in regards to anything that is against the law."

Weinstein was a reasonable man. He met hundreds of men who were never going to amount to anything, and he recognized possibility when it showed up in his court. The judge intervened, and by April 1974, when Burt's daughter was thirteen years old, he got an early release. This was it for Burt. He promised the judge that his family came first, that he no longer felt the need to gamble, that he could earn an honest living. He was going to make it without breaking laws.

He was out of prison when he got a telephone call from a friend from Lewisburg who was also just getting out, and the two of them decided it was time to buy a decent leisure suit. Burt knew of a flea market in Brooklyn where you could buy clothes at seriously discounted prices. It was not clear precisely where these clothes came from or why they were so cheap, but Burt was not the kind of guy who asked a lot of questions. He and the friend from prison were looking at the leisure suit when his friend from the flea market who was selling asked him how much Burt thought they were worth.

"I asked him if he wanted a price for swag, which is stolen, or legitimate. He said swag. And I said twenty dollars. He said to me how would you like to buy these legitimate for twelve dollars? I said I would love to buy a lot of them, and I said, could I borrow some for a few hours? And he said yes."

He and his friend from prison loaded up a truck and drove up to Connecticut to a discount store owner Burt knew. When Burt asked the store owner what he thought the suits were worth, the owner asked the same question Burt asked: stolen or legitimate? Burt said stolen, and the owner guessed the suits were worth twenty dollars apiece.

"I said, 'How would you like to buy a lot of them for eighteen dollars or seventeen dollars?' And he said, 'I'd like to buy a lot. How many do you have?' I said, 'The guy has three thousand.' He said, 'I'll buy them all.' "

The next day the deal collapsed because snow crushed the discount store owner's roof. There was a frantic phone call or two, but Burt got another idea. He rented out a vacant fruit store on New Utrecht Avenue in Brooklyn, built racks with two-by-fours and pipe, and bought a thousand leisure suits at twelve dollars apiece from the flea market on credit. Starting at 5:00 A.M. and working like a dog, he started calling around to friends and associates, telling them he had swag leisure suits for eighteen dollars apiece. By 1:00 P.M. he sold them all. That was six thousand dollars profit in eight hours.

"We went back and took another thousand and by Sunday we had sold the three thousand suits," Burt said. "I thought this was a very good business and we decided to go into it. We started a hundred percent legitimate."

Slowly, just like thousands of businessmen across America, Burt began to service customers with bigger and bigger wallets. He was an entrepreneur who sold a little bit of glamour to the little people. He bought closeout jeans from Gloria Vanderbilt and Calvin Klein and sold them at a profit to Kmart, Macy's, Nordstrom's, and discount firms around the nation. Because of Burt, working people could walk around in designer jeans just like those glittery people at Studio 54. He opened a warehouse on Staten Island and paid his taxes. He hired lawyers to defend himself against lawsuits. He made mortgage payments, car payments, insurance payments. He put money away for his daughter's college fund. He participated in the economy and obtained the credibility necessary to obtain large sums of credit that would allow him to borrow toward his next clothing sale. He was legit.

And then sometimes he wasn't. With Burt Kaplan, there was no such thing as black and white. There was only gray. He was making good money selling closeouts to discount stores, but he somehow always needed a little more, and soon he found a simple way to get it.

To Burt and anyone else in the business of clothing, it was clear that a pair of denim jeans with the name of an important designer from France or Italy stitched on the back pocket was worth far more than one without the name. Just the name. It didn't matter whether the clothing itself was actually made by Calvin Klein or Gloria Vanderbilt or Champion. This was the perfect moneymaking venture. Buy cheap jeans that are not Jordache, pay some sweat shop to stitch Jordache on the back pocket, then sell Jordache jeans. Or Calvin Klein. Or Gloria Vanderbilt. These were called "knockoffs."

"It's when you take a label that a designer makes or a large company and you counterfeit it, you copy it," he said. "We bought sweatshirts from China, had them made to the exact specifications as Champion, and put their labels on it."

With Burt Kaplan, it was impossible to be 100 percent legitimate. He made too much money selling knockoffs, so he kept doing it. Here was a guy who believed that a man's word was his bond and yet he sold fakery to his customers. Here was a man who believed that informing on your fellow man was worse than murder, and yet he continued to gamble, which he believed was the first step toward becoming a stool pigeon. An informant. A rat.

In a single day, you could have a business lunch with a vice president of Gloria Vanderbilt, and then visit the Nineteenth Hole bar at end of Brooklyn to deliver an envelope to Christy Tic, who was now a captain in the Lucchese crime family.

This was the unexplainable world of Burt Kaplan.

**Las Vegas
October 26, 2004**

A squat man in a suit waited for a priest. The man had thinning black hair slicked back like a saloon owner in a B Western. Clearly he worked out a lot. He filled out his suit. His face was square with tiny black dots where his eyes should be, and he was tan all year round. He indulged in an occasional facial, and he colored his hair at the temples, where it was going silver. He didn't have a wife or kids and he was fifty-one years old. He was an accountant, with a license and everything. It was a little before eleven in the morning, and he was waiting for the priest to come by his office in central Las Vegas and offer a blessing to his workplace. He was a man in the modern world, but he still needed Old World stuff like this. If he thought about it even for a minute, he would have to admit he had an awful lot to tell the priest. In truth, the blessing was something he really could use.

"Hello, Father," he said when the priest arrived.

The squat man's name was Steven Corso. For a long time, he'd had a good run. He was once a partner in a growing accounting firm in Manhattan. He told people he'd always make at least a million a year, and he looked like he was telling the truth. Mostly he handled people's income taxes and gave financial advice on the side. He made so much money he expanded his New York practice to Las Vegas. This had been a mistake. He already had problems with gambling in New York, and coming to Vegas was like taking an alcoholic to a keg party. Twenty days earlier the Flamingo Hotel had entered a judgment against him for the $22,723 he owed. He had reached the point at age fifty-one where all he thought about—morning, noon, and night—was money.

If he chose to, Steve Corso, C.P.A., could tell the priest all about how he began to cheat everybody he met. It turned out it was easy to do. He would write two tax forms for certain clients. One form would show how the client deserved a big refund. The other would show how the same client owed money. He would send the first to the IRS and have the IRS send the refund check directly to Corso, C.P.A. He would tell the client to write the check for the money owed to a trustee account and he promised to send the proper amount to the IRS. This he would forget to do. He would cash the client's check, and in this manner he believed he was smarter than everybody.

He took $285,000 from one client, $465,000 from another, $669,000 from another. It began to add up, and by the morning in 2002 when he was driving to work in Manhattan and his cell phone rang, he'd stolen $5,329,566. On the phone was his office manager informing him that the IRS and the FBI were in his file cabinets at that very moment, placing papers in boxes. Steve Corso, C.P.A., immediately flew back to his four-thousand-square-foot stucco home in Vegas with a pool and two fireplaces and called his lawyer. He didn't mention any of this to the priest.

The priest spoke earnestly about football in a philosophical manner, like Spencer Tracy in *Boys Town*.

"The team that has the best defense is number five and the team with the fifth-best defense is number one," the priest said. "But that's football."

Steve Corso could have stopped the football talk and gotten down on his knees and wept. He could have told the priest how he had been indicted back in Connecticut and that he'd agreed to plead guilty to a long list of criminal activities. He could have told the priest how the IRS decided he stole $5.4 million and that he was about to go to jail for ten years easy. But he didn't have to. Corso had decided he would never spend even a single night in prison. He had begged and the IRS and the FBI had said, All right, you can come with us. That was why as the priest talked about football, Steve Corso had two objects inside his suit coat. One was an envelope with a donation for the priest. The other was a small recording device loaned to him by the FBI to tape conversations.

"In the name of the Father and of the Son and of the Holy Spirit," said the priest. "In his own life, Christ Jesus showed us the dignity of labor and he took to the work of the carpenter and was known as the carpenter's son. By working with his own hands he transformed toil from being an eternal curse into being a source of blessing."

How did this apply to Steve Corso, C.P.A.? Was there any dignity of labor in this little session with the priest and the tape recorder? Was Corso transforming toil from an eternal curse into a source of blessing?

"If we do our work well, whatever it may be, we purify ourselves," the priest continued. "Our work enables us to practice charity and to help those who are less fortunate. Let us bless this place then, that we will be showered with blessings on all who are working in this place. Let us pray. O God in Your wise providence, You have blessed all human labor, the work of our hands and of our minds."

Steve Corso did not suddenly blurt out, "Father, I have sinned!" He did not interrupt his performance and tell the priest he was secretly recording this sacred moment. He did what he was supposed to do. He acted the part of FBI inform-ant, and the priest had no clue.

"Let us proclaim that all who have business in this office will through Your guidance and support make the right deci-sions and carry them out fairly and justly," the priest said. "We ask this through Christ our Lord. Amen. Father, we ask for Your presence that this office may truly be blessed."

The priest gave one more sign of the cross and said Amen, then began describing a disturbing moment he'd ex-perienced recently during a visit to a prison hospital, where he saw an eighteen-year-old boy who was sick and hand-cuffed to a gurney.

"What is the eighteen-year-old kid in for?" Corso asked.

"I don't know," said the priest. "I know he had an eight-to-ten-year sentence."

That was a possibility for Steve Corso. Ten years. He had agreed to record his friends in Las Vegas, and if that produced certain results, he'd have a chance to do less than ten and maybe even no time at all. He was embarking on a new career: FBI informant. He was now Steve Corso, the FBI's secret weapon in Vegas. He was going to root out corruption from its hiding places on the Strip and in the pits. But first he had to pay the priest.

"Thank you, Father," Corso said, handing the priest the en-velope he'd prepared. "That's for the church. I'll call you next week. We can do this again."

The priest took the money and said good-bye. The record-ing machine went silent.

Seven hours after he was finished secretly recording the Roman Catholic priest, Corso drove in his car and talked into his tape recorder. He was getting into this role. He told his FBI handlers listening in that he was off to meet with a guy called Johnny M and two guys Gerry Chilli had sent. Gerry Chilli was a soldier in the Bonanno criminal organization back in New York who had been around forever, and the FBI had come to believe that he and the Bonanno family were in control of certain activities in Vegas. Since tape-recording priests would likely not produce any high-profile press conferences, Steve Corso was clear on his mission: take down the Mob in Vegas.

In truth, Steve Corso was really not much more than an accountant. But his father was a labor mediator who due to his job knew certain gangsters back in New York, and over the years Steve had met a few and acted as their accountant. This was why the FBI and the IRS didn't just throw him in jail for stealing millions from his clients. They needed him, and he knew it.

All he had to offer was a few guys from the Bonanno family who hung around a social club in Vegas called the Italian Senior Citizens Society. It wasn't much, but it was a start. For a year he'd been out there working undercover. Two of his clients were the gangsters who controlled a strip club called the Crazy Horse Too. He did the returns of strippers and bartenders. None of the returns were legitimate, and the FBI knew it. He'd also hooked up with Mike Frate, a big guy from Brooklyn who'd come out to Vegas with the former boss Joseph Bonanno to be his driver. Joe Bonanno had retired and written a book about what a man of honor he was and how the Mafia really did exist, and then prosecutors in New York used the book to indict everybody in the world-famous Commission case. Joe Bonanno was dead but Mike Frate was still around, and Steve Corso put him on his list of targets for the FBI.

On this day, almost precisely two years after the FBI first confronted him with his many sins and he agreed to help them out, Steve Corso exited his car in the parking lot of La Scala, what passed for an Italian restaurant in Vegas. It was 5:13 P.M., just in time for the Early Bird Special. This was fortuitous, because Corso could see the two "guys" sent by Gerry Chilli were two of the oldest people he'd seen since his last visit with his mother at the nursing home.

"How are you?" he said. "You must be a friend of Gerry's."

He addressed a stooped old Jewish guy named Morty, who was wearing shorts and black socks and had a voice like rocks in a bucket. The old man was accompanied by an old woman who sounded like Betty Boop, if Betty had lived that long. They were with Johnny M, who sound like Fred Flintstone or any other guy who felt the need to shout when just speaking would do.

"I'm Morty. My wife, Kina. This is Johnny."

"I recognized you because you wanted to wear shorts," Steve said.

At the bar, Johnny M ordered Cuervo Gold and asked if they had the "Spess-ee-al." To Morty he shouted, "You wanna Patrón?"

"I'm gonna wait," Morty said. "If I start now . . ."

Almost immediately Morty worked in their "friend" back in New York. He called him Gerard.

"When I say Gerard, it's Gerry," Morty said. "Only two people call him Gerard: his wife and me." He ordered a veal chop "with a little sweet peppers," which he pronounced "pepp-iz." They all raised their glasses.

"To health, family, real people. To more men like my friend."

Steve asked, "How did you two meet?"

"She come in for a part-time bar job," he said. "I was sitting at the bar. I fell off the chair when she walked in. I really actually flipped."

Johnny M said, "To the prettiest girl in Vegas."

"I'm not going to argue with you," he said, pulling out his wallet. "You want to see something? Take a look at that. That's my favorite picture."

"That is a great picture," Steve said.

"When I met Kina in '62, '63, I was twenty-one years old."

Morty had a hundred stories, all leading back to Gerry Chilli. There was a guy who insulted Gerry, and Morty went after the guy and Gerry called him an Indian, as in wooden Indian, as in stand-up guy. He thought it was hilarious that his wife didn't know what Indian meant.

"It could mean a hard-on," said the wife.

"That's priceless," Corso said.

Morty remembered a guy coming into a bar and threatening everybody if they didn't put his joker poker machines in that day. Morty called up Gerry Chilli, who called the bar.

"Gerry's in Florida, he calls the bar. The guy runs out the door. We never found out who the son of a bitch was. That was aggravating," Morty said. "There's a couple of names left from the old school, they will not be happy until everybody's behind bars or in the grave. And the Chilli name was one of them. I asked somebody today, I'll do a little gambling. What are they gonna give me, eight months, nine months? I wouldn't even say I'm sorry. Your Honor, I had to make a living. You know what I get a kick out of? Gerry calls me up, it's ten-thirty at night. That's rare. He goes, Turn on the TV right now. He says, Are you watching this shit? No, but I know what you're watching. You're watching Victoria Gotti. He went crazy."

"I watched that show for the first time," said Johnny M.

"And you didn't shut it off?" Morty said.

"Sly," Johnny said. "Oh, yeah."

"Sly? No no no. Not even sly. She shouldn't."

"But she's up there. The money."

"The money? So what?" said Morty, his voice rising. "You know what you gotta be on this earth? You gotta be a slut? I don't agree with that. Paris Hilton is opening a joint now. I wouldn't let my granddaughter watch the show. Paris Hilton. Michael Jackson. You gotta be a slut, a pervert, then you'll make the money. No wonder all these people overseas in the Far East hate us."

"How old?" Steve asked.

"How about seventy-five?"

"Who?"

"My honey," said Morty. "She'll be seventy-six Christmas Eve. I'm on this earth, oh, what an experience. They're all dead, so I can talk about them. While they were alive, I couldn't. I don't meet too many real people in Las Vegas."

"Believe me," Steve said, "neither do I."

December 2, 2004

He was cruising into the lot at Caesar's Palace with the radio on as Patti Page crooned, "Have yourself a merry little Christmas."

Steve Corso was on the job, all wired up and headed out to meet with a potential new client and his wife at Il Molino, an Italian restaurant inside a mall at Caesar's Palace. In New

York, the Italian restaurants are on the street. In Vegas, they're in strip malls.

Corso was here because Mike the driver told Steve the accountant about Lou the cop. Mike said Lou was a detective from way back in the Sixty-second Precinct but he was a stand-up guy. Corso didn't want anything to do with Lou the cop. He didn't like cops; he didn't trust them. But Mike the driver said Lou was okay. His father was with the Gambinos, and so was his uncle until we didn't speak about him anymore. Lou the cop was trying to break big in the movies. He'd written a book and it was going to be a movie, too. Lou was looking for investors in his movies. Mike had coughed up twenty-five thousand dollars in a shoebox. Lou had no problem with twenty-five thousand dollars in a shoebox. It was money, just like the stuff all those guys on Wall Street stole from all those companies. Corso the accountant said he would meet Lou the cop to talk about movies, and Mike the driver set up the meeting.

They had met about six times in the past month, and in that time, Corso had met the entire family of Lou the cop. There was Fran, the wife; Anthony, the son; and Deanna and Andrea, the daughters. Corso hit it off with Lou. He was a big guy with the sagging body of a former weight lifter who could talk for hours about absolutely nothing and make it sound interesting. Also, Corso had fallen for the daughter Andrea. She was, in his opinion, stunning, with her big hair piled high and her big breasts and an ability to say "fuck" and "bullshit" in a way that was almost charming. Lou had a dog, a mastiff named Caesar. Andrea had an English bulldog named Flower. Steve Corso already knew all this and he'd only met Lou a few weeks back.

Tonight he was at Il Molino's because Lou claimed to have four screenplays ready to go and all he needed was investors to make it happen. The first movie was called *Strangle My Love*. The second was about a murder in the town of Youngstown, Ohio. The third was about a young woman named Sandy Murphy, who Lou believed was wrongly convicted of murdering her rich husband. The fourth was called *The Pagoda*, and it was a little vague. During his first meeting with Lou a few days before Thanksgiving, Corso had thought of an idea on how to turn all this into dollar bills. Corso had made quite a lot of money helping people turn private companies into public companies. What if he made Lou the cop into a company? A moviemaking company. He could line up the investors, and Lou could turn out the scripts. Eight days after that first meeting, Lou had formed a corporation called De-An-Tone Productions, including the first few letters of each of his children's names.

"I can't believe you didn't bring Andrea!" Corso said, his voice rising like Lou Costello doing the "Who's on first?" routine. "Call her up!"

At the bar in Il Molino, Lou ordered a Tanqueray martini straight up with an olive and a club soda for Fran, his wife. Fran started up right away. She said, "To get into the valet we waited fifteen minutes."

Corso started to explain an easier entrance to Ceasar's when his cell went off. *The Godfather* theme was the ring tone.

"Excellent martini," Lou volunteered to the bartender. "I find bartenders don't make them the way I like."

Father and Mother Eppolito explained that the daughter Andrea was unavailable because she was having her apartment renovated and was studying business administration and would be done soon.

"Andrea, she's got painters, she's got this, she's got that," said Fran.

"And she wants to go for her masters," Lou added.

"After December twentieth, she'll be able to breathe again," Fran said.

The problem for Corso was that as far as the FBI in Las Vegas was concerned, this meeting with Lou the cop and his wife was a supreme waste of time. The FBI was more interested in strippers at Crazy Horse Too and Gerry Chilli. Corso thought he actually might make some money with this Lou the cop, so he kept at it anyway, and he kept the recording device running because you never know what people will say after a few Tanqueray martinis straight up.

In the restaurant with the wrought-iron chandeliers and the free antipasta appetizers, Corso got right to business. He claimed he had found a major investor, a guy he called

Crucker, to put up some money for Lou's movie company. "He's committed," Corso said.

"He liked it?" Lou said.

"It's not a matter of he liked it," Fran said. "That's what he told you last time."

Fran was an issue. She and Lou had been married since before disco. She didn't like this Corso. She didn't believe he was real. She looked at him as yet another slick-money guy looking to rip off her gullible husband. In Corso's view, Fran was an obstacle to overcome.

"I still do not understand—and I've been doing this for ten years—exactly what your partner is expressing to me because it's unclear," Corso said, addressing Lou. "But he will have cash as opposed to stock. I will have guys—some interesting guys—putting in. I've got one guy done. He can't wait. There'll probably be six others."

Corso was making it up as he went along. After Lou had mentioned the twenty-five thousand dollars from Mike Frate in the shoebox, Corso and the FBI decided he might try to see what would happen if Lou were offered money coming from made-up Mafia guys. Or drug money. Illegal money. Thus the story about the "interesting guys" who'd be putting in cash toward the alleged movie company Lou was going to take public.

Lou complained about two guys in cowboy hats from Texas who'd promised to put up some money and then never returned his calls. Corso assured him he'd have no problems raising money.

"It's been the issue," said Fran.

"These are guys from New York," Corso said. "All of them are going to be Italian."

"I cannot stop writing," Lou said. "You like *Strangle My Love*? I can make that for three and a half million dollars. In Europe, Japan is going to pay six million dollars for that movie."

"I would want only three percent of the first two hundred and fifty thousand dollars," Corso said. "I would spend it on the first date."

"I gotta check you out," Fran said.

"You gotta do like in *The Godfather*, go with you," Lou said.

"Are you okay?" Fran asked.

"He's sweating," said Lou. Then he went on and on about yet another guy coming to him to write his life story and promising him land in Mexico. Corso assured him that his guy Crucker was real, while Fran, the wife, chatted with the Italian waiter who claimed to be from Queens about whether he was really from New York.

"At least you're not from Buffalo or Rochester. They pretend they're from New York," she said. "I have a beautiful daughter if you want to meet her."

"There you go," Corso said. "I'm done."

The meal was over and they tried to find the correct valet but got lost in the mall. They wandered and wandered past shops filled with Christmas trimmings, drifting through the Muzak past waterfalls and thousands of shoppers until they finally found the correct valet. The entire time Lou walked slower and slower. He had heart problems. Fran pointed to a car and asked Corso, "Is that yours, the Porsche?" pronouncing it "Porsh-uh."

"I wish it was," he said. They set up another meeting for next week, when Corso said he'd have heard from the "interesting guys" about how much they were willing to put in. When the Eppolitos drove away, Corso went into a nearby bar and tried to pick up the waitress. He claimed it was his birthday, but she wasn't buying.

December 7, 2004

The house of Eppolito sat in the middle of a planned community out on the western edge of Las Vegas, where the desert starts to reclaim the city. It was the usual southwestern stucco subdivision with pools and tile roofs and a locked gate to keep everybody except the guys who mowed the lawns out. You drove up to a gate and a voice from a little box asked you where you were going. If you checked out, you were buzzed in. Steve Corso pressed the button, and Fran answered. She buzzed him in. As he drove toward the house, he said to the FBI tape recorder, "The wife Eppolito. Genius."

Two dogs were barking inside the house when he got out of the car. Lou stood in the door and Steve asked, "Where does your partner live?"

Lou pointed across the street. "Right there," he said.

The house of Eppolito had it all. The pool out back, the gas grill, the $960 a month air conditioning bill in the summer. Behind his house he had two male neighbors he called "the faggots," one of whom came over and cut his hair regularly. Next door he had a family with what he termed "satanic children." He was planning on putting up cypress trees so he wouldn't have to see them. Across the street he had his partner from the NYPD, Stephen Caracappa. He'd created his own little heaven, living there with the wife, the mother-in-law, and the son, an unemployed six-foot-two rap music fan who sometimes worked as a bar bouncer and sometimes didn't work at all. This was what he had accomplished after leaving New York and all that other business behind.

"I'm a home guy," Lou said. "About seven o'clock, we barbecue. We barbecue all summer. Outside we have that gas thing. Not propane. We got natural gas. She starts that up, she puts that big macaroni pot on. She puts on two big London broils. We sit out there and it's beautiful. The sun's going down. It's cool. I go in the pool and the pool water is ninety-four degrees."

Inside, the mastiff jumped all over Corso. In another room, Fran shouted, "Flower! Flower!" but the dog ignored her.

"I love eating meat," Lou said. "Caesar has enlightened me. Meat meat meat."

"How big is he?"

"Two hundred and seventeen pounds, thirty-seven-inch neck," Lou said. "Caesar looks like a bear, he's as gentle as a lamb. Andrea's dog, Flower, is the Antichrist. He was over the other day, I had him, he did not sleep. He growled at me, I had a fight with a rag with him, he wouldn't get away from me. Caesar's sound asleep. He goes over and bites Caesar right on the nose. Caesar jumps up, he looks at me. 'I didn't bite you, he bit you.' He was blaming me for Flower."

Lou suggested they go to his office in another part of the house. On the way Lou mostly talked about his heart surgery coming up in two weeks. He claimed he was unconcerned but kept talking about it anyway.

They came to one of Lou's Walls of Fame. It was covered with citations he'd received while he was on the job. This was twenty-one years on this wall. There was one for posing as an old lady to arrest muggers who targeted seniors. There was one for ending a hostage situation without anyone dead. Mostly they were internal departmental awards that cops routinely put in for, but there was his Medal of Honor from the time he single-handedly arrested a bunch of armed criminals in Harlem. There was also an award from a Brooklyn synagogue for raising money to clean up a graveyard that had been defaced by swastikas. This was Lou's life, on display.

Corso said, "Now, what you may want to consider with all those citations there, if you get them laminated they'll never discolor."

"I got about sixty more," Lou said.

In the office, Corso promised him he'd have the first seventy-five thousand dollars by "next Thursday, Friday, Saturday, Sunday, or Tuesday." He laughed. "That's probably. Ninety-nine percent of the time it's going to be that." Then he asked the question he'd discussed with the FBI: "Do you care what someone does for a living?"

"I don't give a fuck about nothing," Lou said, as expected. "Here's what I tell people. 'As long as you're not asking me to do it, if this is the biggest drug dealer in the United States, I don't give a fuck, but don't ask me to transport drugs for it. I don't do that.' That's what I tell somebody. If you said to me, 'Lou, I wanna introduce you to Jack Smith, he wants to invest in this film. He says seventy-five thousand comes in a fucking shoe box,' that's fine with me. I don't care. I've had people give me money before. You know what I mean? That doesn't bother me, and I don't question people. Like I said with Mike with the Bonannos, he's the driver, 'I don't give a fuck. I don't give a fuck about that.' I know him, I respect him, he respects me. I have a thing, and stupid as it is, I'm a lot older than you are, I don't put my hand in your pocket, and I don't like it when it's done to me."

Corso said, "Cash in a cardboard box."

"Yeah," Lou said. "I got people from the Gambino family call me all the time. They say, 'Lou, we got money.' I say, 'If you want to give me money, it's not a crime to have money. If you have money, I'll make the movie.'"

Lou claimed one guy came to his house.

"He was sixty-seven. He took a look at my kids, he said, 'I'll kill anyone who fucks with your family. You'll hear about it. You'll read about it. I do that because I loved your father so much.'"

Corso laughed, nervously. He said, "He's in this town?"

"He's in this town. Right now. He'd kill 'em. Wonderful."

"It's good to have friends."

Then Lou started with the names: Jimmy Buffalo, some guy from the Gambino family who was not the boss. Corso pretended he didn't know a capo from a Capulet. Lou got to educate. He said, "He's an earner. He's got much more clout than the other guy because he brings in money."

"He might be scamming," Corso said. "He might be doing this, he might be doing that."

"He might be selling the same six thousand acres to you, your father the same six thousand acres, and the six thousand people that already own it. That's him. So I go over to the place. I don't even know who I'm meeting. You don't even know if you're going to be killed. It doesn't bother me. He comes over, gives me a hug and a kiss. I knew him from when I was working. He's about forty-five. So I said, 'Can't you say your name on the phone?' He says, 'I don't know who's listening.' I said, 'Congratulations.' If they're bugging my phone, they hear my wife talking all day. I don't care. I don't do nothing. I'm fine. But they get paranoid, they get nuts. He says to me, 'I put my two cents into a few things and your name has come up in Manhattan at a place down at Mulberry Street. Down on Mulberry Street a good friend he said you're looking for money.' I said, 'I'm always looking for money.' He said, 'Tell me what the thing is, let me know what you need.'"

Lou claimed he said no to Jimmy Buffalo. He didn't need

the aggravation. He just wanted to make movies. He saw it as his destiny. He spouted more ideas. He wanted to do what he called a "black movie." It was something about a black kid who gets out of prison for armed robbery and a white kid from the neighborhood gets him a job and then the white kid is dying because he got shot in an armed robbery years before and guess who shot him? The black kid.

"Whoa," said Corso.

"Where are we going with this?" Lou asked. "We got a black movie. Always makes money. We got something for the kids. Always makes money. We got nigger rap music. Always makes money. You could do a film like that for six, seven million, it makes twenty-five million."

"Did you ever think that you were going to have this career in 1989?"

"No," Lou said, and there was just a trace of bitterness in that answer. He told Corso all about way back before everything went bad with him and the NYPD, one of his friends from the job told him he could have a $250,000-a-year job as a top investigator for American Express. When he said $250,000 he said it slowly, with an emphasis on the *thousand*. Then came the business with the NYPD file being found in Rosario Gambino's house in Jersey and the suspension and the departmental hearing and clearing. He had survived and still he was dead.

"If you saw my police training, I had certified negotiation, homicide detective, kidnapping detective, tracking so you'd never see that I was there. The whole thing. I done it all by the age of thirty-five. I had this tremendous résumé. He says to me, 'It's yours.' Five months later I was suspended, so I lost it all. He said, 'I can't put you in there.'"

Most would say Lou was bitter, but Lou would say he was pragmatic. He knew people only wanted to be around you when you were winning.

"You say you've got a great horse running in the Preakness, they don't want to know you. It's only when you hit that big thing. I feel it in my blood. I know I'm a very good writer, I have people read my treatments, they say, 'I'll back you on this.' I say, 'You say you will?' I call up, I say, 'I'm ready to write.' They say, 'I don't have the money now. It's Christmas.' "

Corso offered consolation, which in his case was always the promise of money. He kept saying Crucker was real, without being asked. He tried to get him to remember the good old days on the job. He asked about the robberies and the bravery and the shooting of people.

"Did you ever get used to killing people?"

"Did I ever feel bad about killing?" he replied. "No, I never lost a minute's sleep. Problem is, if I knew where they were, I'd go back and kill them again."

He started talking about how different he was from other cops because of his gangster father background. "Some cops would say, 'How many bullets did you fire?' I don't know. Did you see the school bus full of kids? I don't know. Not me. I saw it all because I was a street guy from growing up in the street. I knew. My father would always say to me, 'Look at the people next to you. You walk into a place and see a guy yelling at his wife, be prepared.' My father always protected me. I learned never have a jealous bone in your body. I would leave my wife, I didn't worry. She was hot, she was sexy. My father used to tell me, 'If you're very jealous, very controlling, don't get married. Don't get married. If she wants to walk around like that, it's none of your business. I'd rather have nine guys sitting there and say she's mine, not yours.' "

Corso felt it was time to change the subject.

"You said you wanted to show me your gun collection?" Corso said. "Do we have time?"

They walked all the way through the house to the garage, where Lou had created a room in one corner. All over the walls and in boxes were guns. Hundreds of guns.

"Holy shit," Corso said.

The tour started with an AK-47. Then an eight-hundred-round machine gun, then a 9mm automatic. Corso asked, "How did you get interested in guns?"

"I always loved guns when I was a cop," Lou replied. "I used to say to people, 'There are beautiful guns and then there are beautiful guns.' I've killed eight people in eleven gun battles. I had a hell of a career as a cop."

"Oh, my God. What is this now?"

"That's one of the most powerful guns in the world. If you were in your car and I shot from here into your car, the bullet would go through the car into your body and out the fucking other side."

"Who uses these guns?"

"Hunters."

The tour continued to what Lou termed "cowboy guns." He said, "I love cowboy guns. I go nuts for them." Then he pulled out a Mac 210 machine gun, cocked it, and made a "bup-bup-bup" noise like a ten-year-old.

"You ever fire that?"

"Yeah. I just don't like to fuck with that."

"That reminded me of the gun Al Pacino had."

"It is," Lou said. "In *Scarface*."

Corso thought the .44 was beautiful; Lou said it weighed "less than your tie tacks."

"What's that red dot do?" Corso asked.

"Point it at a picture, it's just like a laser. Wherever you aim that gun, that's where the bullet's going."

"Holy shit."

From upstairs, Fran yelled down, "Honey, I need you."

"Be right there," Lou shouted back, opening yet another box. "Now, this gun is my pride and joy."

And so on. He pulled out a Colt automatic with "September 11" engraved in the grip, then a cigarette lighter that turned into a gun. He'd forgotten all about Fran. Corso had had enough guns. He turned to another wall of fame in the garage, this one covered with photographs of Lou with famous people. Since he left the force, Lou had been able to land small parts in about a dozen movies. The photos were his proof that it was all real, not just another story.

"I gotta look at the wall," Corso said. "I haven't studied the wall. That's your partner, right? How long ago? He looks the same."

"Ten years. He doesn't change. That's one thing about him. I don't ever remember seeing him change."

"DeNiro. Boom Boom Mancini. Oh, Joe Pesci."

"Me and Joe up there."

"Oh, there's Scorcese. One of the *Soprano* guys."

"I did a lot of writing for them."

"Did you? Great show." Corso was edging toward the door, but Lou was still pulling guns out. "Next time," Corso said. "I know you have to leave at six."

Finally Lou put the guns down and walked back to the kitchen. He fixed some espresso he said was thick as oil, the way it's supposed to be. He had just finished showing Steve Corso his private world. Not everybody got to see that. He was letting Steve in. He had to let him in. Twelve years out of New York, his life as a world-famous New York City detective behind him, his days appearing on Sally Jessy Raphaël over, Lou Eppolito was swimming in debt. He had a hundred thousand dollars in credit card debt. His twenty-year-old son still lived at home. He was facing heart surgery. He needed Stephen Corso, a man he'd known for maybe a month who was introduced to him by a gangster. He had to believe in what Corso claimed he could do.

"I said to my wife, I'd really like to see things happen like you said," Lou said.

"The public offering," Corso said.

"Yeah. If that happened, it would be a tremendous boost. That would be the thing to change my life. That would be too good to be true."

December 13, 2004

Steve Corso sat in a hotel away from the Strip with his FBI handler, Agent Sheehan. They were having a conference call. Sheehan introduced FBI agent Geraldine Hart and Assistant U.S. Attorney Robert Henoch on the line from New York. Right away New York started asking questions. There was none of this "How about them Mets?" or "Can you believe the weather we're having?" It was straight to business, in the manner Corso had come to expect from the feds: they ask a lot of questions and answer not a one. Now there were no more questions about Gerry Chilli or Mike the driver or the Crazy Horse Too. All the questions were about Lou the cop, and only Lou the cop.

The voices of the prosecutor and the female agent in New

York asked Corso if he'd been to Lou's house. What was it like? How many rooms? What was on the kitchen table? What was in the office? What type of cell phone did he use? Did Corso notice any weapons?

When the call was over, Corso asked Sheehan what was going on. Sheehan said not to worry about it.

TWO

The applicant for a job as a New York City police officer was a little older than most. He was twenty-seven and had just returned from a two-year tour of duty in Vietnam. He had served in the U.S. Army in a transportation unit, mostly handling inventory. He had been honorably discharged and moved back to Staten Island and into the home where he'd grown up. He had taken and passed the exam required of all recruits, and begun his training at the Police Academy. At the time, the department would begin the vetting process after the recruit had already started at the academy, which in the view of Arthur Hearns made it tougher to get the bad ones out once they had been assigned a gun and a badge.

When Hearns got the application in question, Hearns had been working as an investigator in the personnel screening unit of the NYPD for about a year. His job was difficult but profoundly important. He had to figure out why a man would want to join the New York City Police Department, and if he did, how he might behave. He had to make sure nobody got a gun and a badge who couldn't handle the job. He worked in what was called Squad One and handled about sixteen investigations per quarter.

In this job Arthur Hearns had seen some truly amazing applicants. There was a guy who nodded off during the interview. There was a guy who had needle tracks in his arms. Most recruits weren't like this, but the few who were, Hearns needed to spot and push them back out the door.

"Crazy people want to become cops. They get a gun, want to wave it around," Hearns said. "They love that they can tell you what to do."

With the twenty-seven-year-old Vietnam vet, Hearns did the usual background check. He sent letters to area mental hospitals to see if he'd been a patient. He sent letters to schools to check on purported degrees, called up former employers for references, checked up on citizenship, pulled the military record.

"All these pages we sent out to the schools, the Selective Service, the military, they're all put together. It's actually a book on each guy. You get a very good picture of the guy if the investigator is good," Hearns said. "The investigators in Squad One did great jobs. The bosses read every word you wrote."

And, of course, they checked for any record of prior criminal behavior. This was not as simple as it sounds. A recruit who committed a crime when he was a teenager, for example, might not automatically be knocked out of the running. It depended on what he did, how old he was when he did it, and how much remorse he'd expressed after he got caught.

"If he was a youth, it would not knock him out necessarily. If you see a military court-martial, it depends."

In this case, Hearns turned up what he believed was a very disturbing incident. On January 4, 1960, when the recruit was eighteen years old, he had been arrested and charged with burglary on Staten Island. It wasn't just any burglary. The kid had gone out and rented a truck and leased a storefront. He'd carefully picked his target and then in the dead of night backed the truck up to a construction site and filled it up with thousands of dollars' worth of pink fiberglass insulation used in the eaves of houses to cut down on heating costs. His plan was to sell the stuff from the storefront he'd leased, but he got caught and pleaded guilty. He was a high school dropout, leaving New Dorp High School when he was just sixteen, and he was allowed to become a youthful offender and plead guilty to a misdemeanor. Hearns knew all this, but believed that this was no small-time crime. This was not getting into a drunken fist-fight at a sloppy bar. This was an indication of a certain criminal entrepreneurship Hearns found disturbing.

"He went out and rented a truck. This was a well-planned burglary. He burglarized this stuff and tried to sell it to other contractors. This was no teenage lark. This was well planned."

When Hearns finished his investigation, he wrote a report in which he strongly recommended that the twenty-seven-year-old Vietnam vet not be hired by the New York City Police Department. The report went to the Department of Personnel. Nine times out of ten, they would listen to Arthur Hearns. He was experienced, he took his job seriously. He believed that the department benefited from a conservative approach, that there was a way to make judgments about a man's character, that there was a serious difference between a barroom fight and a complex burglary. He didn't know the twenty-seven-year-old recruit and had no reason to treat him with either favor or disdain. He was just looking at the record and seeing a nineteen-year-old man who had made certain carefully thought-out choices that he found disturbing.

"I recommended that he not be hired as a police officer in the City of New York," Hearns said. "The report was made to the Department of Personnel, and the police commissioner might get a copy. To override my decision generally came from civil service Department of Personnel. The department especially in those days was very strict about who we let in. Usually you get dumped. They put you back in uniform and send you to the ass end of the Bronx so you quit."

Somehow nobody listened to Arthur Hearns. Somehow the recruit officially showed up on the payroll of the New York City Police Department on June 30, 1969, despite the fact that Arthur Hearns had pointed out the serious nature of the crime. The fact that this recruit was then assigned a badge and given a gun seemed to stretch the notion of giving a guy a second chance. Arthur Hearns did not know how it happened, because it happened somewhere above him where he could not see.

The recruit was a thin kid, about five feet, seven inches tall, with a gaunt appearance and an intense stare. He had been born too young for World War II and the Korean conflict. He grew up in the Staten Island of the 1950s. His name was Stephen Caracappa.

Louis Eppolito was twenty-one years old when he started working for the New York City Police Department on August 1, 1969. He'd managed to avoid the draft because of childhood rheumatic fever. He claims that when the NYPD hired him, they knew what they were getting.

"They wanted to know how I got on that job. They wanted to know what did I do? I said I told the truth. There was an investigator. On the back of the application form was a box two inches square asking if anybody in your family was ever arrested, fill in the details. I did like six or seven pages. The investigator said, 'Every class has got a class clown. We've got you. Why did you do this?' I said, 'It's true.' I said, 'What does that have to do with me? I don't have a ticket.'"

Eppolito swears up and down he spelled it all out for the New York City Police Department. He claims he wrote on this form that his father was the late Ralph Eppolito, once a soldier in the criminal organization run by boss of bosses Carlo Gambino. He says he made it clear his uncle was Jimmy the Clam Eppolito, currently a soldier in the same family. He claims he told the investigator a story that he would later repeat in his book.

"I was playing handball in the street and a drug addict knocked an old lady in the street. I chased him and turned him over to a cop. The cop took me home, and when my father saw me with the cop, he slapped me in the face. I told that story to the investigator. He said, 'If you can tell me that story and look me right in the face, I'll give you a chance.'"

This, in Louie Eppolito's recollection, was how in 1969 the son of a gangster got to work for the New York City Police Department and got to stay there for twenty years. The only problem with the story is that it appears to be completely untrue. There is no record of Louie's family history laid out in lurid detail in Louis Eppolito's personnel file at the NYPD. Instead there was a document in his personnel file in which the author claimed to have no knowledge of what his father did to earn a living.

1979

Police corruption is usually a cyclical equation in New York, like the hurricane season. It happens at regular intervals. Somebody gets caught, and that somebody starts talking. There is a scandal on the front pages. Then comes the big reform. Everybody's happy. Then the scandal happens again, and so on. The last time it had happened was shortly after Louis Eppolito and Stephen Caracappa somehow managed to land jobs with the NYPD. Back then the Knapp Commission was formed, and Serpico became a hero to some and a villain to others, and a special prosecutor for the State of New York was appointed to make sure this kind of pervasive police malfeasance never happened again.

For nearly a decade, the special prosecutor investigating police corruption did what he was supposed to do. His investigators tracked down hundreds of bad cops, and his lawyers made dozens of cases. There were plenty of cases to be made. Then the state began to cut back on the funding. The operating theory was that the special prosecutor had done such a great job he wasn't needed anymore. No one said that if the special prosecutor went away, the corruption—like hurricane season—would surely return on schedule.

Now it was announced that with the coming of the New Year, Governor Hugh Carey would again cut the staff. By March of the next year, there would be a staff of 51, down from the 160 of the commission's peak in the early 1970s. According to Thomas A. Duffy Jr., the special prosecutor, this was a perfect example of bad timing.

"There are signs that police corruption is on the upsurge," he replied when asked how the cuts would affect the office's ability to do its job.

The special prosecutor did not mention the case of father and son Sciascias, but he could have.

In May 1979, John Sciascia Jr., a twenty-six-year-old petty thief, was arrested in Brooklyn on charges of robbery first and second degree. The key issue for Sciascia Jr. was witness identification. If the witness could identify Sciascia Jr. as the robber, he would go to prison. If the witness became confused and was unsure, Sciascia Jr. might walk away. The solution to all of Sciascia Jr.'s problems was to make it appear as if somebody who looked just like Sciascia Jr. had committed the heinous act.

Enter Louis Eppolito.

Sciascia Jr. went to his lawyer, Richard Goldberg, and told him that a Detective Eppolito had approached him and offered to supply an array of mug shots that would help confuse and obfuscate. The mug shots depicted other petty thieves and miscreants who looked pretty much just like Sciascia Jr. The detective would provide this service to the Sciascia family for a fee. To the lawyer Goldberg, this seemed to be a preposterous story.

For months, John Sciascia Sr., father of the petty thief, told Goldberg he would be getting the mug shots as soon as he raised the thousands of dollars Eppolito required for the mug shot collection, which was officially the property of the City of New York. Goldberg shrugged and went about preparing the case for trial.

Suddenly Sciascia the father showed up with an array of mug shots, all bearing the logo of the New York City Police Department. And the father had a cassette tape, too. When Goldberg played the tape, he heard his client, Sciascia Jr., talking on the phone with a guy about exchanging money for something, and the guy on the tape was saying he had to be careful talking on the phone because he didn't know if it was bugged. Sciascia Sr. insisted that the guy was Detective Eppolito and that he'd given Eppolito thousands of dollars for the mug shots. The father explained that he'd tape-recorded the detective as insurance.

Now Goldberg the attorney had a problem. Technically, he was in receipt of stolen property. He called up the assistant district attorney in Brooklyn who was prosecuting Sciascia Jr., and said they needed to talk.

The Brooklyn district attorney called the office of the special prosecutor for police corruption and turned over the official NYPD mug shots and the tape with Eppolito and Sciascia

Jr. The lawyer assigned to the case was named Edward McLaughlin. He began looking into what to do about the allegation that NYPD detective Eppolito was selling mug shots to criminals.

At the time, Detective Eppolito had made something of a name for himself. He had been in the newspapers a few times and received some awards. Much of this would fall under the category "cowboy stuff." This was in the 1970s, when the city was spiraling into bankruptcy and criminal anarchy. There were garbage strikes and graffiti on the subways and the Son of Sam running around with his .44. The citizenry needed "cowboy stuff" because it gave them the sense that not all was lost. Detective Eppolito was their man.

He kept a file of his clippings. Here was Eppolito in the *News*, nearly run over by a getaway car. There was Eppolito in the *Post*, single-handedly capturing three skels who beat an elderly pharmacist for two hundred dollars, subduing one by clubbing him down in the street. There was Eppolito in the *Times*, working with a squad of undercover officers dressed up like senior citizens to collar muggers. There was Eppolito in uniform wearing the medals he'd accumulated, holding the door chain of one elderly victim's apartment door. The reporter wrote, "Eppolito is the eleventh-most-decorated cop in the department and has a reputation for quick thinking and possessing 'street smarts,' vital to his position with the team."

Eppolito had figured out early in his career that the bosses loved heroic newspaper stories. As far as the newspaper-reading public was concerned, Eppolito was a hero and nothing else. The idea that he would sell mug shots to one of the skels he was supposedly protecting the public from—well, that would seem impossible.

By now, Eppolito was working the robbery squad with Stephen Caracappa. The two had instantly become friends. Both worked frequently with the Brooklyn district attorney's office, including an assistant D.A. named John Fairbanks. When the Sciascia case bubbled to the surface, Fairbanks learned of it and didn't much believe it. At one point he made a point of mentioning the ongoing investigation of Eppolito to Eppolito's friend and partner Caracappa.

At that moment, Caracappa could have expressed outrage

that anyone would even think such a thing about Lou, but he did not. Instead, Caracappa said, "Thank you," and walked away. Immediately Fairbanks began to think that maybe Eppolito had tried to sell the mug shots after all.

Throughout 1980 and into 1981, McLaughlin of the special prosecutor's office pursued the investigation. The elder Sciascia no longer wanted to cooperate, but they had the tape and the NYPD mug shots as evidence. Most troubling in all this was that a petty criminal had found himself in possession of NYPD property from a department that supposedly has all kinds of safeguards in place to make sure nothing like that could happen.

And then the matter was dropped. On November 17, 1982, Sciascia Jr. pleaded guilty to robbery first and second with a maximum eight-year sentence. The audiotape of Detective Eppolito and Sciascia Jr. went into a file, as did the mug shots provided by attorney Goldberg. Eppolito was not questioned about this. The entire matter never showed up in his personnel file. He was not prosecuted. There were no departmental charges. The matter died a quiet little death and existed only in a box of paper that would one day end up in the basement of the state attorney general's office in lower Manhattan, where it served a new purpose: dust collector.

1979

Maria Provenzano's brother, Robert, died of unnatural causes in Las Vegas, and she wanted to know why. In fact, she became obsessed with knowing why. She began making inquiries. She paid two friends of her brother's, Vincent and Frank, ten thousand dollars of her own money, and they showed up with some Las Vegas police paperwork, or what they said was Las Vegas police paperwork. Maria didn't believe it was real, so she lost her ten thousand dollars.

At the time, she lived at Seventeenth Avenue and Fiftieth Street in the Brooklyn neighborhood of Borough Park. This was the Sixty-second Precinct, which happened to be where Detective Louis Eppolito worked. Maria knew him because she worked for the Brooklyn Terminal Market and had been robbed transporting payroll checks, and Detective Eppolito caught her case. After he questioned her about the robbery, she became his girlfriend. She was a kind of police groupie. She knew all the guys in the Sixty-second Precinct detective squad.

During the time she was Eppolito's girlfriend, he offered to help her find out who killed her brother. He told her that because he was an NYPD detective, he could get the real Las Vegas homicide file. Maria waited.

Months passed and still no file. Then Eppolito told Maria he would need some money to get the job done. This seemed odd to Maria, and she told him so. As a result, as far as Eppolito was concerned, Maria was no longer his girlfriend.

For some time, Maria kept all of this to herself. She was still friendly with other detectives in the Sixty-second Precinct, and in general she liked cops. Then she began a new job that nobody knew about. She became a behind-the-scenes cooperating informant with the Drug Enforcement Agency, providing tips on local drug dealing. During this relationship, she mentioned Detective Eppolito trying to shake her down for cash to get police information on her dead brother.

The information about Detective Eppolito was written down and conveyed to the New York City Police Department. Nothing came of it. Detective Eppolito continued on his way through the department, getting his name in the paper whenever he could.

June 27, 1982

At 2:00 A.M. in Bensonhurst, Brooklyn, a thirty-seven-year-old Czech immigrant named Frank Fiala parked his eighty-five-thousand-dollar Rolls-Royce a block away from the Plaza Suite disco. Inside, hundreds of people were just warming up. Frank Fiala knew he wouldn't have to wait behind the velvet rope. He was going to buy the Plaza Suite for a million dollars down in a few weeks. He was going into the disco business. He was going to be the boss of the guy at the door.

Frank Fiala could afford it. He had achieved extravagant

success in the business of selling ship parts. He was a million-aire many times over. He owned planes. He had a fleet of luxury cars. He was impulsive. The way he decided to buy the Plaza Suite was a good example of this trait. One night he was there dancing till dawn and he didn't like the service, so he decided to buy the place. Now he was getting ready to dance till dawn again as he approached the door of the disco he would soon own.

While it could be said that Frank had a good head for business, it could not be said he was a good judge of people. In fact, he was terrible at it. When he got involved in the disco deal, he was made aware that one of the owners was a Brooklyn contractor named Salvatore Gravano, a short, squat man who was a rising star in the Gambino crime family.

The deal had been moving along swimmingly until Gravano suddenly showed up as a partner. Fiala felt Gravano had not been treating him with the proper respect, so earlier that day he had gone to Gravano's office with a small machine gun. He had gone right into the office and, finding Gravano was not present, he sat at Gravano's desk and called Gravano on the phone.

When Gravano showed up with his brother-in-law, Eddie Garafola, Faila was sitting behind Gravano's desk, going on and on about how he wasn't going to be treated like a jerk and that he'd done deals with "the Colombians." Frank Fiala pulled out the machine gun and pointed it at Gravano and his brother-in-law, Eddie. Then he put the gun away. At that moment, Fiala had proven that his judgment of people was lacking.

Now as he approached the club entrance, before he reached the door the bouncer suddenly stepped inside and locked the door.

From out of the early summer darkness came several men wearing ski masks. One came up behind Fiala and tapped him lightly on the shoulder. When Frank turned, a second man pulled him to the ground. The first man hopped on Fiala's chest and pulled a pistol from his shirt. He fired one shot into Fiala's right eye. He looked around and then fired a second shot, into Fiala's left eye. Then, as a parting gesture, he fired a third bullet, into Fiala's mouth.

The men in the ski masks all seemed to evaporate into the night. The line of patrons at the disco had seen the whole thing, but their stories were less than helpful when the detectives from the nearby Bath Street precinct house showed up. One of the first on the scene was Detective Louis Eppolito.

Within the hour the city's crime reporters were all over the disco. Eppolito was happy to be quoted.

"It was a methodic execution," Eppolito told the *Daily News* reporter. "Money apparently was no object for him."

Across the street from the disco and the cops and the reporters, two men stood watching the scene: Salvatore Gravano and his brother-in-law, Eddie Garafola.

A week after Frank Fiala died on the sidewalk, Detective Eppolito walked into a check-cashing store in Bensonhurst, Brooklyn, owned by a man named Joseph Ingrassia. Ingrassia cashed checks for Gravano's construction business and was known as someone who could contact Gravano. Detective Eppolito flashed his badge and said he was working on answering the question of who shot Frank Fiala in the eyes.

Detective Eppolito asked Ingrassia a lot of questions about Gravano and several other members of organized crime, and then he went away. A few days later, Eppolito came back and asked more questions. The third time he appeared there were more questions, all having vaguely to do with the late Frank Fiala. Then Eppolito returned a fourth time, and the first thing he said was, "Is this place bugged?"

Ingrassia said no. Detective Eppolito stepped into the bathroom of the store and gestured for Ingrassia to join him. He turned on a shower and a sink and said in a hushed voice, "I can make life miserable for your friend Gravano."

For five thousand dollars, Eppolito promised he would go away. He then left the store.

Ingrassia got in touch with Gravano. Gravano heard the business proposal from Eppolito. A few days later, Gravano walked into Ingrassia's store with a fat envelope that appeared to contain a stack of bills. Ingrassia got in touch with Eppolito, who showed up the next day, picked up the envelope, and went away. After that, Ingrassia did not hear about Detective Eppolito again, until a few years later, in the fall of 1991, when Gravano decided to give up his life of crime and become a cooperating witness against the Mafia.

It was not clear when precisely the federal government became aware of Eppolito's shakedown of the gangster Gravano. But it was clear that this incident had absolutely no effect on Eppolito's rise within the New York City Police Department.

November 1, 1984

In the NYPD *Patrol Guide* there is a section devoted to the due process a cop accused of most forms of malfeasance is provided. The section is 118-9. It allows the cop to try and explain himself or herself, to give his bosses a reason not to bring departmental charges that could result in suspension or firing or worse. The cop is given a formal interview in which his or her answers are dutifully recorded and become part of the official record. Detective Louis Eppolito got his on the first day of November 1984.

By now Detective Eppolito would tell anyone who would listen that he was the eleventh-most-decorated cop in New York City history. He considered himself an aggressive cop, with a long list of collars to back up the claim. He had been involved in two shoot-outs and received commendations from the commissioner himself, and now he had to explain why a pile of NYPD records had been found in a gangster's garage.

The previous March, FBI agents coming to arrest a mob associate named Rosario Gambino at his home in suburban New Jersey knew that when you arrest people, you never know what you'll find. They found Rosario as expected, handcuffed him, and took him away. They also found a folder containing thirty-six documents that included newspaper and magazine clippings about the mob, diagrams of Mafia family trees, surveillance reports, and the criminal histories of Rosario Gambino and other members of organized crime. The agents were surprised to find this material because it appeared to belong not to Rosario Gambino but to the New York City Police Department.

The implications were obvious. The FBI immediately

turned the file over to the New York City Internal Affairs Bureau, which investigates corruption within the department and which began looking into how official NYPD property wound up in the suburban New Jersey home of a gangster. The IAB first checked the documents for prints, and found some on two of the documents. The prints belonged to Detective Louis Eppolito of the Sixty-second Precinct. They began to work backward.

The Internal Affairs people quickly figured out that at 7:40 A.M. on December 13, 1983, Detective Eppolito had signed in at the Sixty-second Precinct station house to work the 8:00 A.M. to 4:00 P.M. shift. At 9:30 A.M., he signed out to go to the NYPD's Intelligence Division in downtown Brooklyn to look into a matter of some concern. The wife of a nasty con named Penny had received a letter in which Penny threatened to kill her for cooperating with police. Eppolito went to Intel to see if Penny had any connections to organized crime. At Intel, he claimed he noticed a wanted poster for Rosario Gambino hanging on the wall. He approached a detective there, Sweeney, to say he'd seen Gambino the week before, in Brooklyn. He even had a story for that. Gambino had been adjusting his genitals when Eppolito happened to drive by, and Eppolito took this as a sign of disrespect. He told Internal Affairs he confronted Gambino and threatened to kill him if he did that again. He said Sweeney told him next time, let us know, and Eppolito claimed Sweeney then handed him Rosario Gambino's file containing the thirty-six documents.

His explanation for what happened after that got a little vague. He swore up and down that he returned the file and had no clue how Rosario Gambino got ahold of it forty miles away in Cherry Hill, New Jersey. The NYPD promptly suspended Eppolito with pay and filed departmental charges against him.

Case No. 57873/84 went to a deputy commissioner for trials named Hugh Mo, an attorney who acted as a kind of judge to determine whether the allegations against a member of the NYPD have merit. Often the charges he considered were petty—sleeping on the job, failing to maintain department equipment, cadging a free cheeseburger—violations that never make it into the newspapers. Occasionally the charges were more serious. In this case, Detective Eppolito's suspension had been in the papers. There was a certain amount of pressure in the case on the day of the hearing.

"He is the guy with the media following him around," Mo recalled. "He is a walking, I call it tabloid story. He walks in, I smile. I say, 'Holy shit, this guy is a caricature.' He walks in with his gait, his arms, his gesture, staring me down. Sometimes the cops take on the same kind of persona as those in the criminal world. They dominate the space. When they walk into the room, they dominate the space. He comes in. He owns a lot of space. When he walks into my courtroom, I'm saying this guy is something else. This guy looks like a gangster."

Mo was clear on the nature of Eppolito's explanation: "His defense was that I have no idea how those documents got to that Gambino guy's residence. I have every reason to come across it, I'm an aggressive cop. I was doing my work. What he says is, I don't have sole exclusive possession of the documents. If the department is able to show me that, then I am able to make that leap."

The departmental hearing, like a criminal hearing, consists of a prosecutor, called a department's advocate, presenting evidence, and the defense lawyer attacking the credibility or relevance of that evidence. This usually involves witnesses testifying under oath, where the judge can examine the witness and make a call based on the demeanor of the witness whether there is truth being offered up or something else entirely. Actually observing people who are put under oath is very helpful in deciding who's truthful and who's just making it up as they go along.

None of this occurred in the departmental case against Detective Eppolito. There were no witnesses. Instead, the department and Eppolito agreed to agree on the evidence that was relevant. They agreed that Eppolito had a reason to go to the Intel Division, and they agreed that Eppolito had received the Rosario Gambino file from Sweeney. They even agreed that Eppolito's fingerprints were on two of the documents found at Gambino's home. They did not address the question of what happened from there. This omission left Mo working with what he felt was an artificial set of data.

"I can only work within the four corners of these

documents," he said. "I was shocked. I said. 'What is this, no live testimony?' "

There was no chance to examine the demeanor of the witnesses, to see what would happen to Detective Eppolito's story if he was subjected to cross-examination. Mo was trapped within a limited record.

"If the detective was fully examined subject to direct and cross and the entire fact-finding process, as well as the supervisor, he may be able to give some insight," Mo said. "We have to operate within the rule of law. There are people who are going to get hurt. In the judicial process, people are sometimes judged like a book by its cover. They come in, they have a prior record, they get zapped. In this case, I was not given the opportunity to make additional fact-finding based on demeanor. God knows why the department threw in the towel on this. I never had a chance. You can say not so much, Mo gave him the break. The departmental Internal Affairs and departmental advocate gave him a break."

On the hearing day when Mo learned there would be no witnesses, Detective Eppolito was still allowed to speak his piece, although it was a monologue, not a dialogue involving cross-examination of a witness. Mo remembered Eppolito standing up to deliver a speech he'd obviously spent some time cobbling together. It was not so much explanation as it was a declaration of victimhood.

"He made a very passionate speech about the fact that he was targeted because of his lineage," Mo said. "He said he came to work even with a broken finger. He basically gave me an earful of his years in the department, how true blue he was, how this allegation was false and based on flimsy evidence, and the fact that they followed him for months and they didn't come up with anything. It was bravado. He presented himself as a pure victim. I wasn't looking at him as a victim or a hero."

Neither he nor the members of the department's Internal Affairs Bureau brought up the allegations and evidence of Eppolito getting cash for mug shots from Sciascia Jr., demanding cash to help Maria Provenzano, or demanding and receiving cash from Salvatore Gravano. Instead, it was Louie

Eppolito telling the court, "I have never had anybody ever accuse me of something."

In April 1985, Deputy Commissioner Mo found Detective Eppolito not guilty of leaking a law enforcement file to the Mob, stating flatly that "there was no evidence adduced at trial to connect the respondent [Eppolito] with the transfer of those documents to Gambino."

"This court cannot speculate as to how those documents came into Gambino's possession," Mo concluded. "The mere fact that the respondent was reportedly the last known person who had possession of those documents is certainly legally insufficient to support the charge that he passed them to Gambino or some third party. Based on the foregoing, this Court finds the evidence adduced to be legally insufficient to sustain the charges against the respondent."

Mo's decision was approved the next day by Police Commissioner Benjamin Ward. Detective Eppolito was restored to full duty with back-pay due. A few days later the story was leaked to the press, which did not report that the evidence was insufficient. Instead the story said Eppolito was "completely cleared" of all the charges against him.

At about this time, Chief of Detectives Richard Nicastro wanted to send Eppolito to a neighborhood far away from the five families of New York. Mo remembered Nicastro calling him after his decision was released.

"He's basically telling me, he's dirty. You let him off on a technicality. It was based on his instinct, it was based on his gut," Mo said.

Nicastro had a different recollection. He said his decision to try to keep Eppolito out of the Sixty-second Precinct was less an accusation and more an ounce of prevention. It didn't matter. Eppolito had gone straight to the police commissioner, Benjamin Ward, to try to get back to his old precinct.

"After that suspension I went to the police commissioner, Benjamin Ward," Eppolito said. "He said, 'I don't have any words to tell you about what happened.' Commissioner Ward said, 'I always had great respect for you. You're a street cop.' I said, 'Where I can go from here?' "

Nicastro's decision was overturned, and Eppolito was sent back into the heart of Mafia New York, this time to the

Sixty-third Precinct, in the depths of Brooklyn. It was, in Eppolito's mind, a partial vindication, but he required total absolution. He was a bitter man.

"I'm dead in the water. I realized that now. I was heartbroken. I was just going through the motions," he said. "I kept myself for twenty-one years trying to be better. I had to work two and a half times harder than any other cop I ever met because of who I am. Do you know the first two and a half years I never missed a day of work? I went to work with my hands stitched up, I went to work with broken knuckles."

He became convinced that IAB was continuing its investigation, following him around. He says other members of the Sixty-third Precinct would point them out.

"I'd go home and they'd be on the Southern State Parkway," Eppolito said. "I said, 'Let them follow me. Those guys are cops who are following me.'"

By now, his father was gone, and his uncle, Jimmy the Clam, had been shot down in the parking lot of a school near Coney Island, Brooklyn. There was still one other member of the family who was very much alive: Frank Santora Jr. Frankie Jr., who had just finished a stint at Allenwood prison camp for extortion. Eppolito remembered shortly after he had been restored to his old job as detective of the NYPD, he saw Frankie Jr. on a street corner in Bensonhurst, Brooklyn, talking with two other guys

"These were two men I'd never met before. When I pulled up, the two men walked away without looking at me. I asked Junior why he hadn't introduced the two guys. He said, 'You're a fucking cop. I don't want nobody to know you.'"

"He was very protective of me," he said. "He didn't want me to wind up on some surveillance tape talking to these guys, kissing them on the cheek because of the whole Rosario Gambino thing."

At the time, Eppolito lived on Long Island but would visit his mother once a week in Brooklyn.

"I said, 'Hey, Junior, he was very proud of me, very proud, I go once a week to visit my mother.' After my last tour I'd go and visit her, have dinner, drive back to home on the weekend. He said, 'If you're going by your mother's, stop by.'"

During one of the visits to Frankie Junior's house in Bensonhurst, there was a skinny older Jewish guy there with thick glasses who ran a clothing business. His name was Burt Kaplan.

"Let me tell you how I know Burt Kaplan. My cousin Frank, I'm at his house, this guy says what size suit do you wear? I tell him fifty. He's got the store on Eighty-sixth Street in Brooklyn. I'd go by, I'd pay for them. Thirty-five dollars a suit coat. I'd buy two. All this money they're talking about, four thousand dollars? It's nonsense. I'd buy two. I'm a fighter. I'm a big guy. I'm not afraid to wrestle you if you don't wanna go. I'd tear my underarm, I'd need a new shirt. Burt would say, 'Come by the store. What's your size? A twenty-inch neck? That's big.' I'd go to the store, he'd call me and say to stop by. I'd say, 'I can't. I'm working four to twelve.' He'd say, 'Stop by after, on your day off.' I don't remember if he called me, or Frank my cousin called me. I probably bought forty shirts."

After that, Eppolito says he gave Burt his phone number just in case he had any good shirts in.

THREE

Designation day for Frankie Santora Jr. He was sentenced to four years for shaking down Lundy's, the world-famous seafood restaurant in Sheepshead Bay, Brooklyn. If he behaved himself he could be out in three and a half years. When it was time for the U.S. Bureau of Prisons to designate where he would spend his time, he got lucky. The crime he'd committed was extortion, which under normal circumstances involved at least the threat of violence. With Frankie, his mere presence involved the threat of violence. He was a big, charming guy with a perpetually dark tan, shiny black hair, and a huge white smile. But he could turn in a minute, and then you knew where you really stood with Frankie. That was his method for collecting weekly payments out of Lundy's: implication and innuendo did the trick with Frankie. Because of these implications, it was likely Frankie would end up at the very least in a medium-security prison and maybe even a maximum-security prison, where the real hard cases wind up. Nevertheless, Frankie Junior requested Allenwood.

If you were a New York City gangster and you had to do time, Allenwood was where you wanted to be. It wasn't too far from the city, in rural mid-Pennsylvania, and it was the lowest-level security in the system. It wasn't even called a prison. It was a camp. There was no fence around the perimeter, no cell blocks, just dormitories, like college. The college of criminal knowledge. You could wear street clothes. You could sit on nice picnic tables in the sun with your family on visiting day. Your fellow inmates were usually white-collar criminals, stockbrokers gone bad, corrupt lawyers, CEOs who had wandered from the path. If you behaved yourself and did a good job, you could go on a furlough for up to five days. It was extremely minimum-security. You could just walk away any time you liked. For Frankie, the only problem was that Allenwood did not take prisoners involved in violent crime.

Nevertheless, he'd requested Allenwood. Everybody who knew anything about the Bureau of Prisons asked for Allenwood. Since it was minimum-security, it meant life would be a whole lot easier for three and a half years. And on designation day, Frankie Jr., who had threatened to kill the restaurant owner, got to be a very lucky gangster indeed.

The day he arrived at Allenwood, he was assigned to Dormitory 7. He got a job in what the prisoners called the powerhouse, which was another name for the boiler room. Inside, there were plenty of guys from New York. There was Anthony DiLapi, a Lucchese shylock from the Bronx, and Michael Bloom, a bank burglar affiliated with the Colombo family. Affiliations and associations were important. If you didn't know a guy but knew a guy he knew, you were okay. In Frankie Jr's case, he knew guys with the Gambino family. He wasn't a made man; but he was a capable guy.

A month in he got a bed reassignment to Dormitory 6, where he met another guy with certain associations. He was a skinny little forty-seven-year-old Jewish guy who had bad eyes and arthritis and who was with Christy Tic Furnari, a man respected by Frankie and all the others. His name was Burt Kaplan.

It was an odd match. Frankie was built like a subcompact car with a head. He was not afraid to use his hands, or whatever else was available. Burt Kaplan was probably five-eight, maybe 160 pounds. He was balding and wore thick glasses, suffered from hay fever, and was allergic to penicillin. He looked like what he was, which was a Garment Center businessman.

Frankie had his hands, Burt had his wallet. Burt got along with a select group of people at Allenwood because he had money, and he was associated with Christy Tic.

Burt the businessman was doing three years for trying to sell quaaludes that were no good. How the Garment Center guy got into quaaludes was a little twisted entrepreneurial tale. He had been selling designer knockoffs when he ran into a chemist who claimed he could make knockoff hair products that would sell in Africa. It was just crazy enough to work. Kaplan the businessman ran the numbers and hired the chemist. The venture was almost immediately a bust. The product went bad during shipment, and Kaplan was out a lot of money. The chemist said he could make it up. He knew how to manufacture quaaludes, a drug that was very popular in 1980 with certain young people.

Burt didn't know quaaludes from interludes but decided to try drug dealing when someone explained the profit margin: about 2,000 percent. Again he failed. The homemade drugs were useless; he couldn't sell one. Worse for Burt, he got caught, and the chemist did him one more by deciding to cooperate against him.

As it happened, Frankie Jr. and Burt were not only dorm-mates but also both worked in the powerhouse, which was where they got to talking about their old hometown haunts. As fate and the fact that Brooklyn is really a small town would have it, Burt and Frankie Jr. lived about two blocks apart back in Bensonhurst. Burt knew the same people Frankie knew. Burt had installed an air conditioner for Frankie's cousin, Jimmy the Clam Eppolito, and used to play cards at Jimmy's social club.

Frankie bunked three beds away from Burt in Dormitory 6. Burt arranged to pay another inmate to clean Frankie Jr.'s cubicle (and his own). Frankie and Burt ate most of their meals together, and introduced their wives and children to one another during visits.

"I didn't think he was the swiftest guy in the world, but I liked him," Burt said. "He was a big, tough guy who was loosely associated with the Gambino family, although he wasn't put with anyone in particular. I know that he was a hoodlum. I know that he shook down Lundy's seafood people who owned it and got quite a bit of money out of it. I knew he was a tough guy in every bit of the word."

Slowly Frankie got more comfortable with Burt, and became more open about his business with members of organized crime. Once Frankie confided in Burt the tough time he had after his cousin, Jimmy the Clam Eppolito, and his son, Jimmy Jr., had been shot dead in the parking lot of a high school near Coney Island. That could have been a problem for Frankie. He told Burt that he got called in by the hierarchy of the Gambino family, and they asked him if he had any bad feelings about Jimmy the Clam. He answered no, which Burt felt was the right thing to say.

Then Frankie Jr. brought Burt a little business proposition. "When he brought me the proposition," Burt recalled, "I had known him for two years in prison and you get to know somebody in prison in two years a lot better than if you know him in twenty years on the street."

Frankie let it be known that he had a cousin, Lou, who was a detective in the New York City Police Department, and that he could be helpful in certain ways.

"He offered to get me information on any investigation that was going on, and if I had a serious problem in the street, he offered to do murders for me," Kaplan said. "If I wanted, his cousin could search around and find out if I had anything pending against me or if I was under any kind of surveillance. He said his cousin had a partner that had a prestigious job, and between the two of them, they could help me, and if I had any problems physically, they could help me. He told me that he had done things with them previously and that they were good, stand-up guys and that he would have no fear of doing anything with them."

The way Frankie Jr. saw it, this could be good for Burt and good for Frankie Jr. Frankie would charge a nominal fee, depending on the service requested, and Frankie would serve as the liaison to the cops. Burt wouldn't even have to meet them.

At this point in his life, Burt Kaplan was forty-seven years old. He had been arrested four times. This was his second stint in prison. He had a wife and a daughter and a business and employees. True, he was also associated with the Lucchese family and was now doing time on a narcotics conviction. He had spent a lot of money on lawyers, and now he was determined that this would be his last time in a federal or any other prison. He said no to Frankie Jr. In a word, he did not trust cops.

"Number one, I wasn't doing anything at that time where I needed that help," Burt said. "Number two, I told [Frankie] I didn't want to do business with any cops. I felt it was something that could come back and haunt me and I didn't want to do it. It would come back and haunt me with my friends on the street, the friends that I had in organized crime, and possibly could come back and haunt me if one of the [cops] would later on in life become an informant."

Burt was in Allenwood two years and twenty days for the quaaludes. He was supposed to be out in February, but one morning early one of the inmates charged with janitor duty came around sweeping Dormitory 6 before wake-up call, and Burt told him to go away. Words were exchanged, followed by fists. Burt and the inmate were both transferred to segregation in Lewisburg medium-security for four days, and he wound up doing an extra month.

On March 11, 1983, Burt Kaplan walked out of a federal prison for the second time in his life. His wife, Eleanor, picked him up. He was headed back to Brooklyn to see what was left of his clothing business, Bay City Distributors on Bay Sixteenth Street. When he went into Allenwood, he estimated he had about $750,000 worth of inventory. He left his friend Tommy Irish in charge, which was a big mistake. When he arrived on Bay Sixteenth Street, Burt saw the warehouse had been padlocked by the tax man and that Bay City no longer existed as a viable business. He would have to start all over.

In Burt's mind, when he said good-bye to his friend Frankie Jr. and his little proposition about the cops, he was finally turning his back on the criminal life.

Early 1985

The telephone rang at three in the morning at the Kaplan residence in Bensonhurst. It was a beige brick single-family home squeezed between apartment buildings, with a tiny front lawn hemmed in by a chain-link fence, a little slice of Brooklyn heaven. Burt had managed to find it while still incarcerated, and now he lived there with his wife, Eleanor, and only child, Deborah, a twenty-four-year-old woman who was finishing law school. At this time, the phone would ring at three in the morning regularly, but for Deborah Kaplan, who often had to answer it, it was still a frightening experience.

As usual, it was Monica. Monica was the wife of Tommy Galpine, who was one of Deborah's father's closest employees. Deborah's father had known Tommy since he was a teenager stealing appliances off the backs of trucks. He was a tall, gangly guy with a thin mustache and a larcenous heart, and although Deborah was his only true progeny, Burt often called Tommy "my son." Monica was his wife, which was an arrangement that was not working out well for the Kaplan family's ability to get a full night's sleep.

On the phone Monica was hollering that her husband till death do us part Tommy was hitting her, slamming her face into the wall. The usual scenario.

"She was incoherent, screaming, yelling, cursing," Deborah remembered. "There was an emergency situation, that we had to come right away, that I had to get my parents up and we had to rush over to her home."

On this night, the Kaplan family—father, mother, and daughter—pulled themselves out of bed, got dressed, and drove to the Galpines' house, a few blocks away. There they found Monica, drunk. Tommy wasn't home. "She never had a mark on her, no injury," Deborah remembered. "There was nothing wrong with her, except she was drunk."

At the time of this middle-of-the-night rendezvous, Deborah Kaplan was preparing to enter a new phase of her life. Three years earlier she had graduated with a Bachelor of Arts degree from the State University of New York at Albany. Subsequently she enrolled in the law school at St. John's University in Queens and was soon to be graduating to a new life as a respected member of the bar. Her father and mother had never finished college. She was their only child. She was taking the Kaplan name to a new place. She was also about to get married to a lawyer she'd met in law school, Harlan Silverstein. She was finally going to move out of her parents' house. But first she had to deal with the very drunk Monica Galpine.

The Kaplans took Monica back to their house on Eighty-fifth Street to spend the night. Deborah offered her room, but Monica wanted to sleep in her parents' room. Deborah offered her a T-shirt, but Monica wanted to wear Deborah's pajamas.

"She said, 'I'm not wearing that,'" Deborah remembered. "I want to sleep in what the princess sleeps in."

Monica passed out, and the next day everyone got up and went off to work and that was that until the next phone call at three in the morning. This was the House of Kaplan. This was—for the moment—Deborah Kaplan's life.

August 17, 1985

Lawrence, Long Island. A glorious summer Saturday. While half of Manhattan had abandoned the city to lie on sand in the Hamptons, the reception room of Temple Israel was packed. The event was the marriage of the princess herself, Deborah Kaplan, to Harlan Silverstein. The band played in the corner, three-foot-tall floral arrangements obscured the view on all the white linen tables, waiters circulated with wine. Most of the men wore tuxedos, the women designer gowns and hair piled high in the manner of Brooklyn and Dallas, Texas. Both bride and groom had just graduated from St. John's University School of Law. The mother of the bride, Eleanor Kaplan, was as proud as could be. Her daughter was soon to be part of an honorable and respected profession. The princess was preparing to take the bar exam. Life was good.

Working his way across the crowded room, Judd Burstein wasn't sure he should be there. He was a respected member of the New York bar, a graduate of New York University Law School. He made it a practice never to get personally involved with his clients, most of whom were criminals.

"I remember being uncomfortable about going because the problem I had was not to be the lawyer who goes to the parties and the social clubs. I had no desire to be photographed by the FBI," he said. "I went to this because of Eleanor and Debbie."

At the time, Judd was very popular with the Kaplan family. Three months earlier, Judd helped turn Burt around. Burt was out of prison for the quaaludes charge almost two years when the FBI had come at him again. This time they hit him with the worst charge of all: conspiracy to distribute heroin. The father of the bride had been arrested and handcuffed on March 24, 1985, on a federal complaint. Heroin! Was there anything worse than heroin? Scourge of the city. Destroyer of souls. But Judd had consoled the Kaplan family. He pointed out it was just a complaint, not an indictment, which meant that he might still get it killed before it went to the grand jury. The U.S. attorney had thirty days to get an indictment. Burt insisted he had nothing to do with any of this, which made Judd's job a lot easier.

Judd got him out of the heroin charge. Somehow he convinced the prosecutors that while Burt may have done some questionable things in the past, he was not involved in any way with the sale of heroin. The charge was nonsense. The prosecutor went to his boss and came back with a nolle prosequi—a "decline to prosecute." This was extremely rare, and perhaps a sign of good things to come.

As far as Judd could tell, Burt was a new man. He had served his time and was now determined to get it together, for the sake of his daughter and his wife.

"He looked like a Jewish businessman from the Garment Center. He was really trying to get on the straight and narrow," Judd said. "He used to describe himself as a degenerate gambler, but he had been going to Gamblers Anonymous from about 1982. I never knew him to gamble during that time. He used to talk about it as mistakes he made in the past."

Judd liked Burt. "I grew up in Lawrence and he reminded me of a lot of fathers of kids I grew up with who worked in the Garment Center. There were a lot of people in Lawrence who did very well in the Garment Center who were not well read. He didn't care about books and theater. He was a very humble guy. He was completely devoted to his daughter. He really wanted her to succeed."

But Judd was not naive. He was aware that the humble, doting dad had been arrested repeatedly for dealing in stolen goods and had done time for the attempted distribution of narcotics. At the end of the day, Judd knew that Burt was really just a street guy, a guy who lived by his wits. Some of those guys did very well for themselves and never went to jail. Some did very well for themselves but also went to jail. Above all, Judd was aware that Burt embraced the street rule that you never rat on your friends—no matter who they are, no matter what they've done.

"He had a street ethic. I used to laugh about the fact that it was the Jew that had the strongest street ethic. He used to laugh about it. He felt you look someone in the eye, you give them your word, you always live up to your word. If you do something wrong, you don't solve your problems by turning on somebody else. A friend is someone you can rely on."

Judd could see that the father of the bride had spared no expense. There were massive floral arrangements on every table and an open bar—and he didn't even drink. Deborah was his only daughter, the best thing that had ever happened to him, his greatest achievement in life. He had invited everybody he knew because he wanted them to see what it was like to be proud of your daughter on a happy day.

Burt was riding high. He'd somehow picked up his bankrupt clothing business and started all over, making money legitimately. It was as if everything before never really happened. He was doing business with the major labels. Their vice presidents were sitting here at Temple Israel. Here was a vice president at Calvin Klein. There was a vice president of Gloria Vanderbilt. Big shots, and best of all, legit.

Of course, life was not quite that simple.

Burt Kaplan was a complex guy. He presented himself as a hardworking businessman but he surely loved that glamorous gangster life. A friend of the Kaplan family noted that he loved to read about crime. He loved Tony Hillerman and Nelson Demille and, of course, Elmore Leonard. Elmore Leonard would certainly have been captivated by Burt Kaplan. Elmore Leonard certainly would have loved this wedding.

Here was Burt, still in the middle of his five years parole from the quaaludes case. That meant he was strictly forbidden from meeting with or associating with members or associates of organized crime. That would have been difficult to explain if his parole officer happened to wander into the middle of the wedding reception for Deborah and Harlan at Temple Israel.

Anthony Casso and his wife, Lillian, sat at one table toward the middle of the room. Here he was, a soldier in the Lucchese crime family, eating and drinking and having a great time on Burt's dime. At the same table was his best friend in the world, Vic Amuso, another Lucchese soldier. The parole officer might also be interested in Frankie Santora Jr. He was there with his wife, Elaine, having just finished at Allenwood. There was a guy named Whitey with the Bonanno crew. There was even a guy there known as Tony Crime.

And, of course, you couldn't help but notice the slight, elderly man with the thinning brown hair, the only guy at the table wearing a necktie instead of the black-tie formal wear everybody else had on. It was Christy Tic Furnari, the consigliere of the Lucchese crime family. He was one of the main defendants in the ongoing Commission trial along with all the leaders of New York's five organized-crime families. The parole officer would surely be interested in his presence.

For Burt Kaplan, Furnari's presence at the wedding of his only daughter was a powerful measure of respect. Burt had known Christy Tic for years, and he knew that Christy hated to go to weddings.

"In my life, it was an honor," Burt said. "It was nice for him to come. He didn't go to many affairs. He's a quiet guy."

At one point, Christy Tic and Anthony and Vic all made little pilgrimages over to the happy bride to hand her envelopes of cash. Who could say where that cash came from? Extortion of a construction company? Skimming from a union pension fund? Shylock loans? Sports book? Maybe even a heroin sale? The top levels of the Lucchese crime family did not make their money selling TV sets, unless they had been hijacked from a truck out near JFK.

Regardless, on this day the envelopes of cash were just envelopes of cash, gifts to the bride. She took the money and thanked her guests.

At one point the photographer came around the table with Vic and Anthony and Christy Tic. The group gathered for the formal shot, having to split up a little in the middle because of the massive floral arrangement in the center of the table. In the background there was a big golden harp. It was a very classy affair.

On the far left was Furnari's son, Chris, whom everybody called Jumbo and who was also a soldier in the Lucchese crime family. He had his hand around the waist of his date. He was not smiling, almost as if he didn't like having his picture taken. Perhaps it reminded him of Central Booking.

Next to him stood Vic Amuso, with his arm on the shoulder of his wife. He wasn't afraid of the camera at all. He had a broad smile and was looking straight at the photographer. Next to him sat Anthony Casso in black tie, a thin smile on his face, and his wife, Lillian, standing behind him with her hand on his shoulder. She smiled sincerely. Seated to Casso's right was the consigliere himself, Christy Tic, wearing the necktie. Sammy Kaplan, a huge bald man, stood behind Christy with his hand on Christy's shoulder, as if were there in case anything should happen. His bow tie was askew.

At another point the photographer gathered two smiling couples together in the middle of the crowded reception for a quick shot. Lillian Casso stood to the left, holding a corsage and offering a big smile. Next was her husband, Anthony, with a tiny smile. Next stood Burt Kaplan, smiling so broadly his teeth were showing. Finally there was Eleanor Kaplan, smiling easily, her husband's left hand on her shoulder.

And in the middle of the shot, tough to see unless you squint, the two men—Anthony the gangster and Burt the businessman—are holding hands. It was as if this connection was the strongest in the room. It was a connection that would last forever, no matter what either man desired.

It was one for the books.

FOUR

Three men sat in a dark Lincoln parked by Bay Parkway and Eighty-fourth Street in the Brooklyn twilight. The two men in the front seat wore black suits with wide-brimmed black hats. The man in the back was hatless and dressed in a business suit. An envelope sat on his lap. Inside the houses all around the lone Lincoln, families ate dinner, argued about mortgage payments, relaxed in the blue light of a thousand TV sets. In the dark Lincoln, three men schemed.

Burt Kaplan, businessman, sat in the backseat. He was now making good money in the clothing business—legitimate money, in fact. But when somebody walks up and waves a dollar and says, 'Here, this is for you,' what are you supposed to do?

In the front seat sat one of Burt's business partners, a 250-pound balding jeweler who wore the traditional black hat and suit of the Hasidim. He was Joe, and he lived in the Old World Hasidic neighborhood in Williamsburg, Brooklyn, that is a part of New York and yet separate at the same time. He was a wealthy man with international money connections whose family owned a diamond mine in South Africa. Burt had a lot of things going with Joe. He had, for example, brokered a diamond sale from Joe to a friend who had connections in what had once been Upper Volta. On this night, however, the deal with Joe was closer to home.

In the front seat next to Joe sat another Hasidic man, also a jeweler. Burt didn't know his name and could not see his face. Truthfully, Burt didn't want to see his face. The deal in question involved the sale of a Treasury bill worth half a million dollars. There was nothing legitimate about it.

Kaplan had the actual Treasury bill in question on his lap. He had obtained it from his friend, the gangster Anthony Casso, who had obtained it from an associate of the Colombo family. The Colombo associate worked in a depository. The scam was supposed to be this: the Colombo guy steals the bill and gives it to Anthony to sell before anyone notices it's missing. They had about a two-week window. Burt was sitting in the backseat of a Lincoln with two Hasidim in the gloaming because Anthony had asked Burt, with his connections in China and the Upper Volta, if he could find someone to fence the bill overseas. Everyone involved knew they had to act quickly, which was why Burt was meeting Joe and the jeweler in a car parked about a block from his own home, on Eighty-fifth Street, when everyone else was sitting down to dinner.

Burt had first been put in contact with Joe by a gangster named Frankie Hot. To Burt, a man's word meant everything. If a man said he was going to do something, he'd better do it or Burt would never do another deal with him. Joe had been a man of his word on the Upper Volta diamond deal. Burt was taking a little chance involving Joe in the Treasury bill scheme, but Burt always went with his criminal instincts. He felt that tonight, they were right. Joe had produced the jeweler in the front seat.

Joe said the jeweler knew a friendly banker overseas. If the bill was worth $500,000, Burt would get $250,000 to split with Anthony. Joe would get the other $250,000, to split with the jeweler in the front seat and his connection overseas. Everybody would get paid.

Still, although Burt knew Joe, he did not know the jeweler. Therefore he was doing what he could to limit his liabilities. He had told the jeweler in the front seat not to look around at him. He told the jeweler he would need to know his name and where he lived and where he worked ahead of time, in case the jeweler decided to take the Treasury bill and run away. The jeweler agreed and was about to give his name, but Burt said no, give it to Joe later. Joe would tell him if he had to. Burt did not want to know more than he had to know.

Kaplan handed the envelope with the Treasury bill to the jeweler. The jeweler opened the envelope and looked at the bill. He began to ask a lot of questions. Burt answered the man until he stopped asking questions. Then Burt excused himself and said good night. He got out of the car and walked around the corner, back to his loving wife and happy home.

To the legitimate world that went about its business, paying taxes and reporting for jury duty, Burton Kaplan would appear to be an American success story. He had a wife, and a daughter who was working for the Legal Aid Society. He had a company, Progressive Distributors, that bought men's and women's clothing from major labels such as Gloria Vanderbilt and Calvin Klein and sold them to major retail outlets, such as Kmart. He did enough business that he had a huge credit line with a highly respected "factor" called Rosenthal & Rosenthal.

"You sell Kmart an order for a million dollars, and not too many businesses have more than a million or two in their credit lines. Kmart would take sixty days to pay," Burt said. "So if they took half your credit line, you couldn't go buy more stuff. With a factor you could get eighty percent of the money upon the truck receipt of the goods being shipped and could reinvest that into more sales. Also, the factor took the credit risk. If the people didn't pay, the factor assumed the credit risk."

Not just any fly-by-night Garment Center operator could command such respect. Burt had credibility. He was a man of his word. If he said he was going to do something, he would do it. If he had a debt, he would repay it. He had even curbed his gambling habit and stuck with Gamblers Anonymous. He was living up to that letter he'd written to the judge so many years ago, the one in which he promised, "I promise you that the name of Burton Kaplan will never again come before you or the court or any court again in regards to anything that is against the law."

It was all a big lie.

The true Burt Kaplan was surrounded by gangsters. They were his friends and his business partners. The Treasury bill deal wasn't the half of it. Anthony Casso also had a percentage of Burt's company, Progressive Distributors, which owned the Lincoln Town Car Anthony drove around in. Burt's old friend from Allenwood, Frankie Santora Jr., was working at Progressive as well. He and his family bought blue jeans from Burt at cost and sold them out of the back of a truck.

Burt was even Casso's landlord, although Anthony didn't actually have to pay rent. It was another favor for Anthony. Anthony had come to Burt and said, 'Buy my house, I want to buy another, bigger house owned by the Fortunoff family.' To make this appear to be legitimate, Burt would buy Anthony's house, and Anthony would use the proceeds to buy the Fortunoff house.

Kaplan said, "Anthony, I really don't want your house and I'm happy where I'm at."

Casso said, "Yeah, but I trust you and I'm going to sell you the house cheap and you can make a profit on it and I really don't want the whole world to know that I'm selling my house and I need the money so that I can show it when I buy the bigger house."

This was how Burt showed respect for Anthony, which was to give him something for nothing.

By now Burt was officially with Christy Tic but around Anthony Casso all the time. This made Burt what law enforcement types would term an associate of the Lucchese family. He wasn't actually a member. He couldn't be, because he was Jewish. But he could tell any other gangster who tried to shake him down that he was with the Lucchese family and they would have to respect that. This allowed him to meet members and associates of the other New York families, including the Genoveses, the Gambinos, the Colombos, and the Bonannos. When he invested in a miniature golf course with a Genovese associate named Larry and the golf business shut down, Kaplan wanted his money back from Larry, who suddenly wasn't around. Burt used his association with the Lucchese family to make certain arguments to Larry. Burt got his money.

Six days after the twilight meeting with the Hasidim in the

Lincoln, Joe contacted Burt and said he had something for him. Burt set up a meeting right away.

Joe explained that everything had gone as planned, although there had been one other guy in the chain of guys necessary to choreograph the little Treasury bill dance. The guy was another jeweler who was a friend of the jeweler Burt couldn't see in the front seat of the Lincoln.

Now Burt learned who he was dealing with. The name of the jeweler in the front seat was Herman. Herman had reached out to this other jeweler, whose name was Israel Greenwald, because Herman did not actually have the international connections he claimed to have. Greenwald, a guy Burt had never met before, had been the crucial link to the banker overseas. He had been appointed an honorary consul-general by the president of Liberia and thus had diplomatic status. That would make it easier for him to come and go without being questioned.

Burt was not happy about new people suddenly showing up in his little group, but he was happy when Joe handed over $130,000. Joe promised that the rest of the money would be coming within the week. This had to be the easiest money Burt had seen in a long time. He would have to see if Anthony could scare up another Treasury bill right away.

Israel Greenwald had made it all the way to London and back. He was thirty-four years old, a fairly successful diamond merchant who traveled frequently overseas for his business, Blue River Gems. His diplomatic status helped. He had befriended the president of Liberia, who had bestowed upon him the honorary title of consul-general to Liberia. He was used to working his way through Customs at John F. Kennedy International Airport, and he figured the task would not take too long and soon he would return to his family in Queens. When he presented his passport to the Customs agent, there was some discussion between government employees. Then a woman with a very serious expression appeared and produced a gold badge. She introduced herself as Special Agent Beverly Bartzer of the FBI. She knew Israel's name. This was not a good sign.

FBI Agent Bartzer was all business, no banter. She took Israel into a room with no windows and asked him all kinds of questions about the Treasury bill he'd just sold overseas. Then they waited for Greenwald's luggage to be brought up, and Beverly went through every pocket and discovered packs of bills beneath Israel's socks. If you bring cash into the United States, you are supposed to let everyone know about it, not hide it beneath your socks.

Israel Greenwald was a tall, thin, handsome man who practiced the strict regimen of the Orthodox Jew. He always wore a yarmulke, and after sundown on Friday he never drove. He ate kosher, studied the Torah, and earned money to support his wife, Leah, and two little daughters, Yael, eight years old, and Michal, age nine. His wife was beautiful and bright, a first-grade teacher who worked in the next town at a Hebrew school for four hours a day. Israel Greenwald owned a nice suburban home on the Queens/Long Island border, drove a blue Cadillac, and was a prominent man in the Orthodox Jewish community of Far Rockaway and nearby Lawrence, Long Island. Sitting in the room with FBI Agent Bartzer, Israel Greenwald had a lot to lose.

When he got involved with his friend Herman and the Treasury bills, Israel Greenwald had some idea that the arrangement was not completely above the table. He was part of the deal because his diplomatic status would allow him to come and go without being questioned, which right away told him something was funny. But he was used to funny. In the diamond trade, he sometimes used a second set of identification documents under a different name, Isidore Greenwald. He had two sets of everything—Israel Greenwald Visa, Isidore Greenwald Visa. Israel Greenwald American Express, Isidore Greenwald American Express. This was small-time stuff. As far as stolen Treasury bills were concerned, Israel claimed he had no idea the bill he had just sold in London was stolen. To Special Agent Bartzer, it didn't matter much because of the money under the socks.

Special Agent Bartzer asked Israel what he would prefer: go to jail, or cooperate with the federal government to find out where that Treasury bill came from. This would involve recording conversations with his friend Herman. He would pretend as if the Treasury bill scheme had been a big success and pass the money on to Herman with a smile.

When he discussed the matter with his wife, Leah, she was upset, but it wasn't as if he had much choice.

Burt Kaplan sent his ersatz son Tommy Galpine on another errand. He was supposed to deliver a fat envelope to Anthony Casso at a garage on Flatlands Avenue, near Casso's house. He did this all the time, but on this occasion his boss, Burt Kaplan, was "very nervous. He told me to watch for surveillance, check my mirrors."

This was Casso's percentage of the final money from the Treasury bill. In two weeks, Burt and Casso and the Colombo associate had made $250,000 on one deal. Burt personally pocketed $50,000 and gave the rest to Casso. Easy money—even easier than selling Calvin Klein jeans. Burt told Anthony to get him another bond. Anthony said he couldn't because he gave it to another guy, Leo the Zip, who promptly lost it. Now Anthony had to kill Leo the Zip. Burt did not inquire further.

Then came the phone call from Joe.

"We have a problem," Joe said.

"What's the problem?"

"The banker is being questioned by Interpol."

The way Joe explained it, the second jeweler, Israel Greenwald, had forgotten to pay off the banker who had helped finance the Treasury bill sale. He was supposed to give the guy a percentage of the $100,000 he got, but he forgot. As a result, the banker forgot that he was supposed to keep his mouth shut when Interpol came knocking. Now the banker was cooperating, which led Burt to believe that greedy Greenwald had probably already been visited by Scotland Yard, Interpol, the CIA, and everybody else who would like to arrest Burt tomorrow.

There were two kinds of guys in Burt Kaplan's world: stand-up guys and rats. Stand-up guys were guys who would keep their mouth shut, do their time if necessary, and keep the caper running. Everybody else was a rat. Burt had personally never met Israel Greenwald, but he assumed right away that Greenwald was no stand-up guy. Israel Greenwald was a rat, and Burt Kaplan hated rats.

"I made up my mind that if the guy lied and said he gave the banker the hundred thousand and put the hundred thousand in his pocket, he was a guy that was going to give up Joe and then Joe was going to give me up and I would go back to prison."

This was unacceptable to Burt Kaplan. He had spent years rebuilding his reputation. He was legitimate, mostly. He was doing deals with Kmart and Calvin Klein and Gloria Vanderbilt. His daughter was a lawyer. He was a better man than this rat Israel Greenwald. He was Burt Kaplan, stand-up guy.

Then, of course, there was Anthony Casso. That was a real problem. If Anthony thought that Burt was going to be arrested, Anthony might think Burt was *not* a stand-up guy, and then Anthony would have to have Burt killed. Anthony could do that. Anthony *would* do that. And then where would his daughter the lawyer be? Where would his poor suffering wife, Eleanor, be?

In the world he had chosen for himself, Burt believed he had no choice.

"I asked Joe to get me the jeweler number two's home address, where he worked, what kind of car he drove, the license plate number. I told him that we were going to talk to the guy and try and shake him up, try and get him to go back to the point where he won't cooperate. Just to grab him and show him that we could grab him and tell him that he took money to do what he did. He was a partner in this thing and he was the one who was the liar. If he had given the banker the hundred thousand, there wouldn't have been a problem."

In a few days, Joe gave Burt Kaplan the address of Israel Greenwald's home on Sage Street in Far Rockaway, Queens, plus the address where Greenwald worked on Forty-seventh Street in the Diamond District, the make of Greenwald's car, and the license plate number. Burt had what he needed to find Israel Greenwald, a man he believed deserved whatever he would get.

"This is Special Agent Beverly A. Bartzer of the New York office of the FBI. The date is August 5, 1985. The time is approximately 4:40 P.M. This tape is being used to record conversations between Israel Greenwald and Herman ————.

The tape is going to be turned off and reactivated when the conversation begins."

Israel Greenwald wore a small recording device beneath his conservative business attire. The main object was to get his old friend Herman to say something incriminating enough to justify an indictment. An indictment might mean Israel would get out from under the huge rock put there by the FBI that was pressing down upon Israel and his entire family.

"Who is it?" Herman said. "Israel's here. Here, come in. They're very angry. Very upset."

"What happened exactly to the money?" Israel asked. This was after all the payments had been doled out to Joe, who'd doled out some to Burt, who doled out some to Anthony, who doled out some to the Colombo associate. All Greenwald knew was that Herman got the money (at the direction of FBI agent Bartzer) and then the money went someplace. He needed to know where it went.

"Which money?" Herman said.

"Where is the money at now?" Israel asked.

"The money? The bank?"

"Yeah."

"It's basically [unintelligible]." The FBI agent listening in couldn't hear what Herman said.

"No," said Israel.

"What happened?" Herman asked. He wanted to know why Israel forgot to pay off the banker in London.

"Nothing at all," Israel said.

"What do you mean, they don't know what happened?" Herman asked.

"They don't know what happened."

"What do you mean, they don't know?" Herman said, his voice rising. "I don't understand you. Why are you playing games?"

"I'm not playing," Israel replied. "I don't know what's happening. I'm telling you I don't know. They're just playing games."

"What should I tell them?" Herman asked.

"I don't know what you should tell them."

"Okay, that's enough. Okay, you don't want to give me any

information. You want me to tell the bank nothing, or forget about the whole thing. I don't know what happened to you."

Israel stammered, couldn't find the right words. The tape recording device heard his stammer.

"You're lying to friends," Herman said. "You're not playing."

"I have to go," said Israel.

"You won't tell me what happened," Herman said. "You don't care about me. Okay."

The tape went dead.

Usually when Burt called Frankie Santora Jr. at his home in Bensonhurst, Frankie was home. In the middle of the week in the middle of the day, while most men in Brooklyn and everywhere else were out punching a time clock, earning a paycheck, contributing to the economy, Frankie Jr. was at home. He wasn't a normal-working-hours kind of guy. When Burt reached him, he brought up that proposition about Frankie's cousin the detective and his partner.

"I told him I didn't have a lot of money at that particular time, but he knew I was good for it, and I said, 'Would you take twenty-five thousand dollars for this? I could pay it ten, ten and five, every week.' And Frankie said, 'That's fair. Don't worry about it.' And he took the contract."

Burt gave Frankie all the information on Israel Greenwald that he'd been provided by Joe—where he lived, where he worked, the make of the car, the license plate. Frankie said they would check his house, check where he worked, and pull him over on his way to work.

"He said they would pull him over with a flashing light and they would say that he was wanted for a hit and run and that someone wanted to look at him and if it wasn't him, they would take him back right away."

Burt thanked Frankie and told him he had to go away on a business trip to Arizona. He was buying some land out there with his partner from China and Anthony Casso and he would back in a few days. He believed Frankie Jr. was a capable guy. He believed he could get the job done.

February 10, 1986

On a leafy street on the suburban edge of Far Rockaway, Queens, another day arrived at 1206 Sage Street. It was a bright, frigid day. Inside the brick one-family Colonial, the Greenwald family confronted the quotidian obstacle course that thousands of families across America face each morning. It was the beginning of another busy working week. Every one of the Greenwalds—Israel, his wife, Leah, his daughters, Yael and Michal—had certain expectations about the week ahead. Every one of the Greenwalds believed that this was just another Monday, like all the other Mondays before and all the Mondays to come.

At 6:00 A.M., Israel Greenwald was already awake. He had stayed up late the night before caring for eight-year-old Yael, who had a nasty case of the flu. He was trying to teach her how to not cough. When he awoke, he prayed and made a few phone calls.

When Leah awoke, the couple discussed the day's schedule—a ritual of marriage they had performed thousands of times before. She would be at school from eight-thirty to twelve-thirty, returning home to be with Yael and awaiting the arrival of Michal from school. Israel told Leah his schedule: First he would drop off license plates from an old Cadillac they were selling at an insurance agent's office. Then he had to get to Long Island City in Queens to buy a new car phone. He had withdrawn twenty-eight hundred dollars in cash the previous Friday for this. Then he had an appointment with another insurance agent, this time to pick up an upgraded life insurance policy. After that he was going to drop off a suitcase with a business partner in Manhattan, then return home in time to meet a man who was going to buy the Cadillac.

Leah Greenwald prepared breakfast and then got ready to get out the door and off to her job teaching first graders. Upstairs eight-year-old Yael lay in bed, sick, knowing she'd be staying home from school with the live-in housekeeper, Rosalba. Her nine-year-old sister, Michal, sat in the kitchen in her school uniform, eating breakfast before heading off to fifth grade.

As Leah finished cleaning up the breakfast dishes, the

doorbell rang. It was a magician who'd come to pick up the family's pet squirrel monkey for his show. As Leah walked out the door, she could hear her husband and the magician laughing as they tried to catch the monkey.

Michal stood at the front door in her school uniform, waiting for the bus when her father came rushing down the stairs on his way out. He stopped for a moment, and said, "Bye Michali."

"Bye Abba," she said, and then he gave her a big hug. She giggled and noticed that the hug was stronger than usual. He said good-bye and got in his car, and Michal watched the blue Cadillac disappear down the block.

The Same Day

A short, squat man with a brush mustache and a full head of brown hair sat alone in a tiny shed that resembled a sentry post. This was 2232 Nostrand Avenue in Flatbush, a grim little place called Pete's Towing, with a row of rotten garages that looked like something out of a low-rent horror flick. The paint was flecking, the doors were covered with graffiti. The place looked abandoned. The garages fronted on a parking lot filled with older-model cars. This was Peter Franzone's little kingdom.

Pete Franzone was sixteen years old and still in sixth grade when he decided school was not for him. He quit and never went back. He worked as a tow truck driver for a while, until he saved up enough to buy the garage and parking lot on Nostrand Avenue. He leased out one garage part-time to an auto body repairman, and he rented parking spaces in his lot. He paid drivers to prowl the city in his two tow trucks, and he let a poor soul from the neighborhood sleep in a run-down shed at the back of the lot. His wife kept the books because he hated arithmetic and never was comfortable with the written word. He wore his keys on a little silver chain attached to his belt buckle.

He worked all the time. He'd be in by 6:00 A.M. and work until 7:30 P.M. Monday through Friday without fail. His wife was expecting a baby. The due date was quite near. The Fran-zones rented an apartment around the corner from the garage on Avenue I, and the Brooklyn blocks between home and office were about all there was to Pete Franzone's world. It was fair to say he didn't get out much and he didn't much mind. There was work and his wife and pretty soon a baby, and that was about it.

Inside the shed, Pete Franzone had a view of his entire kingdom. He could see the entire parking lot and each garage. He could see anybody coming in and out. He worked the dispatch radio for his trucks and tried to keep track of the invoices and bills that put food on his table. It was winter and a Monday and unforgiving outside, but inside the shed it was warm enough. At about 4:30 P.M. with only a few hours to go before the end of the day, Pete noticed a cop he'd met recently pull into the lot in a dark-model sedan.

The cop was Detective Eppolito of the Sixty-third Precinct. He'd been introduced to Pete by Frankie Santora Jr. Frankie came around a lot. He hung around with a number of tow truck drivers Pete knew. Pete was aware that Frankie had certain connections. Frankie was nice enough, but Pete was a little afraid of him.

The detective backed the car into a space that faced one of the middle garages, garage four. From where he sat inside the shed, he could see the detective sitting in the parked car. Just sitting, waiting.

In a minute three men walking side by side approached the entrance to the lot. They were maybe twenty feet away from where Pete sat in the shed, and as they walked by, Pete noticed one of the guys was Frankie Santora Jr. He was on one side, next to a skinny guy wearing a suit and a Jewish skullcap in the center. On the other side was a thin guy Pete had never seen before with a pockmarked face and a trench coat. His collar was pulled up to obscure the guy's face, so Pete couldn't make him out too well. Frankie and the trench-coat guy appeared to be holding on to the arms of the man in the middle with the Jewish skullcap.

The three men entered the garage right across from where the cop was parked sitting in the car, and Pete watched as Santora shut the garage door. A few minutes later, Pete watched two of the men exit the garage—Frankie Jr. and the trench-coat guy. The Jewish man was nowhere in sight. Frankie walked toward Nostrand Avenue with the trench-coat guy, and as he did, the detective pulled out and drove away. Moments later, Frankie Jr. returned and walked up to Pete in the shed.

Frankie ordered Pete to follow him inside.

At 6:00 P.M. a man showed up at the Greenwald house on Sage Street to check out the old Cadillac the family was selling. On most days, Israel Greenwald would call his wife two or three times to check in. He'd called the house at about eleven to check on his sick daughter, Yael, but since then there were no more calls, and now he wasn't home to talk to the man about the Cadillac.

"That was when I really really started to worry," Leah remembered. "He didn't call, he didn't show up. That was extremely not like him. He was an extremely organized person."

Leah Greenwald assumed the worst. She knew her husband had been involved in the Treasury bill deal with Herman, and she knew he was working with the FBI to put Herman in jail. Therefore Herman was the first person she called when Israel didn't show up.

"What have you done with my husband?" she said.

Herman insisted he'd hadn't seen Israel in six months. Leah knew this was a lie. She hung up and called the FBI. The agent her husband was working with was not in, and nobody else knew what she was talking about. She hung up and tried the New York City Police Department. They told her she had to wait twenty-four hours before reporting him missing. She told them he was an informant for the FBI. They said they'd be right over.

The detectives who came to Sage Street asked a lot of questions. When she showed them the card of an FBI agent, they called the FBI and tracked down the correct agent. When the FBI showed up at Sage Street, they appeared to be very upset and promised to do everything they could.

When Pete Franzone got home that night, his wife was asleep. He did not wake her up to tell her what had happened. She was expecting a baby in a few weeks, and she did not need this information. He could not forget what he had seen, but he could not tell anyone. He went to church every Sunday, but he knew he could never tell the priest. It was his secret. It belonged to no one else. He would carry it by himself wherever he went. He thought of what Frankie did and who Frankie was, and he thought about why Frankie had made him part of what happened. He decided it was to keep him quiet. If he was implicated in the thing, how could he go to the police? He was caught in all directions. He believed that the secret was something he could never reveal to anyone—not his wife, not his priest—no one. He would live with it like a cancer inside forever.

Arizona had been a disaster. Burt spent hundreds of thousands of dollars of his own money and borrowed millions more to buy land outside Phoenix. He and Joe were going to resell at a profit. Phoenix was supposed to be hot. It was not. They'd spent nearly fifteen million dollars on the land, and now it was worth maybe seven million dollars. Most of the money came from a mortgage, which did not go away. Burt Kaplan had flown to the desert to try to convince his friend Henry Ho, a Chinese businessman, to bail him out. During the trip, Frankie Jr. had called and said he had something to say. When Burt arrived from Arizona, he faced the prospect of meeting with Frankie Jr.

When they met, Burt said, "What happened to the jeweler?"

Frankie said his cousin Lou the detective and his partner had turned on the flashing lights and pulled the guy over on Grand Central Parkway. The cops told the guy he was wanted for questioning in a hit-and-run accident, and that they needed to take him in for a lineup and then if it wasn't him, he was free to go. The guy complied and got in the detectives' car. He handed over his keys, and Frankie got in the guy's car and followed. They drove to a garage somewhere in Brooklyn.

"What happened?" Kaplan asked.

"We shot him."

"Who shot him?"

"I did."

"Then what happened to him?"

"I took him out and I got rid of the body."

"Do the other two guys know where the body is?"

"No," said Frankie. "I wouldn't trust anybody with that information."

Frankie Jr. told Kaplan that he "dropped him in the water somewhere," then dropped the guy's car off at the airport.

It was all very abstract. Until now, Burt Kaplan had been charged and convicted of selling stolen goods and trying to sell narcotics that weren't narcotics. He had gone to prison. He had a criminal record. He once had helped dispose of another body, but that guy was already dead. He had never personally killed anyone. He never met the guy Frankie shot and dropped "in the water somewhere." He only knew his name, his address, and what kind of car the guy drove. He didn't know if the guy had a wife, children, credit card debts, if the guy could play Mendelssohn's Concerto for Violin in E Minor or was incapable of humming "The Star-Spangled Banner." He only knew that Israel Greenwald had not held up his end. This guy had lied to everyone, and then when he got caught, he was not a stand-up guy. This was the ultimate sin, being a rat.

Maybe it was even worse than paying someone else to kill a guy you never knew.

The next day Leah Greenwald filed a report with the NYPD saying her husband, Israel, was missing. They asked her a lot of questions and took his photo. A few days later she got a call that they had found Israel's blue Cadillac at the police pound. It had been left in the long-term lot at John F. Kennedy International Airport. When Leah showed up to get it, she found that the treble button on the radio had been broken off. She also found the twenty-eight hundred dollars he'd taken for the car phone in the glove compartment, untouched.

Throughout all this, she believed that Herman—the man behind the Treasury bill deal—might know where her husband was. She called him repeatedly, and at one point got him on the phone. He ended that conversation by stating, "Do you want me to dig my own grave?"

Numerous people within the Orthodox community in Far Rockaway and Lawrence began to call Herman, to put pressure on him to behave like a man who feared the consequences of his actions. Herman came to Leah's parents and begged them to stop. They did not.

"He's walking around and we had to suffer financially, emotionally," Leah said. "He was the key to the crime being solved."

They believed that Israel Greenwald was dead, but they were alone in that belief. The government that pays benefits to widows said there was no proof. The FBI and NYPD promised to look into the matter, but they could not declare him dead. The children of Israel Greenwald could not provide a straight answer when their classmates asked, 'Where is your father?' He was neither living nor dead. He was just gone.

FIVE

Summer 1986

The Nineteenth Hole was not the kind of bar where the guys wore plaid pants and white golf shoes and recounted the errant chip shot that did them in on the twelfth. It was true that the Nineteenth Hole sat just a block away from the Dyker Beach Golf Course out in Brooklyn, but if you weren't invited, you couldn't be there. In fact, sometimes when you were invited you didn't want to be there. A handful of guys were shot in the head in the back room at the Nineteenth Hole. Unofficially speaking, the Nineteenth Hole was the property of the Lucchese crime family.

On this summer afternoon Christy "Tic" Furnari stood outside the Nineteenth Hole, on the sidewalk. He was the consigliere of the Lucchese family. He was also a convicted heroin dealer and rapist. Also with him outside the bar was Anthony Casso, Christy Tic's enforcer for his shylock operation. Casso was forty-six years old, a short, compact, Brooklyn-born Italian with a full head of black hair who carried himself in a manner that implied that no one except Christy Tic could tell him what to do. Everybody called him Gaspipe, either because he shot a guy at a gas station once or his father worked for the gas company. It wasn't clear, and he didn't say. He was a captain in the Lucchese crime family and he spent a lot of time hanging around at the Nineteenth Hole.

At the time, both Christy Tic and Gaspipe were aware that big changes were coming soon to the Lucchese crime family. As they stood outside the Nineteenth Hole on this summer afternoon, the boss of the family, Anthony Corallo, was headed for trial in federal court in the city along with the leaders of all five New York Mob families. It was called the Commission case, and was expected to go for months. The FBI had planted a bug in the boss's black Jaguar and recorded the boss saying things that would probably put him in jail. Also in that same trial was Christy Tic. If Christy went away, he would never again stand outside the Nineteenth Hole on a summer afternoon. He was facing the very real possibility of life in prison.

If the bosses went to jail, the changes would come.

At some point that afternoon, a tall, skinny man with a receding hairline and a black beard walked up to the men outside the Nineteenth Hole and became the first guy in the group wearing a suit. He was a well-known criminal defense lawyer, Gerald Shargel, and was greeted warmly by his client Anthony Casso. He had won an acquittal for Casso, who bought him a special gold watch with the inscription "From Gas."

As the three men chatted on the street, another client of Shargel, a marijuana dealer named Burt Kaplan, joined the group. He was a skinny Jewish guy who was a major earner for Casso. Kaplan always came to the Nineteenth Hole to pay off his gambling debts to Christy Tic. He wasn't supposed to actually enter the Nineteenth Hole bar because he was still on parole, and the Nineteenth Hole was a notorious place parole officers disapproved of. Instead, Kaplan stayed outside on the sidewalk and chatted with his lawyers and the gangsters.

All of a sudden the owner of the Chinese restaurant two doors down came running over, agitated. He was telling Christy Tic there were these two drunken kids in his place and they had a Doberman and they were causing all kinds of havoc and the customers were afraid and they were leaving.

By now the Chinese guy had created a little scene all by himself, and the other gangsters inside the Nineteenth Hole, all of whom liked a little scene now and then, emerged from the dark bar and came blinking into the light.

Chris Furnari said to a guy, Angelo, who ran the Nineteenth Hole, "Didn't I tell you to straighten this kid out to stop causing problems in the neighborhood?"

"I told him," said Angelo. "I warned him."

"Go in there now and get him out of there," said Chris.

Angelo walked into the Chinese restaurant and came out with two twentysomething young punks from the neighborhood. One of them was a tall, redheaded kid who spent hours working out, holding a snarling Doberman on a leash. The dog barked wildly at Angelo of the Nineteenth Hole.

The kid with the dog was Jimmy Hydell, and everybody in the neighborhood knew him.

He was twenty-six, and he had detectives following him around full-time. A girlfriend of his named Annette had been kidnapped in the middle of the day on Avenue U a day after she testified before a grand jury about the time Jimmy beat her bloody. Annette hadn't been seen since. Jimmy had been charged with the daytime robbery of a coin store on Avenue U, and he supposedly helped his uncle, Mickey Boy Paradiso, a soldier in the Gambino family, hijack trucks. Now he was using his Doberman to terrorize people between the lo mein and the fortune cookies.

The dog wouldn't stop barking at Angelo from the Nineteenth Hole. Every time Angelo raised his voice and jabbed a finger at Jimmy Hydell's chest, the dog would go wild. That was when Casso said the dog shouldn't be allowed to do that.

"Hold on to that dog," Casso said, and Angelo pointed with his finger and the dog snapped at Angelo again. Casso warned Jimmy one more time, but Angelo did what he did and the dog did what he did and Casso turned and walked into the Nineteenth Hole.

In a minute he came out with a semiautomatic in his hand. He put a silencer on the gun as he stood on the street, and then he shot the dog.

Twice.

Jimmy, the punk who hijacked trucks and probably killed his girlfriend, immediately started crying. Anthony told him to get the dog out of here. Jimmy picked up the dead dog and walked over to his car, weeping. He opened the trunk and put the dog in and drove away, all the time tears streaming down his face.

"I told him," Casso said, "but he wouldn't listen."

September 14, 1986

During the day the temperature had risen to seventy-nine degrees. Now it was evening and still warm, in the upper sixties. In Brooklyn, it was a little hotter away from the sea. Anthony "Gaspipe" Casso sat in a black Lincoln Town Car eating a Carvel ice cream cone in the parking lot of a Chinese restaurant called the Golden Ox.

This was way down at the other end of Brooklyn, where nobody can tell if you're in Bergen Beach or Mill Basin and only people from Brooklyn really care. This was the last week of summer.

Anthony sat in the Lincoln waiting to meet a guy to commit a crime. The guy was supposed to be getting him some more stolen Treasury bills, which Casso would unload and then make a lot of money. That was the plan. The stolen Treasury bill caper seemed like an easy score. Anthony Casso had made a clean $125,000 off the earlier Treasury bill caper with his Jewish business partner, Burt Kaplan, the old man who sold huge quantities of marijuana but never touched the stuff. Anthony had found the Treasury bills, and Burt got rid of them. Everyone was happy. Hopefully the guy with the new Treasury bills would show up at the Golden Ox so he could see if he was about to make even more easy money.

At about 8:00 P.M. two cars drove up to Anthony's Lincoln.

From inside one car came a shotgun blast; from the other, fire from a semiautomatic.

Anthony Casso dropped his ice cream and dove to the floor. He had been hit, but he was alive. He managed to open the passenger-side door and roll onto the pavement. Where were the men in the cars? He lurched into the Golden Ox and ran straight to the basement, where he hid inside the walk-in freezer. There was a trail of blood, but he was alive.

He waited before lurching back upstairs. The cars with the guns were gone. He flagged down a car. He was bleeding all over and convinced the driver to drive him to Kings County Hospital up Utica Avenue. He had been shot in the left shoulder and the neck by the semiautomatic. The guy with the shotgun had missed.

The cops came to the hospital. They asked him questions about who would want to do such a thing to him, but he was absolutely sure no one would. He said he couldn't remember the type of cars, how many men were in the cars. He didn't see anything.

The cop, a sergeant named Mark McGovern, started looking through Anthony's wallet. The sergeant pulled out a slip of paper that had numbers and showed it to Anthony. It was some kind of computer printout. The cop asked him where he got it, and Anthony said the same thing: he didn't know anything.

A few days later, while Anthony Casso was still at the hospital with holes in his shoulder and neck, more detectives and an FBI agent stopped by. They asked him about the slip of paper found in his wallet and who gave it to him. He said what he always said to cops: I don't have a clue.

Later, Sergeant McGovern checked up on the slip of paper. He learned it was a printout of a license plate check run through the New York City Police Department's Field Assistance Terminal Network computer. It was, technically, the property of the NYPD. The computer printout indicated that a NYPD cop had checked the license plate of a two-door white 1985 Mitsubishi sedan with the New York plate 3400 BSA. It came back registered to Joseph Morelli, of 60-60 86th Street, Elmhurst, New York. There was no such person at that address. In fact, the plate was registered to the NYPD. It was an unmarked NYPD vehicle, the kind used by the Organized Crime Investigation Division (OCID).

Sergeant McGovern realized that the gangster Casso had a cop running plates of undercover cars.

•   •   •

A few hours after Casso was shot at the Golden Ox, Burt Kaplan was entertaining relatives from Ohio at his home on Eighty-fifth Street in the Brooklyn neighborhood of Bensonhurst. By now Burt was doing all right. He owned a big discount clothing store a few blocks away, on Eighty-sixth Street, and sold knockoff clothing in stores all over America. Some of the stores were little, some were like Kmart. He was a millionaire, legit, but he also loved to gamble. Therefore he spent even more time than ever before with gangsters. Now he was sitting on the second-floor porch with the relatives from Ohio, enjoying the warm Indian summer evening, when a man came to the front yard and called up to Burt. It was dark, but Burt knew the voice right away. He immediately excused himself and went downstairs.

"We got a problem," said the man. "They tried to kill our friend."

"Who?" said Burt. "What?"

"They tried to kill Gas," said the man.

The man was Vittorio Amuso. Burt and everybody called him Vic. He was a skinny guy with a receding hairline, sixty-one years old, a lifelong gangster. It was thought that if the boss Corallo and Christy Tic lost to the jury in the Commission case, Vic might become the next boss. Right now he was a captain in the Lucchese crime family and was the closest friend Anthony "Gaspipe" Casso ever had. He explained all about the guys in the cars shooting at Anthony while he was parked at the Golden Ox and how Anthony managed to get away and was now lying in a hospital bed at Kings County. In Amuso's view, somebody needed to see Anthony right away.

"Vic, I can't," said Burt Kaplan. He reminded Amuso that he was out of Allenwood prison only two years and still on probation from the quaalude conviction and was not supposed to sit bedside at Kings County with a famous felon like Anthony "Gaspipe" Casso.

"If I go to the hospital and talk to him, I'm going to get violated," Kaplan said.

"I didn't think about that," said Amuso. "I'll handle it."

Amuso left, and Kaplan realized he would get dragged into this thing with Anthony no matter what. A few months back, he'd given Anthony a Lincoln Town Car as a gift. The car was registered in the name of one of his garment companies, Progressive Industries. Amuso had said Casso was shot in the car, so the cops would undoubtedly seize the car as evidence and then find out it was registered to Progressive. He would have to explain this to his parole officer. He needed to get the car as soon as possible.

The next day he had his errand boy Tommy Galpine take a letter down to the Sixty-third Precinct to see if he could get the car. The cops took the letter but wouldn't give up the car. The car was a crime scene, they said. They'd let him know when he could come back and get it.

Sergeant McGovern of the Organized Crime Control Bureau looked at the computer printout found in Anthony Casso's wallet. There was a series of code numbers that showed which computer was used to run the plate, and there was also a tax identification number of the cop using the computer for that run.

McGovern figured that the computer was at the Management Information Systems Division and that the information on the printout about the unmarked cop car was requested at 6:18 A.M. on June 24, 1986, at the Seventy-sixth Precinct station house in Brooklyn. The person requesting the information had input Tax ID No. 869928 and a confidential code number that allowed access to the system. The query lasted eight minutes and terminated at 6:26 A.M. As it happened, that was just four minutes before the start of Police Officer Louis Tuzzio's shift at the Seventy-sixth Precinct station house in Brooklyn.

P. O. Tuzzio worked for something called TOPAC, which stood for Total Patrol Concept. What it really meant was scooter patrol. On June 24, 1986, the day the computer was accessed, Tuzzio was assigned to Scooter 3553 out of the Seventy-sixth Precinct station house in Brooklyn. His shift was supposed to start at 6:30 A.M.

Sergeant McGovern of the Organized Crime Control Bureau decided it was time to take a closer look at P. O. Tuzzio. He ordered a pen register on Tuzzio's home phone, which would allow him to track the numbers of those who called P. O. Tuzzio and the numbers of those whom Tuzzio called.

McGovern arranged for P. O. Tuzzio to be surveilled to see who he met with. They wanted to know how that little computer printout with the unmarked NYPD car wound up in the wallet of gangster Anthony "Gaspipe" Casso.

The failed attempt to kill Anthony Casso resonated throughout the tiny world of organized crime on both sides. This involved the people who commit crime that is organized and the people who try to catch them doing it. It was viewed as one of those events that would mean more bodies on the sidewalk. In the loquacious world of gangland, the attempt to kill Gaspipe zipped around the grapevine like a coach's firing on sports talk radio shows. This was, after all, Gaspipe. To try to kill a guy like that and then to fail in that attempt—that was as big a mistake as anyone could remember. It was clear to anyone who knew even a little about Gaspipe that he would not rest until everyone involved in the hit—along with their sons, grandsons, and family pets—was deader than Lincoln at Ford's Theater. Because everyone knew this, word started circulating almost immediately about who might have been involved.

First a guy who knew a guy surfaced to tell Anthony Casso about an ex-transit cop named Bobby Berring, who had come around a bus company near Casso's house asking questions about the make and year of Casso's car. Then Casso got word that the brothers Saparano might have something to add. One of their sons happened to be dating the sister of a local tough guy named Jimmy Hydell, the kid with the dog at the Nineteenth Hole. By mistake, the sister had let her boyfriend know about her brother's involvement in the attempt to kill Anthony Casso. Finally, a member of the Colombo family had even more. They had heard that the hit crew consisted of three men—Bobby Berring, Jimmy Hydell, and a guy named Nicky Guido.

That was all the information Casso needed.

The day after Casso was shot, Detective Louis Eppolito of the Sixty-third Precinct approached another detective at the station house and told him they were supposed to inspect a Lincoln Town Car at the police towing yard. The case involved the shooting of a hoodlum well known in the Sixty-third Precinct: Anthony 'Gaspipe" Casso.

In the Sixty-third Precint in the autumn of 1986, Anthony Casso had accumulated an impressive file. They knew everything about him but not enough to put him in prison. The file noted that his electrical bills were in the name of a woman named Ann and that he was a secret partner in several businesses, including Progressive Distributors (owner on paper, Burton Kaplan). He also had a restaurant in Sheepshead Bay. The file listed several spots where Casso hung out, including the Nineteenth Hole and the El Caribe in Brooklyn and a fish restaurant called Abracamento's on the Canarsie Pier. He had three pager numbers.

The file noted that Casso was born on May 21, 1940, which meant he missed the war by a little bit. He started out on Union Street in Red Hook, a few blocks from the Brooklyn waterfront. He was leader of a street gang called the Tigers, and rigged a silencer to a .22 rifle to shoot pigeons from rooftops. At one point he got a job on the docks. There was a dock worker bragging about his metal-tipped work boots. Casso allegedly picked up a five-hundred-pound box with a front-end loader and dropped it on the guy's feet. "See how good them shoes are now," he said with a chuckle, or so the story goes.

The other interesting story about Casso was that he had a long history of crime without punishment. In 1962 he was convicted of bookmaking. He was fined fifty dollars and sentenced to five days in jail. Between 1965 and 1977 he was arrested five times on charges such as assault with a gun, possession of stolen property, heroin trafficking, bank burglary, and conspiracy to bribe state parole officials. Each time he was acquitted. In the bribery case, the main witness declined to testify after being shot eight times.

Three days before Christmas 1972, Casso, his lifelong friend Vic Amuso, and several others were indicted by the district attorney on charges of bribing parole officials to get out early. By now he was showing up in the file as an associate of the Gambino crime family. Casso and his friend Amuso were charged with trying to arrange early release for three corrupt cops who were serving time for shaking down drug dealers. They were acquitted.

In March 1973, Casso and three others were acquitted in Brooklyn of charges that they were part of a bank burglary gang. Prosecutors alleged the gang paid off a cop who introduced a night watchman to the group. The watchman was paid thirty-two thousand dollars to turn off the alarms for jobs, which netted four hundred thousand dollars in jewels and cash from busted safe deposit boxes at three bank branches. The night watchman cooperated, but before he did was heard on tape with defendants saying he knew they didn't do it. The jury took two hours to acquit.

Then in 1979, Casso was inducted into the Lucchese family. The NYPD file dubbed him a soldier and noted he was under investigation for ongoing activities, including bank robberies and bank burglaries. He was also listed as a "potential murder victim," a reference to what was described simply as the "incident at Golden Ox." The NYPD file also contained a list of names of "persons involved." They included Jimmy Hydell, the kid who cried when Anthony Casso shot his dog.

Although Detective Eppolito was not assigned as the lead detective in the attempted murder of Anthony Casso, he was assigned to help out. This means he had access to Gaspipe's file. On this day, his only task was to head to the yard and check out Casso's car.

Detective Eppolito and the other detective drove to the NYPD tow yard to meet a K-9 unit handler with a narcotics-sniffing dog named Grizzly. They popped the trunk and Grizzly did his job, sniffing and wagging. By the time they were done they had found some white powder in the trunk and some keys behind the glove compartment, including one that looked like it belonged to a safe deposit box from a specific bank. They collected the powder in a bag and placed the keys in a separate bag. He had the other detective type the report, which was then added to the file of the ongoing investigation of the attempted murder of Anthony Casso.

Frankie Santoro Jr. phoned Kaplan to let him know some important news about the car that was sitting at the NYPD pound. He said his cousin Lou told him they had found white powder and a safe deposit box key in the trunk. Suddenly Kaplan got an idea. Casso had told him he was having a tough time tracking down the three guys involved in the hit. Frankie and the cops had been very helpful with the jeweler. Why couldn't they be helpful on this?

When Casso got out of the hospital, Kaplan paid a visit. For the first time, Kaplan told his gangster pal he had two cops who might help find out who had tried to kill him. Casso liked that very much. Burt said he'd set it up.

In a few days, Frankie Jr. paid him a visit bearing a big, fat envelope with photographs and papers stamped with the logo of the New York City Police Department.

"I opened it and I looked in it," Kaplan said. "There was a picture of Jimmy Hydell."

In the envelope were crime scene reports with names of people described as "persons involved." There was Jimmy Hydell's uncle, Mickey Boy, and a drug-dealing Gambino captain named Angelo Ruggiero. There was also a Nicky Guido of the Gambino family. The little packet Frankie's cousin had obtained was helpful. It listed where the "persons involved" lived, what kind of cars they drove, even the license plate numbers.

"This is terrific, Frankie," said Kaplan. "What do we owe you?"

Frankie Jr. shook his head.

"This is a gift from my cousin and his partner," Frankie Jr. said. "This is just to show you the kind of things that they would do. They won't take no money because this was someone looking to hurt you and they wouldn't take money under those circumstances. My cousin and his partner won't take any money for something where somebody close to us got hurt. We're not that kind of people."

When Burt Kaplan walked into a social club operated by a guy known as Swaggy on Thirteenth Avenue in Brooklyn, he found Casso and Vic Amuso at the bar.

"Do you know who shot you?" Burt said.

Casso said, "No, and you don't, either."

"Well, it was Jimmy Hydell."

"You're crazy," Casso said, even though he'd already been told by three other people that this was so. "It couldn't have

been Jimmy Hydell. I just got him a job with the unions and
we made friends."

Kaplan handed over the envelope with the photos and police paperwork and said, "See for yourself."

When his trusted friend Burt Kaplan showed up at Swaggy's
with the packet on Jimmy Hydell, Anthony Casso had some
familiarity with crooked law enforcement. Back in the 1970s,
when crooked cops were as easy to spot as graffiti on subway
cars, a friend of his had asked him for some help regarding
two corrupt officers of the New York City Police Department
who had found themselves on Rikers Island charged on multiple counts. The friend wanted Casso to get one of them out
of there right away. Casso reached out to a crooked Rikers Island guard who had a crooked friend he knew on the parole
board. The guard would sneak gangsters out of Rikers on the
weekends for five hundred dollars. The parole board member
might be able to arrange an early release for the bad cop. The
crooked guard said the parole board member could fix the situation for five thousand dollars.

Therefore Casso was mightily impressed that Frankie Santora Jr. and the cops hadn't charged a dime for the packet on
Jimmy Hydell. He told Kaplan the cops were "good guys" to
do that.

Meanwhile, Burt knew that by handing over the packet and
telling Anthony about the cops, he had entered into a new
contract with the gangster. He had offered his protector a
powerful new weapon, and it was important that he keep the
weapon safe—even from Anthony Casso. Casso did not know
the cops' names, and Burt needed to keep it that way. If Casso
knew their names, he might not need Kaplan around as the
middleman. Plus Kaplan had never told Casso about his use
of Frankie Jr. and the cops with the jeweler in the garage. Burt
had deliberately kept that information to himself. When he revealed his relationship with the cops to Casso, he had merely
said they had done something for him and left it at that. He
knew that once he told Casso the cops' names the cops belonged to Casso.

Burt Kaplan had a good idea about the true Anthony Casso.
He knew very well what Casso wanted to do with the photos

and information in the packet. He knew that Jimmy Hydell's days were numbered, and that Casso would spend probably the rest of his life looking to track down every guy on that list of "persons involved." Since Casso was just a middle-age guy, he would have a long time to do that.

What did not surprise Burt Kaplan was Casso's next request.

"Casso asks if Frankie and his friends can pick up Hydell, bring him alive to him."

Casso felt the cops were the best way to get Jimmy Hydell. Jimmy was likely a guy who wouldn't let just anybody pull him over. Flashing lights and badges was the best possible way to catch reluctant Jimmy off guard. And Casso was very clear about the alive part. He needed Hydell to be alive because he needed Hydell to tell him who else was involved in the attempt to kill him.

The implications of keeping Hydell alive were apparent. This was a big step. This was cops kidnapping an American citizen on the streets of New York and delivering him up to a known psychopath, who would likely take his time with the information-gathering in a dark basement somewhere out there in the night.

Kaplan decided it was too late to turn back. He called Frankie, Frankie asked the cops, and they said they could do it. They just needed a car that looked like a detective's car. They agreed upon a price of thirty thousand dollars. "No problem," Burt said, and the acceleration of young Jimmy Hydell's final days was set in motion.

Casso had a Lucchese soldier who operated an auto body shop buy a detective's car, and Kaplan arranged to have his errand boy Tommy Galpine deliver it to a spot on a Brooklyn street a block or two from Frankie Santora Jr.'s house. There were layers of people between Casso and the cops.

Days went by. Jimmy was nowhere to be found. It was now clear that Jimmy was hiding. He had to be. The way Casso saw things, the attempt to kill him had to be sanctioned by the top levels of the Gambino crime family. That meant the Gambino crime family was also trying to find Jimmy to kill him before Casso got to him. Everybody wanted Jimmy Hydell, and Jimmy had disappeared.

• • •

Sergeant McGovern of the Organized Crime Control Bureau had been very busy. He'd assembled his information, and now he needed to ask some questions of scooter cop Louis Tuzzio.

First, Sergeant McGovern got a copy of the log sheet for the computer at the Seventy-sixth Precinct and discovered that P. O. Tuzzio was the fifth cop to access the computer that day and the only one to access the computer anywhere near 6:30 A.M. According to the log, Tuzzio had signed in at 6:30 A.M.

However, the log was confusing in two respects. First, it claimed Tuzzio had run a different plate. Second, the log made no reference to the earlier inquiry for the undercover car. This was puzzling because the computer showed somebody using Tuzzio's tax ID and confidential password to run the other plate a few minutes before the inquiry he'd made sure to put down in the log. It seemed like he had either forgotten to mention the other run on the log, or he didn't want anybody to know about it.

McGovern went back to the computer records and realized that Tuzzio's 6:30 A.M. request really took place at 6:20 A.M., and that he stayed on just long enough to make the undercover-car inquiry found in Anthony Casso's wallet first, then the inquiry he put down on the log sheet a few minutes later. He was, McGovern concluded, using the other request as a cover.

The log was a lie that the NYPD had missed. The log was supposed to be regularly inspected by the sergeant on duty. Such an inspection might have caught the lie. McGovern checked up on the sergeant and discovered he wasn't doing his job. Though the log was supposed to be inspected four times during a twenty-four-hour period, the sergeant checked it only twice.

Now it was time for an official departmental inquiry into how the printout got into Anthony Casso's wallet. P. O. Tuzzio was summoned to a meeting, and a tape recorder was set up. Tuzzio was asked a series of questions, and the best he could do was say he could not recall running the license plate of an unmarked NYPD vehicle. He did remember making the other inquiry, but on this one, he simply drew a blank. Tuzzio said he had "no independent recollection of that day or the circumstances surrounding his request for the information." He theorized he may have been called into the station house to work the computer, and implied that he may have run the unmarked car plate for another officer. He didn't mention any names. He also claimed he couldn't remember why he ran the other plate.

The NYPD administrative judge who heard the case found Tuzzio's explanation "disingenuous" and "not credible."

And that was that. The NYPD went no farther. They suspended Tuzzio for thirty days, and they put him on probation for a year, but they did not fire him. He even filed an appeal of the department's pathetic punishment, which was summarily shot down by an appeals court that wondered why the NYPD had been so lenient with a cop who'd clearly been caught leaking information to a dangerous criminal.

The Appellate Division First Department's decision noted Tuzzio's misconduct in revealing the unmarked car to the gangster "may have placed the lives and safety of fellow officers working in the Organized Crime Investigation Division at risk.

"Were we free to impose a different, harsher penalty, we would do so."

Tuzzio remained on the force and was able to collect his pension. One of the questions at Tuzzio's departmental hearing was, "Did you have any contact with individuals in organized crime?" He replied, "No, I do not."

At the time he answered this question, his son Louis Jr. was an associate of the Bonanno crime family. On January 4, 1990, a hit team sent by the Bonanno crime family shot the younger Tuzzio inside his own sports car. Many of the press reports at the time noted that Tuzzio's father was a cop, although none made reference to the departmental finding that he'd leaked law enforcement secrets to the Mob.

SIX

Ten days before Christmas, "God Rest Ye, Merry Gentlemen" blasted through the mall at Caesar's Palace. "Remember Christ our Savior was born on Christmas Day," with an emphasis on *remember*. It was dinnertime, about six-thirty, and Steve Corso was headed for Joe's Stone Crab in the Caesar's mall. This was yet another dinner with Lou the cop, this time enthusiastically paid for by the FBI. Forget about Gerry Chilli and Mike the driver. He'd tape-recorded Lou and his entire family for six weeks. He'd paid for enough pinot noir and Tanqueray to fill a fifty-five-gallon drum and enough osso buco and filet mignon to feed a fraternity house.

Inside the restaurant he ordered a mojito. The place wasn't busy yet, and he talked on the cell until Lou showed and started talking about his upcoming heart surgery. It was days away, and he was once again going back and forth from extreme optimism to doom and gloom. At the moment he was on the upbeat side of the question.

"Everything is fine," he said. "The doctor said, I went through all your records, everything is fine. I have to tell you percentages, because that's my job. He said ninety-eight percent chance of recovery," Lou said, and turned toward the bartender. "I'll take one of those Bombay martinis with an olive straight up."

"How's Fran taking this?" Corso asked.

"Today she came home with a smile on her face," he said. "My doctor says you can't eat red meat, I won't eat red meat. He said, 'I just don't want you getting up in the morning and having two hamburgers at McDonald's.' I said, 'I don't eat that shit. I'm Italian.' He said, 'Eat until you bust.' He said, 'I think you're in great shape.' You tell me I got to climb a rope with no hands, I'll do it."

"So Fran is happy."

"Ecstatic. The kids are happy. It's good news. I'm not worried about it," he said.

The waiter arrived and listed the specials. Corso ordered pinot noir, and Lou switched to bottled water.

"I like the bottled water," he said. "What is it, Pellegrino? Tell the French you can kiss my hand."

"You're Italian," said the waiter.

With the FBI's credit card, Corso ordered an appetizer portion of stone crabs and bone-in filet mignon, cooked medium, with creamed spinach. Lou ordered the chopped lettuce and tomatoes and lemon herb chicken breast with grilled potatoes. Corso commented that because Lou had experienced the high-pressure life of a cop, facing heart surgery probably wasn't that big a deal. Lou told a story about being in the ambulance with a cop who was shot and how he had to get a tetanus shot because when he lifted up the cop, the cop's bones had punctured Lou's hands.

"I'm one of the few freaks left in this world who believe in God," Lou said. "To me, God is up there. Jesus is up there."

It was all good news. Lou talked about how at first he thought they would have to stop his heart, but after testing his strength the doctors said they wouldn't have to do that.

"When I walked out of there, the fucking weight of the world was off me," he said. "I don't mind dying, but aside from that, I do not want to die. I had that wiseguy mentality. The doctor says to me you want to be a vegetarian, I'll be a vegetarian. I want to stay around and see my children." He said he told Fran to be straight with the children if it didn't work out.

"When I'm done with this, you tell them what the doctor tells me. You tell them the truth. If the doctor says I've got six months, you tell them. I don't like to start my kids off with bullshit."

Now Corso had to make excuses. He'd promised a lot of things. They were going to do this big public offering in a few weeks, and the investors were going to put up money right away, and none of that was happening. No money had arrived. He gave a reason for this, that Crucker the big-money guy was sick. Lou seemed okay with the story for the moment, although he kept talking about how much money he spends. He said he dropped forty-two thousand dollars on the wedding of his daughter Deanna. There were 150 guests, and he did the same for Andrea years ago, when she married a rich guy who she said treated her poorly. She dumped him, but she still had to live with the mistake.

"I'll tell you one thing," Corso said. "If that's the only mistake that Andrea made in her life, that's nothing. I've made so many mistakes."

"We still make them," Lou said.

"I've made so many mistakes. I said to my mom, 'If Dad were still alive, would I make the same mistakes?'"

"I've been in that spot before," Lou said. "I wish I could have two hours to let me sit with my dad for two hours. All you do is remember. My father used to tell me, 'Your mother as far as I'm concerned is really the Blessed Virgin. If you ever raise your hand to a woman, you never do that.' I said, 'I heard you.' He said 'I don't give a fuck, you walk around the block.'"

"I never raised my hand to a woman," Corso said. "You're not a man if you do that. But in this town, half the broads want you to treat them like shit. I can't understand. I remember coming back from school, when I was going to college in New York, I would have to go home for Sunday dinner, macaroni and lemon and chicken every Sunday my entire life. After dinner we would go and sit in the garden and we'd have a little wine and a couple of slices of chicken and we would just sit there and talk. My father would always say, 'We're not going to talk about the moon and China. We're not going to talk about the weather. Tell me what's going on.' The value my father had, he was an incredible listener. He would sit there and you would never know if he agreed with you or disagreed with you. He would support you. If I went out with a girl he didn't like, he would never tell me he didn't like her. Never. He would listen to what I said and in his own way push me away from her. He'd say, 'Her family's like this.' He knew if I came out and said—"

"I don't like her," Lou interjected.

"You'd go the opposite way."

"That's all kids."

"But he was smart enough and you could tell him anything. Anything. But as I've gotten older, I've realized and I never thought this, it does matter—it matters more than you realize—your cultural background."

"I believe that," Lou said. "They care about Mother's Day. They care about what your family's doing. Is there a problem?"

The waiter showed up and listed the desserts. Corso ordered key lime pie with a double espresso, Lou just the espresso. Then he admitted maybe everything wasn't perfect.

"Andrea cried, 'I can't go on with my life without you. You're too important to me.' I said, 'I'll do whatever it takes.'"

Corso said, "My dad had a heart attack and I would always prepare myself for the day they would call and say my dad had died. When he did die, I realized one thing. I was an idiot because you can never prepare yourself for that moment. All I did was worry. I learned the best thing you can do is enjoy it."

When dinner was over, Lou suggested they stop by Andrea's apartment to see her renovations. He said she went to Macy's and spent two hundred dollars on an artificial Christmas tree with lights on it. Fran didn't like it, but Andrea said she had to go with artificial because of Flower the dog. "Andrea said to me, 'I got the fucking tree for the dog.' She said, 'They don't like my dog, I don't like them.' I said, 'He's so fucking ugly, you have to love him.'"

"Flower doesn't fit," Corso said.

"She loves Flower."

On the way to the car "The Little Drummer Boy" played on the mall Muzak.

At Andrea's, Corso and Andrea walked into a room away from the rest of the family. She talked about renovation—the location of the dining room, the use of mirrors, a chandelier, how she's thinking chocolate brown for the couch. There will be a hot tub and no pool because pools are too much work. "We're going to have medieval things, dripping candles," she said. She said that Flower ripped everything to pieces because he has "separation anxiety." He dragged a tree out of the back-yard into the house.

"All this shit will go upstairs," she said. "I don't do any-thing manual. I don't hang shit, so I'm at the mercy of my friends."

There was a crazy bulldog and medieval decorations and graduation coming, but it was clear there was one thing only on Andrea's mind: her father and his heart surgery. She said out of nowhere, "I'm wishing it was the twenty-ninth so it would be over. I wish today was the twenty-ninth. We got in-vited to a New Year's Eve party in New York. I wrote back, 'I'll be spending New Year's Eve in the hospital with my fa-ther.'"

Corso listened and said nothing. Andrea said of her par-ents, "They both have a tendency to sugarcoat things."

"They're protecting you," Corso said. "But he'll be fine."

"Yeah I know, but—"

"The operation will be done by four. I've had five friends go through this fine."

"Did he tell you the story that my sister told him? You're almost obligated, it's your job to say, 'My uncle was sup-posed to go in, and he decided to wait a couple of weeks and he went home and had a heart attack.' She said, 'What hap-pened?' 'Oh, he died.' My sister was in the office. She was hysterical."

"If they needed to do it right away, they would have," Corso said. He told her a story about a rich older guy and his young wife, and how disappointed the wife was when she re-alized he'd pulled through heart surgery.

"Tell me she was pissed off. Oh, God." She laughed for the first time.

"That's the way you have to look at it," Corso said.

"Everyone says he'll be fine," she said, and now the laughter was gone and she was talking about her mother. "If something happens, her life will be over."

Andrea invited Corso to a party in a few days at her apartment to celebrate the end of her graduate work. He accepted, then got into his car and left. On the way, he turned on the car radio and heard a voice say, "Tell us about your daughter."

"Well, she was in an abusive relationship—"

Corso said, "Wonderful" and quickly changed the station.

December 20, 2004

Andrea's graduation party was packed, but there was no music. Instead, a football game, New England at Miami, blared on the giant-screen TV. All the Eppolitos were there, and Corso was introduced all around.

"This is Steve!" Lou shouted to the crowd. "He's going to get the money for my movies!"

Fran and Andrea darted from guest to guest, handing out glasses of champagne.

"You have to make a toast," Fran said.

"Me?" Lou said.

"We're running out of glasses," Fran said, and everybody laughed.

The room got quiet, except for the football.

"I make a toast to my daughter, who in twenty-seven years—twenty-eight years—hasn't given me one ounce of problems and who made me very proud, who went back to graduate school after all those years. She was determined to get her education, which I'm very proud of. The thing that I'm most proud of is she has her mother's beauty and her father's balls."

The crowd loved it. Cheers, laughter, joy all around. It was Andrea's turn.

"When I was going back to school, all of my friends, everybody was really supportive. But the one thing I remembered is I was leaving my parents' house and my father kissed me on the cheek and said that he admired what I was doing.

When my mother hugged me she said she was accepting all of the things I was going to give up in order to go back to school. It's always true that your parents are proud of you, but respect and admire aren't always two things we hear about. So thank you."

Another great cheer, which almost drowned out Lou saying, "I love you."

Fran said, "Great toast."

Lou took Corso aside in the corner. He was still pumped up from the crowd. He was not a man who doubted his own words. He believed that what he said was important, and he was used to being the center of attention. Corso told him everything with the money was going great, that Crucker was especially interested in the Sandy Murphy wrongful conviction story. Lou was manic, jumping from subject to subject. He claimed he had a real, live Hollywood producer named Willie Cutner who wanted in on the company. Willie had produced a handful of teenager slasher movies in the 1980s and had made some money remaking old fifties horror flicks such as *I Was A Teenage Werewolf*.

Fran swung by and offered food; Corso said he already ate. Lou said, "What is this? Can the dog eat it?"

Fran said, "No, he can't have those cookies."

Corso asked Fran about the traditional Italian Christmas dinner she was preparing, with all the fish and the eight courses. She listed antipasto, fried calamari ("I buy the ones that are all ready.") There was sliced shrimp and shrimp marinara and pasta. The usual fish courses, she claimed, nobody eats. Corso said he had a little gift and handed her tickets to see Kevin Spacey performing Bobby Darin songs to kick off his new movie. She waded back into the crowd.

Lou wanted to know what was going on with the seventy-five thousand dollars.

"I should have an official answer tomorrow," Corso said. "Either he says he transfers it or he says it's in a cardboard box, go pick it up."

Andrea came over and said hello. Corso suggested she needed speakers in her apartment.

"You're such a man," she said. "And maybe get a boom box, put up an AC/DC poster?"

Lou said, "Where's your brother? Tell him Miami is back up."

His son, Anthony, came over. He said, "Every time I hit somebody now my knuckle breaks."

"Me, too," Lou said.

Lou was all excited. He was name-dropping like a gossip columnist.

"I got a letter here, I have to search for it, I have a letter from Tom Hanks wondering what my next project is going to be and wondering if he's going to have an opportunity to look at it. I says, 'When my movie comes out, *Mafia Cop*, I don't need you, I don't need anybody. They'll start calling me.' I said, 'Tom, you don't have any idea the people I've dealt with. One time I was talking to Elliot Gould.'"

Corso said, "Who?"

"Elliot Gould. And Robert DeNiro. Here's their home numbers. Christmas cards. I took out Christmas cards from Gene Hackman. I said, 'These are the people I can get up to.'

"I said, 'Tom, I'm going to shock you. I got friends who are the top Mafia guys in the movies. I tell these guys I've written this, you gotta do me a favor. Like Tony Sirico, he's a good friend. I need you to be in this movie. I'll make a five-million-dollar movie that'll look like a thirty-million-dollar movie.'"

A woman who appeared to have found all the glasses of champagne that were available interrupted to say she had a friend who had triple bypass and was not doing great. She said she worked in what she called "the criminal system."

Lou said, "I love those little pieces of shit. They're all murderers, rapists, and killers."

"I love it," the woman said. "If you're going to do it, do it right. Don't get caught."

"Don't get caught, we wouldn't be having this conversation."

"They get out and they come back in the same week."

"I had one guy in court, he unwrapped the microphone, like a singer," Lou said. "I love them. God put them on earth to have fun and play with."

"They're there for my entertainment," said the woman.

"Just think if there were no criminals, there'd be no jails, no cops, no psychiatrists, no judges. They are wonderful. Leave them alone, let them breed, and play with them."

"For sheer entertainment," said the woman before wandering off.

Corso said nothing.

Another woman started talking about a guy with lots of tattoos she knew who had a penis piercing that he called Jacob's Ladder. That got Lou started up on guys with tattoos.

"Tattoos, mustaches, long hair, they're nothing when it comes to getting punched in the chest," he said. "Let me tell you a story."

He talked about a contractor he hired who was covered with tattoos who was supposed to finish up a renovation job at his house but seemed to have forgotten all about it. The guy didn't return calls, and when he did, he promised he'd be right over and never showed up. He had every excuse you could think of. He was sick. His friend's father died. Everything. When he finally showed up, Lou said he and his son confronted the guy.

"I took the guy, I said, 'I want to talk to you for a second.' I took the hatchet out of his hands. I said, 'Do you think I wouldn't put this through your fucking head?' I said, 'You are nothing but a faggot. Your tattoos don't show me shit.' I said, 'You don't finish this job today or tomorrow, I'm going to personally kill you in front of your friends and then I'm going to kill your friends. I said you're taking kindness for weakness and I'm not weak. I don't do that. If you ever want to push I'll personally kill you, and I'll do that in front of your mother and your father and then I'll kill them. I'll let them have the agony of letting them see you die first. That's embedded in me. I can't help it.'"

He paused for dramatic effect.

Corso said, "Did he do it?"

"Yeah, he finished everything, and then he put out his hand and I said, 'I don't shake hands with you. I don't want you to do anything. I want you to get out. I don't want you with your friends with their berets on, their crooked hats, that don't scare me.'"

Miami beat New England, 29–28. The crowd was beginning to put on jackets. They all wished Lou good luck with his surgery. Fran was saying good-bye and talking about how there was no really good Italian food out here in the desert.

"The first time we came here we said, 'We want the broccoli rabe,'" she said. "They brought us zucchini and we said, 'We don't want this crap.'"

December 29, 2004

At about 5:00 P.M. on a Wednesday it was raining in the desert. Steve Corso was parked over on the side of the road having a little talk with a traffic cop. He'd been pulled over and informed that his license expired in May. He claimed he renewed his license online but had not yet received the paperwork. The cop did not appear to believe him and went back to his cruiser to check this out. When he was gone, Corso turned off the FBI tape-recording device that was capturing this magic moment.

A few moments later, the tape came back on and Corso, exasperated, said, "A ticket, what a day. Still going to Lou Eppolito."

He drove to the Desert Springs Hospital on Flamingo Road and parked. He found him on the second-floor ICU in bed 6. At eleven the previous morning Lou Eppolito had had double-bypass surgery to clean out plaque in the arteries near his heart. They had cracked open his rib cage and he was currently hooked up to several machines. They started him on morphine and switched to codeine. It was clear from the conversation that Corso was doing his best to make it seem as if Lou looked like he always did, although clearly he did not.

"You don't look sick," Corso said. "You look beautiful."

"Doesn't he?" Fran said, her voice filled with fear. She was sitting by his bed, as she had since the previous day. Andrea was there as well, silent.

"You look good," Corso said. "How do you feel?"

"Like shit." Lou said that, but it was hard to hear. It was maybe a little bit more than a whisper.

"You look good," Corso said. He kept saying that. "You got pain?"

Fran answered for Lou, "You know from them cracking the chest bone."

"Did they get you up today?" Corso asked.

"Yeah I was up for an hour," Lou said, again in a near-whisper.

Fran asked Corso, "How's your mother?"

He said, "She's my mother." Corso's cell went off with *The Godfather* theme, and he excused himself and stepped out of the room.

When he came back, Fran said Lou would be back home by tomorrow. They talked about the Kevin Spacey show, and Corso claimed to have obtained the famous actor's famous signature on a program.

"They put on a great show," Lou rasped from the bed.

"So the pain is where the cut is?" Corso asked.

"When I breathe in."

"They used to make a big cut but now they do a small cut and they do it telescopically," Fran offered.

"You got great color. You look great," Corso said again.

"How's the other thing going?" Lou asked. His voice cracked on that one.

"When you feel better, get that stuff together for me."

"What about that other guy?"

"He'll be in."

"As long as I know he's still into it." He started to cough. "I got all the papers he wants. I got the thing from the girl. I'm a very fast healer and I'm not going to overkill myself. I'm not going to overdo it. When I get home I'll get the stuff at the house—"

Fran interrupted, "You're not going to be doing a lot of walking around. They're telling you you can walk three houses down. What do you think you're going to do, get in your car and walk to meetings? You stay home and people come to you. Take a step back."

"Well," said Lou. The heart monitor beeped in the background.

"Is the light bothering you?" Fran asked her husband in the bed. "You want me to shut it?"

The nurse came in to check his blood-sugar numbers. Lou was groaning when she moved him and breathing hard. When the nurse left, he said, "I kept telling everybody I want to get this fucking thing over with. Everybody calls me up, say, 'How you feeling?' I just want to get this thing over with. They had a tube down my throat, I couldn't talk."

"Now remember, this is the worst; every day gets better," Corso said. "The nurse seems very nice."

"Oh, yeah, nice. I wouldn't mind giving her a hump." Lou said this without mirth, as if he was expected to say it. He groaned again. The monitor beeped.

"They want to take him off the insulin but they can't do it without the doctor's permission," Fran offered. She said when the anesthesia wore off in the next twenty-four hours, it would be worse.

"It's a good week to go," Corso said. "Pouring rain, you wouldn't get anything done anyway."

"Terrible week," Fran agreed. "What are you doing for New Year's?"

"No plans. Tell you one thing, I won't be down at the Strip."

"I'll be right here," Fran said.

"Bring a little bottle of champagne," Corso said.

"Don't stay up," Fran said to Lou. "Close your eyes."

Corso said good-bye, and Fran said she had to get her jacket from the car and would walk with him outside.

"All right, I'll go," Corso said. "I'll see you soon."

"All right, buddy," whispered Lou.

In the hospital hallway, Corso said he thought Lou looked pretty good, considering. Fran said she agreed.

"I was very very pleased last night when I saw him," she said. "I thought his head was going to be on his chest, I thought he wasn't going to have any color. But all the tubes are covered up. . . . I was really shocked when the doctor said he only did a double. He's got to go on a diet, modify his eating habits. . . . I said you gotta do what you gotta do."

The younger man and the older woman reached the outside and said good-bye. The hospital was on the edge of the city, and in the twilight it was quiet.

A siren wailed way off in the distance, and Fran said, "Feels like snow, if I didn't know any better."

SEVEN

When Detective Stephen Caracappa worked the narcotics task force in the late 1970s, there was plenty of heroin and a steady supply of marijuana. Then came the 1980s and the discovery by the drug lords of Latin America that Americans with their credit cards and unlimited appetites were willing to pay premium prices for powdered cocaine. The Colombian drug lords set up a criminal network that could provide a steady supply to the streets of New York City, which kept the narcotics task force quite busy.

At the time, one of the biggest problems within the task force was the potential for corruption. The money was astonishing. Caracappa and a partner once busted a dealer who had $250,000 in carefully wrapped $100 bills inside a suitcase. The dealer had said, "That's not my money. It's yours." They declined, but others did not. Plenty of opportunities arose. Plus it was believed that you had to snort cocaine to do the job. If you refused, the sellers would immediately decide you were a narc, and that would either be the end of the deal or the end of you. It was dangerous work with too many temptations.

For Stephen Caracappa, it took its toll. He and his first

wife, Cheryl, had a baby girl who died before she was one year old. There was a funeral, and she was buried on a hill near his mother's house in Staten Island in a tiny cemetery called St. Mary's. The gravestone looked out on a housing project. Caracappa began to drink heavily. He couldn't sleep, so he got a prescription for amphetamines. At some point while he was on the narcotics task force, he took too many pills and drank too much alcohol and found himself in a hospital. This was a turning point for Detective Caracappa. He could have been washed up and sent up to the Bronx. Instead, he became the luckiest man in the world.

When the incident became known to his bosses, Caracappa was pulled off the task force and prohibited from doing any more undercover work. He bounced around jobs in the NYPD.

Detective Stephen Caracappa was a survivor. He was kicked off the narcotics task force because of a drug overdose, but he was not fired. He was just moved around and around like an errant Catholic priest until everybody forgot all about that incident, and then one day he got a call from an old friend, Detective Charles Siriano. There was an opening in the Major Case Squad. Detective Caracappa had to know that his moment had arrived.

For a detective in the New York City Police Department, getting a call from the Major Case Squad was like getting a call from the Yankees. This was the show. The unit never caught the dirtbag cases, only the cases that made it into the newspaper. Major Case had status and fame and the power that comes with both. If the bosses deemed it so, Major Case could come in and take over any homicide in the city, pushing the lowly precinct detectives aside like kindergartners. Despite his drug overdose, this was where Caracappa landed in 1986.

His timing was perfect. By 1986, many of the Major Case–level homicides were taking place in certain neighborhoods of Brooklyn, Queens, and Staten Island where the Mafia still thrived. Anthony Casso wasn't the only gangster in New York trying to kill people. Bodies were dropping all over the Brooklyn and Queens neighborhoods of Gravesend, Dyker Heights, Bensonhurst, Bay Ridge, Mill Basin, Marine Park,

Flatlands, Howard Beach, Maspeth, and South Ozone Park. It was like Chicago in the twenties. Gotti murdered the boss of a family on a crowded Manhattan street. A botched effort to bribe a juror in a Pizza Connection case produced ten bodies; the implosion of a mob bank burglary game produced another half dozen; the Colombo family once again began to fall apart and shoot at one another in the streets over the question of who was in charge. The bosses at One Police Plaza decided something needed to be done to stop it all, and so they turned to Major Case.

The idea was simple: appoint a team of the department's top detectives to investigate only organized-crime homicides. The Organized Crime Homicide Unit, it was called, and Detective Charles Siriano and his friend Stephen Caracappa, a dogged investigator who'd worked hundreds of undercover cases with the elite narcotics task force, were the founding fathers.

The main function of the OCHU was to make sure that the chief of detectives office had all current and updated information related to organized-crime homicides, assist the local squads in all OC-related homicides, and ascertain if any of the OC homicides were related. The squad was run by Sergeant John Hart, with Joseph Piraino, Tom Sorrentino, Chuck Siriano, Billy Byrnes, Frank Pergola, Lee Shanahan, and Stephen Caracappa. Everybody was assigned a family. Piraino and Siriano got the Colombo family, Sorentino got the smallest family, the Bonannos. Byrnes and Pergola got the biggest family, the Gambinos; and Caracappa and Shanahan worked the Lucchese family. Caracappa also was the unit coordinator. He would sign all the monthly reports if Hart was unavailable. He was the liaison between the unit detectives and Hart.

Most detectives started at 10:00 A.M. Piraino remembers on days that he showed up earlier, he'd find Caracappa already at his desk, drinking coffee and reading the newspaper, sometimes by 7:30 A.M.

"He was basically a loner," Piraino recalled.

As unit coordinator, Caracappa had complete access to the NYPD's organized-crime investigation division's files at One Police Plaza and had weekly meetings with that unit. He effectively ran the squad at times, but also got involved

in specific murder investigations involving all the crime
families of New York.

He looked the part. Detective Caracappa stood five feet
ten inches and weighed no more than 160, with jet black hair
cut close and a grim undertaker's mustache. He often wore
black suits, which highlighted his gaunt stare. He rarely
smiled. He appeared to be carrying the weight of the world at
all times. He was the Doc Holiday of the NYPD, perfect for
an assignment that came into Major Case on February 4,
1988.

The job was fairly straightforward. An informant tipped
the NYPD about a guy who wanted to contract a hit. Who better than the undertaker himself? The bosses of the NYPD
who'd told Caracappa he couldn't do undercover work after
his drug overdose changed their minds. On February 10,
1988, the informant introduced undercover Detective Caracappa to the subject as a hit man. After the meeting, Caracappa prepared a report:

"Subject met with UC [undercover]. Hit was discussed.
Nagra tape recorder and video recorded. Price set. Subject to
contact UC when he has money together."

Caracappa had pulled it off. He looked and acted just like
a hit man.

May 5, 1986

At 7:27 A.M. Detective Stephen Caracappa of the New
York City Police Department logged into the NYPD's
computer system to run the name Romuel Piecyk. The system
would efficiently search millions of records to pull up any
trace of a criminal record, as well as home addresses, date of
birth, and physical description. Caracappa ran names all the
time. Detective Caracappa knew the game well. He'd spent
years as a street cop, then years in narcotics. He stayed longer
than everybody else filling out paperwork. He stopped by
stakeouts on his day off. He got to know the suspect's girlfriend to figure out how they guy ticked. Most important, he
did the legwork. He checked for everything just to solve the
riddle. And he knew it was always an art, never a science.

Those guys in ballistics matching up lines had their purpose. The lab tests on blood type played a role. But nothing substituted for hard work—and the intuitive sense that this guy was the right guy.

And this guy, Romuel, was not.

Part of the investigator game involved looking for patterns of behavior, and a typical pattern was often found in the suspect's history. This was one reason why Detective Caracappa ran names through the NYPD computer—looking for patterns. Similar crimes committed in the past. Any crimes committed in the past. Caracappa ran names every day he was on the job. A guy became a suspect, you ran his name. It was as automatic as squeezing out the toothpaste before brushing your teeth. Romuel Piecyk had no pattern of behavior to observe. He was just a working stiff, a refrigerator repairman from Queens with a wife and a mortgage and car payments. There was absolutely no obvious reason for Detective Caracappa to run the guy's name in the NYPD's computer early on the morning of May 5, 1986, before his shift usually started.

Except one.

On September 11, 1984, Romuel Piecyk was trying to drive his car down Grand Avenue in Maspeth, Queens when he found his way blocked by a double-parked sedan. He began beeping his horn. Two men got out of the car and an exchange ensued. One of the men reached over and slapped Piecyk. The other guy joined in. The men then took $325 from Piecyk. Both men threatened to put Piecyk in a box. He walked inside the restaurant, called the police, and the two men were led away in handcuffs.

How could he have known the two men were John Gotti and his close personal friend, Frank Coletta?

Although this was a relatively minor bit of litigation with a fairly simple fact pattern, the trial did not occur until March 1986. In the interim, two things happened. John Gotti became boss of the Gambino crime family by arranging the murder of his boss, Paul Castellano, on a Manhattan sidewalk in front of a steakhouse. Also during that time, the brake lines on Piecyk's sedan were slashed and he received numerous phone calls at home with vague and explicit threats to do harm to both Romuel and his entire family.

The first day Piecyk was scheduled to testify, he didn't show. The second day it was the same. Calls were made, and it was learned that he'd checked himself into a hospital for elective surgery on a shoulder injury. It was not clear when the shoulder injury had occurred or precisely why Piecyk had chosen that particular moment to get it fixed. However, he did finally show up in the correct courtroom in Queens County Criminal Court, escorted by two members of the New York City Police Department. Technically he was under arrest as a material witness.

He settled into the witness dock wearing a sling on his right arm and dark glasses.

On the stand he at first invoked his Fifth Amendment rights to remain silent at the risk of implicating himself, although he had not been charged with any crime. When the assistant district attorney assured him it would be all right for him to answer because they would stop requiring the police escort that had been following him around for four days, he changed his mind and began to answer all the questions.

He remembered the details of the day: where the car was double-parked, what time it was, why he needed to get the double-parked car moved so he wouldn't be late for an appointment. He remembered the $325. Then the prosecutor started asking Piecyk about the men who had assaulted him.

"I don't remember who slapped me," he said. "I have no recollection of what the two men looked like or how they were dressed."

A clearly flustered assistant district attorney asked Piecyk if he could identify his attackers in the courtroom.

"Everything happened so fast," Piecyk said, keeping his eyes averted from the defense table where Gotti and Coletta sat leering. "I don't see them now."

On March 25, 1986, Gotti walked out of court, the first of several acquittals under his belt. He and his best friend, Coletta, laughed as they made their way out into the spring air.

"The confusion has all been cleared up," Gotti told the assembled reporters.

Not quite. Gotti still had another problem pending in Brooklyn, where a jury was about to be assembled to determine if, in fact, he was a murderous, power-mad megalomaniac who thought he was Jesse James. The charges involved ordering murders, etc., and Gotti needed all the ammunition he could muster to make sure he could continue to spend his nights at Regine's and not inside the Metropolitan Correctional Center.

The timing for him was bad. He'd just been named in all the papers as the new boss of the Gambino family, and it was presumed he had murdered his predecessor outside Sparks Steakhouse. Not a whole lot of positive PR surrounded the guy as he faced his judgment day in Brooklyn federal court.

All of this had occurred by the time Detective Caracappa called up the name Romuel Piecyk on the NYPD computer. It was not clear why he did this. He was assigned, at the time, to investigate several major organized-crime murders. He was not assigned to the Gotti case. He had nothing to do with the Romuel Piecyk case.

On that day, prosecutors in the case *United States v. John Gotti et al.* wrote a letter to U.S. District Court Judge Eugene Nickerson advising him that they wished to revoke the bail of John Gotti. They specifically cited the case of Romuel Piecyk. Their fear was that witnesses in their upcoming federal case would suddenly come down with an acute case of Piecyk-itis. They wanted John Gotti back in jail. Now.

Gotti's laughter upon emerging from Queens County Criminal Court now rang hollow. A furious Gotti now faced the prospect of cooling his heels at the Metropolitan Correctional Center. This was something he'd done before, of course, but that was when he was a mere soldier. Now he was the boss of the entire Gambino enterprise, with all the soldiers and the capos and the associates. It wasn't fair; it wasn't right. He'd been boss only five months.

He needed to get back on the street, and Romuel Piecyk was just the man to help out.

On May 14, Romuel Piecyk suddenly showed up at the offices of attorney Bruce Cutler. He was the charismatic but blustering lawyer for Gotti, the guy who was always saying Gotti had the heart of a lion, that Gotti was a man's man, the usual stuff. At one time, Piecyk, a working stiff who'd been beaten and robbed by a gangster, wrote to a judge, "I saw the name of the man who assaulted me appearing in the *Daily*

News and the media printed that he was next in line for God-father. Naturally my idea for pursuing this dropped." Now Piecyk had come to see Gotti's lawyer because Gotti needed Piecyk to keep him out of jail.

At Cutler's office the repairman signed a piece of paper that was more important than an ordinary piece of paper. It was a sworn affidavit, and it was all ready to go when he arrived, fully prepared by the lawyer, Cutler. The affidavit swore up and down that Gotti never threatened him or his family or his dog. There was absolutely nothing to the rumor that Gotti thought murder was a legitimate way to advance one's career. In general, Piecyk swore in his affidavit, Gotti was a great guy.

On May 13, Cutler the lawyer took the affidavit to U.S. District Court Judge Eugene Nickerson, the judge who at first granted and then revoked Gotti's bail. Cutler presented the piece of paper, which the judge found wanting. Cutler promised to have Piecyk show up in court. The judge was un-moved. Gotti was tossed back in jail.

A jury was assembled, a trial begun. On August 27, 1986, Romuel Piecyk showed up in court anyway. He asked Judge Nickerson's staff to speak with the judge. He sat in the front row and waited. Gotti never looked over at him. The court clerk returned and said to put it in writing. Piecyk walked out-side of court and faced reporters.

"I was never threatened or harassed or intimidated by Mr. Gotti," he said with a straight face. "I honestly feel Mr. Gotti should be out on bail."

The sad man had done what he was supposed to do, but it didn't work. Gotti stayed in jail during the trial. The mystery of Detective Stephen Caracappa's involvement in the case of Romuel Piecyk remained just that.

EIGHT

It was a rainy Saturday morning on Bangor Street, and Jimmy Hydell had to be someplace to meet some guys. The Hydells lived on Staten Island, so that meant a car was essential. He couldn't use the gray Lincoln because his little brother, Frank, had to use it to get to work at the bagel store. He couldn't use his mother's sedan because it had been stolen. He had to rely on his friend Bobby Berring, the ex-transit cop, to pick him up. At about eleven o'clock, Bobby pulled up outside the Hydell household on Bangor Street. Jimmy walked out the door and did not say good-bye or what time he'd be home. Jimmy never said good-bye.

"I'm going to Brooklyn, Ma," was all he said.

Jimmy's mother, Betty, rarely knew precisely where her kids were going when they left the house, and she'd given up asking. There was no other reason to remember that morning because it was just like every other morning. All of her kids—Jimmy and Frank and Liz and Linda—were coming and going whenever they wanted. Why should this morning be any different?

"You have to remember you're dealing with a grown-up, not a sixteen-year-old," Betty said. Jimmy was twenty-six years old and still living at home, but she was optimistic. He had been working as an apprentice plumber for seven years and was hoping to get his plumbing license any day. But Betty was realistic. She was aware that just about everybody in the neighborhood either was a gangster, knew a gangster, or wanted to be a gangster. Jimmy was in that last category. Frank wanted to be one as soon as possible, too. The boyfriend of her daughter Liz was already a gangster. So was the boyfriend's father. It seemed like everybody Betty knew was either related to or going out with a gangster. It was normal, like a cop family or a firefighter family. Only it was a gangster family.

Betty did the best she could. Because Jimmy still lived at home, she could know where he was at least some of the time. Jimmy was a self-assured kid typical of the neighborhood, hating every cop he saw and hating rats even more. He was closest to his uncle, Mickey Boy Paradiso, and was always running around getting into fistfights and talking about the next caper. In the last few weeks, though, Jimmy had been subdued.

His sister Liz remembered hearing Jimmy talking with one of his friends, Robert, the former transit cop. The two of them let it slip that they had tried to kill a guy, Anthony Casso, and they had failed to finish the job. Liz could tell Jimmy was upset about this because he said the guy they tried to kill was a homicidal lunatic who would kill Jimmy and Robert immediately if he happened to see them on the street. She remembered that her boyfriend, Frank, also seemed to know about Jimmy being involved in the failed attempt to kill Casso.

"I might have told Frank," Liz said. "Or Jimmy told Frank. I don't remember."

At about 1:00 P.M. her brother Frank Hydell left for work at the bagel store in Jimmy's gray Lincoln. A few minutes later, he returned to the house to say that two guys in a powder-blue sedan were following him.

Most mothers might tell their sons to stay home and hope that the guys in the powder-blue sedan might go away. Or she might call the cops. Not Betty Hydell. She got in her car and began driving around the block. In a minute she saw the powder-blue sedan. It was a silly little car, a Nissan or a Toyota. She wrote down the plate, then pulled alongside.

The driver was a big guy with black hair and a mustache and wearing gold chains and an open shirt. The passenger was a skinny guy with dark hair and wearing dark clothing. She said, "Who are you?"

The driver pulled out a gold detective's badge.

"You should let people know what you're doing," she said, and drove away, the license plate number scribbled on a paper beside her on the seat.

Back at the house, Betty told her son Frank, cops were following him, and he went to work. He later told her he saw the powder-blue sedan on the Staten Island Expressway heading into Brooklyn.

At 2:46 P.M. the phone rang at the Hydell house. Linda Hydell picked up. It was Jimmy calling collect to say he'd be home for dinner.

That same morning, Anthony Casso showed up at Burt Kaplan's house on Eighty-fifth Street. Casso was not happy.

"Are you sure your friend and his cousin are out looking for him?" Casso asked.

Kaplan promised to find out. He beeped Frankie Santora. Frankie called back and said, "We're out looking for him right now."

"Frankie, it's imperative that we get this kid because someone else is going to kill him and we want him alive," Kaplan said.

"We're out looking for him right now."

"Please, Frankie, it's important. Make sure that you try very hard to get him."

Half an hour later, Burt got another call from Frankie Santora. Frankie said, "Can you call me back?" When Frankie answered, the first thing he said was, "We got him."

"You're kidding! I only spoke to you about half an hour ago."

"No, we got him. Where do you want him?"

"Frankie," Kaplan said, "call me back. I'll have to get back to you. Beep me back in half an hour."

Kaplan immediately beeped Casso. He asked Casso the same question Frankie asked: Where do you want him?

"Do you remember the toy store where we used to meet?"

• • •

The gangster Gaspipe stood in the middle of the parking lot at Toys "R" Us off the Belt Parkway in Brooklyn. He observed his partner, Burt Kaplan, pull in and park next to him.

"Where are they?" Casso asked.

"They're coming," Burt said.

In a few minutes a dark-colored sedan pulled into the lot and stopped about fifteen feet away from Casso. Frankie Santora was at the wheel. Casso did not move, but Burt walked over and said, "What's up, Frank?" like they were talking about the Yankees and there wasn't a guy tied up in the trunk.

"He was yelling and kicking in the trunk, so I had to pull over and I punched him to keep him quiet," Frank said, handing Burt the keys to the car with Jimmy in the trunk. "You have to be careful that he don't start screaming and yelling."

Frank said they'd gone to Jimmy's house in Staten Island and talked to his mother, then driven back to Brooklyn and found Jimmy at a laundry on Fifteenth Avenue and Eighty-sixth Street. He had surrendered peacefully because he knew Eppolito was a detective from prior incidents, and they handcuffed him and drove him to a garage off Nostrand Avenue in Brooklyn. Inside the garage they switched him to the trunk of the car Frank was driving, which was where he was at that very moment.

Kaplan said thank you and walked over with the key to Casso, who hadn't moved. Casso said, "What are they doing here?"

Kaplan turned and saw two men sitting in a car at the entrance to the Toys "R" Us parking lot. He didn't recognize them, but he knew who they were. There was a big guy with gold chains and an open shirt and a skinny guy with dark clothes. He walked over to Frank and asked what they were doing there. Frank said they were back up because Jimmy was making so much noise in the trunk. It was hard to imagine what kind of story they would have told if somebody had pulled over Frankie with Jimmy hollering in the trunk, but there they were.

"Tell them to get out of here," Casso said. "Tell your friend to get out of here and you get out of here."

• • •

It is difficult to imagine what Jimmy Hydell was thinking handcuffed in the trunk of a car being driven all over Brooklyn. That morning when he'd left his mother's house he'd been summoned to a meeting between the Gambino family and the Lucchese family regarding the attempt to kill Anthony Casso. He was truly a man in the middle whose life was a matter of debate. His uncle, Mickey Boy Paradiso, was going to represent his version of events. The meeting was supposed to take place at a ballfield off Fourteenth Avenue to resolve the dispute, but the meeting had not occurred, and then he was arrested by the cops and put in this trunk. He must have known what was going to happen.

Casso drove to a house in Mill Basin owned by a close friend named Jimmy Gallo, who was away for the weekend. Casso parked in the garage, closed the door, and popped the trunk. Inside was Jimmy, handcuffed and bleeding from the mouth from where Frank had hit him to quiet him down. Casso pulled him out and dragged him down to the basement. At the house was Casso's close friend Vic Amuso. They were locked together forever, Vic and Gas, by events such as Jimmy Hydell in the basement. Whoever shot at Anthony Casso was, in a way, shooting at Vic Amuso. It was important to Vic to learn from the handcuffed guy in the basement who was behind the whole thing.

Hydell was down there for a long time, maybe twelve hours. Into the next morning. During the session in the basement, Hydell admitted many things. He confirmed that he and Bobby Berring and Nicky Guido had tried to kill Anthony Casso and that his uncle, Mickey Boy Paradiso, was the one who wanted it done. Hydell complained about his uncle. He had decided that Mickey Boy had set him up because Mickey Boy was the only one who supposedly knew about the meeting place at Eighty-sixth Street and Fourteenth Avenue when he got kidnapped by the cops.

All of this was information Casso and Amuso needed to hear, but they also needed members of the Gambino family to hear it, too. They decided that Mickey Boy Paradiso, a mere soldier in the family of John Gotti, could not have ordered the death of Anthony Casso without permission of the bosses. Casso and Amuso wanted those bosses to know what they knew, but they were aware that they couldn't just call them on the telephone and explain everything. Instead, they summoned two of them to the basement to hear it straight from Jimmy's mouth.

While waiting for the Gambino family representatives to show, Jimmy Hydell—bound and bloodied and in his final hours—said to Casso, "I'll tell them exactly what happened, but I want you to—I know you're going to kill me, Anthony, but I want you to promise me one thing: You'll throw my body in the street so my mother can get the insurance policy." Casso gave him his solemn word that he would honor the son's final request for the sake of a mother.

The Gambino family representatives showed up in the dingy basement and were presented the trussed Jimmy Hydell. He admitted everything, confessing his sins and laying the blame squarely at the feet of the family that John Gotti now ruled.

The Gambino representatives left, burdened with the knowledge that although Jimmy Hydell was certainly finished, Anthony Casso surely was not. At the door of the house, the Gambinos assured Casso and Amuso that they would inform the boss, John Gotti, about this unfortunate situation. Then Amuso and Casso turned and descended once again into the dark basement with the handcuffed man and a .22 in hand. Casso had told Jimmy Hydell he would put him in the street, but he didn't give a damn about Jimmy's mother and all the insurance she stood to collect.

Betty Hydell had dinner ready at six, but Jimmy didn't show. "That was not unusual. I really didn't think anything of it." That night, at about ten, Jimmy's friend Bobby the ex-transit cop showed up. He asked Betty if she'd seen Jimmy, and he seemed nervous. He handed her a jogging suit that Jimmy had bought that day because he was planning to go for a run. When Betty asked Bobby what the problem was, Bobby said, "Nothing's the matter," and left. Next morning when his bed was empty, she started to worry.

First she went looking for him. Now Bobby the ex-cop was not around. She tried his other friends, but nobody had seen him. She waited until Monday and went to the 122nd Precinct station house near her home. She tried to file a missing-persons report, but the cop on duty told her because Jimmy was an adult, she couldn't file such a report. She then got a visit from her cousin Philly Boy Paradiso. What he told her made her very upset.

Philly Boy claimed that his brother, Mickey Boy, had been arrested for his own protection because the FBI had heard there was a contract on his life. Philly had attended a hearing for Mickey Boy, during which an FBI agent named George Hanna had testified that Jimmy Hydell had been kidnapped, tortured, and killed by Anthony Casso. Betty called FBI agent Hanna, who told her it never happened. She didn't know what to think.

She ran the plate she had through a friend who worked at a driving school, and it came back to a car that was completely different from the powder-blue sedan with the cops. This indicated to her that the car that was following Frank around was an unmarked cop car.

Jimmy's brother, Frank Hydell, went out and got a tattoo on his back that said, "Fuck Anthony Casso." That was his way of remembering his older brother, Jimmy.

Two weeks after Jimmy disappeared, she got a visit from a detective from her Staten Island precinct. He showed her a key chain he said belonged to Jimmy. She said the key chain looked familiar, but she wasn't sure. The detective left with the key chain. Betty Hydell was left with the jogging suit Jimmy bought the day he forgot to say good-bye. She decided to keep it in case he came home.

NINE

Anthony Casso was a thorough man. He did not believe it was right to leave loose ends. Three men had been in the car that day trying to kill him, which meant three men would have to atone for their sins. One already had: Jimmy Hydell in the basement. The second, the ex-transit cop Berring, had disappeared. The last man standing was Nicky Guido. It was a matter of logistics. Casso had never met Nicky Guido formally. He wouldn't know him if he shook his hand. He needed information. Where did Nicky Guido live and work and play?

Casso already had some information from the packet Kaplan had provided that had Hydell's mug shot. He began to ask around about Nicky Guido. First he talked to a drug-dealing soldier in the Colombo crime family, Greg Scarpa Jr. Casso was aware that for years Scarpa's father, Greg Sr., had a law enforcement source he called "the girlfriend." Scarpa Sr. was a profoundly treacherous and secretive man, and Casso had no idea about the identity of "the girlfriend," but Casso did know that Scarpa Sr. often had tremendous information that only could have come from law enforcement. He asked Scarpa Jr. about Nicky Guido, and Scarpa Jr. came back with a good description of Guido and the tidbit that his father was a longshoreman out of South Brooklyn. Casso also learned the Nicky Guido, who'd tried to kill him, lived in the Court Street area near the old South Brooklyn docks in a neighborhood once known as Red Hook.

He was also told that Nicky Guido had a small red car.

Casso sent a team of the usual killers, George and Frank and Joey, down to Court Street to find and kill Guido. They hung around for a few days and never saw the guy. The team did spot a small red car and wrote down the plate. Casso had cops run the plate, and Kaplan came back with a new Brooklyn address several blocks away from Court Street. It wasn't in Red Hook, but it was in Brooklyn, there was a small red car, and the car was registered to a Nicky Guido.

Casso wanted to make sure, so he had Kaplan go back to the cops to double-check the information. This time Frankie Santora Jr. told Kaplan he needed four thousand dollars for the trouble of making sure it was the right Nicky Guido. Kaplan said he would get back to him.

On November 11, 1986, a day before the jury began deliberating in the Commission case, Detective Stephen Caracappa showed up at the Major Case squad room before everyone else. He was usually there when everybody else wandered in at about 10:00 A.M., and there when they left. Some of the detectives there thought he was a bit standoffish, a tad grim. It was fair to say that he appeared to love his work. On this day he was on the New York City Police Department's computer system, looking up criminal records.

The system he tapped into allowed him to see if an individual had ever been arrested in the City of New York for any crime or misdemeanor. If a person had a record, the NYPD Criminal History computer would reveal the type of crime and whether there was a conviction. It also would reveal a person's known addresses, including home and work. If a person had ever applied for a job with the City of New York, it would show that, too.

At 8:01 A.M., Caracappa typed his name and his tax number into the system to begin the inquiry. He requested a records check on one Felix Ancugua without specifying a date of birth. He was required to let the department know what case the inquiry was related to, so he put down Case 341. Five minutes later he typed in a second name:

Nick Guido. Under date of birth he entered February 2, 1960.

He assigned the same case number, 341, to that inquiry.

There was a Nick Guido the NYPD was interested in. A few days earlier, an investigator from the Brooklyn district attorney's office also had put the name Nicholas Guido into the NYPD Criminal History computer. That case number was listed as 1184/86, which was the ongoing investigation of the unsuccessful attempt to kill Anthony "Gaspipe" Casso outside the Carvel store. That Nicholas Guido was believed to be one of the shooters who'd failed to kill Casso. That Nick Guido, however, had a different date of birth: January 29, 1957.

As for the Nick Guido Caracappa had typed in, there was no such thing as Case 341. The Nicky Guido Caracappa was looking up did not know Anthony Casso or Jimmy Hydell or Bobby Berring or anybody else in any crime family. It was a different Nicky Guido living in Brooklyn a neighborhood away from the correct Nicky Guido. Caracappa had typed in the wrong Nicky Guido.

It was not clear whether this information ever got back to Casso. When Kaplan got back in touch with Casso with Frankie Jr.'s demand for four thousand dollars, Casso blew up. He said the whole thing was a shakedown by the cops. The cops' information was okay when it was free, but now Casso didn't want it because he believed he already had it. Casso told Kaplan he had a source at the gas company who could track down the last man standing in the attempt on his life, one Nicky Guido of Brooklyn with a small red car.

November 19, 1986

It was a Wednesday, and the jury had been deliberating for six days. It had been a long trial, with dozens of witnesses and hours of tape-recorded conversations. It was called the Commission case, and it was in the newspapers every day. In the afternoon, the jury came back: guilty on everything.

When the case was announced in February 1985, it was billed as history. The bosses of all five families were charged all at once in one case. It was the first time that everybody was put into one group, the Commission, the Mafia's board of directors. The Commission would meet to work out disputes among the five families, and the jury had decided that that should stop.

For the Gambino family, the two bosses indicted were Paul Castellano and the underboss, Aniello Dellacroce. Both were dead. Castellano had been killed by John Gotti after his mentor, Dellacroce, had died of cancer. The Genovese family saw its supposed boss, Anthony Salerno, convicted, as did the Bonanno family with its boss, Phil Rastelli. The Colombo family's acting boss, Gerry Langella, who was acting because the real boss had a trial of his own going on, was convicted, too.

That left the Lucchese family, and none of the others felt the impact of this jury verdict more than they. The real boss, Anthony "Tony Ducks" Corallo; the underboss, Salvatore "Tom Mix" Santoro; and the consigliere, Christopher "Christy Tic" Furnari, went down on everything. That was the entire head office, all in one day, and with the way the sentencing system worked, it was highly probable that none of these guys would ever sit in a restaurant or go to the movies or go for power walks in the mall ever again.

The experts predicted immediate anarchy within the ranks of the highly sophisticated secret society that had been caught on tape in a Jaguar. William Doran, chief of the Federal Bureau of Investigation's Criminal Division in New York, talked about a "power vacuum." He and other government workers wondered aloud about the future of organized crime in America. It almost seemed like they wouldn't have anything to do anymore.

Regardless of the FBI's predictions, there were two men in a position to benefit from this verdict more than anyone else: Vic Amuso and Anthony Casso. Vic and Gas. It had already been arranged that if Corallo and Santoro and Furnari were convicted, Vic would become the boss and Gas the underboss of the Lucchese crime family. It was at this moment that everything changed forever for the family formed a long time ago by Gaetano "Tommy Two-Fingers Brown" Lucchese.

For years, the Lucchese family had lived in the shadow of the bigger, more powerful family begun by Albert Anastasia and expanded by Carlo Gambino. It had started when Tommy Gambino married Tommy Lucchese's daughter, and went from there. When Tommy Lucchese lingered in a slow death from brain cancer, the Gambino family had moved in on many of his operations. As Lucchese lay in a hospital bed, still alive but unable to communicate, the leaders of three other families met at Lastella Restaurant in Queens. There was Carlo Gambino and Aniello Dellacroce of the Gambino family, Tommy Eboli and Mike Miranda of the Genovese family, and Joe Colombo and Crazy Joey Gallo of the Colombo family. The meeting was called Little Apalachin, after the infamous meeting in the 1950s at an upstate farm. When it was over, the Gambino family came out on top.

The day the boss, the underboss, and the consigliere were all convicted, the Lucchese family was forced to split with the Gambinos all the money made on the Lucchese family's two most lucrative illegal activities: stealing from the Garment Center in Manhattan and stealing from the garbage haulers on Long Island. For every dollar they made, fifty cents went to the Gambino family.

Now that Vic and Gas were in charge, maybe that would change. Vic and Gas were very different from Tony Ducks and Tom Mix and Christy Tic. The way Burt Kaplan saw it, those guys were old-time gangsters who understood the necessity of being reasonable when you're stealing from people. Even gangsters frowned on excessive greed. These guys worked out deals with people. They knew how to balance things. When things got out of balance, that's when you had problems. That's when people would get arrested, and sometimes the people who would get arrested would become rats, and more people would get arrested, and pretty soon the whole thing crashed down around you. That was how Burt Kaplan saw it, anyway.

The change that was coming could not be good.

"At the time Mr. Furnari went to jail, I was close to him and Mr. Furnari would never let me get involved in the things that Mr. Casso did," Kaplan said later. "Casso didn't have the appeal that Mr. Furnari did. He was a lot lower-class than Mr. Furnari."

1986

In the office of Progressive Distributors on Staten Island, Monica Galpine was screaming and hollering and ripping things up. She ripped up salesmen commission sheets, she ripped up forms the factors required. She was expressing her feelings as Eleanor and Deborah Kaplan looked on. Monica had just asked Eleanor for a raise in her job as a clerk at Progressive, where she spent most of her time filing paperwork. Eleanor had said, we don't have the money for that right now.

"The screaming and yelling and throwing things in the office, it was really terrible," Deborah Kaplan recalled. "She said my mother and father would be sorry that she was not given the proper recognition and wasn't treated right."

She stormed out of the office, her threat lingering in the air.

Christmas Day 1986

A spotless red Nissan Maxima sat on Seventeenth Street in Brooklyn, light rain collecting on its brand-new roof. This was Windsor Terrace, a neighborhood of working New York. Here lived firefighters, Department of Motor Vehicles clerks, paint store managers, Snap-on tool salesmen, hunkered down in row upon row of moderate red-brick one-family and two-family homes with tiny lawns and, this time of year, plenty of plastic Santas. This was a place where people lived forever. They clipped supermarket coupons on Sunday to make the mortgage each month and continued to believe that they might actually get ahead. Nicholas Guido, age twenty-six, believed this. He installed phones for AT&T and lived at home with his parents to save money. He was not married, had no children. On this afternoon, Christmas Day, he believed he was ahead of the game. He had just bought himself a brand-new red Nissan, and he couldn't wait to show it off.

It was parked a block away, and the depressing Christmas Day rain didn't help. Inside the Guido family household, the entire extended Guido clan had just finished up at the holiday table. They were sated with manicotti, safe from the elements outside. Nicholas's mother, Pauline, had begun clearing the table and stacking dishes in the sink. Nicholas's older brother, Michael, was there with his wife. His uncle, Tony, was hanging around the TV set with his father. The tree twinkled in the parlor; presents lay scattered on the floor.

That morning Nicholas had received a gold Christ's head from his mother, some checks from his aunts, and a brand-new white winter jacket. But what he really wanted to show off was the new car.

For Nicholas, owning his own car was a big deal. The new Nissan would give him more freedom to come and go as he pleased. It was proof that he could do things for himself, that he was a grown-up who could take care of business without help from his parents. It was all his, and he really wanted to present the evidence to his Uncle Tony.

This was a warm spot on a chilly, miserable day, so Nicholas's task was not easy. Who needed to go out in this mess? They ate, they drank, and throughout the meal, Tony kept putting him off. But the meal was finally finished; it was after four o'clock and nearly dark. These were the shortest days, and Uncle Tony had run out of excuses.

Okay, the uncle said. Nicholas put on his new white winter coat and stepped out into the frigid rain.

The two men sat in the parked car at Seventeenth Street and Prospect Park West. It was 4:25 P.M.; darkness was complete. No other cars moved on the block. Even the Prospect Park Expressway, a sunken highway that lay below them, remained silent. This was Christmas, and every sensible soul was at home, where he belonged. Nick sat in the driver's seat; his uncle sat next to him.

At first they didn't notice the man in his thirties, about five-eight, wearing a gray knit cap and dark jacket, approaching the car. They really didn't see him, in fact, until he was right in front of the car heading toward the driver's-side window, pulling a .38 out of his jacket.

Nicholas must have seen him first because he was able to push his uncle to the floor of the car. The man walked up to the window and emptied nine shots into the car.

The shots hit Nicholas Guido in the chest. In all, he was hit by nine bullets. Not one missed.

Nicholas lay on his side in the front seat of his brand-new Nissan, his blood pooling in the brand-new seats and on his new white jacket. The gunman turned away. A blue sedan pulled up, the gunman jumped in, and the sedan sped away. Uncle Tony was doubled over, his head buried into his knees, covered with his nephew's blood, unhurt. Outside the rain thrummed on the roof of the brand-new Nissan, and Nicholas Guido lay dead.

Officer Michael Cugno of the Seventy-second Precinct was the first to arrive, responding to a "shots fired" call. He had been on the force all of one year and had never seen anything like this. He approached the car and saw Nicholas slumped over, covered in blood. He and his partner began placing yellow police tape around the car to keep bystanders from contaminating the crime scene.

Casso believed he was the victim of bad public relations. It was one thing when gangsters shot gangsters. The newspapers expected that, the taxpaying citizens expected that. Nobody got too upset. But to shoot a telephone repairman on Christmas Day? This was nothing but bad news for the carefully cultivated image of the five families of New York. This undermined the idea that gangsters were really just antihero men of honor instead of criminals like all the drug dealers and pimps and assorted hustlers that La Cosa Nostra purported to disdain. Casso summoned his trusty hit men, George Zappola and Frank Lastorino and Joey Testa, to ask what happened. Frank Lastorino insisted he believed it was the right guy, right up to the moment when Testa walked up to the kid in the little red car and shot him dead in front of his uncle. Casso was not particularly concerned about the dead kid in the car. He was mostly concerned that he looked like a fool.

Frankie Santora Jr. couldn't resist.

"Frankie Santora reached out for me and I met him and he said, 'You know, your guys killed the wrong Nicky Guido,'" Kaplan said. "He said, 'Maybe Gas should have paid the four thousand dollars and got the right information on Nicky Guido.' And Gas got it off of somebody who worked in the gas company and he got the wrong guy."

TEN

A young black man in gray sweats and blue sweatshirt padded along toward the highway at the place where the borough of Brooklyn meets the great wide-open sea. He ran in the middle of the afternoon in the middle of the working week on a path leading under a highway called the Belt. His plan was to follow the bike trail along the edge of Jamaica Bay just east of Coney Island. Here there was no civilization. This was a place where the thrum of passing cars blasting down the Belt Parkway drowned out the roar of the surf. It was not a destination, a place where people chose to be. Even the seagulls seemed lonely out here.

His name was Peter Mitchell, and he ran by himself. He had recently moved in with his brother in a one-bedroom apartment in the neighborhood called Mill Basin. Peter had just finished seven years in the Marine Corps. He was a twenty-seven-year-old with little work experience and a minor-league criminal record. He was single, had no kids. He worked part-time at a supermarket, making deliveries. Mostly he was unemployed, which was why he was able to go for his run in the middle of an afternoon in the middle of a work-week.

He was small and thin and liked to keep himself in shape as best he could. This meant he chose to run, usually three or four miles, twice a week. He would run down along the highway by Jamaica Bay, turn around, and come back. Usually these runs would be uneventful affairs. He would see no one save an occasional dog walker. He would listen to the sounds of the cars, and when traffic ebbed, his own footsteps pounding along the lonely bike trail. He would work up a sweat, return home, shower, and continue on with his life.

On this afternoon he ran into a breeze both steady and mild. He had run down Rockaway Boulevard, now under the Belt, and on to the bike path toward the Mill Basin bridge. He planned to run just past the bridge, turn around, and head home. Today he felt strong; he decided to run a little farther than usual.

He had just run past a horse riding academy between the harbor and the highway and come to a spot in a hollow by the road where a single walnut tree stood, alone against the ocean wind. Mitchell noticed a black Buick Regal parked at the end of a lot. As he got closer, he could see a guy who looked just like a guy in *The Godfather* sitting in the front seat. It was quite remarkable. The guy was older and had a white pompadour and looked exactly like the old Jewish movie mogul who tells the Corleone family lawyer to go screw and makes nasty remarks about "guineas and wops" before waking up in the morning with a bloody horse head in his bed. The guy in the Buick had a distinctive look. He was in the driver's seat with his arm over the shoulder of a younger black woman sitting in the passenger seat next to him.

Mitchell jogged by maybe five feet from the front bumper of the car. The man was looking away, so they didn't make eye contact. Then he turned and looked at Mitchell. It was about 1:00 P.M., so there was plenty of light to see what was what, especially the old guy with the white pompadour. Mitchell kept going toward an abandoned airfield called Floyd Bennett Field.

It was more than a mile to the field, and on the way back his knee was hurting, so some time had passed since he first saw the black Buick. Now after he turned around at the airfield and ran all the way back to the horse academy, he could see that the Buick had moved to a different, more isolated spot. Now a stand of trees and bushes blocked the academy's view of the car. There were no other cars and no other joggers or bike riders anywhere in sight.

Mitchell slowed his running as the guy with the pompadour got out of the car. It struck him that it was somewhat odd that this guy would be out here at this time of day, in the middle of nowhere. It didn't seem wrong. It just didn't seem right. Peter hung back by the bridge. He believed he was out of sight, about fifty feet away. The Buick was parked with its trunk sticking out toward the bike path.

Mitchell guessed the guy with the pompadour was probably five-eight in height. He had a paunch and wore a black leather jacket with dark slacks. He checked the front left tire, then walked around behind the car, opened the trunk, and took something out. He slammed the trunk, walked around to the passenger side, the side facing Mitchell, and opened the door. There sat a woman wearing a fake white fur jacket, a short skirt, flats. She wasn't moving even a little bit. Mitchell stopped jogging and watched.

The guy pulled the woman out of the car like a sack of dirt and dumped her body on the ground, the flats toward Peter. Peter's heart began to quicken. The guy dropped a handful of beer cans on the grass around the girl, then walked around—casually, Peter noticed—got back in the Buick, backed out, and drove away. Peter kept looking at the girl and only glanced at the license plate. It was orange New York State, he remembered, but he missed the numbers.

When he was certain the guy was gone, Peter walked toward the body on the grass. He saw now she had an orange-brown shirt under the fur jacket, that she was black, with an Afro, pretty young, maybe twenty or so. He also noticed that she appeared to have a purplish stripe of bruises that ringed her neck. Her eyes were dry.

In everyone's life there are moments when a single choice will change everything. To take a job, to go to college, to have one more drink, to pull into a rest area instead of driving on. Another popular choice is just to walk away. This was heavy upon the mind of Peter Mitchell as he stood there with the cars whizzing by unaware and the dead girl in her fake fur coat splayed upon the hard Brooklyn ground.

He turned, and he found himself walking back toward the horse riding academy. He walked inside and started to tell the receptionist about the body. The receptionist told him to wait a minute. The manager came out, and Peter told the whole story. The manager called the precinct. After he hung up, the manager asked Peter, "This is what you want? Go home or help the cops."

He thought about the woman lying on the grass and he asked to be driven back to the scene. The manager did what he asked and dropped him off.

When they got there the cops from the precinct were already there. One was in a suit, and Peter figured he was a detective. The other two were uniformed cops. Peter watched them walking around the body, paying no attention to the beer cans strewn all around. He was thinking they should check the beer cans for fingerprints. It was something he'd seen on TV. The detective's name was Richard Canderozzi from the Sixty-third Precinct, and Mitchell gave him a general description of the guy he saw dumping the body. He told him about the white pompadour and how the guy looked like the character in *The Godfather*, and Canderozzi wrote it all down in his notebook.

Then another guy in a suit showed up. He was a big guy, probably a bodybuilder, with a gray suit and a tie draped around his neck that had probably never been tied. He had black wavy hair and a black mustache and looked a little like Jackie Gleason, only with gold chains. The other cops seemed to defer to the big detective with the gold chains. Peter told the same story to him and mentioned the fingerprints on the cans. As he did, he watched the uniforms pick up the cans with their hands and dump them in a trash can.

This was the first sign to Peter Mitchell that maybe he had made a wrong choice.

A park officer in a Smokey the Bear hat showed up, and now the big detective with the gold chains was pressing Mitchell into an unmarked car. They were going to go looking for the bad guy.

In the car, Peter told the big detective all about the guy

from *The Godfather* with the white pompadour dumping the girl on the grass and spreading the beer cans around. The detective did not appear to be listening.

They pulled into a housing project and slowed down. They came to a stop as an overweight white guy with a receding hairline and stringy gray hair lumbered out of one of the apartment buildings. The detective pointed at the guy and said, "That's the guy, right?"

Peter Mitchell did not understand. He said, "That's not the guy. The guy had white hair. He was older."

The detective pushed him. "Are you sure that's not the guy? Are you absolutely sure?"

The detective pulled away and now drove Peter to a precinct house. Peter wasn't from Brooklyn and he had no idea where he was. He was taken into a room in the back with a big glass window looking out into the holding cell area of the station house. There he saw the fat guy with the receding stringy hair sitting in a cell. He wondered about the due process of crime and punishment for a moment or two.

The big detective ushered Peter into a windowless room. It was cold in there, and Peter sat there in his running sweats. Other cops came and went. Sometimes he was alone. The big detective said, "This guy's a piece of shit drug addict. He likes little girls."

Peter Mitchell brought up the white-haired man he had seen dump the girl. The detective said, "I don't give a shit about the white-haired man."

Then it was "good cop, bad cop" all in one guy. First the detective talked about his devotion to the job, took out pictures of himself in uniform with medals on his broad chest. Then his voice got hard. He demanded to know where Peter lived. He said he could find out anyway, so Peter told him. The detective said, "I want you to do this for me."

At this time, Peter Mitchell recalled that he had what could only be termed a "probation problem." After getting out of the Marines, he had drifted to California and got arrested trying to pass a forged check. He had pleaded guilty and served four months, and now he was on probation. The problem had to do with where he lived. When he left California, he was supposed to check in with a probation officer in the City of New

York. He had failed in this respect. The image of the big detective checking into Peter's record and then making certain phone calls came to mind. This image alternated with the image of the girl in the fake fur coat lying on the cold ground.

The big detective said, "I want you to nail this motherfucker."

Peter said, "What about the white-haired guy?"

"Forget about the white-haired guy," the detective said. He didn't raise his voice. He was calm, extremely confident. Then he mentioned, "I wouldn't want anything to happen to your family."

The detective said the fat guy with the stringy gray hair was named Barry Gibbs. That's who dumped the body, not the white-haired guy. Peter knew that he had never seen Barry Gibbs dump anything anywhere.

"He was calm. He had me. I didn't want nothing to happen to me, my brother, my family. I had a choice. Take an asswhippin'. The guy could have beat me like Emmitt Till. I could be found up on the side of the road. I'm thinking if I'm not going to the cops, I'm going to end up like the dead girl. I'm not saying anything. I'm just trying to figure out how I'm getting out of this."

In the cold room the detective began yelling, "That's the guy! That's the guy!"

And then it came to Peter Mitchell. The choice. He did not see it as a question of what is right and what is wrong, of honoring someone's daughter, of putting the wrong guy in jail. He saw it as him or the dead girl.

Peter Mitchell said, "That's the guy."

He thought, "I put my feet on Jesus' face. Fucking hero cop. I will send that guy away." He had never met Barry Gibbs. He did not know if he had children, a wife, friends, acquaintances, coworkers who would now think of Barry Gibbs as the guy who killed that girl. It was Peter Mitchell or the dead girl.

It was now two in the morning. The big detective suddenly got nice, offered to drive Peter Mitchell home. He dropped him off in front of his brother's apartment and handed him his card. It read:

"Louis Eppolito
Detective, Third Grade
New York City Police Department."

"If you need anything," he said, "just call."

When Detective Canderozzi got off his shift he was told that Detective Eppolito would take over the homicide by the Belt. The victim's name was Virginia Robertson. She was a young girl who had experienced much trouble in a short time. She took drugs and sometimes took money for sex. She had a mother and she was upset, but hardly anyone else came around worrying about her death. It was not a high-profile case, and Eppolito was getting it merely because the brass didn't want to pay Canderozzi overtime.

The day after the girl's body was dumped by the highway, Canderozzi noticed a guy at the precinct who seemed to fit the description of the guy the witness had said dumped the girl. He knew the guy was named Brigante. He was a low-level hoodlum with a salvage yard in Canarsie who had various associations with organized crime. He was there in the Sixty-third Precinct station house with a lawyer, and Canderozzi asked Brigante a few questions. The guy was vague and evasive, and when Canderozzi got a good look at him, he noticed something else. This guy did not have white hair. Instead, he had a unique feature that the detective took note of. His hair was shiny black, as if it had just been dyed.

The guy walked out of the precinct, and Detective Canderozzi wrote up his report about Brigante and his dyed hair and filed it with Eppolito. After that Canderozzi didn't think of it again.

For Peter Mitchell, it was a question of sticking to the story. It was easy to describe almost everything. The run. The weather. The lone tree. The Buick Regal, black, with orange plates— all that could stay the same. So could the movements of the afternoon. The guy gets out of the car, pulls beer cans out of the trunk, scatters them around, pulls the girl out of the passenger seat, dumps her next to the cans. She still wears the same fake fur coat.

It was the guy that was the issue. He had to make sure to remember what Barry Gibbs looked like. He'd seen him at the housing project, and then again at the holding cell. And Detective Eppolito had shown him photographs of the guy. He used that to create his description of the guy who dumped the girl at the side of the Belt Parkway. The guy with the white hair from *The Godfather* was gone.

Only Peter Mitchell couldn't forget that guy, and he wondered where that guy might be. Was Detective Eppolito trying to protect this guy, or was he just trying to keep his numbers up? Another prostitute murder solved by hero cop, etc. Peter Mitchell could not be sure. He began to look over his shoulder a lot when he was out and about. For the first two weeks after that morning, he wouldn't run the same route.

All these distractions made Peter Mitchell's big lie tougher to pull off. He flubbed a photo array. The Brooklyn district attorney had required that he ID the guy in an array of six photos of similar-looking miscreants, and he picked the wrong guy. When it was time to do the lineup, Detective Eppolito took no chances, showing Mitchell a Polaroid snapshot of Barry Gibbs just before Mitchell went into the room with the big one-way mirror and picked out Barry Gibbs on the first try.

November 18, 1986

Before he was to appear in front of the grand jury, Peter Mitchell had lunch with Detective Eppolito. The detective had pastrami, Mitchell had a cheeseburger. The cop gave him twenty dollars for transportation and said, "You're doing the right thing." When he appeared in the room in front of all those taxpaying citizens weighing the fate of Barry Gibbs, Mitchell was careful not to mention the white-haired guy. The prosecutor, Andrew Dember, went along, unaware of Mitchell's deception. Mitchell did Louie's version of "the right thing"—he was asked questions, he gave answers.

Shortly after Mitchell's testimony, the grand jury heard more testimony that Barry Gibbs did know Virginia Robertson, had done drugs with her, and had had sex with her. He admitted that, although he denied again and again killing her.

Barry Gibbs was a drug user. He couldn't say for sure where he was that afternoon. There were witnesses who had him near his apartment at about the same time, but that still gave him plenty of time to dump a body less than a quarter mile away on the Belt Parkway bike path.

The grand jury did not hear any testimony about the guy with the dyed black hair showing up at the precinct. Detective Canderozzi's report about how the guy at the precinct fit the description that Mitchell had given him was nowhere in sight. Canderozzi was not called as a witness. The grand jury had heard enough.

They indicted Barry Gibbs on charges of murdering Virginia Robertson. He was held without bail due to the brutality of the crime. The poor girl had been strangled, and her body was left by the side of the highway. The case against Barry Gibbs would go forward, relying heavily on the testimony of the people's star witness: Peter Mitchell. The wheels were engaged. The machine shuddered into gear. There was no stopping it once it got started.

ELEVEN

On a Thursday at two in the afternoon, Corso showed up at the house of Eppolito with briefcase and a calculator. Caesar jumped up and down and Corso said, "Caesar, my baby!" in a high-pitched voice. Fran said, "Happy New Year. I'm on my last nerve today."

Lou gave Corso a kiss on the cheek. Corso said, "He's walking faster than you now?"

"He's walking faster than me," Fran said.

They sat in the kitchen, Fran brought out espresso, and they talked about Lou's amazing recovery. Fran announced that Lou had combed his hair that morning by himself. Lou went to another room and returned with some papers. They got down to the business at hand, which was to figure out why exactly Lou and Fran forgot to mention $1 million worth of income on their taxes for the past decade. Lou put it another way.

"I lied and cheated the past ten years on taxes."

The Hollywood dream had not been quite the end of the rainbow for the Eppolitos. When he retired from the New York City Police Department, Lou had his three-quarters pension from the heart condition and—as far as steady income went—that was it. He had the book contract, which he told people was a nice $200,000 bump. And he was doing the acting business, which was a paycheck here, a paycheck there. He was counting on hitting it big. He thought he knew all these big people in Hollywood and that would be enough. It was only enough to land bit parts and "technical consultant" gigs, but that wasn't paying the air-conditioning bills. He'd convinced the boxer Boom Boom Mancini to contribute toward one of his projects, the Youngstown, Ohio, story, but that wasn't enough, either. He needed something more.

He needed Steve Corso and his million-dollar promise about public offerings and Crucker and the stock jumping from $1 to $5 in no time at all.

But first he had to clean up the mess he'd made in the past ten years. Corso told him he needed to hear everything—all the income he didn't declare, why he didn't declare it, what he spent it on. The Lou Eppolito income pattern was all over the map: one year Lou made $411,000, the next $131,000, the next $103,000, the next $76,000, the next $228,500. On one form he didn't declare his police pension; on another, he did. He was an IRS audit waiting to happen.

"Why didn't you do it in the past?" Corso asked.

"We couldn't," Lou said.

"We were in over our heads," Fran said.

There were all these unexpected expenses. There was the wedding for Andrea, the wedding for Deanna, the Cadillac for their semiemployed son Anthony. Then Andrea got in a car accident that put $20,000 on the credit card. Pretty soon the credit card had maxed out, so they got another one. They were now carrying $100,000 in credit card debt, and the interest payments were killing them. They might as well have gone to a loan shark. They were about to pay a $30,000 penalty on a no-questions-asked loan they took out to cover previous debts. They were swimming in it.

"We paid for the honeymoon, we paid for the furniture," Lou said.

"Because you're Italian," Corso said. "Other people would say, 'Get the fuck out of there.' Irish people would kick 'em out."

"Yes. One hundred percent," Lou said.

Corso said, "When you didn't declare that, you knew that that was wrong."

"Yeah," said Fran.

They discussed the Eppolito credit rating. "Two years ago," Fran said, "it was fabulous. Now it's a B. Right now the debt-to-income ratio is no good for us."

"Now we go forward," Corso said. He offered to set up offshore accounts. The money goes there and nobody knows anything about it. Fran said, "That doesn't sound illegal to you?"

"No," said Lou.

"Yeah, it probably is," Corso admitted, "but no one is going to know about it. Everyone does it. I'm not saying to do it, but the option's there. No one can ever trace it."

"How do you access it?" Fran asked. She had moved beyond "illegal."

"You can go down and pick it up. You can have it wired in small amounts," Corso said. "I'm just telling you the real world. I'm not saying right or wrong. When people have that much money—"

"They don't want to give it up," Fran said.

"I don't care," Corso said.

"I don't care," Lou said.

"I don't either," Fran said.

"This is how it's been for twenty-eight years," she said. "I'm not going to make excuses for it. This is how we are."

"There's a great virtue in anonymity," Corso said.

"What does that mean?" Fran said. "I know what *it* means, but I wanna know what *he* means."

"I just like to go about my business, keep my head down, and duck the bullets," Corso said.

"If they don't know who you are, the better," Lou said.

"You make me nervous," Fran said to Corso.

"I make you nervous? If I make you nervous, you're in trouble."

"I don't know you."

Corso shifted it back to the big public deal and all the money that was just around the corner. He wanted everybody to be happy. He suggested Lou's friend Steve Caracappa, the former partner in the NYPD who lived across the street, might be able to get in on the stock deal, too. He suggested they set up a meeting, and Lou thought that was a great idea. It was clear that Lou believed every word and Fran believed not a single one. Corso said, "I could sell it. There's no problem doing this funding of this deal. I want you to try to do this deal." He faced Fran. "I know you're skeptical."

"I am."

"This is a done deal," he said. "I can sell anything. What I need is the truth. Whatever the truth is, I can sell it. This is my world. I can sell it."

Then Lou said something that stopped Corso's usual Dale Carnegie you-can-do-anything shtick dead.

"She's always worried about me being handcuffed."

"You mean arrested?" Corso asked, tentatively.

"Yeah," said Lou. "Because of who my family was back in Brooklyn, they're still coming after me. I saw cops sitting across the street."

When he said this, Lou was aware that his cousin, Frankie Jr., was long ago dead and gone. He was aware that Anthony Casso was now viewed as a ranting maniac sitting alone in a prison cell in the middle of America, useless as a witness for the government. He was aware that Burt Kaplan was sitting in a prison cell, keeping his mouth shut like the stand-up guy he had always been. The only other person who knew anything about everything that had happened lived across the street, and he wasn't about to start talking to anyone. He was free and clear, and yet he never stopped thinking that somebody was watching. Lou didn't say it to Corso, but he had convinced himself that he'd recently seen a guy sitting in a car when he was coming out of a restaurant. He thought the guy might be following him, but on the way home he checked the mirror and the guy was gone. He parked the car, went into the house, and realized he'd forgotten to pick up some milk. As he was pulling out of the driveway, he swore he saw the guy in the car sitting on the street staring at his house. A few weeks back Andrea thought she saw someone following her and cut across the parking spaces in a mall lot to escape.

"You think they're still coming after you?" Corso asked. "I mean, I don't care. It doesn't matter."

"Yeah," Lou said. He didn't say who "they" were.

"For what reason?" Corso said. He waded carefully into dangerous waters with the question, but Lou did not rise to it.

"I was with this woman, drop-dead gorgeous. I didn't do a thing. I'm not cheating on my wife. I don't do things like this. So it's boring," he said. "When the FBI goes after people, they say, 'I know you from somewhere.' You know me from somewhere? Unless you're sitting across the street from my house, you don't know me. I don't go to clubs. I don't hang out with wiseguys. The main reason is that it will come back and bite you in the ass."

"Have you ever been investigated?" Corso said to himself. To Lou he said, "What do you think you were investigated about?

"That's okay, that was police business. As a police officer, headlines in the paper. That was during . . ." He trailed off. Then he said, "I was never arrested, never charged with anything in my life."

Lou then pretended to be filling out a form. He asked himself, "Are you under any major investigations right now? No. Have you been in the past? Absolutely. I'm away from that. Absolutely not. Never. Do you attend places that wiseguys go? And the answer is no."

Corso said, "I do."

He tried to assure everyone that everything was going to be all right. He promised that their secrets were his secrets. He made it seem as if they were all in the same boat, and that if they went down, he'd go down, too.

"In essence, you don't like this part, Fran, you're going to have to trust me and I'm going to have to trust you," Corso said. "Because there's no privilege in this stuff. You've told me that you've got almost a million dollars in untaxed income. If someone put a gun to my head, I'm never gonna say anything, but you have to understand there's no privilege and I don't have any privilege with you. So we're in bed together, much as you don't want that to be true."

Fran laughed bitterly and said, "Can I get you back? Don't tell me we're not going to have to pay. We're going to have to pay."

"You misunderstand me. What I'm saying to you clearly is, if you can't pay it, there's nothing they can do. They put a lien on your credit report, that's it. When the ship came in, you could always just pay them. When you don't declare a million dollars, that could get you in trouble."

"That's been a fear of mine for five years," Fran said.

Lou offered a more philosophical take on the question of guilt and innocence, crime and punishment. He said, "I'm not looking to cheat and lie. You're not going to have that. Up until now, I had to do what I did to survive."

Corso asked Fran, "You think you put a lot of pressure on him here, Fran?"

Fran said, "There's a lot of things that aren't being said."

TWELVE

Once again Pete Franzone was working late on a Friday at his garage in Brooklyn, Pete's Towing. In twenty minutes he'd park the tow truck in the garage and close up for the night. He was inside his little shed, and it was dark and freezing outside. Three days earlier Pete had endured the one-year anniversary of the guy with the Jewish skullcap on the floor.

Since that night Pete had seen Frankie here and there. He'd made a point of being friendly. He didn't want Frankie to think he was going to change his mind about anything. He even went to a sweet-sixteen party for Frankie's daughter Tammy. At the party he'd seen Frankie's cousin Detective Eppolito. Since the night with the guy on the floor the cop had leased a space in the lot for a car he used that looked like an unmarked car. Pete and the cop never spoke about the guy in the garage, as if it never happened. This was one of the reasons why Pete Franzone was terrified of going to the cops. What would they say if he claimed an NYPD detective had been part of the whole thing? No one would believe him. He was a tow truck driver with a sixth-grade education. Eppolito was a detective in the New York City Police Department.

As Pete got ready to head home to his wife and his new-born son, he was looking forward to the boy's one-year birthday on the twenty-fifth. Thinking about that birthday kept him sane. Then out of the darkness Frankie Jr. walked up and said, "I gotta talk to a couple of people."

Twenty minutes later and he would have been home with his wife and child, eating dinner, watching a little TV, going to sleep after a hard day's labor. Instead Pete would not go home just yet. He did as he was told. He opened one of the garage doors for Frankie. As Pete was pulling the chain used to hoist the door, he noticed over his shoulder a familiar sight: Detective Eppolito, pulling his sedan into the lot and backing it into a parking space, with the nose of the car facing the garage.

Just like the last time.

A brown Cadillac pulled into the lot, and Frankie waved him toward the garage. The driver backed in, and Pete could see two men inside. One of the guys in the car was a short, stocky man with a bulky jacket and light brown hair. Pete had never seen him before. Frankie told Pete to go back outside the garage. As he was walking out, two more men approached. Pete said, "Are these the guys?" and before Frankie could answer, one of the guys said, "Hey Frankie."

Pete went back to his shed, as he was told. Detective Eppolito still sat in the car, facing the garage. Five men, including Frankie Jr., had walked inside that garage.

The phone rang inside the shed. It was Frankie. He wanted Pete to come into the garage to turn off the heat. Pete did not want to go into the garage. He told Frankie where the switch was, but Frankie said he couldn't find it and that Pete had to come in.

The first thing he saw inside the garage was the white tarp wrapped around an object. One of the men Pete had never seen before was kneeling down, working on tying up the package with a series of knots, the way a sailor ties down a sail. The next thing Pete noticed was that only four men, including Frankie Jr., were standing. He realized that the short, heavy-set guy with the thick jacket and light brown hair was missing. He shut off the heat and was walking by the tarp when the guy tying the knots touched his arm and said, "Give us a hand with this."

Pete Franzone, who was not wearing gloves, did as he was told. One of the guys in the garage cursed him out and used his own gloves to wipe down the white tarp with the elaborate ropework as it lay in the trunk of the brown Cadillac. When Frankie and the rest of the guys in the garage pulled out in the Caddy, Franzone noticed that Detective Eppolito followed right behind.

February 14, 1987

At 5:20 A.M. Police Officer Sylvia Cantwell Santiago was working the midnight to 8:00 A.M. shift in Brooklyn's Sixty-third Precinct when she got a call about a body in the street. She responded to the intersection of Coleman Street and Avenue U. It was frigid, in the teens, quiet as death. In front of a church an object wrapped in a white tarp lay on Coleman Street between two parked cars. It was about six feet long and roped together with an elaborate set of knots. A foot stuck out one end.

The body appeared to be contorted into a kneeling position. It was frozen solid. The crime scene unit showed up and took a series of photographs. It was noted that there were white scrapings on the body's knees.

At the morgue, the medical examiner determined the cause of death as multiple gunshots to the head. The victim was Pasquale Varriale, twenty-six years old, a low-level hustler affiliated with the Colombo crime family. He was suspected of trying to bribe a juror in a Mob-connected heroin case, and he hung around with people who killed for fun. There were many reasons why he would be dead.

This was how Police Officer Santiago began her Valentine's Day.

April 1987

The New York City Police Department generates hundreds of memos each day. With tens of thousands of officers and far too many chiefs, memos are considered essential proof that actual work is taking place. Without memos, there is no proof. In April 1987, the chief of intelligence of the New York City Police Department wrote a memo to Captain Patrick Harnett, the commanding officer of the Major Case Squad. In composing his memo, the chief of intelligence relied on an age-old tradition common to bureaucrats throughout world: the overuse of lifeless euphemism.

The title of the memo: "Misuse of Confidential Information."

This was a tidy little phrase for a very dangerous business. Of concern to the chief of intelligence was one of the most heinous acts a law enforcement officer could perform: revealing the identities of informants. This was better known as giving up the rats. The nature of this type of confidential information was that it was provided exclusively to law enforcement for law enforcement purposes. To be effective, a confidential informant had to know that if he spoke surreptitiously to the FBI or the NYPD, his dangerous secret relationship must be protected from exposure. The nature of the criminal enterprise is such that anybody caught helping the other side is a dead man walking. For an agent or a cop to reveal this informant to one of his underworld peers is to sentence the informant to death. Any cop or agent knows this. At the precinct level, corruption concerns usually involve petty larcenies on the street. Free pizza slices handed out to officers, cash taken from the stolen wallet. In narcotics, it was usually watching for missing cash and, even worse, drugs. In the Major Case squad's Organized Crime Homicide Unit, the number one issue of concern was always "Misuse of Confidential Information."

Of particular interest to the NYPD's chief of intelligence was the vulnerability of the vast amount of this information stored in the NYPD's computer system. The department was supposed to carefully monitor who had access to the system. Anyone who accessed the system was required to explain explicitly why he or she was using it. That meant tagging a request for specific information to a specific matter under investigation by the specific detective who needed the computer access.

When the chief of intelligence asked about potential problems in this area, Captain Harnett responded with righteous anger. In an April 11, 1988 memo titled "Corruption Hazards and Programs," Harnett insisted his squad was cleaner than Efrem Zimbalist Jr.'s dialogue.

Harnett acknowledged there were problems with monitoring with precision the computer system, which was used hundreds of times a day by his unit. He first noted that the computer terminal itself was kept in a "locked and alarmed office" and was equipped with what he termed "watchdog software." Harnett then admitted, "Deficiencies have been noted in this area in the past."

The term hung in the air and was not explained. What deficiencies? When? By whom? Regarding which detectives and which informants? No matter. Harnett, the commanding officer of the Major Case Squad, had a response without explanation: "Upon investigation it was shown that the inquiries were case-related and the proper follow-up reports were filed. There is no indication either by allegation or evident in any of the current investigations that such information is being misused."

Harnett appeared to say there was always an explanation that could be found to connect an inquiry into the system to a legitimate ongoing case. Given the nature of investigations, this was convenient. Investigations are, by their nature, difficult to explain. You run a name because the guy knows a guy who might be connected to the thing with the guy. It was that vague. In fact, Harnett seemed indignant that anyone would dare question the integrity of his elite detective squad.

"I have a group of supervisors and investigators with the highest level of moral [sic], integrity, and job interest," he wrote. "They all are mature and experienced detectives who have gone through a thorough selective process. They take pride in their assignments and are fully supportive of the department's anticorruption programs. Members of the Major Case Squad are constantly kept busy working on interesting investigations. Their work is monitored closely and there is a narrow sphere of control. My supervisors as mentioned take pride in their work and unit. They are familiar with the program and together we will continue to maintain this high level of integrity."

He seemed to be saying that Major Case Squad detectives were too interested in their jobs to be corrupt. He didn't bother to explain the "deficiencies," instead explaining them away as if to say that such an inquiry would be inappropriate.

This memo was written less than six months after Detective Stephen Caracappa of the Major Case Squad requested information regarding Nick Guido, the telephone repairman who wound up dead due to having the wrong name.

Take the efforts of Sergeant John Hart, the squad supervisor. Blurring the lines of authority appeared to be a Sergeant Hart specialty. Occasionally Hart would send out memos meant for his squad only. The folks at One Police Plaza would not have been amused, for instance, by his March 1988 memo 'To All Members of the OCHU":

> Subject: "The Wearing of Many Hats by Members of OCHU"
>
> Effective immediately: All detectives assigned to the OCHU will be wearing several hats. At times we will be called upon to wear at least four hats at one time. First-grade and second-grade detectives may even be called upon to wear five hats.
>
> At no time should a current member of our unit feel this is an unnecessary burden, as we should all accept our responsibilities as adult men and "not question the boss as to who, but to do as ordered."
>
> Sergeant John E. Hart

In reply to Hart's "Wearing of Many Hats" memo, the detectives of the Organized Crime Homicide Unit came up with a "family chart" detailing their own interpretation of the different hats they should wear. Their view appeared to be that one hat would be as the member of a crime family, so named the Hart Family.

The chart depicted the hierarchy of the OCHU. It showed up in a memo dated March 4, 1988, from one "Sonny Black" to Sergeant Jack Hart. At the top of the chart of the Hart

Family was the boss, "Sergeant" Jack Hart. There was an underboss, a consigliere, one capo, three soldiers, and one acting soldier, who got the nickname "Kid Blast." The acting street boss was listed as one of the founders of the squad, Steve Caracappa.

Valentine's Day 1987

When John Otto Heidel, the Bypass King, met with his handlers in the FBI, he lost his name. In written reports he was referred to simply as "NY 12872-OC," the OC referring to organized crime. The idea was to limit the number of people who knew of the informant's status as an informant. This was in Otto's best interests. He was, after all, a full-time criminal meeting regularly with the cops and the FBI and relating in detail the comings and goings of his so-called friends. In fact, he'd been doing this for more than a decade. Each week he'd arrange to meet with his handlers and tell them the latest scheme. Some of what he related was based on actual conspiracies in which he himself participated. Some of it was stuff he heard on the street. This was a common arrangement in law enforcement. In many ways this little dance between criminal and cop kept the system of criminal justice from crashing down. This allowed Otto to go about his business believing he would not be arrested, and the FBI to receive information that resulted in arrests and career promotions.

On this day, Otto was meeting with his latest handler, Special Agent Patrick Colgan of the FBI, a man who'd devoted years of his life to chasing after the Lucchese crime family. Recently Colgan had been working with an NYPD/FBI task force that was very interested in ending a string of overnight burglaries that were making everyone in law enforcement look like a bunch of amateurs. These criminals weren't breaking into homes in Queens. They were breaking into banks and jewelry stores and getting away with millions of dollars' worth of what cops liked to call "ill-gotten gains."

In Brooklyn in the mid-1980s, this type of sophisticated bank burglary had become big business. The gangs were highly organized. They would enter the targeted business at midnight on Friday and spend the entire weekend carefully selecting what they wished to steal. They'd bring food and drink and make a little party of it. They'd empty out safe deposit boxes, fill bags with gold and silver and precious stones, and crawl back out into the night to sell their acquisitions. The key to their success was bypass—finding a way around complicated and expensive alarm systems installed by corporate overseers to keep people out. The gangs needed somebody with a working knowledge of electronics. Otto was their man.

At forty-six, Otto probably could have been a successful union-scale electrician. He was a Brooklyn-born neighborhood guy with a good mind for the details of electronics. He could fix anything. If he'd been born to a dock worker in Portland, Maine, or a shrimp boat captain in Galveston, perhaps he would have made a legitimate and decent living repairing TV sets or wiring condominiums. Instead, he grew up in certain neighborhoods of Brooklyn South where getting over was more important than getting by.

He started with simple tasks: hijacking trucks out at John F. Kennedy International Airport, on the edge of the sea and Queens. He worked his way up to big-score burglary, the highlight being a career-making caper busting into a midtown Manhattan jewelry store called Charles Friedman & Sons and exiting with four hundred thousand dollars' worth of gold and precious stones. To make this happen, Otto had become an expert in bypassing burglar alarms. He was the Bypass King.

In his middle age, Otto had equipped himself with a working knowledge of electricity and its uses in the field of security. He could get around three separate burglar alarms to get himself and his partners into the Friedman jewelry store and numerous banks around New York. He was an electrical genius. This, of course, meant his quest for simplicity was history.

His genius reputation put him in the newspaper. He and his pals had gained a nickname for themselves: the Bypass Gang. It was all great fun, having a nickname, breaking into banks and jewelry stores, and walking away with bags of money and jewels. But having no name was always better than having a nickname. Nicknames always attracted the attention of law enforcement.

Long ago Otto had been caught and secretly agreed to work for the FBI.

Now he was out there, swinging in the wind. He was aware that if his secret work as an informant were discovered, he would be murdered, probably in a very public manner to send a message. But he had to keep making these tapes until he brought in a big name. Wannabes and associates weren't good enough. The FBI wanted it all, and he had to deliver. In the meantime he was all alone, swimming in an open sea of complications.

The FBI especially wanted the greedy men who ran organized crime, who had decided to get their piece of the Bypass Gang. That meant that the Bypass Gang had acquired certain friends to represent their interests and ensure that they could keep at least a little of what they stole. In the case of Otto Heidel, he had more "representatives" than could fit in a school bus. On the actual jobs there was a soldier in the Lucchese family, "Georgie Neck," and his gangster brother, Vincent. Behind the scenes collecting a percentage there was the street boss of the Lucchese family, Vittorio "Little Vic" Amuso, and his lifelong friend and consigliere, Anthony "Gaspipe" Casso. And that was just the Lucchese family. The Colombo family and even the fractious Bonanno family also were involved. Practically every family you could want. Together they had pulled off numerous bank burglaries in the past year, with Otto Heidel the key to the unlocked doors on many a lucrative night.

Keeping this high-wire act on track, however, had not been so simple. Otto had, in fact, been caught and confronted by the FBI. He could have gone to trial or pleaded guilty and done his time, but he chose a different route: he agreed to become a confidential informant, working with the Lucchese family, the Colombo family, and the Bonanno family by night and telling the FBI all about it the next day. He was around a lot of information that was useful. At one point he heard Anthony Casso go on and on about the time he personally tortured and killed Jimmy Hydell. When he told the FBI about it, Otto recounted Anthony Casso's story about Jimmy's final hours this way: "After a number of hours of beatings and other tortuous activities, Hydel admitted to Casso that he did in fact try to kill him."

It was a dangerous job, but it kept Otto out of jail.

On this day, February 14, Otto had another little Valentine for his friends at the FBI regarding Anthony Casso. He was again meeting with Agent Colgan, and was now relating something quite disturbing that he'd picked up from Casso. When Otto was done with his tale, Colgan typed a report consistently misspelling Casso's name:

"Source stated that Anthony Gaspipe Caso has a contact in the Sixty-third Precinct who is a detective and who will frequently supply Caso information on ongoing investigations. Caso also informed the source that he requests this detective friend of his to oftentimes call other police agencies and departments in order to determine ongoing facts concerning investigations. Apparently this detective can obtain much of this information Caso desires simply by his position as a detective in the NYCPD. Source does not know the name of the detective nor does he expect to find his particular investigative assignment out in the near future. However, if he does so, he will immediately contact the [FBI's] New York office with this information."

May 15, 1987

A group of men pulled up in a van outside the Bulova Watch warehouse in Astoria, Queens. It was near dawn; there were no security guards in the back or on the roof because the building was considered impossible to enter. It was protected by a sophisticated network of alarms connected directly to the New York City Police Department precinct a few blocks away. The building itself was a fortress in a tough-to-reach spot in the middle of a residential neighborhood hard by the intersection of the Brooklyn-Queens Expressway and Grand Central Parkway. The men who jumped out of the van were not impressed. They had with them a secret weapon: Otto Heidel, the Bypass King.

On the night of the Bulova job, Otto looked at the system

and knew exactly what he had to do. While the rest of the crew sat around in the van in the parking lot, trying to stay quiet, Otto worked his way through the schematic inside his head, essentially rewiring the alarm system to make it think it was still functioning. When he was done, he was assigned to sit in the van and listen to the police scanners. He had a Bearcat scanner tuned to the Brooklyn South precinct, several two-way radios, and a "black book" with a list of supposedly top-secret frequency numbers from within the NYPD, including the frequency of the deputy commissioner and the Major Case Squad. One of the guys on the job that night, Vic Amuso, was hungry, and he decided to go for take-out while the burglars burgled away inside the Bulova warehouse.

"Do you want anything?" he asked.

"Soup," said Otto. "Some nice, hot soup."

For the next eight hours the crew carefully picked out what they wanted, or more importantly, what they could easily fence. By the time they left the next day they had acquired goods worth half a million dollars. Boxes and boxes of watches, twenty-four to forty-eight per box. They had to pull up a truck to fit it all.

The next morning Gaspipe and "Georgie Neck" and Otto Heidel pulled into an empty garage in Staten Island and unloaded twenty-five boxes of watches. Burt Kaplan's drug-dealing accomplice Tommy Galpine, a tall, lanky kid with a mustache who looked more like a cowboy than the drug dealer he was, helped out. Burt knew some people who knew some people who could get rid of the watches. It wasn't as good as cash, but it was eventual cash.

"Casso told me that this same gang had broken into Bulova's warehouse in Queens and that if I wanted, he could get me the watches from that burglary to fence," Kaplan recalled. "It was a fairly reasonable price, and I said okay, I would do it. And he said, 'Don't worry about the money. I'll vouch for the money.'"

A day later, Kaplan realized there was a problem. Several of the fences who were trying to unload the boxes of Bulova watches were getting visits from the FBI. This was not considered to be good news for anyone. He told Tommy to go back and move the boxes from the Staten Island garage. Tommy did as he was told, and the following day a bunch of guys wearing FBI windbreakers showed up at the garage and found nothing.

It was clear that whoever touched the Bulova watches got a visit from the FBI. It was clear that one or more among them was meeting in secret with special agents. This scenario presented two options: find the informant and kill him, or get ready to spend some time in the yard at Lompoc. The Bypass Gang had done so many jobs together that if one guy went bad, the whole thing would come crashing down.

There were more rumors on the streets of Brooklyn than in a *Daily News* gossip column. Who was the rat? The information was extremely vague, which was a problem. If you couldn't say for sure who had flipped, then everybody was a suspect. This did not make for an atmosphere conducive to team spirit. It was a snake pit. Paranoia governed your every move. Who could you trust? Who was listening when you spoke? Who was watching? When would you hear the knock on the door?

El Caribe

If you were a respectable gangster in the mid-1980s, El Caribe was the place to be. It was a big catering hall on the edge of a fetid canal and next to a parking lot full of school buses down in Mill Basin at the far end of Brooklyn. There were so many FBI surveillance vans outside the parking lot day and night that resentful neighbors sometimes called the local precinct. Often the vans were parked in tow-away zones for hours on end.

In the summer of 1987 Burt Kaplan sat at the bar waiting to meet with a tenant of his who had a job selling food inside El Caribe. On this night he was sitting at the beach club near Tommy Karate. In most criminal organizations there is a really scary guy who does the worst of the worst jobs. He's usually a guy who enjoys killing. In the old Murder, Incorporated, there were a bunch of guys like that. In the Gambino family, it was a guy named Roy Demeo. In the Lucchese family, it was Anthony Casso. In the Bonanno family, it was Tommy Karate. He had a bar in Brooklyn off McDonald Avenue where he would take people to kill them. If you got an invitation to this bar, you knew it would be the last place you'd ever see. In the back room, Tommy would take the body, place it in a bathtub, and cut it open to drain out the blood. Then he'd chop off the head and hands to make identification difficult, and chop up the rest into trash-bag-size pieces for removal to a bird sanctuary on Staten Island.

On this night, Tommy Karate was sitting with Burt when a guy Burt knew only as Otto walked over to where they were sitting. Otto had been playing racquetball; he still had his sweats on. Burt had seen the guy around—a middle-aged guy who spent all his time in gyms. Like a lot of guys at El Caribe.

"Tommy Karate was standing with us and Otto Heidel walked over and he was playing racquetball in the facilities. And Tommy Karate says to him, 'You know something, Otto? I think you're a stool pigeon.'"

This is the kind of accusation in which one of the two participants almost always ends up dead. If you make the accusation and can't back it up, you're dead. If you can, the other guy is dead. Burt remembered, "Otto Heidel got very affronted by it. He said, 'Why are you talking like that, Tommy?' And Tommy says, 'It just seems that every time we do something when you're involved, somebody gets pinched or they know we're coming in before we get there and nothing ever goes right. I personally think you're a stool pigeon.'"

This was not the kind of thing you said to somebody as a joke. Kaplan perceived that Otto was frightened out of his wits. Everybody knew what Tommy Karate did in the back room of his bar. Otto denied and denied, but the more he denied, the more Burt Kaplan began to think about the Bulova watches Otto had helped unload in Staten Island and the FBI agents showing up the next day.

Burt did what he always did when he felt someone could do him some harm. He went to Gaspipe and told him all about it. He knew Gaspipe had done several burglaries with Otto.

"I told him exactly what happened, the exchanges between the two of them, and I said, 'You know, I know you're close to this Otto Heidel,' and he says, 'Yes, we've been friends and doing things together for years. We never had no problems with him.' I said, 'To me it didn't look right, the conversation.' He said, 'Well, why don't you ask our friends to find out what they could about Otto?' "

A few days later, Kaplan says Detective Eppolito paid him a visit.

"Otto is hot," was all Eppolito had to say.

September 3, 1987

At 4:20 P.M. two men walked past the busy shopping area on Bath Avenue in Brooklyn, talking. One was a younger man, in his thirties, Carmine Varriale, a soldier in the Lucchese crime family. The other was Frank Santora Jr., older, in his fifties, a big man by any standard with shiny black hair and a year-round tan. It was Thursday, a weekday, and there were people on the sidewalks shopping and going about their business. They all stopped what they were doing when Varriale and Santora reached the sidewalk in front of the Bath Avenue Dry Cleaning and Tailoring Shop.

A white guy walked right up behind them and shot them both three times in the head. The man, wearing a hooded sweatshirt, jumped into a waiting sedan and sped away.

Though there was still plenty of sunlight left heading into this Labor Day weekend, not a single witness got a plate number or a good look at the assailant.

Varriale died on the sidewalk. Santora held on for a bit, but was pronounced dead later at Victory Memorial Hospital.

In trying to figure out what caused this mess on Bath Avenue, detectives knew right away that many people would want to shoot Carmine Varriale in the head. First of all, he was a soldier in the Lucchese crime family who was known to associate with Anthony "Gaspipe" Casso. Next, he had been involved in several bad drug deals. Plus he had problems with his gangster half brother, Pasquale Varriale, the guy they found in front of the church in the white tarp. Pasquale had been associated with the Colombo crime family, so detectives feared the death of Carmine so shortly after the death of his half brother Pasquale could turn out to be the first shot in a war between the Lucchese family and the Colombo family.

Frank Santora Jr. was another matter. In the Major Case Squad files Frankie was listed as "loosely associated" with the Gambino family.

Within an hour after word got out about the double homicide, Detectives Eppolito and Caracappa showed up at the Sixty-second Precinct station house uninvited. Eppolito was furious, ranting and raving about his cousin. Detectives working the Varriale/Santora homicide were just beginning the investigation, going through the DD5s, the forms used to take down witness statements at the scene of a crime. It was a tedious business, especially in certain neighborhoods where nobody ever sees anything. One of the detectives doing his DD5 work, Joe Piraino, knew Eppolito was related to one of the victims, so that would explain why he was there. But he felt it was odd that Caracappa had shown up. Piraino had been assigned the Varriale/Santora homicide by the unit's sergeant. Caracappa really had no business being there.

Eppolito, Piraino noted, was nearly foaming at the mouth.

"They got them all!" Eppolito hollered to no one in particular. "They took everybody!"

Detective Eppolito and his friend Detective Caracappa both attended Frankie Santora Jr.'s funeral. Under most circumstances, this might have caught the attention of the Internal Affairs Bureau of the NYPD, but because Detective Eppolito had a blood tie, everybody looked the other way.

Pete Franzone the garage owner showed up at Frankie's funeral as well. He had always been afraid of Frankie and he was also aware that he had committed crimes with Frankie. He had helped Frankie do certain things. He needed to attend the funeral to show everybody else there that just because Frankie was dead, that didn't mean Pete Franzone was going to start remembering what went on inside his garage.

Burt Kaplan, who was still on parole, did not go to Frankie Santora Jr.'s funeral. He did, however, mention the death of Frankie to Anthony Casso, noting that "our friend" with the cops had been whacked on Bath Avenue.

Casso's reaction was a surprise.

"I didn't know that was 'our friend,'" Casso said of Frankie Jr. "If I knew that, I could have stopped it.'"

The shooting of Frankie Jr. had been a big mistake by Anthony Casso. He had problems with Frankie's friend Carmine Varriale for a number of months, and Frankie had just been unlucky enough to be walking next to Carmine. By mistake, Casso had cut off his connection with the very useful NYPD detectives.

A week after Frankie Jr.'s funeral, Mrs. Frankie Jr. suddenly showed up out of the blue at Burt Kaplan's clothing store on Eighty-sixth Street. She had a simple request, Kaplan recalled: "She says, 'Would you like to meet Frankie's cousin the cop?'"

For the first time, Burt Kaplan was going to meet face to face with Louis Eppolito. He'd seen him before a couple of times. Once Eppolito had been at a social function but Burt had not introduced himself. He'd seen him at Toys R Us the day they snatched Jimmy Hydell. Now Frankie's wife had arranged it for Burt to come to her house on Seventy-ninth Street in Bensonhurst and meet cousin Lou.

When Burt showed up, Mrs. Frankie brought him into the dining room and introduced him to Lou. She left them alone in the dining room.

"I'm pretty sure you know who I am," Eppolito said.

"I know who you are," said Burt.

Eppolito got right to business. The arrangement he had with Frankie and Burt had worked out well for all concerned. Just because Frankie, God rest his soul, was gone, that was no reason to terminate the contract.

"I think we could make this simple. We could make this a business arrangement. You could put me and my partner on a four-thousand-a-month pad, and we'll give you everything that we get on every family, any bit of information we get about informants, about ongoing investigations, wiretaps, and imminent arrests."

Detective Eppolito explained how he worked in the Sixty-second Precinct, but he had a partner who worked on a task force where "there was a lot of information that came across. He was in meetings with the FBI and that that would all become part of the four thousand a month and the only exception would be murder contracts would be above that. Lou told me that his partner was the key to the whole thing, and that Louie could only get us information from the precinct that he worked in or if he heard some scuttlebutt from other detectives, but that his partner was sitting in on these organized-crime meetings all the time."

Sitting at his dead gangster cousin's dining room table, Detective Eppolito made one point clear above all others. Although he was a cop, he shared Burt's profound hatred of informants. Burt had been brought up to believe that there was no lower form of life than a rat, and Lou the detective could not agree more. As Kaplan put it, "[Eppolito] told me he liked doing things with us because when he gave us information people got taken care of that deserved it, and that in the past he gave information to other people and they never acted on it."

Burt said he would talk to his people to see if the arrangement could be continued, but he didn't see why not. He felt it might not be a good idea to call the cops directly, so they needed a way of communicating if something came up quickly—say, word that Burt or Anthony Casso or anybody else they cared about was about to be arrested. Burt adopted the means he used to communicate with Gaspipe, which was for Eppolito to beep him to a pay phone and then Burt would go to a pay phone and call the number. That way you'd have pay-phone-to-pay-phone contact. No phone records to connect the dots. Burt scribbled down Lou's beeper number in his black address book and even put down Lou's home number on Long Island. He came up with a code name in case anybody looked in the book: Marco. Lou was now Marco. If he needed Lou, he'd call the number marked Marco.

Kaplan gave Lou the number his daughter, Deborah, had when she lived at home. She'd moved in with her lawyer husband now, but the number still existed. If Kaplan beeped Lou, he would always punch in the prefix of his home phone number at the end—259—so Burt would know who was beeping him.

The deal was struck. As Burt left Frankie's house, he noticed a thin guy with black hair and a mustache sitting in a sedan near the driveway. Kaplan looked directly at the guy, who turned his head away quickly. Kaplan assumed it was Eppolito's partner, whatever his name was.

Casso immediately agreed to the four thousand dollars a month. It was a bargain, but he wanted it to be his and his alone.

"He said, 'Tell them if they want to do this, and we go forward on it, that they have to work exclusively for us,'" Kaplan recalled. "We don't want them giving information to other guys in other families, and possibly have a problem back from it which will eventually come back to us."

Thus the marriage continued, with one less middleman. Most of the time when Burt would meet with Detective Eppolito, the detective would come to his house at about 10:00 P.M. Kaplan would put out the porch light, and Detective Eppolito would tap on Burt's front window. If Burt's wife, Eleanor, was asleep, they would talk in the living room. If she was still awake, they would go to the back to where his daughter had lived as a child.

Sometimes they would meet elsewhere, if Louie wasn't in the city. They'd meet at rest areas on the Southern State Parkway or the Long Island Expressway. At times they'd meet at the apartment of one of Louie's girlfriends. In time Louie introduced Burt to Steve. Their first meeting was at the parking lot of a Perkins Pancake House on Staten Island. When they arrived, Burt and Steve agreed it was not a good idea for them to all be seen together in this parking lot with all these people driving in and out. Burt got in the car with Steve and Lou and they drove to a small cemetery near housing projects and around the corner from Steve's mother's house. The cemetery was empty almost all the time.

That way if anybody was watching, they'd be easily spotted. It was a perfect arrangement: for a mere four thousand dollars a month, the Lucchese crime family would be getting unprecedented access to the inner workings of the FBI, the NYPD, the DEA, the Brooklyn district attorney, and everybody else who had an ongoing investigation into the people who ran that organization.

How could anything go wrong?

October 8, 1987

By 4:15 P.M. the sky was beginning to darken at the far side of Brooklyn. This was Marine Park, a neighborhood of civil servants and shop owners miles from the skyscrapers of Manhattan, a small town of one- and two-family homes so close together you could answer the *Jeopardy* questions posed by the TV set next door. This was where the crowded streets of Brooklyn bumped into a wild and lonely marshland of cattails and sea grass and jarringly open space known as Gateway Recreational Park. Here was an incongruous juxtaposition of gritty urbania and Mother Nature in all her glory, where sea breezes mix with the acrid perfume of the B48 transit bus passing by on Avenue U.

Here also was a man with a problem. His name was John Otto Heidel, a stocky 170-pound middle-aged guy wearing a gray sweatshirt and blue jogging pants. Otto had just finished playing a sweaty game of racquetball, which was not a problem for him. He was in great shape for a guy whose forty-seventh birthday was just five days away. It was a Thursday; the weekend was coming. It had been an unusually warm day, in the mid-sixties, with no rain, no wind, a beautiful slice of Indian summer, and now Otto was heading back to his eight-year-old blue Pontiac Bonneville parked on busy Avenue U three car lengths from East Thirty-fifth Street. The car was still there—that was good—but there was a problem: the right rear tire was flat.

To most taxpaying citizens of Brooklyn and elsewhere, this would seem a simple matter: get a jack, get a spare, fix the flat. To Otto Heidel in the fall of 1987, a flat tire was never just a flat tire.

In the last few days Otto had decided that the Lucchese family was going to kill him. Two days previous, when Otto wasn't home, two of his partners in the Bypass Gang had stopped by claiming they needed to discuss an unspecified matter. This was a surprise, and Heidel did not like surprises. In fact, the Bypass King had been avoiding the Bypass Gang for a while now. Otto was a full-time paranoid guy. As Otto approached his Pontiac with racquetball gear in hand, he could not afford to view a flat tire as a mere flat tire.

Otto opened the trunk of his Bonneville and removed the spare and the jack. He placed the equipment on the street next to the ruined tire. He then took a .9mm Walther PPK from his waist and placed it on the street next to the jack. It was loaded, easy to reach. Otto began working the lug nuts off the tire with the tire iron. As he did, a light blue 1983 Oldsmobile with two men inside pulled on to Avenue U from East Thirty-fifth Street.

It all happened quite fast. One of the men in the Olds jumped out of the car and began firing at Otto. Heidel picked up his .9mm and fired four shots as he ran down Avenue U and onto East Thirty-fifth Street. The guy with the gun, wearing a dark hooded sweatshirt, chased after, the Olds following close behind the wrong way down the one-way street. Otto tried to hide behind a parked car but was hit again and again. He stumbled back another ten feet and collapsed on the street.

A woman living nearby ran out and tried to stanch the bleeding. It was October in the gloaming, the sky was beginning to darken. Otto the Bypass King lay in the street, his heart barely beating. He had been hit in the chest, back, and buttocks. He was still alive. There was still a pulse. All those hours of racquetball had paid off.

First a squad car showed up, answering a call for 10-34, "Shots fired." Over the radio, they requested help.

"Male down in the middle of the street. No ID on perp. Shot in chest. Male bleeding heavy. Male still has a pulse. Rush EMS."

By the time EMS showed up, Otto Heidel was gone.

In the squad room at the Sixty-third Precinct, Detective Ed Scott worked the Otto Heidel homicide. Scott sat at his desk, asking pedigree questions of Otto's son James Heidel, just a few hours after Otto had been murdered. As Scott took down background information on James's dead father, a detective Scott knew only a little happened to walk by the desk. The detective was a big guy who always wore gold chains and a tie that he never tied around his neck.

"That cop is dirty," James said.

Scott said nothing. Perps and their children often accused cops of being dirty. It happened almost every day. But for reasons he could not explain, this statement by this kid at this particular moment stayed with Detective Scott. The big detective with the gold chains was Louis Eppolito. A lot of guys in the Sixty-third Precinct weren't too crazy about Eppolito. Detective Scott didn't have much interaction with Eppolito, and he didn't particularly want to. He considered Eppolito to be a loud guy who talked about breaking heads and how many broads he'd screwed. Detective Scott did not much like him, which probably contributed to his remembering what the son of the Bypass King had to say.

The evening Otto was shot down in the streets of Mill Basin, FBI Agent Stephen Carbone got a call at home. He and another agent had been working Otto as a source as part of an FBI-NYPD effort called the Joint Bank Robbery Task Force, whose aim was to eliminate the Bypass Gang from the pages of the newspapers. Otto was a very important source. He'd recorded conversations and given the squad a blow-by-blow of the gang's comings and goings, and he was going to be a star witness when the indictment came down. Now he was no longer available for such a role. This was a big kick in the task force.

The next day, Carbone and his partner went to Heidel's apartment in Brooklyn with detectives from the Sixty-third Precinct, including Ed Scott. There they found Otto's Greatest Hits: microcassettes and regular cassettes, hidden inside a secret compartment in the bathroom. A quick listen showed the tapes were mostly Otto at work: Otto recording police scanners, Otto at the scene of bank burglaries talking to his coconspirators. A decision was made for Detective Scott to take the tapes back to the Sixty-third Precinct for safekeeping. If they were sent to the NYPD property clerk, it could take days to get them back. Instead of being vouchered as evidence, the tapes were dropped in a black plastic bag and kept in the office of a sergeant at the Sixty-third Precinct. The keys to Otto's apartment were kept in Detective Scott's storage cubby. Detective Scott would later say that anyone in the precinct would have had access to both the tapes and the keys.

• • •

"After Otto was killed, Louie came to my house and he handed me two minitapes," Kaplan said. "He said, 'This will prove that I was right, that the guy was cooperating, and that he was taping people.' And I didn't have a tape player to play that and I gave the tapes to Casso. Louie said, 'I got them out of Otto's apartment, while I was doing the investigation, and I put them in my boot.'" Kaplan said Casso listened to the tapes and said, "You were right. There is a conversation from a bank burglary, and Vic Amuso's voice is on the tape, saying to Otto, 'Do you want anything?' It was a cold night. And Otto was in a van listening to police radios, and Otto said, 'Yes, soup.'"

On October 9, 1987, Detective Joseph Piraino was assigned to the Otto Heidel homicide. Nobody else from Major Case was given this task, which was designated Case 113. Nevertheless, a day after the death of Otto Heidel, another detective from Major Case filled out a Request for Records Check form, seeking a criminal-records inquiry on two men: Phillip D'Angello and Peter Spotto. Both were low-level street criminals who just happened to be Otto Heidel's codefendants in an earlier bank burglary case. The record check revealed everything you could want to know about D'Angello and Spotto, and Otto as well, including where they might be found and the names of all their known associates.

The detective who made this request was Stephen Caracappa. He sought information on Otto's living associates and had Sergeant Hart of the Major Case Squad sign off on his requests. He put down a case number, 113, the number for the Otto Heidel investigation, signed his name, and retrieved the information.

If you were a member of the NYPD's Major Case Squad, the elite of the elite, you could ask for anything and nobody asked why. All you had to do was put down a number. The key was to come up with a number—say, Case 113. That was good enough.

Of course, numbers were like fingerprints. They were useful later in the business of connecting dots.

• • •

The death of an informant is a serious affair for the FBI and the NYPD. It is extremely bad for business. The implications are profound. The message is clear: your secret cooperation is not secret. The government cannot protect you. You can hide but you cannot run.

Documents generated by the NYPD Major Case Squad detective assigned to the case days after the sudden unexpected demise of Otto the Bypass King make clear that the cops had no clue who had figured out Otto was a cooperator. Detective Piraino had listed Otto as "closely associated to Lucchese crew" and as a guy with a sizable file in the NYPD's Safe Loft and Truck Squad archives. "Vault burglary and electronic bypass jobs" were noted as what the NYPD coyly dubbed Otto's "criminal specialty."

It was important to figure out who killed Otto, for then it might be possible to figure out who gave Otto up. The odds of resolving these questions seemed, at the time, daunting. Eyewitnesses described the shooter as a male, white, in his thirties, wearing dark clothes. This could apply to approximately forty-five thousand people living in Brooklyn alone. Witnesses said the shooter jumped into a waiting Chevy, or maybe an Olds, late model, driven by another male, white, wearing a "dark blue hooded-type sweatshirt."

As one NYPD report explained, "NO LICENSE PLATE # OBSERVED AT THIS TIME."

Detectives Scott and Piraino found a .9mm Walther PPK near Otto's auto, its serial number, 241398, intact. Nearby were four ejected .380 rounds, which they believed came from the gun. They popped Otto's trunk and found all kinds of police scanners and internal NYPD lists of frequency numbers. They ran his license plate and came back with the alias Michael Rosen. They discovered he'd last been busted earlier that summer by the FBI, and they even learned he had an outstanding parking ticket dated July 14.

There was, notably, no formal mention of the fact that Heidel was at the time of his death cooperating with the FBI, but everybody in the Sixty-third Precinct seemed to know it.

On the day Otto died, there was concern within the multiple law enforcement agencies pursuing the Bypass Gang that there was a leak in law enforcement. Informants were telling their handlers about wiseguys in the Lucchese and Colombo families boasting about "friends" in law enforcement keeping them up to date. Wiseguys often claimed to have friends in the NYPD and the FBI, but in this case the informants said they had seen certain documents that seemed to corroborate the claim. All of this was very vague and very worrisome.

Plugging leaks is no simple task. There were cops in three different area codes out looking for the Bypass Gang: the Brooklyn district attorney, several of the FBI's New York organized-crime units, the FBI's bank robbery squad, the NYPD's Safe Loft and Truck Squad, the NYPD's Major Case squad, and even the Suffolk County district attorney, way out on Long Island. You could fill a movie theater with all those cops, and the more cops and agents involved, the higher the likelihood of a leak. One supervisor of the FBI's bank robbery squad recalled telling his agents not to talk to the Brooklyn DA. One assistant district attorney in Brooklyn told his guys not to go near a certain FBI agent he believed had compromised an organized-crime informant in a separate case.

Paranoia afflicted the good guys. Supervisory agent John Coleman of the Joint Bank Robbery Task Force, known as C-19, admitted, "There was some concern about informational leaks regarding this investigation and as a result, members of my squad and myself were reluctant to discuss this investigation with people not assigned to C-19."

Strange coincidences would occur that could not be easily explained. Detective Joseph Lamendola was a member of the Safe Loft and Truck Squad of the NYPD. This was the unit that spent its time going after people like Otto Heidel or anyone else who felt the best way to make a living was to break into other people's places of business and take everything that was not nailed to the floor. In the middle of the Bypass Gang investigation, Lamendola and the unit had obtained permission from a judge to monitor the phone numbers that came into or went out of Anthony Casso's phones. They didn't actually listen in on his conversations, but they could see who he was calling and who was calling him. As they checked the numbers Casso was calling and vice versa, they connected him to other Mafia members and associates. Step two was to actually listen in, and with their web of phone numbers they got a judge to authorize a wiretap on Anthony Casso's phone.

Days after the bug went in, Casso stopped using that phone.

Finding the leak was complicated, made more difficult by the nature of the job. Within the NYPD, all kinds of rules were designed to track who was asking for what information. If you asked, you were supposed to have a good reason, and somebody was supposed to write it down. Requesting anything from the Intelligence Unit meant following a long set of guidelines that all detectives were required to follow.

There were all sorts of rules to follow regarding using the departmental computer, because what was in it was, to say the least, highly sensitive information. Criminal history back to the time you were a teenager, and that included arrests that had been sealed by the courts; all known addresses and some not known; boyfriends, girlfriends, friends, enemies, mothers, fathers, sisters, brothers, cousins, second cousins, etc. Social Security number, date of birth, place of birth, mother's maiden name. A detailed description of the tattooed hula-skirted babe on your left bicep. It was all there, including— under the category most highly sensitive—the list of all those dedicated felons who'd decided to secretly cooperate with the NYPD, the FBI, the DEA, or NASA.

This information was a treasure trove for organized crime. Besides identifying which of your best friends was secretly cooperating with the FBI, the system also contained just the right information to track down a rival, his family, and his girlfriend. Having trouble finding a reluctant loan shark victim? What better spot than the NYPD's massive computer? How about figuring out that you're about to be arrested? The NYPD computer can help you plan the perfect time to take that long-needed Mexican vacation in the sleepy town of "On the Lam."

The idea that this stuff could get into criminal hands was a nightmare for any law enforcement agency, so there were safeguards to make sure this never happened. To access the computer, a detective had to fill out a form and get it signed by a supervisor. He had to put down his tax registration number and identify the case number that would explain who

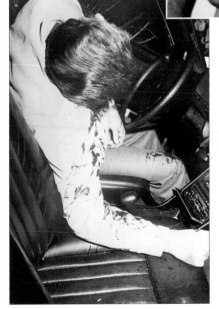

Eppolito's gangster cousin, Frank Santora Jr., who first proposed the unholy marriage between the mob and the two cops.
Government exhibit

The late Eddie Lino, Gambino soldier shot down in his car by Caracappa because Anthony Casso wanted revenge for an attempt to kill him.
Government exhibit

The late John Otto Heidel, member of a bank burglary gang murdered after mob cops identified him as a police informant. *Government exhibit*

Caracappa's lawyer Edward Hayes (left) chats with Eppolito's lawyer Bruce Cutler during a break in court proceedings outside Brooklyn Federal Court. *Todd Maisel, New York Daily News*

Prosecutors Mitra Hormozi and Robert Henoch during a break in trial. Henoch oversaw the questioning of key witness Burt Kaplan.
Debbie Egan-Chin, New York Daily News

DEA Special Agent Mark Manko (left) and DEA Supervisor John Peluso, the two investigators who were crucial to the prosecution of the two mob cops, emerge from court minutes after Caracappa and Eppolito were sentenced.
Debbie Egan-Chin, New York Daily News

Anthony "Gaspipe" Casso (left), homicidal underboss of the Lucchese crime family, next to Burt Kaplan (right), his liaison to the cops, at the wedding of Kaplan's daughter. Kaplan would ultimately emerge as the prosecution's star witness.
Government exhibit

James Hydell, gangster wannabe who failed in an attempt to kill Casso. The cops kidnapped Hydell and delivered him to his death at the hands of Casso.
Government exhibit

Anna Lino, wife of slain gangster Eddie Lino, shakes hands with Barry Gibbs, who spent eighteen years in prison for a crime he did not commit because of Eppolito. Lino's son, Vincent, stands between them on the day the cops were sentenced.
Debbie Egan-Chin, New York Daily News

The body of Nicholas Guido, a telephone installer, who was killed because he had the same name as a gangster who tried to kill Casso. Guido had nothing to do with the mob.
Linda Rosier, New York Daily News

Stephen Caracappa, outside Brooklyn Federal Court after making bail. He was furious that the media took his photo nearly every day of the trial. *Mike Albans, New York Daily News*

Louis Eppolito with his wife, Fran, arrives at court during trial. Hours before the jury found him guilty, he told photographers that he felt great. *Linda Rosier, New York Daily News*

Louis Eppolito's house in Las Vegas, paid for with drug money borrowed from Burt Kaplan. Informant Stephen Corso recorded hours of conversation inside this house.

Debbie Egan-Chin, New York Daily News

needed the information and why. The rules for keeping this classified material safe from unauthorized eyes sounded impressive: "Access to its consoles must be limited to authorized personnel. Computer programs may be coded to restrict retrieval to those who know the code. The computer should be programmed to refuse direct outstation inputs or retrieval. The computer room must be protected from unauthorized entry which could lead to the damage of the machinery or the data."

In truth, the NYPD computer system seemed to have more leaks than a congressional subcommittee. You were supposed to put a case number down that served to explain why you were inquiring. Plenty of times there was no case number. Detectives routinely swapped passwords to access the thing. They'd call up and request information as a favor to check up on some car their girlfriend was seen in with some guy. The guy retrieving the information would sometimes write down who asked for it, and sometimes just write down his own name. As highly secure systems go, this one was not.

In June 1985, for example, Detective Stephen Caracappa of the Major Case Squad ran the name Monica Singleton. He entered her date of birth, but he didn't bother to put a case number in. The NYPD computer dutifully discovered that Monica Singleton had no criminal record. Good thing. Monica Singleton was Stephen Caracappa's girlfriend, soon to be fiancée, soon to be wife.

THIRTEEN

When Peter Mitchell was called as a witness for the prosecution in *People vs. Barry Gibbs*, he walked into the fifth-floor Brooklyn courtroom of New York Supreme Court Justice Ronald Aiello and saw Gibbs for the first time in fourteen months.

"He didn't look like the same guy I seen in the lineup," Mitchell said. "He was fatter, bigger." He sat in the box and was sworn in. Assistant District Attorney Andrew Dember then began direct examination of his most crucial witness. His questioning lasted no more than forty minutes.

Prosecutor Dember began with a recitation of Mitchell's misdeeds, including a drunk driving arrest (misdemeanor) and the bad-check charge (felony). Dember did it so the defense lawyer wouldn't. Dember then had Mitchell take the jury to the edge of Brooklyn where the highway meets the sea and Peter Mitchell the lone jogger came upon a white man and a black woman sitting in the front seat of a gray Oldsmobile Cutlass—not a black Buick Regal. He asked Mitchell to describe the face of the man who dumped the body.

Mitchell said, "White, big nose, baggy face."

"'Baggy'?" asked the judge. "Did you say 'baggy'?"

"Yeah," Mitchell said. "Like a prune."

"Did you notice anything else about him?" the prosecutor asked.

"Just the big nose," he said. The hair was "salt and pepper" and "frilly on top." There was no mention of the man in *The Godfather* or a white pompadour.

This time he said the guy wore red pants and a plaid shirt with a paunch. That was different from the black leather jacket and dark slacks with a paunch that he actually saw. He also claimed the guy saw him and then drove off quickly.

"Did you get a look at the face?" Dember asked.

"It was right in my face," Mitchell responded.

"Do you see that man in the courtroom?"

"Yes," Mitchell said, pointing toward Gibbs at the defense table. "The man sitting over there in the middle, brown suit."

The jury broke for lunch. In the afternoon, he came back and testified that he never saw Detective Louis Eppolito at the scene with the body but that he did talk to him at the Sixty-third Precinct station house. He made no mention of driving around the projects with Eppolito and spying Gibbs coming out of a building. He said nothing about Eppolito's instructions. He just said that days after Mitchell came upon Virginia Robertson's body, Eppolito called him up and told him to show up for a lineup.

Dember asked Mitchell before the lineup, "Did you have any conversations with Detective Eppolito on the fourteenth of November?"

Mitchell said, "I don't recall."

"Did anybody, before you viewed that lineup, anybody tell you who to select from the lineup?"

"No."

Assistant District Attorney Dember then made sure to have Mitchell point out that he did not know Barry Gibbs or Virginia Robertson, and then that was the end of the direct testimony.

Cross-examination took three days. Gibbs's defense attorney, Ira London, asked Mitchell a hundred questions to shake his memory. He started by asking Mitchell if he had any "feelings" about Detective Eppolito, like he and Eppolito were "on the same team." Mitchell said no, then later said he was "with the prosecution." London the attorney noted that his private investigator, Knudsen, visited Mitchell at his house and Mitchell had declined to discuss the case. London asked, "Did you have something to hide from Mr. Knudsen about that incident?"

"No," Mitchell said, and then he went on to describe seeing the red light of the private investigator's tape recorder and ending the interview. The case was adjourned for the day. The next day, before the jury and Mitchell were allowed in the courtroom, London accused him of making up the whole story about the red light and the tape recorder. He said he could prove it was a lie by playing the tape.

London produced a blown-up photo of the jogging path and photographs of the view from the bridge to where Mitchell claimed to have seen the Cutlass and the man in the red pants. The photographs appeared to make Mitchell's statements evaporate. Then he got Mitchell to claim he wasn't breathing heavily after running six miles in thirty minutes, which would have been faster than some Olympic athletes. Then Mitchell admitted he had talked to Eppolito at the crime scene after claiming he first talked to him at the precinct. Then London the lawyer asked Mitchell, "Do you remember telling these people different things about observations you say you made that day, right?"

"'Different things'?" Mitchell replied. "What, you saying I'm lying?"

On the third day Mitchell admitted he told the detectives at the crime scene one story and the jurors another about first seeing the man with the big nose the first time close up and then seeing him again from far away. At first he had insisted it was the same man but now admitted he wasn't sure. London pointed out that Mitchell described the man who dumped the body as 150 to 175 pounds, while Barry Gibbs weighed more than 200 pounds. London the lawyer made it clear that Mitchell also did not mention the "large nose" at the crime scene; that only came much later. This rattled Mitchell's cage.

"No," he said in an agitated state. "I give the same description I'm saying now until I die."

"Did you tell Eppolito at the scene that he had a big nose, that the white male had a big nose?" London pressed.

"Yes."

"You sure of that?"

"Faintly," Mitchell said. "Faintly."

Mitchell admitted he had conversation with Eppolito at the precinct before viewing the lineup. First he said it wasn't a private conversation, then he admitted it was. He also admitted that just before the trial, he began to dream about the face of the man who dumped the body.

"It was not the face of the man that you saw on November fourth, am I correct?" London asked.

"False," Mitchell responded.

At some point during the three days Mitchell sat on the witness stand, he saw Detective Eppolito standing in the entrance to the courtroom, nodding at him. He took this to be a signal that Eppolito was watching. At another point, Mitchell became convinced he saw the guy who actually dumped Virginia Robertson's body sitting in the courtroom.

"I'm looking around the courtroom and I see the fucking white-haired guy sitting in the courtroom. The judge said, 'Mr. Mitchell are you okay?' I couldn't be sure, but it was the same white hair, same paunch. He's wearing shades, though. I'm thinking this might be the Mob. I had a chance to save Barry Gibbs. I wanted to say, 'He did it!'"

After he was done, Dember took Mitchell outside and told him he was a great witness and that they had an inmate who would testify that Barry Gibbs had admitted that he killed Virginia Robertson. Mitchell was shocked.

"I was like, what the fuck is this? I thought, this is bigger than me. I knew he didn't do it, but I gotta get out of there now."

Peter Mitchell walked out of the Kings County courthouse in downtown Brooklyn alone. He believed he had been instructed by the system of criminal justice to subvert the system of criminal justice. He knew what he had done. He had lied in court in front of all those people. He had noticed Barry Gibbs frowning during cross-examination. It was quite possible that the man would go to prison for no good reason at all. This was Peter Mitchell's heavy burden, placed upon his shoulders by Detective Louis Eppolito, the eleventh-most-decorated cop in New York Police Department history.

A few days later Barry Gibbs was convicted of murder in the second degree and sentenced to spend the next twenty years with the State of New York.

1988

Burt Kaplan never liked cops. He had come to believe they did not have his best interests at heart. But there were cops, and there were cops. There were certain cops who treated him with some respect. When they would arrest him, they would be polite about it. They would tell him all the bad things he was doing and he would try to convince them either that he had nothing to do with the bad things or that they really weren't bad at all. With the quaaludes, he had failed. With the heroin, he had succeeded. One thing Burt Kaplan really hated: cops who talked trash behind your back.

In all his years, Burt had not run into this problem with the many detectives he knew in the NYPD or the agents he'd encountered from the Drug Enforcement Agency. The FBI was different. Now he was on the phone with his factor, Rosenthal & Rosenthal, and he was learning of a visit the FBI paid to the company that kept Burt in business.

Rosenthal & Rosenthal were concerned about the visit. The agents said some things about Burt being involved with organized criminals and how Burt was an ex-convict and a known drug dealer. That kind of thing. These were all true statements, but they were not statements Burt needed his factor to hear. Rosenthal & Rosenthal did not really want to talk about this over the phone, and Burt agreed. He said he'd be in right away. At rush hour he drove to Manhattan and met Rosenthal & Rosenthal at a diner on First Avenue.

"I have to ask you a few questions, Burt. Do you mind?"

"Of course not," said Burt.

"Were you in prison?"

Burt looked Rosenthal & Rosenthal right in the eye and said, "Of course not."

"Are you involved in organized crime?"

"No," Burt said, again with the look in the eye.

"I'm glad to hear that," Rosenthal & Rosenthal said, "because I had a visit, and if what they told me was true, I would have to cease my relationship with you in the near future because my bonding company wouldn't allow me to continue."

Burt assured Rosenthal & Rosenthal that there was nothing to worry about. He got in his car, drove home to Brooklyn through the traffic, arrived home, and immediately regretted everything he'd said. Here was a guy who looked on Burt as a man of his word. He believed Burt because Burt gave him his word that he only told the truth, and now he had lied, lied, lied. If Burt didn't have his word, he didn't have anything. At five o'clock in the morning the next day, Burt was standing in front of Rosenthal & Rosenthal's office. He had a written guarantee from his factor for an eight-hundred-thousand-dollar letter of credit with Calvin Klein. He was prepared to rip it up. The guy showed up at five-thirty and they went around the corner and had a cup of coffee.

"I was in prison before," he said. "I have some friends in organized crime, but I'm not controlled by organized crime." This was how he saw it, anyway. He was not "controlled" by organized crime. Maybe he controlled organized crime. Rosenthal & Rosenthal didn't care. He was grateful that Burt remembered the truth.

"Well," he said. "I appreciate you telling me that."

Burt took out the Calvin Klein letter of credit and offered it to his factor.

"No, I wouldn't do that to you," he said. "I'll give you ninety days to try to find yourself some other financing, and you can use that."

Burt walked away from the meeting feeling that he had done the right thing and that the guy from Rosenthal & Rosenthal had done the right thing. As far as Burt was concerned, the only performer in this little morality play who didn't behave well was the FBI. Burt was beginning to really hate the FBI.

"Louie came and told me that there's a guy by the name of Domenic Costa that's involved in the Bypass Gang that's co-operating," Kaplan said. "I passed that on to Anthony Casso."

October 12, 1988

A few minutes before midnight and Ann Caramonte was filled with the anger of a girlfriend fed up. She sat alone in her two-story red-brick Bensonhurst apartment on Bay Ridge Parkway, thinking about the dinner she'd cooked for her boyfriend, Domenic Costa Jr. He was supposed to be home hours ago, and now he was not where he said he would be. She'd beeped him and he returned the call, claiming he was still at work and would be home in forty-five minutes. Definitely. That was ninety minutes ago. True, he was a hard-working guy. Or at least that is what he claimed. He had told Ann he worked three jobs, including a new gig doing house calls for a locksmith in Brooklyn. This was not a nine-to-five job, working for the locksmith. People locked themselves out of apartments at all hours of the day and night. But ninety minutes, this was not like the Domenic she knew.

Of course, what exactly did Ann know about her Domenic? What exactly did her Domenic do in all those hours when he wasn't around? He was always so vague about the wheres and the hows. She was aware that he was very good at getting around things. He could pick locks, crack safes, figure out how to get through hundred-thousand-dollar alarm systems. She knew this because he told her, and just about anyone else who would listen. He loved to talk about his abilities, although he always left out certain details, such as where precisely he practiced his God-given skills.

Of course, being on time was not one of his skills. Here it was, 11:59 P.M.—one minute to midnight—and no Domenic.

Then she heard it: Pop! Pop! Pop! Like fireworks, only right outside her window. Three times, maybe more.

Ann walked outside in the October chill and noticed that the garage door was open, the front of Domenic's brand-new white Pontiac sedan visible. She could see the plate, RGG 961.

As she walked closer she could see that the front windshield was shattered. As she walked closer, she could see her Domenic, now slumped over the steering wheel, his blood everywhere.

"Domenic! Domenic! Domenic!" Ann screamed, her high-pitched hysteria rising over this supremely quiet neighborhood. And no one answered, save a woman walking her dog.

The woman seemed to come out of nowhere. Ann screamed at her to help, and she rushed over. She tried to see if Domenic was alive, then rushed away to call 911. Within minutes, there were cops everywhere.

The woman with the dog said her name was Dorothea Lazar, and she had seen just about everything. There were two guys; one walked right past her. He had a gray sweatshirt on. She hadn't paid him any mind until she heard the shots; then she turned and saw the guy jump into a gray sedan and speed off down Twenty-first Avenue.

Oh, yeah, and one more thing. The guy slumped over the wheel? He's still alive.

Carmine Sessa and his friend Bobby sat in a gray sedan, waiting for a white 1987 Pontiac. It was nearly midnight on Bay Ridge Parkway in Bensonhurst. Carmine was looking for plate RGG 961. His timing was perfect. The car pulled past them and pulled in front of the driveway at 2102 Bay Ridge Parkway, stopped, then backed in toward the garage.

The driver got out, pulled up the garage door. He got back in his car, then slowly began backing into the garage, his headlights pointed outward. Carmine Sessa was already out of the sedan, walking down Bay Ridge Parkway toward the car in the garage. The .380 in his waistband was already in his right hand.

The way Carmine Sessa saw it, the reason Domenic Costa Jr. had to go was simple: he was no longer of value. For a long time, Domenic had been quite valuable. He had cracked hundreds of safes for Carmine Sessa, many of them inside bank vaults throughout Brooklyn. He had been doing this for years. Of course, he would only practice his skills after hours, usually after he and his pals blasted through a wall and went to work. He was a professional safecracker and a member of a gang the press called the Bypass Gang. As in bypassing alarm systems. Three hundred of them, in fact, for a take of seventy-five million dollars. He was very good.

In exchange, Carmine and another full-time gangster named Anthony "Gaspipe" Casso had offered Domenic certain protections. Carmine did this as a soldier in the organized-crime family that was named after Joseph Colombo; Anthony did this as a captain in the family named after Tommy "Two-Fingers Brown" Lucchese. Carmine and Anthony were able to offer Domenic the advantage of not being taken advantage of by certain other families who might wish to lay claim to Domenic's percentage.

For Domenic, there were certain disadvantages to this arrangement. When you are in a crime with other people, you are linked forever to these people, whether you like it or not. Forever you are both friend and enemy of your coconspirators, for at any moment your friends could decide that you have become a government informant and thus are no longer their friend.

This, in fact, is what was happening within the Bypass Gang. Carmine Sessa and "Gaspipe," had learned certain facts about members of the Bypass Gang. In the case of Domenic Costa, the facts were somewhat distressing.

In July or August, Domenic had decided to become a confidential informant for the FBI. Carmine knew what this meant. Domenic had been secretly meeting with an FBI agent who'd become very interested in the Bypass Gang. It was well known that the U.S. attorney in Brooklyn was preparing to indict a lot of people Carmine knew, and it was clear that Domenic was helping out.

It also was clear that Domenic would have a lot to offer the U.S. attorney. He'd been involved in nearly all the bank burglaries that Carmine and Anthony Casso had benefited from, and he was a guy with a knack for detail. He could remember the proper way to bust into dozens of different brands of safes, so remembering who was around during jobs with Carmine wouldn't be too much of a problem.

Carmine quickened his pace, holding the .380 to his side as he passed a woman walking a dog. She didn't seem to notice. Carmine walked up to Domenic Costa, who obviously didn't see him coming. He began shooting as he stood in front of the car, moving around to the driver's-side window, pumping five bullets into the car. He turned away and walked back down the driveway, where the gray sedan was now waiting. He jumped into the car and sped off into the night. It's possible that as he turned the corner he heard a woman screaming "Domenic!" over and over, but he wasn't sure. As far as he could tell, he'd hit the guy in the head. He'd done the job he'd been sent to do.

October 17, 1988

In the intensive-care unit on the third floor of Kings County Hospital, a man lay in bed, tubes in his nose and arms, a respirator clipped over his mouth. Doctors and nurses came and went. They figured there were at least three bullets that had entered the man's cranium and remained there, which meant chance was now part of the equation.

Outside the door, two plainclothes detectives chatted with two uniformed cops from the Seventy-first Precinct. Detective Piraino of the Major Case Squad was on hand. The order was for twenty-four-hour-a-day, seven-day-a-week coverage. They'd run the guy's name, and it came back under the heading "Specialty: Burglary, bypass alarms." Based on the eyewitness accounts and the fact that there was no robbery, it was clear there was what the squad liked to call an "OC element" in play.

At 9:45 A.M., a Dr. Tronolone emerged from the room to inform Detective Piraino that a bullet had surfaced in the eye of the patient, Mr. Costa, and that emergency surgery would be needed to remove the object immediately. The doctors went to work; the detective waited for the evidence.

When the surgery was complete, the doctors handed the detective what he wanted: a copper-jacketed .380 slug that had spent the previous week swimming around inside Domenic Costa's skull. Detective Piriano now just had to figure out who put it there and why.

The search started with one of Piraino's colleagues on the Major Case Squad, Detective Charles Siriano. Siriano had been on the squad a year and was one of three investigators looking at the Bypass Gang who first convinced Domenic Costa to cooperate. Now there was an allegation that Siriano was dirty, either on purpose or by mistake.

The allegation was that Siriano said something to another informant he had cultivated, a guy named Chickie. Whatever it was he said, it made it clear to Chickie that Domenic Costa was an active, cooperating informant within the Bypass Gang. When confronted, Siriano denied this, and Chickie was brought in for questioning.

The first time he was given a polygraph, Chickie either failed or the results were inconclusive because Chickie was on heart medicine. It depended on how you wanted to look at it. A second polygraph was administered, and this time Chickie passed. As a result, the NYPD decided that Detective Siriano had passed, too.

The investigation of Chickie, however, raised certain questions about how secret information about informants really was. When he was being questioned about Chickie, Detective Siriano made it clear that Major Case informant information stayed within the Major Case Squad and was not registered with the NYPD's Intelligence Division.

Within Major Case, Siriano was sure he'd told the sergeant in charge, Hart, about Domenic's status as a cooperator.

He also made it clear that others in Major Case probably knew, especially one guy in particular: Detective Stephen Caracappa. Siriano portrayed Caracappa as involved in most of the investigations going on in Major Case. He was the "go to" guy within the squad.

FOURTEEN

Major Case Squad room, 6:57 A.M. Detective Stephen Caracappa sat at the NYPD computer, running a name. At this hour, it was rare for anyone to be in the office, much less running names on the computer. But as a member of the newly formed Organized Crime Homicide Unit within Major Case, Caracappa frequently requested information regarding all sorts of members and associates of the underworld. In the world of the detective, you really didn't have to explain yourself every time you ran a name.

As required, Caracappa typed in his name, his tax ID number, and the name Peter Savino. He supplied no date of birth for Savino and no case number. It was not clear from the record precisely what he received in return, although at the time Savino was listed as a sometime confidential informant who tipped off the NYPD and the FBI to activities within the Genovese family. In February 1987, Caracappa's request was somewhat unusual. He was, at the time, not assigned to the Genovese family. He had no obvious reason to request information on Peter Savino.

November 24, 1987

In the predictable world of gangland, there are dozens of Tonys, a gaggle of Guidos, a busload of Vinnies, and not a small number of Tommys, Mikeys, and Petes. Rare is it that one encounters a Barclay. Barclay you find at the country club with the G&Ts. Barclays wear belts with little whales, shoes without socks, maybe silk ascots even. It's tough to envision a Barclay digging a guy up from a basement in the middle of the night. But on a quiet afternoon just after Thanksgiving 1987, NYPD detective William Mitzeliotis, FBI special agent Leo Farrell, and Assistant U.S. attorney Greg O'Connell sat in a windowless room in downtown Brooklyn listening to Barclay Feranga describe the guys he'd helped bury.

The detective, the agent, and the prosecutor wrote down whatever came out of the mouth of Barclay—officially known as File BO 2458-348. A big, bald guy with tattoos and the dull expression of a kid with a short attention span. Barclay was a career criminal who had decided on a career change, and the detective, the special agent, and the prosecutor had to listen patiently, without emotion, scribbling down each atrocity as it emerged from the tar pit of Barclay's history.

There were certain expectations. The government workers knew going in that Barclay was an associate of the Lucchese family, but when it came to drugs, he worked with everybody. Barclay was a major-league drug dealer. His cocaine supplier was a Colombian known as Al, a kilo-weight supplier. They had worked out a system. When Barclay contacted Al on his beeper, he punched in the code number 011773. If he wanted Al to call him back on his cell, he punched in 1517. If he wanted a callback to his beeper, he punched in 3217. It was amazing that a guy like Barclay could keep all those numbers straight.

There was more. There was the unexpected. Barclay had three bodies he wished to be held accountable for. Barclay had been involved personally in three homicides, and he could name the two other guys who helped out.   •

The first murder was of a contractor named Richie, an associate of the Colombo family who had made a mistake in choosing an employer. Ten years back, Richie agreed to do plumbing work for Funzi Tiere, a captain in the Genovese family. Tiere wanted Richie to install another toilet in his Brooklyn home, but he didn't want to pay any money. Richie, who was under the impression that you should be paid when you install a toilet, had the temerity to demand payment for his work.

This infuriated Funzi, who ordered his subordinates to beat the hell out of Richie. Somehow Barclay and two others got the job. Barclay recalled that the problem with administering a beating to Richie was that Richie was "a real tough guy." He simply would not submit. As a result, Richie got shot in the head.

Murder victim number two was a guy named Shorty, a drug dealer whom one of Barclay's associates believed had ripped him off. Shorty got shot in the head as well. The same basic scenario unfolded with murder number three. This time Shorty's brother, Ralph, was shot in the head as he left his apartment in Brooklyn.

Barclay was only too happy to tell prosecutor O'Connell who besides himself had helped in the matters of Richie and Shorty and Ralph. One was a psycho named Gerry Pappa. This was no surprise. He was well known to the NYPD and the FBI. The other name was definitely a surprise: Pete Savino.

As far as the FBI knew, Pete Savino was a businessman, the owner of Arista Windows, a window installation company in Brooklyn that had made Savino and the Mafia of New York a lot of money. Pete Savino also was a sometime cooperating witness for both the NYPD and the FBI. Somehow in all his cooperating, Pete had forgotten to mention the murders of Richie and Shorty and Ralph.

Pete apparently also forgot to mention that, in all three cases, the bodies were buried under the floor of Pete's company, Arista. When Arista moved, Pete Savino, businessman, helped dig up all three—Richie, Shorty, and Shorty's brother, Ralph—and move them to the company's new location, a warehouse in a bleak section on the Brooklyn/Queens border. Pete helped bury Shorty and Ralph in a yard area of the warehouse, while Richie the contractor, perhaps because of his expertise as a plumber, wound up under the toilet. And Pete Savino was there when it happened.

Pete Savino's concept of "cooperation" now seemed in doubt. Pete had some explaining to do.

A few days after Thanksgiving 1987, a team of FBI agents and NYPD detectives worked up a sweat inside a decrepit old warehouse on Scott Avenue in Brooklyn. It was a desolate neighborhood on the Brooklyn/Queens border where eighteen-wheelers roamed and packs of dogs wandered. Men with shovels in FBI windbreakers were an unusual sight.

For twenty-four hours, the teams worked their way through the warehouse. They hammered the concrete floors into powder and plunged shovels into Brooklyn dirt. They first went to a yard behind the warehouse and, one by one, Shorty and Ralph emerged from their shallow graves. Then they moved on to a bathroom and discovered the skeletal remains of Richie the contractor beneath the toilet.

The dispute over Funzi's toilet had put in motion certain events that could not be stopped.

O'Connell the prosecutor called a lawyer representing Pete Savino. He requested to see the man to discuss certain developments retrieved from under the concrete on Scott Avenue. It was time, O'Connell made clear, for Pete the businessman to take on a new role: confidential witness.

For years, Savino had secretly provided information to the government as a "confidential informant." A confidential informant could just phone in tips and go about his felonious business, as long as it wasn't too obvious. Since 1974, this had been Savino's role: whispering information about his fellow gangsters to both the NYPD and the FBI without having to reveal his many sins. It was communion without confession, and it served him well. A confidential witness had to go much farther. He had to reveal every crime he'd ever committed, name every criminal with whom he'd done business, secretly record conversations with friends. Always he had to agree to go public at the end and testify in court.

Presented with three bodies in the basement, Savino had a sudden change of heart.

He was forty-five years old; divorced twice, the new father

of twin boys. It was time to become a full-time cooperating witness. For days Pete Savino was debriefed by the FBI. He was not arrested, and the agents made sure to allow him time to run his business, Arista. He began by letting them know everything he'd been holding back.

He was a millionaire thief with not one but three Mafia families in his corner. He was closest to the Genovese family, so trusted by the boss, Vincent "Chin" Gigante, that he often sat next to him at the Triangle Social Club in Greenwich Village. He also was close to Peter Gotti of the Gambino family and to the Lucchese family street boss, Vic Amuso, and his underboss, Gaspipe Casso. Savino was making so much money that he was able to pay off not one but three Mafia families.

And it all happened at his business, Arista Windows. There he'd made a fortune installing thousands of windows in the housing projects run by the New York City Housing Authority, inflating costs, rigging bids, generally ripping off the taxpayers in any way he could. This allowed him to be rich and kick up a percentage to his many Mafia bosses.

To prosecutors, this windows business was a major flaw in the allegedly secret society of La Cosa Nostra. Here was one place where three separate families came to do business. Savino had become so good at the window rip-off, he could lead to Gigante and Gotti and Amuso and all the rest. Savino knew everybody, and everybody trusted him.

The idea was simple: bug the offices at Arista. See who shows up.

Arista was the Rosetta stone with a microphone. The Pete Savino Show was pure entertainment.

On tape, Savino says to a colleague, "Remember *Casablanca*, with Humphrey Bogart? They should make *Casa Window*, because there's more intrigue."

Throughout 1988 and into 1989, Savino recorded thousands of words. Everywhere he went there was a microphone. His office was bugged. His car was bugged. He was bugged. Wherever he went, the words of anyone who spoke within earshot became part of an official record. Words about crimes personally committed in his presence. Words about crimes committed outside his presence. Words about crimes committed by best friends. Words about crimes committed by people he'd never met. Thousands and thousands of words, each one a little brick in the wall assembled by the prosecutor, O'Connell.

There was bid rigging. Savino and four other window installers got together and divided up contracts at the Housing Authority. Contractor A got job one; contractor B got job two, and so on. It was illegal and did a wonderful job undermining the competitive bidding process that was supposed to save taxpayers lots of money. Pete Savino was very open about it all. He made sure to explain himself clearly.

"Let's say a bid came out tomorrow and we flipped a coin, okay?" he told one associate. "This is ten thousand windows. All right, you won the coin toss, you get that one, the next one I get, whatever it is."

"And we go back and forth," says the associate, "like it used to be."

Savino bribed Housing Authority inspectors. The FBI observed. Savino recorded a corrupt business agent of the union he'd been affiliated with for years. The FBI observed. The business agent demanded and received a dollar a window to let Arista use nonunion help. This allowed Arista to bill the taxpayers for union scale wages but pay less-skilled nonunion workers far less, a crafty and completely illegal way of inflating profits. Later the corrupt union business agent demanded two dollars a window.

Throughout it all, a percentage of the scheme floated upstream to the bosses of the Genovese and Gambino and Lucchese crime families. Payments were discussed and disguised. A Lucchese soldier, Fat Pete Chiodo, set up a trucking company, Tiger Management, as a cover for some of these payments. Tiger pretended to be a "consultant" on the windows jobs but in reality was a money washing machine.

Savino with his microphones did his best to implicate. The more of his associates he could capture in various conspiracies, the better chance he had of walking away without prison time. Mostly he implicated the Genovese family, the group with whom he was officially affiliated. But he also implicated others.

At one point he recorded the Genovese family telling him

he had to repay a million dollars his associates owed to the Lucchese family leaders, Vic Amuso and Gaspipe Casso. He and his representative in the Genovese family, a captain named Joe Zito, showed up at the Nineteenth Hole bar in Brooklyn with a Sunkist orange box stuffed with five-, ten-, and twenty-dollar bills. Vic and Gas were furious.

"What's the difference?" Zito said. "You got a quarter of a million dollars."

Vic and Gas wanted more. The money coming out of Local 580 had caught their attention, so they decided they wanted the local for the Lucchese family, which is to say for themselves. There was a sit-down. Vic and Gas won. Local 580 now belonged to Vic and Gas.

The tape recorder went to work; the assistant U.S. attorney, Greg O'Connell, went to work. Throughout 1988, with Savino working full-time for the government, prosecutors began to lay the plans for a big federal press conference that would ruin the mornings of the leaders of three of the city's major crime families. To keep it simple, they'd name it after the item that was making the Mafia rich: Windows. As the tapes rolled, the prosecutors could see the two top names on their indictment clearly:

Vic Amuso and Anthony Casso.

"Louie brought me a piece of paper, a report, a police report, and it said that Pete Savino was cooperating with the government," Burt Kaplan said. "It said that he was cooperating with them for a few years, and that he was cooperating originally with a detective in the Sixty-second Precinct and that when the government came to him and started asking the questions about the window business, he took them immediately down to the basement, where he showed them where some bodies were buried. It was a report of the background of the whole interview with Pete Savino, that he was originally an informant with somebody in the Sixty-second."

Kaplan made sure to get the reports about Pete Savino to Casso, but before he did, he ripped the letterhead off the paperwork. It was very important for Burt Kaplan to keep Casso from ever learning the identity of the cops. The way Burt saw it, if Casso knew their names, Casso wouldn't need Burt Kaplan anymore.

The problem with organized crime is that you just can't trust anybody. Anthony Casso certainly didn't. On any given day, he would imagine a long list of names of those who would do him harm. Of late, one of the names happened to be the man who'd brought him up through the ranks: Christopher Furnari. Now that Christy Tic, the CFO, and Tony Ducks, the CEO, were away, Vic and Gas were running a very dysfunctional borgotta. There had always been a low-key rivalry between the guys from the Bronx and the guys from Brooklyn, but now that the old-timers were gone, there was a sense that certain unavailable opportunities had suddenly become available. With the bosses away, Vic and Gas—born and raised in Brooklyn—began to think that the guys from the Bronx were trying to push them out.

Casso convinced himself that the guys from the Bronx were secretly visiting with Christy Tic in prison, plotting behind his back in the visiting room at the Federal Correctional Institution in Oxford, Wisconsin. Furnari's son, Chris Jr., a hothead everybody called Jumbo, was coming back from these visits with his father claiming his father had ordered this guy killed and that guy killed. Certain efforts were made to ascertain the truthfulness of Jumbo's alleged messages, and they were found to be purely alleged in the mind of Jumbo. Jumbo was put on the shelf—essentially kicked out without being rubbed out. All of this increased the paranoia of the full-time paranoid Gaspipe Casso, so he reached out to his friend Burt.

Kaplan was tasked to quietly find out who was visiting Christy Tic in the heartland of America. He consulted with Detective Caracappa.

"I spoke to Steve and asked Steve if he could write a letter, through his job, to get the prison visiting records, and I also said to him, 'If this is going to come back and be a permanent record of something against you, I don't want you to do it.' And he said, 'No, it's no problem. I can do it. I'll put it into a current investigation.'"

December 17, 1987

Captain Patrick J. Harnett, commanding officer of the NYPD's Major Case Squad, wrote a letter to the warden of the Federal Correctional Institution in Oxford, Wisconsin:

Dear Sir,

The Major Case Squad is currently conducting a long-term investigation into the activities of the five organized-crime families in New York City. It is respectfully requested that you provide this command with the following information concerning the individual listed below:

Christopher Furnari, Inmate No. 19815-054.

Persons with whom he is corresponding with, Visitors list, Recent photograph of inmate.

This information will be used for Police Department purposes only, therefore Freedom of Information Act does not apply.

Sincerely, Captain Harnett

A week or so later, Kaplan said Caracappa the detective came back to Burt with a list of names, which Kaplan turned over to Casso. In a little while Casso came back and said the only ones visiting Furnari were his family and that nobody was contacting him about anything that was going on in the street. All the plots against him, all the scheming by the Bronx faction—all of that was inside Gaspipe's troubled head. In a way, it was sad. Now the man Kaplan had respected all those years, Christy Tic, was just a man, a consigliere in name only, cut off from the power and fame he had in certain shrinking circles. He had lived by the rules and refused to cooperate with the government and now he was forgotten, a counselor to no one but his children and his wife, waiting for the end of his life in a room in the middle of nowhere.

April 19, 1989

In the extremely glamorous world of law enforcement, as seen on TV, detectives almost always spend their nights chasing down bad guys in daring gun battles in abandoned warehouses. Sometimes they have a shot of Jim Beam and suddenly reach a Sherlock Holmes epiphany that cracks open the case. In the background is a Coleman Hawkins-type saxophone. It is unclear whether Victoria Vreeland of the New Jersey Division of Criminal Justice believed such moments would ever be hers as she sat in an empty room looking down on a beat-up old work trailer in an industrial section of Newark as she did five days a week, Monday through Friday, nine to five.

This was her glamorous job. She was supposed to watch the trailer as part of a team looking into the illegal dumping of medical waste by a company called Tiger Management. There was a video camera running there, and she had to make sure it was working. She also took notes of who was coming and going. The trailer she was assigned to look at was a Tiger trailer. The guy she was seeing coming and going from the Tiger trailer was easy to spot. He weighed probably 350, maybe 375, and wore track suits. He had glasses and tended to walk slowly wherever he went. His mother had named him Peter, but everybody called him Fat Pete. He was Pete Chiodo, captain in the Lucchese crime family. He had set up Tiger to deal with Arista Windows, the money machine for the Lucchese family run by Pete Savino. Pete Savino had told Victoria and her team all about Pete Chiodo Tiger Management, and they planned on putting him in jail as soon as possible, by means glamorous or otherwise.

To do this they installed tiny electronic devices inside the base of the trailer that could monitor conversations inside. They'd also bugged the phones in the trailer, which had provided them with hours of meandering conversations that here and there implied criminal intent. A lot of stuff like, "Did you talk to the guy?" and "What about the thing with the guy?" Enough to keep the wires hot.

On most days, Fat Pete would pull up in his black Lincoln Town Car and roll into the trailer. A parade of gangsters and gangster wannabes would follow.

On this particular day, Victoria was suddenly aware of an odd sight: a giant mobile home had pulled up outside the trailer. It was huge. A guy in a dirty T-shirt and fedora emerged and went inside the Tiger trailer.

A minute later he emerged and started poking around under the back side of the trailer. Victoria, at that moment, became alarmed. The spot he was poking at was precisely where the government-salaried technicians working for the New Jersey Division of Criminal Justice had installed the bugging devices. Precisely. She was afraid he might spot the devices, which had little wires poking out that implied Big Brother was listening.

Then it got worse. The guy with the fedora came out from under the Tiger trailer and started gazing with furrowed brow at one of the telephone poles right in front of the trailer. The giant mobile home was parked right next to it, so the guy with the fedora climbed up a ladder in the back onto the mobile home's roof and began poking around at the box on the top of the pole. He had a device the phone company uses to dial into lines from poles. On most days it would be odd under any circumstance for a citizen to climb on top of a mobile home to inspect a telephone pole. In this particular case, the pole in question happened to contain yet another device funded by the taxpayers of New Jersey that was quite helpful in listening in on gangsters.

In a word, Victoria knew she'd been made.

She watched the guy get off that mobile home, drive it a little up the street to the next pole, and repeat his procedure on every pole to the end of Port Street. This went on for forty-five minutes. It was embarrassing. At one point, the guy brought a ladder up to the roof of the mobile home to get to a pole he couldn't reach. It was the middle of the afternoon, and though cars occasionally drove by, nobody said a thing.

The next day, the wires went dead. They tracked down the guy with the fedora and found out his name was Mario. They asked Mario what he was doing up there on the roof of his mobile home in the middle of a workday fooling around with telephone poles. He said he had climbed up to get a better look at the airplanes flying out of nearby Newark International Airport.

The way Gaspipe saw it, any self-respecting Mafia family where the boss runs around in a bathrobe and slippers had to be a band of idiots. He'd given the Genovese family the information about Pete Savino being a rat. He told a guy named Benny Eggs, who reported back that they took Pete Savino down into a basement and put a gun in Pete's mouth. Somehow Pete Savino was still alive. He had convinced the Genovese family that he would never cooperate, and they had believed him. Gaspipe was furious, but that was only one reason to be furious. Nobody seemed to know how to behave. After Kaplan's friends in law enforcement had told him about the bug in Pete Chiodo's trailer, he'd told Pete about it. He expected Pete would just stop talking inside the trailer, but he was wrong. Instead Pete had stupidly had the wire removed. How obvious could you be? It was like telling the cops there was a leak. To Gaspipe, the information from the cops was more important than one bug in a trailer.

Usually when gangsters take control of a union, they find multiple ways to screw over the hardworking men and women who are supposed to benefit from collective bargaining. They are never satisfied to steal from the union in merely one way. They steal in as many ways as they can dream up. One way is to make the union put members of organized crimes on jobs where they don't actually show up but still get paid union scale. No-show jobs. That was what James Bishop, secretary-treasurer of District Council 9 of the Painters Union, was supposed to do.

"Fuck Jimmy Bishop," said Anthony Casso.

Casso was meeting in a small room over a pizza parlor near Utica Avenue and Flatlands Avenue, down the street from his house. Fat Pete Chiodo and another captain, Al D'Arco, were there. Casso was furious that Bishop had stopped doing what he was told to do. He was supposed to put

certain associates on the books as no-shows, and he was not
doing it. He was ignoring phone calls and other forms of communication designed to get him to behave. Casso immediately
suspected Jimmy had gone bad and become a rat. Later he
would ask his friend Burt to ask his friends the cops if Jimmy
Bishop was a rat.

Burt came back right away and said yes.

May 17, 1990

At 6:11 A.M., Thursday, Jimmy Bishop emerged in the wet
spring dawn of Queens. He was a married man, a busy
man, but he had found time to spend the night with his girlfriend. She lived in a high-rise on Powel Cove Boulevard in
the 109th Precinct. Jimmy found the time to stop there whenever he could. He always parked his car in the same spot by
the driveway to the high-rise. He always drove the same car,
a gray Lincoln Town Car, paid for by his union, District Council 9 of the Painters Union. He made no effort to hide his comings and goings. He was a man in charge of his own destiny.

At the moment, his destiny appeared to be impressive. He
was a six-figure man as secretary-treasurer of District Council 9 and district leader in the Queens Democratic Party. It was
convenient for fund-raising purposes of certain Queens politi-
cians that he was both. He owned a half-million-dollar man-
sion, also in Queens. He also was an associate of the Lucchese
crime family.

The Lucchese family had controlled the painters union
since forever. Although Jimmy Bishop was the boss of his
household, the master of his destiny, answering to no one, he
also was a hired hand who did what he was told. When Anthony Casso and Vic Amuso said jump, he quickly said, "How
high?"

Or at least, he did until recently. Recently he had been
caught up by the Manhattan district attorney's investigation of
the Mafia. They had come to him quietly and played some
tape recordings and convinced him that he was about to go to
jail for the rest of his life unless he helped out. He decided to
help out.

On this spring morning as he emerged from his girlfriend's high-rise, Jimmy walked with self-confidence because he believed that very few people knew he was secretly an informant, a cooperator, a rat. His lawyers knew. The guys in the DA's office knew. Maybe his mistress, probably not. In truth, Jimmy's change of heart was known to more than a few.

A few months earlier, a top investigator in the inspector general of the Metropolitan Transportation Authority noted that although the DA would not divulge the name of its new "top union official," the inspector general had "received information" that the new informant was, in fact, Jimmy Bishop.

Jimmy Bishop got into his Lincoln, put the key in the ignition, and then got shot seven times in the head. Jimmy Bishop, union leader, mob associate, government cooperator, was no longer cooperating with anybody.

May 25, 1990

Louie called me and told me he had to meet me," Burt Kaplan said. "It was very, very important but he couldn't come into New York, he had a previous appointment, he had to be someplace else, and he asked me if I can meet him on the Long Island Expressway, and I said yes. I went out there and met him. He told me that the following morning everybody involved in the Windows case was going to be arrested, including Anthony Casso and Vic Amuso. I tried to reach Anthony Casso and he was out of town, and I called Vic Amuso's house and he was out, and I told whoever answered the phone, I said, the minute Vic comes in tell him it's an emergency and reach out for Mr. Eagle, that was the code name I had with Vic and Gas, and to call me no matter what time of night it is when he comes in. He called me about one-thirty in the morning. I told him I had to see him. He said, 'Okay, I'll see you tomorrow morning.' I said, 'No, I got to see you right now, it's important.' And he came to my house. I told him that I don't even think he should go home anymore tonight, that he's definitely going to be arrested tomorrow morning with Gas and a lot of other people, and that if he does go home, just get whatever clothes he needed and leave immediately, go on the lam."

May 27, 1990

Two men stood alone in a city park in the shadow of the Verrazano-Narrows Bridge in the Brooklyn neighborhood of Bay Ridge. It was the middle of a Sunday on Memorial Day Weekend, and it was hot and sunny. Bicyclists and joggers cruised by on the path under the bridge. An oil tanker floated on the glittering Narrows under the huge bridge; weekend traffic pooled on the Belt Parkway nearby. The two men met as they always did, by a Civil War cannon pointed at New York Harbor. They walked together out in the open, so it would be easy to see if anyone was nearby, watching. One of the men glanced around nervously as he talked.

"Vic and me are getting pinched," said Anthony "Gaspipe" Casso. He was a compact man in his late forties in good shape, with a full head of black hair. He walked with the confidence of a man who was comfortable with himself, who felt himself capable of doing just about anything and then sleeping without interruption that very night.

He was walking and talking with Al D'Arco, a captain in the Lucchese crime family. D'Arco was the smaller of the two, a wiry, older man who had become an associate of an organized-crime family in the 1950s. He once hit a guy in the head with a piece of metal cable because he forgot to bring a gun.

"Vic is already gone," Casso said.

"Why aren't you gone?" D'Arco asked.

"I got till Monday," Casso said. "The bulls told me."

Casso said he had learned from his friends in law enforcement that he and his lifelong pal Vic Amuso were to be included in a federal indictment related to the Mob's involvement in the installation of thousands of windows in New York City Housing Authority projects. Sometimes he called his law enforcement friends "the bulls," sometimes "the agent," and sometimes "my crystal ball." He told D'Arco that the crystal ball never made a mistake. Amuso was already in hiding, and now Casso was preparing to be so himself.

Casso told D'Arco that he and Amuso believed they could beat the Windows case if they were tried separately from the rest of the defendants. Their plan was to evade law enforcement for as long as possible, given that cases like this take months to resolve. In the meantime, Casso told D'Arco that he and Amuso would still be in charge of the Lucchese crime family. Considering that it was already somewhat difficult to manage a bunch of criminals when you were around, trying to do so when you were hiding out in safe houses and avoiding most forms of electronic communication would make the job seem worse than being mayor of New York. Casso, however, had a solution.

D'Arco would be the point man. He would take a list of pay phones, each of which was assigned a number, and when one of Casso's associates called D'Arco, he'd say the number and D'Arco would have to get himself to the correct pay phone in an hour. It was a pretty clever system, albeit one that relied on favorable traffic patterns.

Casso prepared to go. He appeared to choke up a bit as he said good-bye. Then he composed himself and said, "Mike Salerno is a rat."

This was extremely alarming news for D'Arco. Salerno was considered a reliable captain in the Lucchese family who had always and without question done what was asked. D'Arco saw Salerno as a loyal member of organized crime, just as Alfonse D'Arco saw himself.

"That can't be right," D'Arco said.

Casso insisted it was true and made clear that the boss, Amuso, wanted Salerno to go. D'Arco said he didn't think this was a good idea because the proof of this allegation was questionable, but he agreed to take care of the Salerno matter because that was what you did. If they asked, you did. He said good-bye. He was just doing what he was told.

May 30, 1990

Memorial Day weekend was over. Hot dogs and beer were over, baseball was over, parades were over. It was a Wednesday, rainy and gusty and time to go back to work. For about two hundred FBI agents and NYPD cops, work started early.

At about 6:00 A.M., the agents and cops started hitting

houses from Staten Island to Brooklyn to Queens to Long Island, adding to somebody else's Memorial Day weekend hangover. One by one, they were attempting to arrest a long list of guys included in an indictment unsealed that morning by the U.S. attorney for the Eastern District of New York. The indictment was known as Windows.

This was one of those indictments that showed how the Mafia reached into everybody's pocket. It was like a tax. They stole a little bit on all the tens of thousands of windows installed in City of New York housing projects. It was a lot of windows. The federal government had made it stop by recruiting a key player, Pete Savino, and using his company, Arista Windows, as a fly strip. For more than a year, before he got found out, Savino managed to secretly record hundreds of hours of banal but incriminating chats with numerous members of the Genovese family, the Lucchese family, and the most powerful family in America, the Gambino family. There were hours of conversations with corrupt union business agents and dirty Housing Authority employees and gangsters. Bribes were paid, schemes where hatched, tribute kicked up. The FBI had it all on tape, and now all those many months of hard work were paying off. The sweep had begun.

Assistant U.S. Attorney Greg O'Connell, who spent more than two years of his life supervising the Windows investigation from beginning to end, was pleased that the work of all the agents and detectives and prosecutors was finally in the public eye. He also was somewhat dismayed. Before a takedown, the government likes to figure out where people are going to be so they're not caught running around looking for some guy who happened to be on vacation in Disney World and nobody knew. In this case, there were more than a dozen defendants.

Most of these had been easy to locate. The Genovese family boss, Vincent Gigante, lived with his mother in a cramped apartment in Greenwich Village. There he maintained his elaborate charade as the "oddfather," hoping to evade the law. On this morning, he was standing in a running shower holding an umbrella when the agents showed up. Peter Gotti, the none-too-bright former sanitation worker brother of John Gotti, was at his home in Howard Beach. Fat Pete Chiodo, the

350-pound owner of Tiger Management, was at his home on Staten Island. And so on down the list they went, throwing in a capo here, a soldier there, and a busload of associates for good measure.

There were, however, two significant blank spaces on the Windows list.

The top two names—Vittorio Amuso and Anthony Casso—were nowhere to be found. This wasn't like the guy who gets the coffee at the social club. This was the boss and the underboss of the Lucchese family. This was embarrassing. The FBI had believed they knew where these guys were going to be, and when they went to make the arrests, they found nobody home, with no forwarding address. All those months of preparation and on the day of the debut, the star performers were unavailable. O'Connell was furious for a specific reason. O'Connell was a firm believer in the maxim that there is no such thing as coincidence.

In weeks, law enforcement lets it be known in the newspapers that Casso and Amuso were in the New York area. FBI agents found a 10.5-carat diamond ring valued at half a million dollars and two hundred thousand in cash stuffed inside a dog food box inside a safe deposit box in name of Casso's wife, Lillian. They let this information out because they wanted Anthony Casso to know they were coming for him as soon as they could.

June 5, 1990

Six days after the arrest of half of the Mafia in the Windows case, the Forty-ninth Precinct in Brooklyn got a series of phone calls complaining about a bad smell attacking passersby near 2741 Westervelt Avenue. The source appeared to be in the trunk of a parked Olds. Two uniforms arrived, popped the trunk, and discovered a white male who'd been in there for a number of days. Since it was June, this had created an odor similar to the gateway to hell. A preliminary investigation concluded that the male was one Michael Salerno, a made member of the Lucchese crime family. An NYPD memo written by the precinct detective who showed up noted that Salerno was shot once in the chest, and under the category motive the detective wrote: "Having something to due [*sic*] with the past indictment in the Windows case."

The detective added this: "It should be noted voice box was cut out."

Louie Eppolito and Burt Kaplan were having one of their meetings where he talked about a new suit Louie needed right away, and then other things came up. Kaplan remembered Louie asked, "Can you ask Gaspipe to do me a favor?"

This was a first. Usually the gangster asked the cops for this and that. Now it was the cop asking the gangster.

"What is it, Louie?"

"A friend of mine owes Bruno from Canarsie some money, and this is the same kid that has the auto repair business that let us use his place, and that Bruno from Canarsie is pressing him and abusing him and if you would speak to Casso to speak to Bruno to get him to take the pressure off the kid."

It seemed like a reasonable request. The guy who owned the auto body shop was a working guy in a jam, and Louie the cop was trying to lend a hand. Bruno from Canarsie was a criminal, and the guy with the auto body shop was just a gambler and a friend of Louie the cop. There was a certain logic to the whole thing.

"I'll take care of it," said Burt.

Kaplan took the request to Casso. He told him one of the cops—he didn't mention names—needed a favor. The cop would appreciate it very much if Anthony would speak to Bruno to take the pressure off the kid because the kid is a good kid. As Kaplan remembered it, Casso thought about it for a few minutes and said he would speak to Bruno. Later Casso said Bruno gave him a little bit of a hard time but finally agreed to do what Casso asked. When Burt told Louie what he'd done, Louie the cop said, "Tell Anthony thank you very much."

That wasn't the end of it.

Kaplan got another visit from Louie. This time Louie was saying Bruno from Canarsie's name had come up in an investigation. There was an arrest coming down, a big investigation in the jewelry district uptown, and Bruno from Canarsie was to be named but not to be arrested. That meant he was to be listed as an unindicted coconspirator. That meant the prosecutor thought Bruno was a really bad guy—a criminal, even—but couldn't prove it. So he dumped his name into the indictment and called it a day.

Louie the cop didn't see it that way. Louie felt Bruno was hot. Kaplan wasn't so sure. "To my belief, an unindicted coconspirator doesn't make him an informant, and I questioned Louie on that and he said, 'Trust me. I know the guy is an informant.'

When Burt told Gaspipe what Louie had said about Bruno from Canarsie, Casso wasn't so sure what to say.

"You got to be kidding me," Casso said. "I know Bruno a lot of years. Are you sure that your friend isn't just trying to get even with Bruno based on the fact that he was abusing his friend, the kid with the repair shop?"

"No," said Burt. "I brought that up to the cop myself and he says that Bruno is definitely hot."

"Well, at this point I got to believe him because they've been believable on everything else," said Casso.

August 1990

The gangster Louie Bagels had finally figured out what to do about the dead canary. He was supposed to kill a guy and then put the canary in the mouth of the dead guy. This was no simple task. When you were killing somebody, you couldn't make an appointment. It happened when it happened. So you if you were planning on just killing a canary, then killing the guy and putting the canary in his mouth, that might work out just fine, and then again it might not. Timing was everything. Ideally you had to have a dead canary ready at all times. Louie Bagels had come up with a solution: a frozen canary.

Louie got the canary and threw it in the freezer. He made sure nobody came near the freezer for a while, and pretty soon he had what he needed.

Bruno from Canarsie had to go. Anthony Casso and Vic Amuso had ordered it. They said he was an informant. Casso was already mad at Bruno from Canarsie, who he believed was making friends with certain members of the Gambino family who had tried to kill him. A dead Bruno was not good enough. Casso didn't want him to disappear. He wanted Bruno to be found and identified as a rat. In his fury, he ordered the canary.

Bruno from Canarsie was an old-time gangster. He'd been around forever, and he was surrounded by capable guys. There was one brother, Louie, who was crazy, and another brother who was really crazy whom everybody called Tarzan. There was Al Visconti and Larry Taylor, two tough guys who enforced Bruno's loan-shark business. Bruno would be tough to kill.

On the day of the event, Louie Bagels removed the canary from the freezer. He had convinced Bruno to show up at his bagel store on Cross Bay Boulevard in Howard Beach, Queens, to discuss some business. When Bruno the alleged informant entered the back room of Louie's bagel shop, Louie Bagels shot him in the chest, then in the head. The frozen canary went in Bruno's mouth. They wrapped Bruno and the canary in a rug and dragged him into the back alley, where he was deposited in the trunk of a sedan, which was parked on a street in Brooklyn.

At about 5:10 P.M. on August 30, several calls started coming into the Sixty-third Precinct. There was this sedan parked in front of 1029 East 55th Street, and you couldn't walk past it without gagging. The odor was tremendous. The uniforms sent to the scene popped the trunk and reeled. Inside was Bruno from Canarsie. He'd been in there for days, in August. When they got him to the medical examiner, the assistant preparing the report wrote, "Unknown object found in mouth."

FIFTEEN

Steve Corso did not like the wine the FBI was paying for. He sat at the bar at yet another Italian restaurant in Vegas; this one was Piero's. It was huge. He'd arrived at a little before six to meet Lou Eppolito and his partner Steve Caracappa. The reservation was under Caracappa's name because he had suggested the place so they could try the veal. He said it was "his place," that he came here all the time. Caracappa was running the Las Vegas office of a New York private investigation firm, and this was where he took clients. It was supposedly known for its Las Vegas celebrities, like Steve and Eydie or Wayne Newton or Jerry Lewis. A scene from *Casino* was shot in there. On the menu, the owner vowed, "No one gets bothered at my restaurant. I don't care who the celebrity is or what they have done." Now the bartender at Piero's had suggested a wine, and it wasn't working out.

"I don't know if it's bad or if it's me," Corso said.

"What do you want, a Chianti?" asked the bartender. "Try it. If you don't like it . . ."

The feds wouldn't tell him anything about why they were so interested in these two aging retired cops living out their Social Security years in a city where ATM machines are always near the one-armed bandits. They gave him general directions. They told him to keep the gangster investor story going, emphasizing that the money would be cash and come from some illicit activity, possibly drugs. And they made it clear they needed Caracappa to be part of the story. Now they wanted Corso to take it one step farther. They wanted him to see if they would participate in an actual drug sale.

Between the FBI and Corso, C.P.A., they came up with a new story about some of Corso's celebrity clients coming to Vegas to party. They would be young Hollywood guys, including some famous names that Corso couldn't really mention for reasons of privacy, and they would need some Ecstasy and speed for the trip. The view seemed to be that Lou Eppolito had a weakness for name-dropping, yet another vulnerable personality defect they could manipulate to bring out the real Lou.

The Hollywood story seemed plausible also because of Caracappa, who had long ago served as an undercover doing buy and busts for an NYPD narcotics squad. This would mean he would likely claim to have up-to-date knowledge of drugs, even though he hadn't been on the street since the days when *Miami Vice* was a cool TV show. Multiple drug fads had come and gone since then, from crack to Ecstasy to crystal meth, so it would be interesting to see what Caracappa would claim to know.

Caracappa would not be as easy as Eppolito. Eppolito was the kind of guy who had a story for every occasion. He couldn't prevent himself from talking. He believed himself to be a street guy, smarter than the gangsters and detectives he admired and the chiefs and FBI agents he reviled. Guys who think they're smart think they can talk and not get caught in a lie. Really smart guys, like Caracappa, know that silence is the best weapon a man can possess.

A week earlier Corso met him for the first time, and during the entire session, Caracappa hadn't said a thing about himself. Eppolito talked loudly and with total self-assurance, listening to his own words and hearing little else. Caracappa spoke quietly, deliberately, saying almost nothing and listening carefully to everything Corso said. Even worse, Caracappa was able to get Corso to go on and on. The first question Caracappa asked was, "Where did you grow up in New York?"

In most places, this would seem like a harmless query. In New York, it was always a challenge. There was New York, and there was New York. If you claimed to be a New Yorker, you better be legit. Corso was not. The question forced him to do a contorted verbal dance in which he recounted the history of the entire Corso clan going back to Ellis Island, and how his father and mother grew up on Mulberry Street in Little Italy but how they got the hell out of there by the early 1960s when little Steve Corso, C.P.A., was still just an idea. The truth was that Corso grew up in the mean streets of Hackensack, New Jersey. Even worse, he actually attended and even graduated from college. The conversation with Caracappa did not start out so well.

At one point in that first meeting, Caracappa actually said, "This is not the third degree." But it was.

Lou and Steve arrived at Piero's right on time.

"How's your mom?" Lou said. It was a month after his surgery, and he was back on his feet. "Give me a Tanqueray martini, straight up with an olive."

"What are you drinking?" Caracappa asked Corso.

"Chianti."

"A chianti," Caracappa said. A little gesture of peace.

They talked about their respective mothers and then clicked glasses.

"Cheers," said Corso.

"*Grazie,*" said Lou.

"Do you know why you buy wine?" Caracappa said. "Just to compare to beer. I really enjoy the veal here, I think it's better. I think it's all in the taste. My wife is a decent cook, an excellent cook. She buys veal, she prepares it this way She cuts the veal herself. She looks at it, says this is going to be good."

They found a table and everybody did what they were supposed to do. Corso talked about the best Italian restaurants in New York to get veal. Lou talked about an Italian restaurant he went to with Robert DeNiro and Nick Pileggi and how he told them John Gotti loved the place (he just called him "John"). Caracappa talked about how much he missed all the Italian restaurants in New York that he couldn't go to because he was stuck here in Vegas. It was clear he had made a place for himself out there in Vegas. He had a routine, going to bed by eight every night and race-walking around his gated community every evening. He and his wife, Monica, were on the community's board of directors. But he still thought of New York every day. He read both the *Daily News* and the *Post* every day online.

"You like the city?" Caracappa asked about New York.

"Yeah," Corso said.

"I hate it," Lou said.

"I miss it," Caracappa said.

Lou said when Caracappa was in the Major Case Squad of the NYPD, he was the king of the city. They could go anywhere, do anything. Lou then said he needed five thousand dollars cash right away to buy some guns. Steve said no problem. Then Corso repeated the story about the money coming in any minute from the four gangsters. In their first meetings Corso had built up the story by refusing to reveal their names, then dropped them into the conversation so everybody knew what was what. Nobody seemed to care, and that was good for Corso. Corso made yet another promise to Lou: "If you have financial pressure it's done because you're gonna have a steady stream of money. You probably are going to be earning more than you've ever earned."

"Definitely," Lou replied.

The waiter read the specials: "Spinach ravioli and linguini, tenderloin of beef with mashed potatoes, fish is cod in lemon butter or Atlantic salmon with pesto. We also have the best veal and pasta that is cooked in the whole city. Our prime rib is superb. Our soup tonight is pastini with homemade cheese ravioli or you want a salad we have the Beefeater tomatoes."

Lou and Caracappa ordered the veal Milanese. Though Caracappa specifically had suggested Piero's for the veal, Corso ordered arugula and Dover sole. Caracappa ordered more Chianti.

Corso the accountant was also Corso the salesman. He tried to ask questions that got people talking about themselves. Most people loved to talk about themselves. Lou certainly did. As part of his routine, Corso asked every couple he met how they came to know each other. He knew that was a question everyone couldn't wait to answer. He tried it with Lou and Steve.

"The first time I went out with him we sort of like bonded," Caracappa said. "We just had a lot of laughs. We became friends. The guy had balls, and I like balls on a guy. And he didn't mind me because I could sit in a car for six hours and not say a word. I'm a moody guy. He was so open. What impressed me about him more than anything was all he talked about was his family. His wife and his kids."

Thirty years later they were living across the street from one another. It did seem a bit odd, but Caracappa had set up shop as a private investigator working for a former detective who ran an agency back in New York City. He was the Vegas branch office, and he mostly handled security for wealthy clients and celebrities coming out to Sin City. Cher and a bunch of wrestlers. The Rock. The Undertaker. People like that.

"Back in New York, we have two totally different reputations," Lou said. "Me? You would not want me after you."

Corso said, "I don't want either of you after me."

"I will hunt you down," Lou said. "Him I wouldn't want looking at me. He'll tell me what I had for breakfast three months ago, when I shit, what color it was, and what was in it. You don't want him investigating you. Because as an investigator, there was none that were as good as he was. I would go through the door and choke you and he would put you in jail."

That got Lou off on one of the clients, a drunken state senator who hooked up with two prostitutes who were shaking him down. Lou said he went into the room and the two prostitutes were standing there, as he put it, "buck naked."

"I says, 'Listen we have a little problem.' And she looks at me drunk and she says, 'No, we don't; he does.' I said, 'She's not going to the fucking newspaper.' I said, 'Let me talk to her.' I hit her across the fucking chest with my hand, boom! I said, 'I'll go to the fucking Club Paradise and tell them you were fucking up a client,'" he said. "I says, 'Don't fuck with me or you're dead in this fucking town.' Her and her girlfriend got dressed. The client said, 'Did I give you five hundred dollars? Here's two hundred more.'"

Caracappa described how he met his wife, Monica. He was working a robbery case and canvassing an apartment building. When she came to the door she was wearing hardly anything and said she didn't have time to answer questions because she was late to meet somebody. He offered to drive her, and she said yes. He got her number and called her for eight weeks. On the eighth week she said yes, and now they're married. They lived in an apartment in the West Twenties in Manhattan and life was good, until one day when, Steve said, "I just wanted to get out of New York." He didn't say why.

His wife was a businesswoman, making lots of money as a fashion buyer. For some reason, he kept referring to her in the past tense.

"She was a progressive woman. She flew all over the world," he said. "She was an interesting girl to be with in Manhattan. She knew all these places. She knew these different—"

"Elements?" Corso said. "Social groups?"

"Yeah. Let me ask you a very personal question," Caracappa said to Corso. "I've been here nine, ten years now. Who's your barber? Because you got a very good haircut."

Corso told him about Al, who cuts his hair, gives him a shave, and colors the gray hair at his temples. Lou said, "You like that pampering shit?"

"Yeah, I do," Caracappa said. "I get facials all the time. I do all that stuff. I mean, come on, Lou."

"Not me," Lou said. "Cut my hair, get away from me. Don't touch me."

"I have to admit I'm somewhat of a faggot in my own way," Caracappa said. "I like my hair done a certain way. I like to be pampered. Why not? Why shouldn't I be pampered, Lou?"

"I say don't put your fucking hands on me," Lou said.

"Who you got cutting your hair?" Caracappa said.

"I have somebody come to the house to cut it. I'll pay through the nose. Twenty dollars. With tip."

"Is that the same barber who cuts the dog's hair?"

It was like a routine they did—the haircut routine. They knew each other since the 1970s. They could finish each other's sentences. One was garrulous and loose-talking, the other quietly funny but very careful. One was fat, the other skinny. One liked to talk about shooting some guy in the face, the other about how he got to work every morning before everybody else. It was hard to see the connection.

The connection was the old neighborhood. Neither Steve nor Lou had to go through the song and dance about being New Yorkers that Corso was forced to perform. Both had grown up in the heart of Brooklyn surrounded by gangsters. Lou's father and uncle and cousin were gangsters. Caracappa's relatives were not in any Mafia family, but his neighbor across the street growing up in Bensonhurst was Tommy Billotti, who would eventually rise to the top of the Gambino family. Tommy was the guy with Paul Castellano when John Gotti's hit crew emerged in the pre-Christmas dusk and shot them both down on a Manhattan street. To people who followed the comings and goings of gangsters, Tommy Billotti was a big deal.

"When I went to school, you could tell then I'm with a group of guys we all knew there was two ways to go," Caracappa said. "You either went civil service or there was the Mob. Or you went to join the army. There was nothing for you. Nobody was intelligent enough to get an education at that time. We were stupid. But Tommy everybody knew. This guy was the toughest."

Caracappa chose the army and eventually civil service. Tommy Billotti made the other choice. Caracappa was vague about why they might get along, and he certainly did not bring up his own arrest for the construction site robbery he'd organized when he was a kid. He just put it like this: "He took a liking to me. He never beat the shit out of me."

"I can't imagine losing my best friend," Corso said. "How bad do you feel when he gets hit?"

"Not bad at all," Lou answered for him.

"No, you know why?" Caracappa said. "He used to say to me, 'Stevie, you should have come with me. You could have made a lot of money. Stevie, you should have come with me. I said, I can't go to jail, I can't do the time. I felt very, very bad only for the central reason that I understand what happened and why it happened."

The way Caracappa saw things, Tommy Billotti didn't

need to be a gangster, but he just couldn't help himself. He had the "wiseguy mentality" that everybody is a sucker. But just like Lou, Caracappa agreed that not everything was black and white.

"One day him and I were having coffee in my mother's house. We were just talking about girls. Girls we knew during high school and he always respected the fact that I was a cop. He never asked me for anything, but he also knew that if he needed a favor, if I could do it, I would do it."

There it was for Corso and the FBI. Caracappa the retired detective still collecting his disability pension from the City of New York said he would do favors for a Mafia killer. He didn't say he did this favor or that favor, just that he would if he could. Corso needed to go a little farther with this. He started yammering like Larry King, asking the two retired cops whether drugs ruined the Mafia. They both thought this true and inevitable. There was too much money to ignore. The question got them both started.

"Look what the feds did to the Mafia, with John Gotti and what brought him down," Caracappa said. "Drugs. There was so much money in drugs and Gotti's family, long before he went to jail. Thousands of guys were making tons of money on drugs. I had a good, good friend of mind who passed away. We hit a place one time. Raided a place, there must have been a hundred and twenty thousand dollars on the floor. I'm talking late seventies. I don't even think it was the eighties. Whoever seen that kind of money? Especially guys like us. The guy said, 'That's not my money.' He said, 'Take it.' We could have walked away with the money if we wanted. We could have had a killing. There was so much money there. You can't trust nobody. Guy looked at me, I looked at him. You wanna kill him? I'm not willing to kill him. You lock him up. You walk away from that."

"That's the one thing you don't want to do," Lou said, "is hurt anybody."

"Yeah, you don't hurt nobody," Caracappa repeated.

"That's the worst thing you do is hurt somebody," Lou said. "If you do, look at me, he's a fucking lowlife. He's a piece of shit. You say, You lock him the fuck up. You can always make that money later."

They seemed to be opening up a little here and there. At one point, Caracappa joked, "I'm not the most honest guy in the world, I'll be the first to admit it." Corso threw out the Hollywood punks story, just to see what would happen.

"I got these young clients, kids making a shitload of money, coming to Vegas. A couple of guys who say, 'Where can we get this stuff and that stuff?' They give me these terms, I have no idea what they're talking about. From them the hot stuff now is speed."

"Speed is very bad," Caracappa said.

"Ecstasy," Corso said.

"Ecstasy is very big," Caracappa said. "You know what it is, Steve? It's like anything else. It's business. If you look at it as a business, you could make a lot of money. A lot of legit guys, a lot of ex-cops got into the business. They made their money and they got out. Back in the late seventies, if you had the balls to do it, you could have made millions. Not thousands. Millions."

"You could still make as much money?" Corso asked.

"Oh, yeah," Caracappa replied. "You can make a lot of money on drugs."

He started remembering his cowboy days when he looked like Serpico with a full beard and was working on a joint task force with the Drug Enforcement Agency and the NYPD busting drug dealers around the world.

"You live the life," he said. "We went down to South America where coke was coming in. When I first started in the sixties it was heroin, then it was coke, and when it first hit, it was great. I'll tell you, everybody was on coke. You know what it was? It was a party drug. It went into different circles. There was so much money to be made. With the feds, you had the money from the government. You could travel. You could do this, you could do that. The New York City Police Department, you had to borrow fifty dollars to make a buy. Them, they'd just give it to you. This was Nixon. Great times."

Corso the provocateur asked Caracappa what would happen if he happened to catch an Italian in the narcotics trade. Caracappa answered immediately and with enthusiasm.

"I wouldn't touch it," he said. "I had an opportunity, though. There was a made guy in the Bronx, guy by the name of . . ." He trailed off. "He was an old-timer. He was buying clothes—amphetamines. Uppers. Stuff like that. It came down to him and I was like, I walked away from it. It was like family."

"They were okay for that?" Corso asked about the NYPD.

"They had no choice," Caracappa said.

"I had this cousin, this guy would take your eye out," Lou said. He didn't say the cousin's name, but it was clearly Frankie Santora Jr. "My cousin said, 'You want to go into narcotics?' I said, 'Me? No. I can't. I'll get killed.'"

Caracappa was back in his old undercover days.

"You know what it was?" he asked, expecting no answer. "It was a game. You're an actor. You read a person and you know it's greed. That perpetrates the whole thing. It's the greed. I mean during the years, I don't know speed and I don't know Ecstasy, but I know heroin and I know coke. Heroin I wouldn't touch because I'm afraid of needles. Coke, if you were a successful undercover, you did coke. If you didn't do coke, you weren't going to make it."

"If you said no, you would get killed," Lou said.

"Was it addictive?" Corso asked.

"You gotta control it, Caracappa said. "You gotta control it. It's wonderful. It's the best thing in the world. But the point is, you could see how people could get addicted to it. The same with money."

Caracappa was on a roll. There was an explanation for everything. He did drugs because he had to. It was okay— wonderful, in fact—as long as you could control it. The undercover memories put him back in his glory days, and he liked it. He started talking about a detective he knew who once decided it would be a good idea to rob banks and the shah of Iran's wife.

"He got away with it?" Corso asked.

"No! He went to jail," Caracappa said. "We were in narcotics together. Back in them days, nobody gives a shit."

The war stories were winding down. They were returning from the gunfire and dirty needles and "Ford to City: Drop Dead" of Gotham City in the seventies, when nobody gave a damn, to thirty years later and the strangeness of an Italian restaurant in the middle of the desert. Corso had to go, but he promised to take the two of them out the next Sunday night. He said he'd pick the place.

"You don't have to take us out to dinner every week," Caracappa said. "I just wanted you to taste this veal because I couldn't believe you hadn't had it."

"He got the fish," Lou pointed out.

"Yeah," Caracappa said, "but I had to tell him about it."

SIXTEEN

Detective Caracappa was in communication with the Los Angeles Police Department homicide unit. The two departments were discussing Anthony DiLapi, a fifty-three-year-old former business agent of Local 522 of the Teamsters from Brooklyn now believed to be living somewhere in or near LA. DiLapi was a soldier in the Lucchese crime family who in 1980 had been sentenced to a five-year sentence in federal prison after his conviction on obstruction of justice and conspiracy charges. He had lived forever in the Bronx and after doing his time had suddenly disappeared from New York.

The record on these communications is unclear. Either Caracappa was interested in anything LAPD might have on DiLapi or LAPD was interested in anything Caracappa might have on the guy. Either way, there was a back-and-forth paper trail that included Caracappa at one point writing a note to his counterparts on the West Coast. The undated note on Major Case Squad letterhead was in Caracappa's handwriting. It listed Anthony DiLapi as "nephew of Santora, presently on federal parole," a misspelled reference to the former Lucchese underboss Tom Mix Santoro. It listed DiLapi as "Lucchese soldier," and included a 1988 address in Hawthorne, New York. It also listed information from SDNY, the U.S. attorney in Manhattan. That included DiLapi's FBI number. The note stated, "Owns dinner in California," another misspelled reference to the fact that DiLapi ran a restaurant out in LA. The note finished by describing DiLapi as "Potential target of hit—From Jim Mullens, Man. D.A." At the bottom of the note was NYPD boilerplate language about the information being "confidential" and "Property of the New York City Police Department."

Prominent on the note was DiLapi's home address: 803 5-4 Canny Avenue, Resada, California.

"Casso said he called for Anthony DiLapi to come in and tell him what he controlled up in the Bronx," Kaplan said. "Anthony DiLapi was into the Joker Poker machines and bookmaking places, and Anthony DiLapi said he would come in the following week and give Casso that information. Instead, he sold all his stops and he left town. Casso asked if our friends the cops could help find him. I made an appointment with Steve and told Steve the situation and asked him if he could write a letter to his parole officer because when you leave one jurisdiction and go to another, you have to be assigned to a different parole officer, and he said he could do that. Again, I asked him, 'Steve, will this come back and hurt you in the future because it's going to be a permanent record?' And he says no, he's not worried about it. He could do it. He would put [DiLapi's] name in with five or six other people in a real investigation going on at that time. [Later] Steve said DiLapi moved to California and gave me a business address. Casso said he sent three guys to California but DiLapi made them and fled. Casso wanted another address. I said, 'I think that's dangerous for him to do that, but I'll ask him anyway.' And I spoke to Steve and I said, 'Steve, please, if this is going to come back and haunt you, don't do it.' Like always, Steve said, 'I could do it.' And he did it."

February 3, 1990

Anthony DiLapi wanted to see his grandson very much. His daughter, Mary Ann, had been living in Hawaii when he was born, and so Anthony had never met him. Now Mary Ann was moving back to the mainland. Not to the Los Angeles suburb of Reseda, where Anthony was living, but to Salt Lake City, Utah, which was at least closer than Hawaii. Mary Ann was flying in today, a Saturday, and there was a layover in Los Angeles before flying to Salt Lake City. Anthony had suggested they have a quick get-together at the airport so he could see his grandson for the first time. Mary Ann did not think this would work, so they agreed that he would come to Salt Lake City later in the spring. The visit at the airport was not to be.

There could have been a number of reasons why Anthony DiLapi felt an urgent need to see his grandson, but the most likely explanation had to do with the guys who'd shown up at a car dealership where he sometimes worked. He'd spotted the guys and he knew right away that they weren't there to buy a car. These were guys from back in Brooklyn, and they had forgotten to make an appointment. These days, Anthony DiLapi had no desire to see anybody who didn't make an appointment.

Anthony DiLapi had come a long way from Arthur Avenue in the Bronx. Anthony DiLapi had grown up in the Bronx, lived almost his entire life in the Bronx, and now here he was in a state known for Hollywood movie stars and earthquakes. Nevertheless, he was a free man in Reseda. At least for a while, anyway. DiLapi had chosen to escape the Bronx and all its ramifications for a new life on the Left Coast. It was tabula rasa for Anthony. He had reasons.

Back in the Bronx, he was a good worker for the Lucchese crime family with a good future. He was an earner. He controlled Local 522 of the Teamsters. Plus he had a rabbi. His uncle was Tom Mix Santoro, the family underboss. It was nothing but promise for Anthony, siphoning millions from a union with your uncle as the underboss. He was well paid and completely corrupt, a business agent in name only for the Teamsters. He offered an organizer from another union six thousand dollars to stop trying to organize a Garment Center trucking company that was in the Lucchese pocket. When this did not work, DiLapi threatened to kill the organizer. This was the heart and soul of what the Lucchese family did, and he had done it for years.

Then he got caught and was out of the picture for five years. Being out of the picture can change everything. When he was convicted, his uncle was still in charge. At his sentencing, he dutifully claimed to know nothing about any Mafia, stating, "Maybe someone told them that because I'm Italian I'm in the Mafia." Then came the big Commission trial and his uncle went away for a long time. Suddenly DiLapi's prospects within the Lucchese crime family were null and void. The new bosses, Vic Amuso and Anthony Casso, were from Brooklyn. They never went to the Bronx. They didn't like the Bronx. As a result, when Anthony DiLapi emerged from prison in 1985, he had come to believe they wanted to kill all the guys from the Bronx.

Almost immediately after he stepped out of prison, Vic and Gas summoned him in for a meeting. He went to the meeting, and he heard them say they expected payments from his Joker Poker machines and everything else he had going. Only they wanted more payments than in the past. DiLapi figured out what he didn't really want to know: Vic and Gas wanted him to stop paying so they would have an excuse to make him dead. These were guys with whom he'd shared many a laugh and plenty of cash, and now they were against him entirely. The second time they asked him to a meeting, he didn't show up. He understood what this meant.

California seemed like the perfect place. Nobody was really from there. Everyone was a stranger. DiLapi left New York and didn't look back. He left his wife, his daughter, his son, even his girlfriend, and moved into a rented apartment under a different last name. He even got a part-time job working for a car dealer. He was making it legit. For a while, he thought the Bronx was something he could forget all about.

Then the guys showed up at the car dealership. He was lucky that he'd recognized them. This was followed by an FBI agent showing up to tell him what he already knew, that somebody back East wanted to see him dead.

Six months earlier he told his daughter, Mary Ann, "It's black and white. If I go back to New York, I'll be killed. It's just that simple." Of course, it wasn't that simple. His wife was very sick back in New York, and he wanted to go back and see her. His brother, Sal, who knew some of the guys who knew Vic and Gas, had made some quiet, informal inquiries to try to figure out what would happen if Anthony went home. He had not heard back from anybody.

He began to act differently. He took up jogging and began to lose weight. It was almost as if he were preparing for something. He began to look for more guys from New York suddenly showing up in California.

February 4, 1990

Late on a Sunday afternoon a light winter rain fell on Canny Avenue in Reseda, chilling the air and coating the date palms with a twilight glitter. Inside a darkened basement parking garage of a modest apartment building, a man hunched in the corner, a .38 in his hands. His name was Joseph D'Arco, and he had flown all the way from Brooklyn to do a piece of work.

Joseph D'Arco's father had told him to do it, though not as a father telling a son to take up accounting so as to have a steady income. This was a different paternal decree. Joseph's father was Alfonse D'Arco, a captain in the Lucchese crime family who had dedicated his life to organized criminal activity. Alfonse was a true believer in the notion that the Mafia was a place for men of honor, where certain rules were followed diligently and one did as one was told for the greater good. The order to go to California with .38 in hand was a corporate decision handed from supervisor to employee, as well as from father to son. D'Arco the elder had decided that believing in La Cosa Nostra meant including your blood family in that belief.

It was likely that Joseph D'Arco was trying desperately to please his father the gangster. The boss of the family, Vic Amuso, had specifically told D'Arco the elder to include his son in the California job, and Joseph D'Arco was not about to let his father down. The plan was choreographed weeks in advance, with D'Arco the younger chosen as the shooter and two other guys waiting around the corner in a stolen car for him to emerge. The operation was complicated. They brought a guy out who specialized in boosting cars, and they'd stolen three just for the job. They were obsessed with helicopters. The LAPD used lots of helicopters, so the gangsters from New York figured they might have to switch cars a few times after performing the task they had set out to do.

D'Arco the younger was to personally do the job, drop the gun, walk out of the garage and into the waiting car, and disappear into the Hollywood night. Now all he had to do was wait for the appearance of DiLapi the union guy. DiLapi was the piece of work.

D'Arco waited for an hour, maybe two before he saw what he needed to see.

The Lincoln DiLapi always drove had wheeled into the underground garage and was headed for its usual parking space. Funny how that worked, how a guy who knew he could be killed at any moment would use the same parking space every day. D'Arco watched the car come to a stop, the taillights flicker off. He watched a guy in his fifties, probably around his father's age, shut off the car, fumble around, probably pocketing the keys. As the guy moved to open the door, D'Arco stepped forward from the shadows.

D'Arco raised his .38 in the belief that his father would be very pleased.

March 2, 1990

Almost a month had passed since Anthony DiLapi had been found lying face down in the garage of his apartment building, and the Los Angeles Police Department was nowhere near understanding how this had come to be. Detectives Wermuth and Bassett of the LAPD's Hollywood Division had interviewed a number of individuals they believed could have been responsible, but had come to no conclusions. The fact was a lot of people had reasons to prefer DiLapi dead. They were asking questions about these many people to Anthony's daughter, Mary Ann.

They had come all the way out to Salt Lake City to interview a daughter about her murdered father. It was not an easy trip. The daughter was very open and had no desire to deny that her father was a gangster. She kept referring to the Lucchese family as "his organization," as if it were the Rotary Club or the Masons. She was obviously sad about it, but she expressed different theories as to who would want to kill her father.

She said right away that before he died, her father was a very frightened man. Although he was never straightforward in speaking about such things, Anthony DiLapi had let his daughter know that things weren't going so well for him back in New York with "the organization." The organization had new management, and they did not appear to appreciate his skills. That was why he was in California, and that was why he told no one—not even his daughter—where he lived.

Recently another friend of his from New York had disappeared. She didn't know his name but referred to the friend as "Buddy," and noted that at first her father had kept Buddy's disappearance from her. Then he admitted he was afraid when Buddy was missing.

She described this friend and that friend, voicing concern that certain "friends" did not show up at the funeral. She called one friend a "loan shark" and assured the LAPD detectives that although her father's siblings were "normal people" who had nothing to do with "the organization," if they knew who killed him, they would certainly not tell the police. Her father was a grandfather, but he was a criminal grandfather, and she knew all about it.

"A long time ago, I found guns, silencers, gloves, etc., in our house," she told the LAPD. "I confronted Dad and he, in a roundabout way, told me he killed people as part of his living." She described her father's criminal ways as if describing woodworking projects in the basement: "Dad used to like to hide his guns and cash in two ways. He would conceal them by cutting out the interior pages of books and removing windowsills." She made it clear he thought he was being watched: "Dad was very careful about his habits."

Perhaps she always knew it was going to be this way. She told herself he was in the Teamsters union and involved in the construction trades, but she also knew he was arrested and charged with bribery and went to prison for a long time. He had made "occasional references" to organized crime. He mentioned a meeting in Las Vegas, and then he mentioned that the boss of the Lucchese crime family had ordered him to a meeting and he'd refused to go. He'd recently mentioned that an FBI agent had come to see him and told him his life was in danger and offered him protective custody. He'd refused.

Mary Ann probably was a victim of wishful thinking. When he moved out to California, her father had just wanted to be left alone. But in this way of life, nobody gets left alone. And she remembered one other odd comment he'd made.

"If I die," he told her, "cops were involved."

SEVENTEEN

For decades, El Caribe has been the Le Cirque of La Cosa Nostra. There were no air kisses, just pecks on the cheek by men who would never use the terms "fabulous" or "ensemble." It was where members and associates could hang around the bar and talk about how broke they were and all the money they were going to make tomorrow. The Colombos, the Lucheses, the Bonannos, the Gambinos, the Genovese family—it was like Oscar parties, only in track suits. Everybody knew who was in there on any given night. This was the place where Tommy Karate accused the late Otto Heidel of being a rat, and Burt Kaplan was there to hear it all.

Therefore it was the perfect spot to honor the retirement of Detective Second Grade Louis Eppolito.

There he was at the Mob hangout, a changed man. Six years had passed since he was "cleared" by Administrative Judge Hugh Mo and the rest of the New York City Police Department. He had been reassigned to Brooklyn's Sixty-third Precinct, and had met Robert DeNiro during a stakeout in Manhattan. He won the bit part of a gangster called Fat Andy in *Goodfellas,* mostly because he looked like a gangster more than a cop.

NYPD sergeant Arthur Hearns remembered Eppolito the

movie star walking around the Sixty-third Precinct station house with autographed copies of his photograph, a head shot of Louie smiling but serious. By then, Hearns had forgotten all about the fact that nearly twenty years previous, he'd recommended strongly that the department not hire Eppolito's lifelong friend Stephen Caracappa. That was a long time ago. Sergeant Hearns liked Louie.

"You gotta understand something about a cop. A cop deals with people. While a guy's talking, you gotta size him up. Is this guy using me? You got to know who is bullshitting you. With Louie, he was shoveling it with a shovel. But he was likable," Hearns remembered. "He was giving out pictures of himself as the Hollywood actor, signed, like Gregory Peck, 'Best Regards, Louie.' He thought he was the next Humphrey Bogart. He was in *Goodfellas*. They cut most of that out."

For what they left in, Louie got a check for nineteen thousand dollars—about half his salary as a detective second grade, all in one check from Warner Brothers.

The check did it. Detective Second Grade Eppolito—a bitter man—decided he'd had enough of the NYPD. Although he'd remained on the job for four years after his suspension and departmental hearing, he was still furious about that event and believed it had changed his prospects within the NYPD irrevocably.

"I really took a bad, bad attitude after that happened. There were so many people who had things to say about me that were derogatory. I had one inspector say to me, 'I'm sick and tired of dealing with your kind.' I said, 'What do you mean, "your kind"?' He said, 'You know what I mean.' I kept myself for twenty-one years trying to be better. I had to work two and a half times harder than any other cop I ever met because of who I am. Do you know the first two and a half years I never missed a day? I went to work with my hands stitched up, I went to work with broken knuckles. Then they sit me down they treat me like an animal. After that suspension I went to the police commissioner, Benjamin Ward. He said, 'I don't have any words to tell you about what happened.' Commissioner Ward said, 'I always had great respect for you. You're a street cop.' I said, 'Where I can go from here? I'm dead. I'm dead in the water.' I realized that now. I was heart-broken. I was just going through the motions."

He put in his papers and applied for and got a disability pension that would allow him to collect three-quarters—not the usual half—of his last year's salary. It was all going to work out. He would become a movie star, turn his knowledge of the street into a real paycheck. Back home on his Wall of Fame in the suburban palace on Long Island was the proof: his three medals of honor, his forty-two citations, his fifty awards for excellent police work. Now at El Caribe, his pals in the Sixty-third Precinct were gathered for their annual dinner, and Detective Eppolito—three months off the job after seventeen years—was to be honored. They presented him with a two-foot statue of a cop rescuing a woman that could stand right next to all the rest of the awards and citations. It was a happy affair for a bitter man with a whole lot of secrets.

For four years, Anthony Casso was a man tormented by the desire to kill anybody he believed was against him. He wasn't always sure who was against him and who was for him, but then he decided it didn't really matter if it was true. And the one event in his life that made him crazier than anything else was the afternoon of September 14, 1986, when the car pulled alongside and the bullets flew as he ate his Carvel ice cream. He had lived, and yet he had not survived. He was plagued by the notion that those who were responsible continued to go about their daily lives unpunished. It drove him mad.

In the four years since that day, he'd succeeded in killing only one of those involved. That was Jimmy Hydell, the low-level hoodlum who was only doing a job somebody smarter told him to. All other attempts at retribution had failed miserably. The wrong Nicky Guido was killed on Christmas Day. The right Nicky Guido, the one who actually shot at him, was now safe in prison. The transit cop, Berring, who drove the car that day, was now cooperating with the government. This left Casso with the guys who ordered the hit, which meant he would, if he could, kill the entire hierarchy of the Gambino crime family.

He had come to believe that the family now run by John Gotti was behind the attempt on his life, and he was not a man who could just let things go. Of course, killing John Gotti was not so simple. He was a boss, although he wasn't considered a legitimate boss (of an illegitimate enterprise). He had become a boss by killing his boss, and that was not allowed. Many people in the other New York families were plotting to rectify this parliamentary faux pas, but it would take time. The way it was explained to Casso, they were going to kill everybody around Gotti first, leaving him all by himself.

Casso focused on Gotti's minions.

First there was Salvatore Gravano, Gotti's underboss. He was a short, profoundly deceitful man who would kill his mother if he thought he could make a little money out of it. Gravano figured out that the alleged rules of the Mafia were easy to use for your own purposes. If he felt some guy owned a construction company that was legitimately competing against him for jobs and winning, he would say the guy was a rat and then get permission to have the guy killed. One might have thought Casso would admire a guy like that, but in fact Casso loathed Gravano. So Casso asked Kaplan to get the cops to kill the man.

It seemed like a good idea. Casso was aware that killing a guy like Gravano would not be easy. Gravano had killed quite a few guys in his day, and he was almost never alone. Casso figured if members of the Lucchese family tried to do it, there could be a big mess. He would see it coming. Then he remembered about the two cops and Jimmy Hydell. Jimmy had been a guy who was being hunted by everybody, and the two cops had managed to put him in a car and deliver him like a stuffed bird. Why couldn't they do the same with Gravano? Better yet, why not just shoot the guy themselves?

He asked Burt to set it up.

For weeks on end, between shifts, on weekends, whenever they could find the time, Eppolito and Caracappa watched Gravano. At one point they were sitting outside Gravano's construction company, Marathon Construction, on Stillwell Avenue in Brooklyn, when a detective doing legitimate surveillance of Gravano spotted them and asked them what they were doing. They claimed they were waiting to meet a guy and left soon after.

"They didn't think they should go to that spot anymore,"

Kaplan said. "They followed him to his house and from his house on a lot of occasions, but they could never catch him alone. They told me he was always dropped off by people or picked up by people in other cars. And they didn't have a chance to fulfill the contract."

Casso tried another approach. If you can't kill Sammy, the number-two guy, kill one of Gotti's closest friends, Bobby Borriello. He was inspired, in part, by a tape recording brought to Casso by the cops in which Borriello made certain statements of ill will toward Casso.

Kaplan said, "Louie brought me a, I guess you call it a cassette, a small tape, and he said, 'Here, listen to this. You could keep it.' And I had a cassette player underneath my kitchen cabinets. It was one of the ones that went flush up against the cabinets, and I plugged it in and I heard, I didn't know whose voice it was, but I heard a guy saying, 'These guys missed with Casso and they better take care of this thing or I'm going to get mad and I'll drive right into his driveway and kill him and his whole family.' When Casso heard the tape, he said, " 'That's Bobby Borriello.' "

Bobby Borriello was a mountain of a man who didn't care about anybody. He figured he was always the biggest guy in the room, so nobody would get in his way. He often drove his boss, Gotti, around, and it was believed that he would kill you merely because he felt at that moment it was something that should be done.

The cops followed Bobby around for a while, until one afternoon on Court Street in downtown Brooklyn yet another detective who knew Louie walked up to Louie and Steve sitting in an unmarked car waiting for Bobby to emerge from an office building and said, "How are you? What's new?" How often would that happen in downtown Des Moines? That was the end of that off-the-books stakeout.

Finally Casso settled on Eddie Lino. If you have to kill somebody, it might as well be Eddie. Eddie was a lifetime gangster from a family of gangsters. There was his cousin Frankie, his cousin Bobby, and his cousin Bobby's son, all gangsters. He was also one of the shooters Gotti used in the 1985 murder of Castellano that occurred in front of a steak restaurant in time for the evening news. He was a captain in the Gambino family and a drug dealer. Casso was a drug dealer, too, so he couldn't really hold that against him. But he could always say that was the reason you killed somebody. It was convenient.

When Burt put the question to the cops about killing Eddie Lino, they agreed, but they wanted more than twice the twenty-five thousand dollars they were paid for the Jimmy Hydell matter. This was due to inflation. Their fee was now sixty-five thousand dollars. Plus they wanted guns and a car.

"Jesus," said Casso, "don't these guys do anything for themselves?"

Casso got them a revolver and a semiautomatic and gave them to Burt, who delivered them to the cops. Burt said he'd take care of the car. He had his errand boy Tommy Galpine arrange to pick up a purple/blue two-door 1987 Olds with a dark blue vinyl top that could easily be mistaken for an unmarked cop car. He was supposed to get it in Bensonhurst and drop it on a street corner in Staten Island. It didn't work out. Kaplan got a call from Tommy, who was sitting in the Olds on Fourth Avenue near Ninety-seventh Street in Bay Ridge, Brooklyn, waiting for the tow truck. The transmission had imploded just before the entrance to the Verrazano-Narrows Bridge. Kaplan had to pay to have the car towed, repaired, and cleaned. It cost him thirteen hundred dollars. The cops said they'd get their own car.

November 6, 1990

It was past the dinner hour on the edge of Brooklyn where the sea breeze blew strong and warm. A drizzle fell on the Belt Parkway, a major highway that divides Brooklyn from New York Harbor. It is a way to drive around Brooklyn, to avoid it completely. Like any other highway, it is a place where you can stand by the side of the road with ten thousand cars streaming by a few feet away and you stand alone. It was a Tuesday night, and the Belt was still packed with blinking red taillights streaming endlessly toward John F. Kennedy International Airport or farther out on Long Island. It was about 7:00 P.M., and most of those people were probably going home. One of those people was Eddie Lino, a captain in the Gambino crime family, who had just left the Cabrini Social Club on Avenue U in Bensonhurst and was headed to his home on Fort Salonga, Long Island.

He drove alone in a 1988 black Mercedes on a service road heading toward the entrance to the Belt. He was forty-seven, had three kids, a wife, and a full head of hair. He was a heroin dealer and he sometimes killed people for his boss, John Gotti. He was one of the guys who shot down Paul Castellano, the guy Gotti replaced. In February Eddie had been acquitted of heroin trafficking. It was his third trial on the same charges. The first time there was a mistrial and allegations of jury tampering. The second time there was a hung jury. The third time there was an acquittal but also an investigation into a note placed on the door of one of the alternate jurors that led to that juror's dismissal from the trial. Eight years in court, same drug charges. Now he was just another commuter heading home, ready for a drink before dinner, a little TV.

He was steering east on the service road between West Fifth Street and Ocean Avenue when another car, a Crown Victoria, pulled alongside. There was a flashing red light on the dash, and as the car pulled up, the guy on the passenger side—a thin, dark-haired guy in his forties with a thin mustache and eyes that were not smiling—flashed a gold detective's badge. Eddie braked but did not put the car in park.

"Frankie?" the driver behind the guy with the badge said. It was dark and tough to see the driver.

Eddie Lino knew right away what was going on. It was two cops looking for his cousin Frankie Lino. This did not happen all the time, but then again, cops were pretty stupid, so it was understandable. He said, "I'm Eddie. Frankie's my cousin."

The one who was driving, now Eddie could see he was a big guy with a mustache—they all seemed to have mustaches, these guys—he said something like, "What's that?" and pointed into Eddie's car toward the passenger-side floor. The skinny guy with the mustache in the passenger seat was closer to Eddie as he looked toward the mat on the floor of his 1988 Mercedes.

• • •

Michael Salsano, a thirty-seven-year-old guy from Brooklyn, drove east on the service road of the Belt Parkway when he found his way blocked by a Crown Victoria. He figured it was double-parked in the middle of the street. He started to pull around it when he noticed a skinny short guy run to the back passenger side door of the Crown Victoria and jump in. When he did, the Crown Victoria took off onto the entrance to the Belt and vanished into the traffic. It was dark, so he couldn't make out the plate or even the precise color of the car.

Now Salsano looked over and saw a 1988 black Mercedes that he hadn't seen before. It seemed to drift across the road and crash into a chain-link fence and come to a stop in the bushes at the side of the Belt. Salsano stopped and parked and walked over to the Mercedes.

Inside was a middle-aged guy in a two-tone jogging outfit slouched over the wheel. There was blood all over. The car was still in gear. Salsano did not touch anything.

In a few moments, the uniforms and detectives of the Sixtieth Precinct arrived at the scene. They set up a crime scene perimeter with yellow tape. Eddie Lino had at least five holes in him, including four entrance wounds in his head, almost all on the left side of his face. He also had bullet wounds in his left arm and upper torso and one in his lower left back. It appeared as though someone were standing over him as he sat in his car and blasted away before he had a moment to react. In all, five bullets were recovered inside Eddie, and one inside his jacket.

A Detective Mutterperl of the Sixtieth Precinct interviewed Salsano, and he told the story about the Crown Victoria and the guy jumping in the backseat and speeding away like Jesse James. Another officer on the scene tagged the property retrieved from inside the car: $1,316 cash, including twelve $100 bills, an AmEx card, a Delta frequent-flier card, a portable phone, and four lead bullets inside the interior, including one embedded in the car's front-door speaker. All came from a .38, which fires a maximum of six shots. This would indicate that there was more than one shooter, or one shooter with two guns.

On the street nearby was a Pulsar wristwatch with a black band. Its crystal was demolished. The time had stopped at just before 7:00 P.M. The watch was dusted for prints, but none were found. A small hair was caught in the wristband, dark in color. It was sent for close examination to people who enjoy examining hairs found in watches on the streets next to a dead man.

November 8, 1990

Burt Kaplan was not well. He had just turned fifty-seven a few weeks earlier. He had arthritis, temporalis, Reynaud's disease, high blood pressure. His was a litany of complaints, with a daily regimen of narcotics. Prednisone for the temporalis. Norvax for the high blood pressure. He lost much of his hearing in the navy. He was on his third detached retina, which was why at nine-thirty at night on November 8, he lay in a hospital bed at New York Eye & Ear, recovering from eye surgery. He'd checked in the previous day and had surgery at 10:35 A.M. on this day. The surgery was over in two hours, and he'd been sent back to his room, where he'd been sleeping off and on ever since. He was on codeine and Tylenol.

The surgery had occurred much earlier that morning, but he was still groggy from the drugs. He had a patch over his right eye. Visiting hours were over.

Kaplan: "It was about nine-thirty or ten o'clock at night, and I was sleeping. I had gotten my operation that day, and Louie came in the door and he tapped me on the foot and he woke me up and he says, 'I got good news.' First I jumped up when I seen him. I thought it was bad news. And I said, 'What's the matter? What's the matter?' He said, 'No, no, take it easy. I got good news.' I said, 'What?' He said, 'We got Eddie Lino.'"

Kaplan: "What do you mean, you got him?"

"We killed him," Louie said.

Louie pulled a newspaper story out of his pocket. It was the *Daily News*. The headline writer had written, "Cohort of Gotti Slain in Brooklyn." A smaller headline said, "The Belt Parkway Was a Dead End." There was a photo of some guy slumped over the wheel of a car that appeared to be parked inside a big bush. The caption stated, "Bullet-riddled body of

Edward Lino in Mercedes found on Belt service road." It was right over a story about a "busty transsexual" who got a twenty-five-thousand-dollar settlement because she'd been forced to do time in a men's prison.

Eppolito told the tale sitting at Kaplan's bedside with the old man groggy and one eyed covered. He said he and his partner, Steve, had followed Eddie from his social club on Avenue U, and before he got on the Belt, they turned on the red light and pulled him over.

"I walked over to him and I said, 'Hey, Frankie, how are you?' And Eddie got all happy. Then he says, 'I'm not Frankie Lino. I'm Eddie Lino.' 'Oh, we thought you were Frankie Lino.' So I pointed across to the passenger floor of the car and I asked Eddie, 'What's that?' And Eddie bent down to look and Steve shot him a number of times."

Kaplan: "How come Steve shot him?"

"Steve," said Louie, "is a much better shot."

The man with the hat brought a box for a cake. The man rang the doorbell of Kaplan's house on Eighty-fifth Street, and Kaplan's wife, Eleanor, said, "Won't you come in?" The man said, "No, I don't want to come in." He stood on the doorstep with the hat, a baseball cap, pulled down low down over his face and the box in his hand.

"This is from Gas," the man said, handing over the box and walking away. Kaplan thought it was Casso's close friend Georgie Neck, but he wasn't sure. He took the box inside and opened it.

Inside were packs of hundred-dollar bills. There was seventy thousand dollars, which was five thousand dollars more than the cops had requested to do this job. This was maybe Casso testing Kaplan. Kaplan decided to give the money to the cops anyway, all of it, and tell Casso what he did. If it was a test, then Kaplan would count the extra money against the cops' next monthly payment.

EIGHTEEN

Al D'Arco was a small, wiry guy who worked in the fish market in lower Manhattan, owned a restaurant in Little Italy, La Donna Rosa, and had five kids to support. He started associating with Paul Vario of the Lucchese crime family in the 1950s, at a time when it took a lot of years of work before anybody proposed you as a member. In Al D'Arco's case, that meant almost thirty years. During that time, he sold heroin, 76 percent pure. He sold quaaludes that turned out to be no good. He robbed what he called "freelance shylocks." He hijacked trucks, "not every day, whenever it came up." He burned down a paper-box factory but first checked to make sure nobody was home next door. Every type of crime except pimping and pornography. That was not considered kosher by criminals he looked up to. Finally, in 1982, he was told to go somewhere. At the time, that meant you'd either get to join the secret club, or you'd get murdered. If you refused to go, you'd be murdered anyway. So you went. He went, and was made a member of the Lucchese crime family.

At the time, in Al D'Arco's worldview, the Mafia had rules that were meant to be followed. There were traditions, there was respect. Informants were unusual or dead. It was an institution where your word meant something. Sometimes he didn't understand the rules. At the time he was invited to join, it was forbidden for made members to wear any clothing that had the color red in it, because red was for some unknown reason thought to be worn by "rats." That was the way it was, and Al D'Arco wasn't one to question the rules. So he didn't wear red until the rule changed.

He rose through the ranks. He was from Little Italy in Manhattan but was put wih the Brooklyn faction of the family, first with Paul Vario and then with Christy Tic Furnari. When Christy Tic went away, he wound up with Vic and Gas. Al D'Arco was a guy Vic and Gas could count on. He was made a captain in 1988.

On this day in 1991, D'Arco was summoned to an anonymous apartment building in Bensonhurst to get the word from two of America's most wanted, Vic Amuso and Anthony "Gaspipe" Casso.

When the entire FBI and NYPD have you targeted for capture, arranging a little business meeting is no simple task. A trip to the corner store could involve four or more surveillance vehicles, with agents and detectives operating under the assumption that any trip offered the possibility of catching Vic and Gas. Their absence from the Windows case stuck like a piece of sand in the eye of the U.S. attorney in Brooklyn. Vic and Gas were well aware of this. So they got together only occasionally, and made sure that nobody was watching. When they summoned D'Arco to this meeting, they knew he would check his mirrors the whole way.

The choreography had to be precise. D'Arco, after all, was followed around all the time by an assortment of law enforcement agencies: the FBI, the NYPD, the Brooklyn district attorney. Everywhere he went he had an unwanted entourage. Both sides performed their respective roles: the cops pretended not to been seen, the gangster pretended not to see. On occasion, the gangster would disappear and reappear the next day or a few hours later.

On January 9, D'Arco managed to slip his entourage and show up at the appointed spot without being seen.

Inside a room sat the boss and underboss, two middle-aged men living out of suitcases, moving from place to place late at night, constantly waiting for the moment when they'd be surrounded by agents with guns drawn. From the start of the meeting, it was clear that the two men—who were living a transient existence apart from one another and every other member of the Lucchese family—needed to get down to the important business of finding a way to work under these trying circumstances.

The first item on the agenda was to make D'Arco acting boss of the family.

As acting boss, D'Arco would be the voice of Vic and Gas. They would relay messages to their troops through him, continuing the complicated pay phone arrangement. He was to make day-to-day decisions regarding disputes with other families and between captains, and he was to make sure the tribute was coming in. He could move people from crew to crew, discipline soldiers for infractions, handle the numerous bureaucratic decisions that emerged day to day. But he could not induct new members without consulting Vic and Gas. He could not order a hit. As boss, only Amuso could do that.

By now there had been quite a few hits. There was Michael Salerno with the voice box and Bruno Facciola with the canary. There were the two union leaders, Jimmy Bishop and another guy named Sonny they feared would turn informant. There was a drug dealer named Red Calder and Anthony DiLapi out in seedy California.

At the meeting in Brooklyn, Casso let D'Arco in on a little fantasy he'd had of late. He wanted to have a dinner for forty guys he despised. He would invite them to a meal and then kill them all. He wasn't too specific about who was on the list, but he didn't have to be. D'Arco got the general idea.

In nearly all of these cases, Casso told D'Arco he'd learned of the alleged informant status of all those on his hit list from his "crystal ball." D'Arco was not exactly clear on the nature of this source. Sometimes Casso referred to an "agent" when discussing the "crystal ball," sometimes to a cop. Casso never mentioned a name, and as far as D'Arco could tell, not even the boss of the family knew the true identity of Casso's alleged crystal ball. All D'Arco knew was that whoever it was, his information was leading to a string of murders the likes of which had never afflicted the Lucchese family since he'd been involved in it. And in D'Arco's case, that would be about twenty-five years.

Casso told D'Arco the "crystal ball" had learned of another that might be of interest to D'Arco: a plot to kill Al D'Arco as soon as possible. The plot involved revenge. The brothers of Bruno Facciola were not at all happy that their sibling had been found in the trunk of a car with a bird in his mouth, and they now wished to come back at Al D'Arco, his sons, and all of D'Arco's crew, including Louie Bagels and everybody else they believed killed their brother, Bruno the loan shark. Casso claimed he'd even heard a tape in which Bruno's brother Louie discussed this plot. The tape was detailed enough to identify everybody involved in the scheme, including all the Facciola brothers, Louie, Nicky, and "Tarzan," and two unrelated Lucchese associates, Al Visconti and Larry Taylor, an armed robber who specialized in ripping off jewelry salesmen. Casso ordered D'Arco to kill Visconti and Taylor before they killed D'Arco.

Within two months, both men were dead. Visconti died as he entered the lobby of his apartment building. He was shot three times in the head and once in the testicles, which detectives decided was the result of the belief that Visconti—whose bad toupee earned him the nickname "Flounderhead"—frequented homosexual clubs. Taylor was shot in the head as he walked down a street in Brooklyn by two men blasting away with a shotgun and a .9mm from a moving sedan. The Major Case ran the sedan's plate through the Department of Motor Vehicles. The squad report noted that the car came back to a residence used by a Lucchese soldier and that witnesses described two men in the car, one of whom "appears to be Alphonse D'Arco."

May 1991

Al D'Arco was acting boss of the Lucchese crime family, and he couldn't be more unhappy. It should have been a career fulfilled. He'd been doing this since 1950 and had dedicated his life to it. He had power, he had respect, he had a driver. He still had to find his way to pay phones all over kingdom come and take orders from a man who seemed to be losing his grip on reality. On this day D'Arco was driven out to a pay phone on Glen Cove Road somewhere in the heart of Long Island. He was supposed to be at the phone at the appointed time. Of late, these phone calls had been disturbing, being that pretty much every one wound up with yet another order for a piece of work. At the pay phone on Long Island, D'Arco listened as Casso once again made it clear he needed more people dead.

Now it was Fat Pete Chiodo's turn. For weeks, Casso had become increasingly angry at Fat Pete, who for years had been his most trusted associate. Pete secretly owned a Brooklyn bar called the Nineteenth Hole. Casso and Amuso had ordered him to transfer ownership to them so they could realize some income while they were in hiding. Chiodo had neglected to follow through. Casso was claiming Chiodo had cut a deal with law enforcement and would soon agree to testify against the entire Lucchese family. This would be extremely bad news, given that Chiodo had been around forever and knew, more or less, everything there was to know. Chiodo had to go. Casso was furious.

In Casso's worldview, everyone was either a rat or about to become one.

As the phone call was winding down, D'Arco felt there was both good news and bad news. The good news was that he was acting boss. This was, in a way, a career goal. He had dedicated his life to organized criminal activity and now he had received the ultimate compliment: a promotion. The bad news was that he would still be reporting to two of the most wanted men in America, who would have a tough time managing while on the run. In fact, D'Arco felt at the time that this arrangement was a surefire way of ensuring that the Lucchese family would soon fall apart.

D'Arco got off the pay phone and wondered to himself: When does it end? When is it my turn to wind up dead?

May 8, 1991

Fat Pete Chiodo stood over his sedan at a gas station on Staten Island, fiddling with the oil stick. He had been indicted not once but twice in the past few months, first in the Windows case and then in a Manhattan district attorney's investigation of a corrupt painters union. He had stopped going to social clubs, stopped going anywhere. He'd moved out of his Staten Island home and now kept a low profile, staying here and there but never for more than a few days. Now he was standing in a parking lot when a car filled with guys in baseball caps and sunglasses pulled up next to him.

The exact number of bullets fired was difficult to ascertain. There were a lot. It helped that Fat Pete was, in fact, fat. He weighed between 350 and 375 pounds, and the excess baggage was enough to absorb enough of the bullets that when the sedan with the guys sped out of the gas station, Fat Pete lay on his side on the oil-soaked cement, leaking out all over the place but not quite enough to kill him. He was forty-one years old, he had been shot twelve times, and he was still alive.

That afternoon, Joseph D'Arco called his father, the acting boss of the Lucchese family. He said he and a guy, Fat Frankie, had pulled up on Chiodo at the gas station but Chiodo had spotted them before they got out of the car. Fat Frankie froze up and wouldn't get out of the car, so Joseph D'Arco said he walked over and shot Chiodo again and again. Joseph was not convinced he'd accomplished what he'd set out to do.

September 19, 1991

It was a sunny day, hot, a Thursday. Alfonse D'Arco and his son Joseph drove on the Long Island Expressway to his mother's house. He had put his other four children on a plane to Hawaii. He was driving all the way out on Long Island so no one from Mulberry Street would see what he was about to do. He had made up his mind to cooperate with the FBI after nearly 40 years in organized crime. He had started when

Eisenhower was president, and now it was over. He hadn't even been arrested, and he was still doing this.

Maybe it was the meeting he'd been summoned to at which Gaspipe and Amuso told him he was no longer acting boss, that the Lucchese family would now be run by a three-man panel that did not include him. They implied that he hadn't been kicking up what he was supposed to. Maybe it was Fat Pete Chiodo. Or his old friend Mike Salerno. Or Di-Lapi in Hollywood, or Bruno the loan shark with the canary in the mouth. Or who knows how many others? Probably it was the architect Anthony Fava, who had been working on Casso's house in Mill Basin. It was a palace, this house, with costs going up and up. Anthony Fava was found lying in the backseat of his sedan parked on West Seventh Street in Brooklyn's Sixty-first Precinct. He was found at about nine-thirty in the morning by a man walking by who thought there was a guy asleep in the backseat. The precinct uniforms found a man who'd been badly beaten, stabbed, shot, and tortured. There were numerous cigarette burns on the man's inner thighs. As far as Al D'Arco could tell, the guy was just an architect, and Anthony Casso just didn't want to pay the bill.

"I was told, 'They're talking behind your back.' That's Anthony Casso's method. Make a guy a rat, then kill him. That makes Gas a rat to do that. . . . I wanted to give him some revenge. I couldn't catch him. He was too smart. I was getting calls from the government. I wouldn't cooperate. My son Joseph got a call from Frankie Lastorino. He said, 'We trunked the architect.' I said, 'What am I to fight for? This is going to happen again. I never double-crossed anybody in my life. I never got involved in anybody's family.' I said, 'I'm washing my hands of this.'"

At his mother's house, D'Arco called his lawyer, who called the FBI. On the day D'Arco made his choice, he could say he was once the acting boss of the Lucchese crime family. He had been in organized crime since the early 1950s, involved in murders, shylocking, bookmaking, extortion of unions, stealing whatever he could whenever he could. He had brought his son Joseph into this mess and involved him in murders. He was fifty-nine years old. A second career seemed out of the question. The FBI told him they'd be out there immediately, probably an hour, depending on the traffic.

Mike Campi, FBI agent, New York:

"Why did D'Arco cooperate? D'Arco was then making easy money for the Lucchese. The Colombo war is brewing. D'Arco was brought in as intermediary by the Luccheses, meeting with Gambino and Genovese family, putting the Colombo family on notice. When he was questioned [by Casso] with regard to the money he was bringing, he was thinking, 'Now I'm demoted.' He's got the experience of watching [Casso and Amuso] mismanage everything and their solution to everything is to always kill everybody. They're on the run. They're paranoid, distrusting everybody. . . . That's where Al D'Arco is saying, 'Look at the decisions you're making.' Then all of a sudden Al D'Arco, who considers himself a loyal member of organized crime, he gets demoted. How do you feel when a guy says he wants to invite forty people from the family to a dinner and kill them all? You have to ask yourself, 'What did I get myself into?' He was a great witness. The best witnesses have good memories. A lie is not going to come out the same. That's the one thing about Al D'Arco. He's instrumental in getting other guys to cooperate. . . . If a witness doesn't look like Al D'Arco, you're going to have problems. The one thing with D'Arco is his stuff is always the same. If you ask him today, maybe he mixes things up, but his details are the same over and over. . . . It's not uncommon to be surprised by the additional details. When you have somebody who's on board, you have to ask the questions. Sometimes you don't ask about something, it comes out anyway."

In the fall of 1991, the FBI in New York was busy writing things down in notebooks. Al D'Arco was spending hours of the day trying to remember everything he had ever done that might be of interest to prosecutors throughout the metro area. There were numerous murders and attempted murders and beatings and extortions and union shakedowns. There was the infiltration of the city windows business, with the two dollars per window at every housing project from Canarsie in Brooklyn to Mott Haven in the Bronx. D'Arco met with numerous agents, giving information on dozens of guys he'd done crimes with over forty-one years. His debriefings were lengthy and at times strange.

Once D'Arco tried to explain the Mafia kiss. In the reports, D'Arco was always referred to as CW for "cooperating witness," as in, "Greeting each other with a kiss is another LCN custom which goes in and out of vogue. The CW explained it was a ritual imported from Europe which enjoyed varying degrees of popularity in the United States. In terms of who kisses whom, whether the participants kiss on one or both cheeks, or whether a handshake is also involved, these details have no meaning and are not a reliable indicator of a person's status within the family. In fact, word was passed recently that members should refrain from kissing each other, at least in public. The reason for this is that the government, at various racketeering trials, was producing surveillance photographs showing members kissing each other. The photos seemed to lend credence to government assertions that the LCN was a highly organized secret society and this was hurting the members' cases."

Then Al D'Arco took a little unexpected turn.

At the time, the FBI, the NYPD, and just about every other law enforcement agency in New York down to the Parks Police, had become increasingly annoyed and even upset by the consistent feeling that there were moles in their midst. The Bypass Gang was only one source of leakage. There were numerous investigations where the gangsters suddenly stopped talking on a particular phone, where somebody would disappear the day before a sweep, and—the worst of all—where an informant would show up under the dirt in Staten Island. Al D'Arco told them one reason why.

Throughout the mid-1980s, gangsters in several of the five New York families had secretly bought off law enforcement sources. There were uniformed cops in New York, cops on Long Island, detectives in several precincts, FBI agents. It was hard to quantify, but the more D'Arco gave examples, the more obvious it became that at least some of what he was saying was true and ongoing. Cops leaking information about wiretapped phones. Cops tipping off gangsters to upcoming arrests. Worst of all, cops revealing the names of informants. The implications were obvious and disturbing.

D'Arco went into great detail, and even explained to the FBI how complicated such an arrangement could be, where criminals pay off cops to become criminals and require that they be scrupulously corrupt.

"A corrupt law enforcement officer might find himself in difficulty with the Mob," read one summary of a D'Arco interview. "If an officer were fabricating evidence or otherwise not playing by the rules in dealing with them, it is possible that the LCN would find some way of letting the officer's superiors know. In even the most extreme circumstances, however, it is unlikely any physical harm would come to him."

D'Arco named names.

There was Sal Avellino, a wealthy Lucchese captain who controlled the carting industry on Long Island for both the Lucchese and the Gambino families. He was called behind his back "The Golfer." As D'Arco told it, the Golfer was investing four thousand dollars a month from all the money he was shaking down from garbage carters on Long Island to pay off a federal agent who was somehow involved in the unit of the FBI New York office that looked at John Gotti and the Gambino crime family. This agent would provide information on wiretaps and the schedule for pending arrests.

In a January 7, 1992, interview with two FBI agents at an "undisclosed location," D'Arco claimed the Golfer told him "he was very nervous when meeting" with the corrupt agent, whom he would meet the first week of each month somewhere on Long Island. At one point, he recalled, "Avellino informed him the federal agents were attempting to place a bug in [D'Arco's] restaurant, but the judge declined to sign this order since the government was unable to specify where the meetings took place."

During his secret meetings with the FBI, D'Arco insisted that the Golfer's law-enforcement contact was an FBI agent because Avellino was "quizzed on a number of occasions and advised that this money should be going to a federal agent and not a cop. It would have been suicidal for Avellino to have misrepresented this fact." He even presented the bureau with a slip of paper on which a series of numbers were written:

15750—4000—1000—1500
9250

He claimed this was a breakdown of how he distributed the
money he took each month from garbage haulers on Long Island. The $15,750 was his monthly take. Of that, $4,000 went
to the FBI agent; $1,000 and $1,500 for certain personal expenses, including a wedding. The $9,250 was the remainder,
which was handed over to D'Arco, who split it with Casso
and Amuso.

Then there was a "law-enforcement guy" on the Mob payroll at some police agency in California. D'Arco knew no
more about this, nor could he identify the name of the drug-
enforcement agent who was allegedly feeding law-enforcement
information to a Lucchese captain named Little Stevie Crea. A
captain named Danny Cutaia claimed to have a source within
the NYPD.

D'Arco was equally vague about a law-enforcement agent
who supposedly supplied information to Frank Lastorino, a
Lucchese soldier. All D'Arco knew was he met the source at
a diner. Lastorino met his source, Tony, who had a girlfriend
in the Brooklyn district attorney's office, in Canarsie near a
car wash he controlled.

Then there was Lucchese soldier George Zappola—
"Georgie Neck," he was called. His brother was a retired cop
who had been busted for burglary. He supposedly still had
contacts back in the NYPD.

Finally there was Gaspipe. D'Arco said Casso seemed to
have particularly helpful contacts in law enforcement, although he did not know their names. Nor could he be sure of
what was true when Casso referred to his "friends" in law enforcement. Sometimes Casso referred to an "agent," implying
he had an FBI agent on the payroll. At other times he referred
to "the cops" or "the bulls," which D'Arco took to mean
members of the NYPD. Never, in all the years he had known
and dealt with Casso, did D'Arco ever hear Casso mention the
names of his cops or agents or whoever he was paying. All
D'Arco knew was that when Casso claimed to have information from a law-enforcement source, it almost always turned
out to be right.

Casso's source was nearly legendary within the Lucchese

family. Fat Pete Chiodo, before he began cooperating with the FBI and was shot twelve times, referred to Casso's source as the "crystal ball." The crystal ball had known precisely when the Windows bust was going to occur. The crystal ball knew where Anthony DiLapi lived in California. The crystal ball knew about Bruno Facciola, about Mike Salerno, and even about Fat Pete Chiodo. He was pretty sure only Casso knew the identity of the crystal ball.

Somehow none of this got out. D'Arco's secrets about law enforcement, about corrupt cops and agents stayed secret. The newspapers and TV paid no attention to Al D'Arco and his revelations about multiple law-enforcement leaks in the NYPD and the FBI. It was just Al D'Arco talking. In truth, D'Arco's timing was off.

D'Arco just happened to drop these revelations about corrupt cops in the fall of 1991 at the same time as *United States v. John Gotti et al.* was unfolding in Brooklyn federal court. Gotti was all over the papers, the gangster who thumbed his nose at the FBI, who'd beat the feds three times. That was where the cameras were. They were playing the tapes, they were bringing out Salvatore Gravano, the squat sociopath who was testifying against his boss. John Gotti was headlines, the cover of *Time* magazine. Al D'Arco and all his talk of corrupt law enforcement was lousy TV.

The crystal ball and all the rest would go into a file under a case marked "Open."

NINETEEN

In the bar at a restaurant called Forlini's, Lou Eppolito was having a rough night. Steve Corso had his Pinot Noir and Steve Caracappa was drinking his Chianti, but Lou couldn't hector the bartender about the perfect way to make a Tanqueray martini because of his heart problems. He was stuck with Pellegrino. Plus he did not have his public company yet, which was supposed to have happened five days ago. He still had not seen one dime of the $250,000 salary Corso promised way back in December. That was a many weekly bills to pay ago. His Hollywood dreams were fading to black before the first reel started. Where was the money? Where was the fame? Where was the adulation he believed he so richly deserved?

A lot had happened since he met Steve Corso and all his promises. His rib cage had been cracked open for a double by-pass. His daughter, Deanna, was due to give birth in May, and the doctors had seen something wrong with the baby's heart. This would be Lou's first grandchild. Now he was hearing that the father and son with the Bonanno family, the Frates, the guys who gave him the shoebox with $25,000 way back when, now all of a sudden they wanted to claim a percentage of Lou's big movie company. In Lou's view, this was outrageous.

And to make it worse, he had a cold.

"He thinks he's a partner or something," Lou said. "I says, 'You read the papers? You got nothing to do with this.' He said, 'Well, I talked to Steve.' I said, 'Steve didn't make the deal. Crucker made the fucking deal. Steve gets paid because that's what he does. It doesn't come out of his pocket.' He said, 'I know what you're saying.' I said, 'I know what the fuck I'm saying. That's never gonna happen. Never.'"

"He said we need to be on the payroll, too," Corso said.

"No," Lou said. "It's never gonna happen."

To add to Lou's headaches, Corso was now saying that the gangsters from Florida who had promised to send Lou money right away hadn't sent anything. This made Lou more upset. He threatened to drive down to Florida to get it that night. Corso—knowing that there really were no gangsters in Florida and that the late payment was simply because the FBI was a massive bureaucracy where civil servants argued about who was supposed to sign the check—said that Lou probably shouldn't drive down to Florida. Corso then made up yet another story, this time about being afraid to call the guys in Florida back again.

"I'll get whacked," Corso whined.

"If you called me up Wednesday and said I gotta problem, somebody's going to come down here and kill me, I'm going to say, 'Sit in the office all day, nobody's going to hurt you,'" Lou said.

"Steve, no one will ever hurt you," Caracappa said. "Trust me."

"I trust you."

"Does he realize?" Caracappa said to Lou. "You don't."

"How can I realize?" Corso said. "I've known you guys a month."

"Nobody will hurt you," Caracappa said. "You pick up the phone, you call me, he calls me, we'll take care of everything."

Corso the salesman could see he was losing his mark. He needed to get both of them back on track, pumped up about the public offering that would make them all rich men. He turned to one of his usual weapons: guilt. He made it seem as if all this pessimism was a result of Lou and Steve's Italian heritage. He referred to this as the "why me?" syndrome, as in why would somebody be offering me a million dollars? In reality, this was a reasonable question. But Corso made it seem unreasonable.

"I'm here because you are going to make me a lot of money. Crucker is here because you're gonna make him a shitload of money. And you're gonna make a hell of a lot of money. That's the reason," Corso said. "You've got to get off the thing it's an old Italian concept, 'why me?'" Corso was just warming up. "Fuck 'why me?' People aren't doing you any favors. They're doing it because you're making them a lot of money. You are making me money. If you were an asshole, and you were Italian, trust me, I'd love you but I wouldn't be here. It's about money. I don't know how plain I can say it."

Lou excused himself to go to the bathroom. Caracappa tried to reassure Corso that everything would be all right. This was the informant's ultimate goal: get the target to do the sales pitch.

"You gotta understand one thing and believe me when I tell you this: Don't put too much pressure on yourself," Caracappa said. "It's gonna happen. You believe it's gonna happen, it's gonna happen. Calm yourself down. I'll tell you why. You're gonna make yourself sick over this. I've been in this business a lot longer than you. I know what I'm talking about."

"Steve," said the FBI informant, "if I don't have my word, I got nothing."

"I believe you or I wouldn't be sitting here with you and you wouldn't be sitting here with me and Lou."

Corso had a theory to explain Lou. In his view, all of Lou's problems led back to Fran, the wife. She didn't believe a word Corso said, and it didn't help that his plan had changed. First he said he was going to get Lou seventy-five thousand dollars up front. Then it became payments of just under ten thousand dollars over several weeks. Then the payments hadn't shown up.

"I told him five to six business days and today's the seventh business day and he got upset," Corso confided to

Caracappa while Lou was away. "Why did he get upset? A reasonable guy ain't gonna get upset. But a guy who's hearing it from a girl—nying, nying, nying, nying, nying—he's gonna get upset. He doesn't tell me this. This is what I'm figuring out," Corso said. "He's gotta filter out Fran. He's gotta put her out of his mind. I don't ever discuss this but I see her hitting and hitting and hitting and then he goes under pressure and he gets upset."

"I'm glad you told me that because I'll take care of it," Caracappa said. "Listen, nobody knows this guy better than me. The potential is there. He is hurting for money. I know he's hurting for money."

"She's going nying, nying, nying."

"Let me tell you. Bronx girl. No education. She been on the balls of her ass with this guy, and she's made money with him. She's scared. The guy just had a bypass operation. I don't know what kind of insurance he has. Do you know what I mean, Steve? She's scared."

"I know."

"You got to understand the mentality of a woman."

"But he's gotta be strong enough to say look . . ."

"He's not, he's not. Because she influences him so much."

"I don't give a shit. It's for him. I may be off a day or two here, but it happens."

"You know what happens since he took the operation? He's become a pussy. Trust me."

"I trust you."

Lou reappeared and they discussed the upcoming Academy Awards, how *Sideways* was good for giving Steve Corso the idea to order Pinot Noir but not good enough to win an Oscar. Everybody liked *Million Dollar Baby*. Lou explained that Clint Eastwood couldn't act but he could direct.

"How's the other girl doing I can't get to first base with?" Corso asked of Lou's daughter, Andrea.

"You can get to first base with her," Lou said.

"You can get to first base," Steve agreed.

"I haven't even gotten to down the line," Corso said. "I can't even bunt."

The waiter appeared and they ordered more Pellegrino, Chianti, and Pinot Noir. Corso pronounced it "Pee-no New-are." Lou had the pasta fagioli with bruchetta appetizer, Caracappa had the chicken Milanese, and Corso went for the osso buco. When the dinners arrived, Corso cleared his throat.

"The other thing I want to talk to you about and I don't know. Don't take it the wrong way," he said. "I got these four guys coming in. They're young Hollywood punks but they're my clients. Two are famous. They're coming in this weekend. These are the guys who are going to invest. They may need protection, but I didn't talk to them about that. The reason I had to get in touch with the Gweedster . . . Did you get in touch with him today?

"Who?" Lou asked.

"Guido."

"I have to see my son," Lou said. "My son knows him."

"These guys have been my clients three years." Corso began chewing his veal. "They're younger. Two are famous. They're twenty-nine, thirty. They're coming in for the whole weekend."

"How famous?" Lou said. "What do you mean by famous? They actors?"

"Yeah. You'd know their names. And they're gonna invest, okay? So it's not my problem, but my thing is that these guys, being young, like to party and they do things I have no knowledge about. Basically that's designer shit, designer drugs."

"Tony can help you," Lou said. "My son, he can bring them to all the places. The top places."

"They don't want to go to the places," Corso clarified, following his FBI instructions as best he could. "That's why I was thinking of Guido. They want me to get them either Ecstasy or speed. I don't know what that is."

"Gotta ask Guido," Lou said.

"Guido's the guy?"

"Those kids," said Lou.

"Guido can handle it," Corso repeated.

"All those places, yeah," Lou said.

"Okay," Corso said. "So I just gotta get in touch with this guy, that's why I was trying to get in touch with him. That and to see if I can do any accounting with him."

They digressed to other topics, but Corso kept circling back to Guido, who could get the drugs. Corso wanted to test the question of whether Lou and Steve were really vouching for, as he put it, the Gweedster.

"I can trust this guy Guido?"

"Oh, yeah," Lou said.

"You know why I trust him?" Caracappa added. "Let me tell you why I trust him. I wanted him to come into my house. I let him use my computer, fool around with my wife, teach her the computer, what she has in her brain with the computer. He's a very . . . what I see in the kid is, he's a very respectable kid, he's loyal to Lou's son."

"Yeah," said Lou.

For four months the FBI listened to conversations and knew all there was to know about Caesar and Flower and all the rest of what was going on inside the house of Eppolito. They heard waiters read off the dinner specials at every top restaurant in Las Vegas, knowing they had to pay the bills. They had heard Lou and Fran admit they were tax cheats and that Lou kept every photo of himself with any celebrity on his wall. They heard Lou Eppolito agree that he didn't care if the money that would support his Hollywood dream came from Pablo Escobar or Don Corleone, and they heard Lou talk about getting cash in a shoebox. Now they had what they believed was evidence of Lou Eppolito and Stephen Caracappa, two former New York City detectives, participating in a drug deal. This was what they needed to hear. This was conspiracy to distribute. When confronted with a direct request to purchase illegal speed and Ecstasy, Detectives Eppolito and Caracappa did not throw their hands in the air and scream, "Drugs! How can you talk of drugs?!" It was, "Guido—he'll do that." Corso said he'd call Lou's son, Anthony, to get in touch with Guido. He set up another dinner.

"I can't make it on Thursday," Carcappa said. "This is my last dinner with you guys."

"Next Friday then," Corso said. "I gotta do these dinners. I can't live without them."

Walking to the parking lot, Caracappa noticed Lou was breathing heavily.

"You're huffing and puffing," he said. "You're like a

money machine. I gotta keep you alive for ten years to make some money."

"I plan to be around more than ten years," Lou said.

"Talk to Andrea," Corso said.

"You take care of yourself," Caracappa said.

"Don't kiss me," Lou said.

TWENTY

For NYPD detective Richard Scattaglia, it was time to turn up the heat on Burton Kaplan. It was clear Detective Scattaglia really wanted to put Burt in jail, but he was having a tough time of it. Throughout the 1980s and now into the 1990s, numerous law-enforcement agencies had tried without success to get Burt: the NYPD, the FBI, the DEA, the Brooklyn district attorney, and Detective Scattaglia, doing his part with the Staten Island district attorney. It had been a long time since Burt had seen a prison cell, which was where the army of law enforcers felt he belonged. He was last successfully convicted of a crime in 1980, and since his release from prison in 1983 nobody could touch him. The heroin charge that evaporated had been the last real attempt. Now it was Detective Scattaglia's turn.

He was trying to get a judge to expand the investigation of Burt, whom he believed to be trafficking in massive amounts of knockoffs. To do this, Scattaglia had to present the judge with some evidence that Burt deserved to be investigated. Scattaglia needed probable cause. There didn't seem to be much probable cause around.

For eight months Scattaglia and his team sat outside Burt's

warehouse on a forlorn edge of Staten Island and didn't see much of anything. That was a lot of sitting. They watched the warehouse from 8:30 A.M. to 5:30 P.M., Monday through Friday, starting February 1, 1991. That would work out to approximately 150 days sitting inside a van with the engine off, drinking vats of coffee. Sometimes you watched your breath cloud in the winter air. Sometimes you wiped the sweat off your brow before it dripped onto the camera and messed up the shot. Thousands of rolls of film were expended watching the three-story cinder block building. Dozens of people pulled up without packages, entered the building, and left a moment later with packages. Most everybody went through a rear entrance. As far as the NYPD could tell, this was the evidence they had that Burt was yet again running a major counterfeit clothing operation—guys coming and going with packages.

Some of the guys had criminal records. Of course, Burt did. So did Tommy Irish, his partner. But Tommy hadn't been arrested since the 1970s, and that was for unlawful dealings with fireworks. There was another guy who also had a criminal record, dating back to the early 1960s, but his last arrest was in 1968. The worst of the worst stopping by for a package was Frank Buscemi, a repeat offender who was still on probation after doing time on a racketeering conviction. He had the most impressive criminal résumé—felonious assault, receiving stolen property (booze), truck hijacking (ladies' apparel), truck hijacking again (Japanese radios), more truck hijacking (TVs), attempted grand larceny (trying to defraud a clothing store), distribution of quaaludes, and finally an attempt to rip off a casino.

Detective Scattaglia listed all of these offenses, and told the judge he'd seen guys like Buscemi coming and going from Burt Kaplan's warehouse a lot. "There has been at least one occasion when I have observed within five hours approximately fifteen automobiles and their occupants engage in the above-described activity."

He also described Burt Kaplan arriving at the warehouse before anybody else every day, and having watched him open the warehouse door with a set of keys and go inside. He made sure to tell the judge about this.

At times individuals could be seen leaving the warehouse

with clothes over their shoulders or in their hands. Sometimes they'd leave with cardboard boxes wrapped in "what appears to be duct tape."

"Based upon my experience and training as a New York City Police officer, the activities I have observed are consistent with the manner in which stolen property is sold and sampled or displayed to potential buyers for future purchases of larger quantities," Scattaglia wrote. He then requested what's called a pen register, a device that would monitor the four phone lines Kaplan used at Progressive. This would allow Detective Scattaglia to see who called Burt and who Burt called.

Good enough, said the judge. Start tracking those numbers.

July 28, 1992

It was a Tuesday, a workday. Most New York City taxpayers had packed themselves into sweaty subway cars and trudged to their jobs in the stifling heat. Not Steven Lenehan. Work was not part of his personal philosophy. He preferred the life of a knockabout guy, living by his wits, scraping by day by day, getting over in any way he could. A dreamer and a schemer. On this day he cruised past the compact Staten Island ranch houses of Sommers Avenue in the air-conditioned comfort of his black Lincoln Continental. He was driver today, picking up Gerald Chilli, captain in the Bonanno crime family.

Gerry Chilli was a legend among a certain set. A garrulous middle-aged gangster who'd crawled and clawed his way up the ladder, he was loved by many, feared by some. Always he insisted he was inches from bankruptcy. He had turned fifty-eight two days before, an age when many men are doing the math on retirement and working on the golf swing. Instead, Gerry Chilli was scheduled to meet a guy that afternoon to buy two pounds of marijuana imported all the way from Mexico.

The seller was a guy named Burt Last Name Unknown.

Lenehan had never actually met Burt Last Name Unknown, but Gerry had vouched for the guy as somebody you could trust. He operated some kind of clothing business related to the Garment Center, and the FBI was very interested in getting him. That was where Steve Lenehan came in.

Situated deep within Lenehan's Lincoln was a device known as a Nagra, a recording device that could tape hours of conversation without interruption. It was technically the property of the FBI. In fact, Lenehan himself was the property of the FBI. Like a lot of other guys driving Lincolns around Staten Island, he'd been caught doing various crimes and decided he could live with the decision that it is far better to give up your best friends than to spend even a day in federal prison. He was a government cooperator, and today he was going to work.

If a passerby happened upon him as he sat in his Lincoln parked outside the home of Gerry Chilli, they would have observed a man alone, talking to himself.

"It's Tuesday, the twenty-eighth of July," Lenehan said to his secret friend Nagra. "I'm at Gerry Chilli's house. It's five after eleven in the morning."

A few minutes later Chilli emerged from his home and hopped in the car. The first words out of his mouth were, "I'm walking around fucking broke."

"If it goes right," Lenehan replied, "we'll be in good shape."

The plan was to pick up two pounds of marijuana at a warehouse in Staten Island owned by Burt Last Name Unknown. Burt was known for his high-quality marijuana, but in the Lincoln, Lenehan and Gerry Chilli worried a little about whether these two pounds would hold up their end.

"He says it's definitely skunk," Lenehan said. "I said, skunk, don't worry."

"We don't know if it's skunk," Chilli said. "You shouldn't have told him that."

Lenehan: "It's a different kind of skunk. It's Staten Island skunk, it's not the same as Jersey skunk. Hey when he waved that five thousand in front of me . . ."

Chilli: "Yeah, you didn't want to know nothing."

Lenehan: "I would have gave any name he wanted."

Chilli: "Yeah, you're terrible. We ain't gonna pay him now anyway."

Lenahan: "I know, we gotta make a maneuver here."

Chilli: "We can't show we got the money already." The Lincoln slowed almost to a stop. A line of traffic stretched to the horizon, as it always did in this section of Staten Island. "What is this fucking traffic?" Chilli commented.

Chilli felt this was a good moment to let Lenahan know what a great guy this guy Burt was, regardless of what kind of maneuver they were pulling. He said Burt had recently staked him a thousand dollars.

"He says, 'I got something going.' He says, 'I'll help you out a little, I know you're in trouble.' "

Lenahan: "So he seems like a real good guy."

Chilli: "Ah, you can't beat him. When I tell you, a fucking honorable Jew."

Then Chilli made a remark that caught the FBI's attention. He made reference to Vic, the boss of the Lucchese crime family, and by implication Vic's best friend, Anthony "Gaspipe" Casso, a man they were very interested in finding. Gerry Chilli was making it clear that this guy named Burt was close to Vic and Anthony of the Lucchese family, so the FBI might be able to put a big marijuana arrest onto these two characters and go from there. Vic Amuso had been caught after a year on the lam, and Casso was still out there somewhere, a thumb in the eye of the FBI.

"See Vic and them, they're in trouble over there," Chilli said. "I guarantee Burt will send fifty, a hundred thousand like nothing. That's the type of guy he is."

Lenahan: "If you got a good Jew, you got a good person."

Chilli: "Yeah, this one is a good Jew. I know him long, I know Burt."

"He seems like a hell of a nice guy," Lenahan says, encouraging Chilli to talk more about Burt.

"Ah, man, he told me, 'Chilli, I ain't lyin' to ya.' He said, 'I'm giving to the wholesalers big stuff, big amounts. I'm giving fifteen and change.' He said, 'I ain't lyin' to ya, Chilli, you know? I got nothing to lie to you about.' I said, 'I know you ain't lyin'.' " Chilli said Burt staked him a twenty-five-thousand-dollar credit.

"Nobody gives you credit like that," Lenahan said.

"No more today," Chilli said. "Forget this guy. God bless him."

The Nagra spun and spun.

Lenehan pulled into a lot around the back of Burt's warehouse. They rang the bell at the back door and waited. A guy named George let them in. Inside, Chilli introduced Lenehan to Burt. The guy was older, probably fifty to fifty-five, medium build, maybe five-eight, 140 pounds, balding with brown fringe. The guy George looked Italian, about forty, with a stocky build, a mustache, and wearing a bright red shirt. Without a word, Chilli and Burt walked upstairs, while Lenehan waited with George. George said nothing and disappeared into the back of the warehouse.

In a while Chilli and Burt and George returned, saying nothing in front of Lenehan. George handed Lenehan a box. Chilli and Lenehan then left the building, placing the box in the Lincoln's trunk.

They drove to Chilli's house and opened the box. Inside were two clear plastic bags filled with marijuana and stuffed inside a white "I Love New York" bag. The plan was for Lenehan to take the drugs to his house for safekeeping while Gerry Chilli stayed at home to get in touch with his dealers. Lenehan took the "I Love New York" bag with the two pounds of pot from Burt Last Name Unknown and placed it in the trunk of his Lincoln.

Alone again on the highway and headed to New Jersey, Lenehan talked to the tape recorder in his car:

"I'm leaving Gerry Chilli's house in Staten Island to meet Agent Joe Gilson at Newark Airport," he said. "I have in my possession two pounds of marijuana."

Two pounds of probable cause.

July 8, 1992

Betty Hydell was at home all by herself with the TV noises on Bangor Street in Staten Island. It was a weekday, and none of the kids were around, so the TV was her friend. Her son Jimmy had disappeared long ago, and Frankie was out and about. Linda and Liz were working. It was Sally Jessy

Raphael on the box and there was a lot of applause and then there was this fat guy with a pompadour and a mustache who looked a little like Jackie Gleason sitting down to chat with Sally. Betty stopped what she was doing and paid attention.

Sally was going on and on about the fat guy being a decorated cop who had grown up around the Mafia. The camera zoomed in on a book with a detective's badge on the cover next to the title *Mafia Cop*. Betty could not believe her eyes.

There, talking to Sally on the TV like he was somebody famous, was the fat cop she'd seen six years ago sitting in that powder-blue Toyota with the gold chains and the open shirt. Six years ago on October 18, 1986, when her son Jimmy Hydell, walked out the door and was never heard from again. She listened to Sally call the guy Detective Eppolito and ask him all kinds of questions that let him say how brave he was. She could tell that the cop was nervous, that he didn't belong on television. He looked like the kind of guy who was used to everyone thinking he was charming and now it wasn't working.

She scribbled down the name of the book, *Mafia Cop*, and decided it was time to go to the bookstore. Inside the book she found a photo of Eppolito in a sleeveless white T-shirt to show off his biceps. The caption read, "Detective Louie Eppoltio, 'always ready to go.'" Another photo depicted Eppolito sitting in a squad room with his friend and partner Stephen Caracappa. They were described as "The two Godfathers of the NYPD." When Betty saw that, she knew right away the other skinny cop she had seen the morning her boy Jimmy disappeared was this Caracappa.

Now she knew their names, both of them. The publication of the book had allowed Betty Hydell to put names to faces.

And she told exactly no one. She still had another son, Frankie, to worry about. Like Jimmy, he was headed in a bad direction. She believed that if she came forward and made a lot of noise about two detectives being involved in a Mob murder, she'd be putting her other son in harm's way: "When I recognized them and realized they were detectives, who was I gonna go to? I was afraid if I did go to anybody they'd go after my other son."

She wondered what made Eppolito—a guy she believed

had gotten away with murder—dare court publicity by writing a book. She remembered that morning clearly; she remembered the way they flashed their badges and looked back at her as if she had no business asking them what they were doing there. At the time, they were nameless. But now she knew their names.

Mafia Cop made it on to the *New York Times* best-seller list for a short period in 1992. Detective Louis Eppolito wrote it with a *New York Post* reporter named Bob Drury after Eppolito retired from the New York City Police Department on December 14, 1989. The book was supposed to clear Eppolito's name once and for all. It described in detail his many daring deeds as a detective in the New York City Police Department, and the terrible crisis of loyalty Eppolito faced being raised by gangsters and choosing to be a cop. He would tell friends the book was supposed to be called *Man in the Middle*, but his publishers at Simon & Schuster insisted on the much catchier *Mafia Cop: The Story of an Honest Cop Whose Family Was the Mob*.

The book was remarkable less for what it said than for what it did not say.

It made mention of a "crack hooker whose murderer [Eppolito] spent his off-duty hours tracking down." This appears to be a reference to his pursuit of Barry Gibbs, although the book does not mention Gibbs or the witness against him, Peter Mitchell. The book mentions the time Eppolito was assigned to the 1983 homicide of somebody he said was named Albert Veriali. The spelling was wrong. The correct name was Albert Varriale, who happened to be a cousin of Pasquale Varriale, who'd been murdered in Pete Franzone's garage. Albert also was related to Carmine Varriale, who'd been murdered walking down the street with Lou Eppolito's gangster cousin Frankie Santora Jr.

The book makes no mention whatsoever of Frankie Jr., which is most remarkable considering that it spends much time discussing other gangsters in Eppolito's family such as his father, Fat the Gangster, and his uncle, Jimmy the Clam. He had no problem mentioning them. For some reason, Frankie Jr. was left out.

The book does quote Eppolito's father making fun of cops for corrupting themselves for pathetic amounts of cash, but the book makes no mention of the five thousand dollars Eppolito got from the Sciascia father and son for the mug shots he nicked from the NYPD, or the five thousand dollars Eppolito got from Sammy Gravano to stop investigating one of Sammy's many murders. Perhaps most importantly, the book makes no mention whatsoever of Burt Kaplan, or Burt Last Name Unknown, the Garment Center businessman and part-time marijuana dealer who was handing Eppolito and his partner Caracappa four thousand dollars a month and whom the FBI, the DEA, the Brooklyn district attorney, the Staten Island district attorney, and the NYPD were pursuing relentlessly when *Mafia Cop* hit the bookstores.

Eppolito dedicated the book like this: "For my father Ralph. Thanks for making a man that no other man could break." In the narrative, Eppolito concluded that the underworld was, in many ways, a more honorable place than the ranks of the New York City Police Department. He wrote that he was driven off the job because of his name, and that when he was down, many of his fellow cops weren't there for them, while the gangsters he grew up with offered a helping hand. The final line read, "The New York City Police Department had finally managed to rid itself of one of its worthiest cops."

Soon after the book hit the shelves, retired detective Louis Eppolito was a new man. He was famous, a little. He had chatted with Sally Jessy Raphael, had eaten dinner with Robert DeNiro. And then he was informed that he soon could be receiving the American version of knighthood, the goal to which all good Americans aspire, the Holy Grail of American success: *Mafia Cop* was optioned for a movie.

He gave a copy to Hugh Mo, the NYPD administrative judge who'd tossed out the departmental charges against him. On the front inside cover he wrote, "To my friend, Hugh Mo. I hope you enjoyed the book as much as I did writing it. It tells of honor—respect. It is my HONOR to know you a man who could JUDGE you on truth and have the guts to put me back on the job when others saw fit to get rid of me. You have also won my friendship and respect just by being a REAL MAN! And that is always something I will remember about you."

He gave another copy to Burt Kaplan, writing, "To my good friend Burt." In Brooklyn, Anthony Casso saw the book and recognized the two cops he'd seen that afternoon six years back in the Toys "R" Us parking lot with Jimmy Hydell in the trunk of the car. He bought the book. He read it and saw the photographs and, at some point, he asked Burt Kaplan, "These are the two guys in the Toys 'R' Us parking lot?"

Kaplan looked at Casso. He was aware that it would not be in his interests to confirm this information, nor would it be a good idea to deny it. Lying to Anthony Casso was usually not a good idea. He was in a bit of a jam.

"Anthony," Burt said, "I'm not going to get into that. I would never tell you their names. You can surmise anything you want."

The giant white van would fit right in at an RV park in Arkansas. In Bensonhurst, it looked like P. T. Barnum had arrived. The van was parked in front of Burt Kaplan's house on Eighty-fifth Street on a sunny Saturday afternoon, and Louie Eppolito seemed proud to show it off. He had stopped by Burt's on his way out of town. He and his wife, Fran, were headed to Vegas, one-way.

"I was shocked," Kaplan said. "It was white, pure white, and I felt very conspicuous standing out on the sidewalk with Louie, him being a retired detective and me being a criminal, with this big white van and on a Saturday afternoon with a lot of people driving by. I didn't say that to him, but I was nervous, and I said, 'Louie, it's a beautiful van and I did what most people did at that time. I went in my pocket and I had a—I used pay phones a lot, I had two, three dollars' worth of quarters and I threw it on the floor of the car, which meant good luck.' He told me that his mother-in-law and the kids were going to fly and that him and his wife were going—they had some animals—and that he was going to drive across country to Vegas in that van that he bought."

It was a strange meeting. Burt and Louie had a little falling out, in which Louie came to Burt's house and demanded more money and a chance to meet Anthony Casso. Burt thought this was a stupid idea. Louie offered to stand behind a door and talk to Anthony. Burt still felt it was stupid. There had been some yelling, and Burt—skinny, arthritic Burt—had pushed Louie out the door and told him never to come back. Later Steve came to Burt with a box of cookies, and now Burt met only with Steve. And here was Louie with the van, hoping for a final blessing from an old friend as he transformed himself from a Brooklyn guy into a Las Vegas swinger. It was strange.

When Louie and Fran drove away, Burt was left with his problems. Ever since the FBI came around and talked about him behind his back, Burt had been having a tough time in the clothing business. Champion was suing him for selling knockoffs. Everybody was looking for his money, so if they asked, he was broke. During a deposition in one of the many lawsuits, he told a lawyer who asked him how old he was. He replied, "56 physically, 102 mentally." He claimed to have lost millions on the Phoenix land deal, and was walking around saying he made only forty thousand dollars.

"I must have done some good to some people in my life for them to have this kind of respect for me, and the fact that I am doing so bad," he complained.

Burt knew he was capable of making a decent living 100 percent legitimately, but it was just getting too difficult. You could make an even better living if you cut corners here and sold knockoffs, clothing that pretended to be designer clothing but was really just clothing with designer labels. He had recently discovered a new way to make unbelievable profits, 1,000 percent returns.

Marijuana.

Since the quaalude debacle, Burt had stayed away from drugs. Everyone around him was in it, and the profits were unbelievable, but he stayed away. One of his partners in the clothing business, Ray Fontaine, was the guy who finally turned Burt around. Ray explained that marijuana was the way to go because marijuana was not heroin or cocaine, both of which would put you in prison forever and usually involved very crazy people. Marijuana was somehow not as violent as heroin and cocaine, and it was much better quality than it used to be, which meant you could sell less of it for more money. That was convenient. What you needed was a big clothing distributor warehouse on Staten Island where it could stay out of sight until it was sold.

By 1992, Burt Kaplan had decided he could not be in the clothing business without also selling hundreds of pounds of marijuana. Personally he did not like the stuff. He tried exactly two puffs in prison many years back, and had stayed away from it since. He did like the economic return.

Inside the warehouse on any given day, Burt could move a hundred pounds of marijuana. He kept two books and was meticulous about tracking supply and demand. He labeled everything as if it were clothes. Errand boy Tommy Galpine would travel all over to pick up the packages and bring them back. Once Tommy brought his wife, Monica, and two young sons to Durango, Colorado, and brought the pot back in an RV like a middle-class family on a road trip. Sometimes Tommy would deliver pot in a diaper bag or wrapped like a Christmas present. The Burt Kaplan marijuana operation did whatever it took. Always Kaplan insisted on top-quality product. He had connections in Texas, in Oregon, in Juárez, and made a point of storing surplus for dry spells. Quality and availability were Kaplan hallmarks—like a hotel chain. The dealers knew that they could always turn to Burt and their dope-smoking customers would always stay satisfied.

At the warehouse in Staten Island, Burt was maniacal about security. He posted cameras at the entrance to track who was coming and going. He suspected everybody was an undercover cop. He made workers wear rubber gloves so they wouldn't get fingerprints on the plastic tape used to wrap the packages of dope. He instructed everyone not to say anything on the phone. He put a high value on trust. He talked only to a chosen few about his business, Tommy Galpine probably being his closest associate. "I love him like a son," he would tell people. With Tommy and a small number of other partners, Burt would candidly discuss legal and illegal affairs, comfortable that they shared his street loathing of informants. If anybody he didn't know entered the room, he would shut up right away.

He also involved his own family in his business.

Galpine's wife, Monica, worked for a time within the Kaplan marijuana empire. She kept drug records, wrapped drugs, traveled with her husband to deliver drugs and money, helped her husband get rid of firearms. In notes to a lawyer, she described the interconnection of Kaplan's personal and business lives. She said Kaplan's wife, Eleanor, would count cash and checks, and at times his daughter, the lawyer Deborah, deposited both. It wasn't clear that they had any idea where the cash was coming from. In fact, the way Burt set it up, it would appear the money was part of the clothing operation. At the same time, Monica said Burt's businesses helped financially support his daughter and her lawyer husband, Harlan. When Harlan was going to law school, Burt helped pay the bills. Burt paid for the couple's car garage in Manhattan after they were married.

Monica told another story that made it clear Burt Kaplan took family very seriously. She heard about this from her husband, Tommy. At some point in the early 1980s, a teenage niece of Burt's was raped. The girl was said to be fourteen years old, and she'd been raped somewhere near Prospect Park in Brooklyn. Somehow Burt learned the rapist's identity and had the guy brought to the family liquor store on Vanderbilt Avenue. There in a back room, Burt allegedly poured gasoline over the man and lit him on fire.

Whether or not this story was true, it had a powerful effect on Monica Galpine. She had a different perspective on Burt than the vice presidents at Calvin Klein and Gloria Vanderbilt. She thought he was a scary guy. She knew the real Burt. His bodyguard, a big guy named Herman Bannerman, carried a firearm. Why would a legitimate businessman need a bodyguard with a gun? Burt, the skinny Jewish guy with the bad eye and the arthritis who was allergic to penicillin, was not the Burt she knew. Although she did not know whether the story was true, she believed Burt Kaplan was capable of personally pouring gasoline on someone and lighting the match.

The letter was written by Vittorio Amuso, the boss of the Lucchese family, as he sat in a prison in rural Connecticut living with the knowledge that he would probably spend the rest of his life looking at the same four walls. He had been caught after months on the run. The letter was handwritten, mostly capital letters, demonstrating a fair acquaintance with spelling and grammar. Mostly it dealt with administrative matters, almost like an internal corporate memo from the CEO to a lower-level vice president.

There was a matter of one associate complaining that another had been given a promotion that just wasn't fair. Amuso, who was not in a position to have a sit-down over this issue, was instructing Anthony Casso on how to deal with it. The Bureau of Prisons assigned people to read all inmate mail, so there were no real names, just pretend names. An associate named Rafie was called Fat Pizza Guy. A soldier named Anthony was called Abbie. A soldier named Frank was called Banana; another, named Sal, was called the Golfer. Banana was supposed to "ball out" Abbie and Fat Pizza Guy and keep in touch with the Golfer.

"Whatever you do always leave the strength in our neighborhood," Amuso wrote, stating his belief that it was important that guys from Brooklyn—not from the Bronx—should be running the family. "Fuck the Big Eyes over the bridges."

Then the real message in the letter became clear. Despite the code words and ridiculous nicknames, the underlying theme was obvious to Anthony Casso: deceit is contagious. Deceit is a bastard child that begets bastard progeny. Vic had been caught and convicted on a Sunday. Black Sunday, he called it. Now he had spent enough time inside a cell to become a carrier of this contagion. The longer he sat, the more he became convinced that his lifelong friend and business associate Anthony "Gaspipe" Casso had used information from his friends the cops to turn him in. In the letter, this was not stated overtly, but it was there.

"I am still very puzzuled *[sic]* how they nailed me on Black Sunday!" he wrote. "I'm surprised you never got the true story. That was my last call there that day. I had new number for you. Too late now but I'm still looking for correct story! Take good care, stay healthy, safe, and especially free! Your true friend always."

To Casso, this was Vic's subtle way of saying he believed Casso had given him up to the FBI. Vic had called Casso the day he was arrested. Casso had a new phone number that day, and not long after Vic dialed it he got a visit from the FBI. Casso's "true friend" Vic Amuso was letting Casso know that he no longer trusted him, that all bets were off. It was no longer going to be Vic and Gas. It was now just Gas, on his own. Gas assumed that Vic would do what Gas would do—have him killed whenever it was convenient.

For nearly three years, Anthony Casso successfully avoided being arrested by everybody. Since Anthony went on the lam in May 1990, his family of gangsters was a big mess. The boss, Vic Amuso, had been caught and convicted and probably would die in prison. Fat Pete Chiodo was now cooperating against Vic and Anthony and the rest of them after somebody shot him and then his sister. Al D'Arco was cooperating voluntarily without even an indictment against him. One of Anthony's closest gangster friends, George Zappola, was a fugitive himself due to yet another case. Casso was reduced to keeping in touch with another Lucchese soldier, Frank Lastorino, and his trustworthy partner, Burt Kaplan. Casso was on the run with no end in sight, hiding from the Windows indictment in a suburban split-level owned by one of his girlfriends, Rosemary, in a woody little nowhere place called Budd Lake, New Jersey. He was still using the pay phone setup to communicate with Burt Kaplan, calling from a cell phone to Burt's beeper, plugging in the pay phone's code number, then calling Kaplan at the designated phone.

Casso had set up a nice system so he could take some time off from the girlfriend to see his wife, Lillian. They would meet at a motel in New Jersey arranged by Burt Kaplan. They would sign in under Burt's name, as Mr. and Mrs. Kaplan. This was a system that was working for a long time, despite the best efforts of the FBI, the NYPD, and several U.S. attorneys and DAs across the New York area.

On this Saturday, Burt was driving Lilian to see Anthony when he suddenly had to go to the bathroom really bad. He happened to be driving near the motel that "Mr. and Mrs. Kaplan" frequented, so he pulled into the lot to dash into the restroom. The minute he pulled in he was convinced FBI agents were sitting in an unmarked car watching for Anthony.

When he left the hotel, he told Lillian what he thought and had her look when they drove by the unmarked car. He was sure it was the FBI, so he drove around for an hour until he was sure no one was following, and then he dropped Lillian off at a mall and told her to contact her husband and tell him what they both saw.

To Burt, this was not surprising. The FBI had gone out of their way a number of times to get into the newspaper that they believed Casso was still in the New York area, which, for what it was worth, was true. They were clearly devoting a serious amount of the taxpayers' dollars to tracking down Casso, and now they had succeeded, somewhat. It indicated that the FBI knew more than Burt and Anthony gave them credit for. It also indicated that "Mr. and Mrs. Kaplan" would not be returning to this particular motel.

January 19, 1993

When the team of agents crashed through the door of the split-level on Waterloo Road in Budd Lake, New Jersey, the fearsome Mafia kingpin stood wrapped in a towel in the bathroom, dripping wet from the shower. It was fair to say that he had not been expecting this.

It had been a long time coming. A week earlier, a federal judge had authorized the wiretap of Frank Lastorino's phone in Brooklyn. For days they listened to Casso order Lastorino to do this and that, mostly having to do with getting more money to Casso as soon as possible. It was apparent that Casso believed nobody could find him if he talked on a cell phone. In this regard, technology was not his friend. The FBI had figured out how to trace calls to and from Frank Lastorino's phone in Brooklyn to a particular cell phone beacon near Mount Olive in northern New Jersey. That was all they needed. They already knew of Casso's girlfriend Rosemary, and thought her pleasant split-level in nearby Budd Lake, New Jersey, might be a comfortable spot for Casso to hide. In the predawn hours, agents surrounded the house and waited in the woods.

They had no idea if Casso was home, but they didn't want to enter while the girlfriend was inside. Watching from the trees, they saw her emerge from the house, hop in a Jeep, and drive away. As soon as she was out of sight, they moved in.

Casso did as he was told. The agents worked their way through the house, discovering two suitcases stuffed with $340,000 in cash, lists of proposed members of the Lucchese and Gambino families, an undated letter from Amuso to Casso, and names of all the current Lucchese crews and their respective captains. They found a package marked "Rat," which contained records pertaining to Al D'Arco. They also found a pile of internal FBI documents related to Anthony Casso and various activities within the Lucchese crime family. There was a list of names that included "Borielo"and "Lino."

There also were some scrawlings on a yellow notepad that the FBI made sure to set aside. At the top of the pad was the name Anthony Rotondo, a captain in the DeCavalcante family of New Jersey. Rotondo was a college-educated gangster who had been around for years without getting arrested. He had some dispute with the Lucchese family over jukeboxes owned by Rotondo. Casso had asked Kaplan to find an address on Rotondo, and he'd come up with one in Brooklyn that was wrong. Casso asked him to check with his friends the cops, and they had found the correct address on Barlow Avenue in Staten Island. That address and Rotondo's date of birth were scrawled on the yellow pad. The FBI noted that somebody—either the cops or Kaplan—also had scrawled a single word next to the address: "Guaranteed."

Whenever one's friends get arrested and face the probability of spending the rest of their lives in jail, the prospect inevitably arises that they'll begin remembering all the bad things their friends did and turn those memories into a key. Burt Kaplan did not see his old friend Anthony Casso that way. If anybody was a stand-up guy, it was Anthony Casso. Casso hated rats. He'd killed a busload of them. Of course, Casso hadn't done time since the 1970s. That was a long time to get used to walking around in the daylight. Still, Burt felt Casso would do his time like his lifelong friend Vic Amuso. Vic faced a fifty-four-count racketeering indictment that included pretty much every crime a hardworking gangster could commit, and he didn't fold. He went to trial, got convicted, and probably would never see the outside of a prison again. Anthony Casso, whom most believed was twice as tough as Vic, would surely take his medicine and keep his mouth shut.

TWENTY-ONE

February 1994

The federal court in downtown Brooklyn is where the gangsters of New York face their moment of truth. They come in, they get indicted, they plan on getting acquitted, but it usually doesn't work out. Then they go to prison and die. Or they do their time, go out on the street, do more crimes, and then come back for another visit. Or they conclude that all of this really isn't working out, and they stand up before their peers and confess their sins in the hope of rising again. They cross that line to die or to become the thing they most reviled in their other life, a rat. In the basement of the courthouse in a room without windows, Anthony Casso was facing his moment.

For the prosecutors, Greg O'Connell and Charles Rose, this little sit-down had been long in the making, going all the way back to the plumber who demanded payment for Funzi Tieri's toilet. The plumber had begat Barclay Faranza who begat Pete Savino who begat the Windows case, which begat Al D'Arco and Fat Pete Chiodo, who in turn begat Anthony Casso. Convergence. O'Connell recalled reminding Casso that he was indicted in the Windows case and in another case that charged him with eight murders. He also let him know that more charges were on the way. O'Connell made it clear to Casso that his former colleagues in the Lucchese family Al D'Arco and Pete Chiodo had been very helpful about recalling all the things Anthony had either done himself or told them to do. To make things worse, Anthony had learned in prison that his old friend Vic Amuso had put out a contract on Anthony. The old team of Vic and Gas was no more. Vic wanted Anthony dead, primarily because he feared that Anthony would do what he was now preparing to do.

Anthony had called up FBI Agent Richard Rudolph, the agent who'd come to the house in New Jersey when he stood there in his towel. He'd told Agent Rudolph he needed to talk, and the federal government made all the arrangements. In prison, if you decide to cooperate with the government, they move you away from everybody else. When somebody gets moved, everybody assumes he's cooperating. Anthony wasn't yet cooperating formally, so they dreamed up a ruse in case things didn't work out. On a day when he had a scheduled court appearance, they had him come in early and sit in the basement of the court with Greg O'Connell and Charles Rose and tell them what was on his mind.

It was clear why Anthony was there. He didn't want to be the last guy standing on the sinking ship. Sammy Gravano had figured that one out. Just like Anthony Casso, Gravano was a scheming sociopath, but he had decided to turn on his boss, John Gotti, and soon he'd be getting out of jail. If Anthony cooperated, he might have the same shot. If he didn't, he would grow very old in prison. The prosecutors had offered him a deal that wasn't much of a deal: plead guilty without cooperation, get twenty-two years. He would be turning fifty-four in May, which could mean he'd be seventy-six years old when he walked out the door. Prosecutors O'Connell and Rose made it clear he could go to the movies or take a leisurely walk in the park much sooner. It was his choice. All Anthony Casso had to do was become a rat.

It was a different world now. Rats were everywhere. Besides Sammy in the Gambino family and Al D'Arco and Fat Pete in the Lucchese family, the Colombo family was infested with them. Carmine Sessa, the consigliere, had surrendered to the FBI in front of St. Patrick's Cathedral in Manhattan and immediately seen the light. Fat Sal Micciotta, a Colombo soldier who weighed nearly four hundred pounds, had come in from the cold. And now it was rumored that Greg Scarpa Sr., one of the most dangerous guys ever to call himself a goodfella, had been working with the FBI for years. Being a rat was becoming almost normal.

There were certain advantages. Clearly Gravano had hit the home run. He admitted to nineteen murders, including his brother-in-law, and the word was he would be out within the year. All he had to do was give up every friend he ever had. His name was reviled throughout Brooklyn, but who was the winner and who was the loser? The boss, John Gotti, would keep his mouth shut and die in jail, while Sammy would walk the streets a free man with a new name. The same with Al D'Arco and Fat Pete. Both of them could be out at any time, as soon as the government wrote one of those special letters to the judge explaining how you may have murdered the sons and brothers of a dozen families, but you were now atoning by telling the truth for the first time ever. Unless he did something about it, Anthony Casso would from now on only see his wife and two children across a table in a prison visiting room with guards watching every moment.

The session in the basement was called a proffer because if it didn't work out, the prosecutors had agreed they wouldn't use the information Casso revealed against him. Everyone would go on pretending like they never had the conversation, with Casso pretending he was wrongly accused and prosecutors pretending that they weren't using the information he had told them. Casso agreed that he would meet with the prosecutors and agents without his attorney, Michael Rosen, who would be showing up at the courthouse later in the day.

O'Connell and Rose were reluctant to talk to Casso. The other informants they worked with made it clear he was a serial killer who liked to torture his victims before finishing them off. He was a sick puppy and would make Sammy Gravano seem like a decent guy who made a few bad choices. The FBI, however, wanted to listen. The other informants had mentioned Casso was always bragging about his law-enforcement source, a guy he always referred to cryptically as "the agent." The FBI needed to know if "the agent" was *their* agent, so the meeting in the basement of the courthouse was arranged.

"He proffered for two hours," O'Connell recalled. "He goes from almost charming and pleasant, a sense of humor, almost jocular, to cold and absolutely remorseless where he drifts into his anecdotes, entertaining himself and laughing at the rememberances. In the late seventies, there was a marijuana boat called *Terry's Dream*. He was telling a story about how he was worried about the captain's son and tells him to come down next to Alligator Alley in Florida. Casso is there with this other wiseguy. Gaspipe shot the kid. When he's telling the story, he said, 'The kid had fallen down on my car and got blood on my car. I had to take the car apart. Then I seen him in the grave and the kid sits up. I took a shovelful of dirt and shoved it in his mouth and held him down until he choked.' "

This was the kind of stuff they would have to contend with if Anthony came over to their side. Still, the FBI wanted to know about "the agent." They kept the questions generic, so it wouldn't seem like they were giving him ideas about what to say. They asked him whether he knew of any connections in law enforcement, prepared to hear him drop the name of a specific FBI agent.

Casso confirmed what Al D'Arco had said years before—that Salvatore Avellino, the Golfer, had been paying an FBI agent for years. He recalled that in 1987, the Golfer met with Casso and Amuso in the Toys "R" Us parking lot off Flatbush Avenue, the same one where Jimmy Hydell spent some of his final hours. The Golfer told them that his FBI source had learned of an associate named Finnegan who was cooperating with law enforcement. Casso and Amuso had never heard of a Finnegan. Avellino handed them a piece of paper with the real name of the informant, Donato Christiano. Casso and Amuso still didn't recognize the name.

Then Casso stopped talking about "the agent" and began talking about something else nobody had been expecting.

There were also these two cops, he said. Detectives in the NYPD for many years. One guy was fat and loud, the other guy was skinny with connections to a task force. Their names were Louis Eppolito and Stephen Caracappa. He knew what they looked like. He'd seen their pictures in a book. They had checked out the name Donato Christiano and found out that he was, in fact, a cooperator. They were extremely helpful in these matters.

In the coming weeks, it got worse and worse with the stories about the cops. Casso began to spend a lot of time talking about the cops. The meetings took place with FBI Agents James Brennan and Dick Rudolph and U.S. Attorneys Greg O'Connell and Charles Rose in the rural foothills of Pennsylvania. These were law-enforcement agents. They had seen and heard a lot of bad things over the years. This was maybe the worst. This was two of New York City's finest getting paid to completely subvert the system they were sworn to uphold. Rudolph and Brennan and O'Connell and Rose were not guys who said "I'm shocked" very often. In this case, they said it over and over again.

It was a festering mess within the New York City Police Department for more than a decade.

No detail was too lurid when Casso described how the cops used their shields to help kidnap Jimmy Hydell.

Casso told the story as if he were sitting around a campfire, trying to entertain with a story he knew would give his listeners nightmares. To Casso, it was entertainment. He revealed that another gangster had told him he had tried for weeks to kill Jimmy Hydell, but the day he finally spotted Jimmy in Brooklyn he saw two guys who looked like cops pick up Hydell in what looked like an unmarked car. Casso described everything—how he saw the cops in the Toys "R" Us parking lot, how he brought Jimmy to the basement of Jimmy Gallo's home, how he brought the two Gambino gangsters over to have Jimmy say in front of everybody how he tried to kill Casso at the behest of the Gambino family. Then, for the first time, Anthony Casso described the end of Jimmy Hydell in the basement.

"Amuso and Casso reentered the basement," the FBI report stated. "Casso took a .22 automatic pistol with a silencer and repeatedly shot Hydell, killing him. Amuso and Casso removed the body from the basement and placed it in the trunk of the green Plymouth, along with the gun. Casso drove the car several blocks and parked near a boat yard." Casso claimed they called two subordinates, who later told him Hydell was "in a parking lot in Canarsie."

"It was very convincing," O'Connell said. "He was anxious to tell us."

He talked about this murder and that murder involving the cops and said there was a lot more and he would explain everything. He claimed he only learned their names for sure after buying the book, *Mafia Cop*. He pointed out that there was another guy out there who would corroborate everything he was saying. His name was Burt Kaplan, an ailing Garment Center businessman who was the middleman between the cops and the Lucchese crime family. Burt, Casso explained, could tell you everything you need to know.

Kaplan was the one who gave him the details of the final moments of Eddie Lino. Kaplan had told him the cops followed Lino for days in an unmarked car with stolen plates and pulled him over on the service road. They shot him in the head. Kaplan claimed Caracappa even exited the car after the hit to make sure Lino was dead and had been seen by a witness as he ran back into the car with Eppolito to speed away.

As the meetings with the FBI and prosecutors progressed, there was a tentative agreement to work out a cooperation deal. O'Connell called Casso's lawyer, Rosen, who was stuck in traffic on the way to the court for what he believed to be yet another appearance in a case that would take a year to settle. O'Connell told him his services were no longer needed. Rosen knew immediately what had happened.

On March 1, Casso stood before a federal judge in the Brooklyn courthouse and pleaded guilty to a seventy-two-count racketeering indictment, including fifteen murders. He had a new lawyer, a new jail cell, and a new identity. He would be better than the guy he always wanted to kill, Sammy Gravano. Like Sammy, maybe one day soon he'd be back out on the street, walking among all those boring civilians who worked for a living he'd always despised.

By the time Anthony Casso started talking about Lou Eppolito and Steve Caracappa, law enforcement in New York was already combating the collective headache caused by numerous revelations and allegations involving bad cops and bad agents all over the five boroughs of New York.

Besides Eppolito and Caracappa and Sal Avellino's FBI agent, Casso also told them of yet another cop on the payroll. In this case a gangster named Sammy Kaplan, who everybody thought was related to Burt but really was not, had his own contact within the New York City Police Department. This contact, whose name Casso did not know, had helped out with an informant problem. The cop had obtained a mug shot of a low-level gangster named Richie the Barber whom Casso and Amuso had decided was cooperating. With the photograph, one of Casso's soldiers was able to track down Richie the Barber for a haircut. During the haircut, he casually learned Richie's work habits and that he drove a Mustang. A few weeks later, when Richie the Barber closed up shop and walked toward his Mustang, Casso walked up and shot him. Somehow Richie survived, but the attempt on his life had been a complete mystery to everyone until Casso opened his mouth.

Over in the Gambino family there was Detective William Piest of the NYPD's Intelligence Division—the unit that collects and analyzes information on organized crime. Piest had admitted leaking secrets to John Gotti for years. In the course of that investigation, the FBI had learned that one of Gotti's lawyers, Mike Coiro, had claimed to have a separate corrupt law-enforcement source who could confirm or deny whether specific individuals had become informants. Coiro the lawyer denied everything and said, like Claude Raines in *Casablanca*, that he was shocked to hear of such allegations, and the matter went nowhere.

In the forever dysfunctional Colombo family the FBI had won over a new informant, consigliere Carmine Sessa.

He was telling the FBI all about another gangster, Greg Scarpa Sr., who had a law-enforcement source he called "the girlfriend." Scarpa Sr. was one of the most violent gangsters in New York, and it had always struck Sessa as odd that he would kill and kill and nobody would arrest him. Scarpa Sr. claimed "the girlfriend" had tipped him off when his son was about to be arrested by the Drug Enforcement Administration (DEA), and he usually could find out pretty quickly where the other side in the Colombo war was hiding out. Here was another gangster talking about Scarpa Sr.'s "girlfriend."

And Sessa claimed yet another Colombo gangster also had his own source in law enforcement. A soldier everybody called Joey Brewster claimed he grew up with an FBI agent in Bensonhurst, and the agent had warned him to stay away from Scarpa. This was another dead end because Sessa only had a first name for the agent, and he wasn't sure why the agent would tell Joey Brewster to stay away from Scarpa, the long-time informant.

And still another Colombo soldier, named Larry Mazza, corroborated Sessa's story about Greg Scarpa and "the girl-friend," but he also indicated there was somebody else in law enforcement whispering to the Mob. He recalled walking around a running track at Otisville prison in upstate New York with a number of other Colombo gangsters, including a capo named Teddy Persico. He claimed he had learned who was cooperating from an Organized Crime Task Force member who was not an FBI agent.

Dinnertime and Burt Kaplan was taking a bath in his home on Eighty-fifth Street in Bensonhurst when the phone rang downstairs. His wife, Eleanor, called up that his lawyer, Judd, was on the phone.

"Tell him I'm in the tub," he hollered down. "Tell him to call back in half an hour."

Judd had been very helpful lately. The FBI had come after Burt again, this time claiming he was trying to sell illegal Peruvian passports to the Chinese. In July 1993 they got an actual indictment and came to his house at 8:30 A.M. As he was walking down his driveway they arrested him in front of all the neighbors. During the arrest, he asked what he'd done. When they told him, he said, "These are bullshit charges and the FBI could get me dead to rights on eighty different things but these passports are legit." He wondered if the agents waited for him to exit his house so they could confiscate his briefcase. He knew that the cops' numbers were in a little black book in the briefcase under the name Marco, but he figured the FBI wouldn't have a clue.

It didn't make sense that Judd was calling about the

passports. He'd successfully blown up the indictment, just like he did before with the heroin. He and Burt had been allowed to travel to China, even, to show that the Chinese government had approved of the sale of the passports. The indictment was voided, and Burt went about his business.

Five minutes later, the phone rang again. It was Judd. Now Burt pulled himself out of the tub and wrapped himself in a towel. He picked up the phone in the bathroom. Standing there dripping on the tile, Burt said, "Yeah, Judd, what seems to be the problem? You said you'd call back in half an hour."

"Are you sitting down?" Judd asked.

"What do you mean? Don't fool around."

"Anthony went bad."

"Anthony Russo?"

"Anthony Casso."

"Are you crazy?" Burt said, his voice beginning to rise. "Are you trying to get us both killed? Why would you say something like that?"

In his nine years of dealing with Burt, Judd had never heard Burt get excited. He was always the same, unflappable, his face revealing nothing, his tone of voice nearly monotone. When he told a joke sometimes it was hard to tell if he was trying to be funny. Now Burt was upset.

"He fired his attorney and he has a government attorney and he definitely went bad," Judd said.

"Thank you very much," Burt said, and hung up.

Burt couldn't believe what he had heard.

"I felt sick because I thought Mr. Casso, if anybody in the world was a stand-up person, I thought it was him. Secondly, I knew I was facing a lot of problems legally. Because Casso was aware of the whole situation that was going on between Louie and Steve. I felt that the only way the government would take someone like Casso as a cooperator, I knew of many, many, many bodies that he had, and later on I found out that he admitted to thirty-eight, but I knew twenty-five at that time, and I felt, being in the street like I was, that why would the government take a guy like Casso who had so much baggage unless he could give them something sensational back? To me it was the relationship between Steve, Louie, I and Frankie, Junior and him."

This was the power of the coconspirator. Kaplan believed Anthony Casso did not know for sure the name of the two cops, but because of that foolish book, he had a pretty good idea who they were. "He could make an educated guess," was the way Burt saw it. This scenario offered little comfort. Burt could not be sure that the FBI wouldn't be able to use enough of what Anthony said to put him and the two cops in jail. He was aware that Anthony would be a tough witness. His behavior with Jimmy Hydell alone would make that so. But he was also aware that the FBI would be very interested in going after two profoundly corrupt NYPD detectives. It was time for Burt to go.

Burt left his house and went to a pay phone down the street. He called his errand boy Tommy Galpine, his gun-toting driver Herman Bannerman, and his fellow ex-con Michael Gordon, to meet him at the house. When they arrived, he let everybody know he was going away for a while and started issuing orders. Some money would continue to go to Tommy Irish's wife, who was sick and needed it. He gathered up as much money as he could, including cash his wife had saved in the house. He told Tommy Galpine to scrounge up some marijuana money to replace it, and then asked Gordon to do him a favor. He needed to see somebody right away, but he did not want to drive his own Oldsmobile.

The apartment building at 12 East 22nd Street in Manhattan was like ten thousand others. No doorman. Eighty-eight apartments where residents know maybe two other people's names. People kept to themselves there. Maybe the only exception to that rule went on in the one-bedroom known as Apartment 10A, which happened to be the number Burt Kaplan was looking for when he arrived at the door.

Kaplan was vaguely aware that Detective Steve Caracappa lived in Apartment 10A with his girlfriend Monica, another tenant of 12 East 22nd Street. He had lived in another apartment on another floor, but they had met in the hall and things developed. Now Steve had moved in with Monica, who sold umbrellas and owned a fat cat. They lived together in Apartment 10A, and it was Monica who answered the buzzer.

"Is Steve in? It's Burt."

"He's asleep."

"Wake him up. It's an emergency."

In the apartment the two men sat down across from each other. Kaplan felt embarrassed.

"We got a real problem," he said, and he explained about Anthony going bad. This was the moment when the ropes that hold the logs together on the raft in the middle of the ocean start to come apart. Everybody runs around, frantically trying to tie the ropes back together, as the fins circle. Burt was here to let Steve know he was going away for a while and that he wasn't going to behave like Anthony.

"Do you need any money?" Caracappa asked. "Do you need me to take care of your wife?"

"No, Steve. Thank you very much. I have money."

"Well, if you ever do need money in the future, just let me know," Steve said. "I'll take care of your wife."

"Can you control Louie?"

Burt considered himself a stand-up guy, and he felt Steve was a stand-up guy. Louie, he wasn't so sure. Over the years he'd always felt Louie couldn't control his impulses. He was always lecturing Louie about his inability to understand the concept of assets versus liability. Burt didn't know where all Louie's money went. Louie was always begging him for more and promising to pay back right away, which he rarely did. Burt called this "flamboyant," which was a nice way to say "unstable."

"Can you take care of the situation with him?" Burt asked.

"Louie's been my partner and I trust him and don't worry about it."

The two men hugged and kissed on the cheek and Burt walked out of Apartment 10A into the spring Manhattan night. He didn't know where he was going or what he was going to do when he got there.

He had a wife and a grown-up daughter and a house and car payments and what appeared to be a life. Millions would envy what Burt had acquired: a reasonable facsimile of success. He had strived to be routine. He got up every morning, kissed his wife good-bye, drove to work in the Olds, and made money any way he could. All to give his daughter the one thing he could never possess: legitimacy. Legitimacy cost money. He paid the college bills, footed the bill for the parking garage in the city his daughter and her husband used. And his progeny had made it. She worked like a slave for paltry wages at the Legal Aid Society, defending the indigent. She had gotten herself appointed as an arbitrator in Small Claims Court, a classic first step for those who wish to become a judge. On her walls hung the bachelor's degree from the State University at Albany and the juris doctorate from St. John's University School of Law. That was achievement. Burt's life resembled a life to which millions of Americans aspired. Now it might all be gone.

Burt knew what he had to do. He needed to chuck it all: the house, the car, the wife, the daughter, the job. All were tied to Burt Kaplan, unindicted coconspirator. Burt Kaplan, whose name was being scribbled down in some FBI agent's notebook even as he left Steve and Monica and the fat cat on East Twenty-second Street. That name had to be erased for the time being. He needed to disappear for a while. He knew a guy in Juárez. He told everybody he was going to China.

TWENTY-TWO

March 26, 1994

For a lot of NYPD detectives, the goal is to put in your twenty years, snag a security job, and collect the pension. If possible, retire to a place where there are other NYPD retirees: Westchester County or way out on Long Island. Spend your off hours remembering the great collars, the wimpy DAs, the weak-kneed judges, the slick defense lawyers, and all the perps and mopes that brought them all together in the never-ending comic opera that is the criminal justice system. Or you could go to Vegas.

Whatever plays in Vegas, stays in Vegas. Wayne Newton. Elvis in his jumpsuit phase. Bugsy Siegel. The Rat Pack. An oasis of venality located conveniently between Phoenix and LA, where the castles of the desert—the Trop, the Sands, the Crazy Horse, Caesar's Palace—offer whatever you could want: slots, craps, roulette, blackjack, promises, promises, promises. The glamour and the sleaze. Not a known hangout for retired cops, but this was where Lou Eppolito landed.

He wanted to move to Hollywood. He would say California, but he meant Hollywood. He envisioned the whole thing: he'd write screenplays, have meetings with big directors, drop names like Scorcese, make the big pitch. People were eating

up cop movies, and he had twenty-one years of stories. He
flew his wife and kids out to LA and they hated it. *Hated it.*
"The people are not like New York people," Fran said. He said
okay. They'd stay in New York. Then his best friend, Steve
Caracappa, happened to mention Vegas in passing as a place
he might want to retire to.

Fran's ears perked up. She could do that. Louie thought
about it for fifteen minutes and put a For Sale sign on the front
yard of his Long Island home. They flew again out West, and
Fran and the kids loved it. Neither Fran nor Louie gambled,
and Louie figured it was 250 miles from LA. Vegas it was.

On February 10, 1994, he sold the house on Long Island.
Four days later, on Valentine's Day 1994, Lou arrived in the
Nevada desert still looking like a guy from Brooklyn. He was
renting a house while he had another one built. It was going
to be the best: five thousand square feet, and it would triple in
value. Las Vegas was the hottest real-estate market in the nation. Everybody was moving out there. People sick of Hollywood were moving. Lou figured he was ahead of the curve.
He was going to turn it all around. The NYPD and everything
he believed they had done to him were 2,200 miles behind
him. He was working on a screenplay and he had a hundred
more in his head. He was setting up meetings in Hollywood.
He had an agent. He had the bit part as Fat Andy the gangster
in *Goodfellas*, about Italian gangsters, then as a cop with Sean
Penn in *State of Grace*, about Irish gangsters. He claimed to
have done rewrites on movies called *Deep Cover* and *Wings
of Steel*. He had small roles in action movies: *Street Hunter*,
Switch, *Predator 2*, *Company Business*, *Ruby*, *Mad Dog and
Glory*, *The Italian Movie*, and *Handgun*. He even showed up
in a Woody Allen film, *Bullets Over Broadway*. He was
telling people he was a "guest star" in a TV movie, *Kojack—
True Blue*. It was nothing but good ahead.

Then he woke up on a March morning and the phone rang
and it was his coauthor on *Mafia Cop*, Bob Drury. Drury
wanted to know if he would speak with a friend of his, Jerry
Capeci, the organized-crime reporter for the *New York Daily
News*. He agreed, and in a few minutes Capeci called and
started asking questions about Anthony Casso. A few weeks
earlier Capeci had reported that Casso was cooperating with

federal prosecutors in the Eastern District of New York. Casso was saying all kinds of things, but one of the things he was saying was that he had two city detectives on his payroll who had whacked a gangster, Eddie Lino, for him. Capeci now wanted to know if Louie had ever heard of Anthony Casso or Eddie Lino. Louie said that of course he knew who they were. They were big-time gangsters. Everybody in the Sixty-third Precinct knew those names. Capeci asked if he ever met them. Had he been told by one to kill the other? "Absolutely not," said Lou. He denied everything and started hollering at Capeci about Casso being from another family.

The next morning Eppolito and Caracappa—who had retired from Major Case but was still working a private security job in New York—saw their names in the newspapers along with Casso's allegations. There had been stories about Casso and unnamed cops, but this was the first one to actually name names. The *Daily News* headline stated, "Hitman Charges Stun Ex-Cop." There was a doleful photo of Eppolito only, wearing his usual gold chains with the open collar.

"I thought it was just bullshit," Eppolito said. "They're just dragging my name through it. It didn't bother me that much. I called Bruce Cutler at his office. I said, 'Did you see that thing in the paper?' I said, 'They're talking about me.' Bruce said, 'Send me five thousand dollars and I'll represent you.'"

November 1994

Three New Yorkers sat in a restaurant in the middle of the Nevada desert. It was in a giant mall around the corner from a giant supermarket next to gas stations with giant signs stretching up into the vast blue sky. This could be in any city in America. There were fast-food restaurants and drugstore chains and an ATM every six blocks. There were no sidewalks or people walking around. This was where everybody drove in cars everywhere. This was Tropicana Boulevard, Las Vegas, Nevada, where there were slot machines in the supermarkets for your convenience.

Steve Caracappa and Lou Eppolito sat with Burt Kaplan, three men trapped in the same narrative. All were going about their lives, making a paycheck as best they could. All were waiting to see what would happen with Anthony Casso back in New York, like that guy under the swinging blade in "The Pit and the Pendulum." Anthony Casso's voice was the ghost that haunted their every decision. Each of the three men felt that at any time, everything they had could be taken away.

From a practical point of view, there was not much they could do except wait. Burt had heard that Anthony Casso had put out a contract on his life, and as a demonstration of friendship, Steve and Louie said that if Casso ever succeeded, they would kill him, and if that didn't work out, they'd kill his son. They tried to think of ways to attack whatever Casso was saying, although they didn't know much about that except what was in the papers. They knew for sure about Eddie Lino. Steve thought of an excuse for the Eddie Lino matter. He had been working the shooting of Meir Kahane the day before, and he had dinner with a famous hostess of a cable TV show the night after. He might be able to get her to say it was the same night that Eddie Lino got his. As for the rest, they would just have to wait and see.

Burt was moving forward with his life on the premise that if he hadn't been indicted a few weeks after Anthony became a government informer, it probably wasn't going to happen. He continued to run his Staten Island clothing business from twenty-two hundred miles away, making sure plenty of money got to his wife, Eleanor, back in Bensonhurst. He was now settled in Oregon after months of traveling around from California to Mexico to Vegas. In Oregon he went to the library and got a card under the name Barry Mayers. He used that to get a card from Triple A. Then he got put on a list at Costco, and they sent him an ID for that. Now he had three valid IDs. He went to Motor Vehicles in Portland, and that was all he needed to become Barry Mayers. His nondriver ID card had a photo of Barry Mayers who looked just like Burt Kaplan, smiling.

With his new identity, Burt was planning on moving to Vegas from Oregon. He was setting up a business, Garment City Warehouse, with some old friends he knew from the business. His name couldn't show up on paper, but it would be his business. His plan was to sell mostly ladies' suits to the women who worked in the casinos. "Give them a good suit for a good value," he said. He was staying at Caesar's Palace but was planning on moving to a condo called Paradise Valley. Now with his new name, Barry Mayers, Burt felt comfortable tracking down his old friend Detective Second Grade Louis Eppolito.

He'd known since the day Louie pulled up with the giant white RV that Louie was in Vegas, and now that Anthony Casso was working for the FBI, Burt was somewhat concerned that the self-proclaimed "Mafia cop" might succumb to certain pressures and join Anthony. Burt was paranoid all the time now. His eyesight was lousy, so he asked his girlfriend there, Louisa, to look up Eppolito's name in the phone book, and there it was. He didn't want to visit him or even call him on the phone because he believed there might be surveillance, so he had Louisa call and set up a meeting. They met at a supermarket near the restaurant where they were now sitting, and they walked around the fruit department pushing wire carts talking about the guy they all had in common back there in New York talking to the FBI.

Steve still lived his life in New York. He'd retired and worked a security job for a merchant's organization on Fourteenth Street in Manhattan, which allowed him to be the only one of the three of them to be there to read in the *Daily News* all about Anthony Casso flipping over to the government side. For a number of weeks, when the stories first came out in March 1994, Steven had been most upset that his aging mother knew of the stories in the newspaper, but he'd hired a lawyer, Edward Hayes, who had tried to get the prosecutors to say if they were going to bring charges. Months had gone by, and so far there were no charges. Now Steve was out in Vegas, too, looking to establish a Vegas office for a private investigative firm he was working for. He offered to do surveillance for Burt, to see if he had anybody following him, but Burt felt that wasn't necessary.

Louie had a few rough months as well when the stories first came out, but his lawyer, Bruce Cutler, offered to have both Louie and Steve take lie detector tests. The prosecutors had refused. Cutler had told him not to worry about it, so instead Louie worried about money, as he always did. He had ordered a five-thousand-square-foot house, and now he didn't want it. He wanted another house that was even bigger, but the builder of the first house said he couldn't give him his down payment back until he actually sold the house. With the threat of Anthony Casso and the FBI sitting like black clouds on the desert horizon, Louie Eppolito mostly wanted to talk about money.

"Listen," Eppolito said to Kaplan. "I need a big favor."

Just like all the times before, Louie just needed to borrow some money for a little while. He'd pay it back as soon as he could. He only needed seventy-five thousand dollars as down payment on the second house he wanted, and he asked Burt to go to a shylock to borrow the money. He was willing to pay a point.

"You got to be crazy," Burt said.

"I'll pay a point," Eppolito said.

"How can you afford to pay seven hundred and fifty dollars a week? That's crazy," Kaplan said. "But you're my friend. Let me make some phone calls and see if I can borrow the money off of somebody that I do my marijuana business with. I also owe the guy a lot of money and he trusts me with large amounts, and I'm going to ask him if I can juggle the seventy-five thousand. This way it won't cost you any interest."

In a few weeks, Kaplan made the arrangements. He borrowed seventy-five thousand dollars from his marijuana connection, a guy he knew only as Dave. One of his friends delivered it the way they always delivered marijuana money: five-thousand-dollar bundles of forty-one hundred bills wrapped as Christmas presents. Burt took ten thousand dollars of it and bet it on Super Bowl 1995, San Francisco versus San Diego. He took the rest and met Louie at Caesar's Palace, where he had been staying for a while.

"Thank you," Louie said.

"I'm trying to keep you out of trouble," Kaplan said. "So try to pay it back as soon as possible."

"You saved my life with this money, and I really appreciate it, and the minute I get the money I'm going to give it to you," Louie said.

At times Burt Kaplan saw Louie Eppolito the way a father views a son who has lost his way. "Louie on occasion came to me and said he needed to borrow money and I said, 'I don't understand you, Louie. Do you have any bad habits?' And he said, 'No, I don't gamble. And I don't do drugs.' I said, 'How come you're always in trouble with money? Your end is two thousand a month plus you have your salary.' He said, 'I collect snakes, very expensive snakes and it costs a lot of money to feed them and a lot of money to buy them and I like doing things like that.' And Louie always wore three, four chains, five, five rings on his fingers, and I tried to preach to him as an older guy that he should be more conscious of the way he spends his money and stop getting himself under pressure all the time."

The San Francisco 49ers beat the San Diego Chargers, 49 to 26 at Joe Robbie Stadium in Miami. Burt Kaplan put down ten thousand dollars that he was supposed to be borrowing for Louie Eppolito, and although he had for years referred to himself as a degenerate gambler and had tried to kick the habit again and again with Gamblers Anonymous, he won. As a gambler, he had to believe in luck.

The marriage was falling apart. It just wasn't working out between Anthony Casso and the U.S. government. It was a difficult relationship from the start, but Casso knew a lot, and the government really needed him to help prosecute Vincent Gigante, the boss of the Genovese family, a rational man who eluded prison for years by pretending to be nuts. The federal prosecutors in Brooklyn tried for years to put Gigante in prison, but his crazy performance worked wonders with a number of highly paid professional psychologists who decided he had to be crazy because no normal person would behave like this for so long, walking around Greenwich Village unshaven in a ratty bathrobe muttering about Jesus. The government entered into the marriage with Casso because Casso could say he was at meetings where Gigante was as clear-spoken as Laurence Olivier doing *Hamlet*. Then the marriage began to fall apart.

When they first pulled him out of the federal lockup in Brooklyn, they flew him to the middle of the desert where New Mexico and Texas meet the Mexican border. The federal facility was called La Tuna, and it was the same spot where

Joe Valachi began cooperating years ago. When he first began his little waltz with the federal government, Casso was charming and happy to help out. He would meet for hours and hours again and again with FBI agents Richard Rudolph and Robert Brennan and assistant U.S. attorneys Charles Rose and Greg O'Connell. All four were experienced men who were fully aware that meeting with the likes of Anthony Casso was always a matter of separating what could be true from what really was true. Since Casso was a criminal, it was difficult to compare his declarations with, say, the written record. One way to test if Casso was telling the truth was to compare what he said with what other informants who came before him said.

At first, Casso freely and enthusiastically admitted that he was personally involved in fifteen murders. The numbers didn't add up. Informants such as Fat Pete Chiodo and Al D'Arco counted more murders. Okay, Casso said. Maybe it was twenty-six. Then they went back to Chiodo and D'Arco and others and realized they might be talking about thirty-five murders. That many victims would fill a school bus. Casso got increasingly vague about this.

There was the matter of Fat Pete Chiodo's sister. Somebody tried to kill her. As far as the murderers and other liars within organized crime were concerned, this was just wrong. It was completely against the "rules" of organized crime that say you don't kill sisters and mothers and aunts. Casso claimed he had nothing to do with this attempt to kill the sister. Unfortunately, the FBI had already heard from several other informants on their payroll that the whole idea of shooting the sister was Anthony Casso's in the first place.

Then Casso provided more stories—in fact, many more stories—in direct contradiction to the words of other former members of the highly disciplined Mafia who had become informants for the United States. Salvatore Gravano, for instance, the former vice president of the Gambinos. Here he was billed by the government as the greatest thing to come out of Brooklyn since the Coney Island Cyclone, the guy who put John Gotti in jail. Of course, it was John Gotti who put John Gotti in jail, but Salvatore Gravano was nonetheless important to the federal government. It was necessary that he be telling the truth. Throughout his hours of debriefings with the FBI,

Gravano had insisted again and again that he was dead set against the sale and distribution of narcotics. He claimed that narcotics were bad for business because they always led to more informants. Prison sentences for drugs were so bad there would surely be dozens of guys lining up to cooperate, and then the whole card castle would crash down. Never, Sammy said, was I involved in drugs.

Ho, ho, said Anthony Casso. He told the FBI right away that he and Sammy and Eddie Lino had been involved in a big marijuana deal when Sammy got busted. They were going to have the stuff brought in on a fishing boat out of Sheepshead Bay called *The Hunter*. He laid it all out, explaining how at the last minute they had to switch from marijuana to cocaine and packed it in burlap sacks on ice marked Seafood. The federal government now had two guys who were supposed to be telling the truth telling two different stories about the same incident.

There were many differences of fact between Casso and Gravano.

"During my debriefings I had told SAs Rudolph and Brennan about a meeting that I attended several years ago at La Tavilla restaurant on 92nd St in Brooklyn along with John Gotti, Vic Amuso and Gravano," Casso later wrote. "During the meeting I told Gotti and Gravano that the two NYPD Detectives on my payroll had given me the name of an informant who provided information leading to the probable cause finding for a wiretap of Angelo Ruggiero, a Gambino family member. John Gotti told Gravano to check it out and take care of it if there was a problem. This individual, whose name I cannot recall, was later found dead in the trunk of a car on a service road off the Belt Parkway just before the Knapp Street exit. I was later told by the agents that Gravano denied any knowledge of this matter and the agents let the matter drop. I understood this to be a signal not to contradict Gravano."

This also occurred with Al D'Arco, the man who claimed to have been appointed acting boss of the Lucchese crime family by Casso and Vic Amuso. Casso flat out denied this, claiming that D'Arco was never acting boss but just one of four men appointed to a panel that was supposed to run the family while Casso and Amuso were on the run. And Casso was now claiming D'Arco wasn't at half the places he'd said he was. Casso also denied D'Arco's story that Casso wanted to invite all his enemies within the Lucchese family to a dinner and kill them all. Worse, he said D'Arco lied about money. D'Arco claimed when he came in to the U.S. government to cooperate, he had only $30,000 to his name. Casso said his son had hidden $250,000 in a shoebox at a relative's house.

Casso then started biting the hand that could free him. Giving up the two NYPD detectives was one thing. They were cops. Going after federal agents was another thing altogether. He claimed that a Drug Enforcement Agency (DEA) agent had been involved in a fairly celebrated theft of heroin seized in the French Connection case.

"I told the FBI how the theft was arranged by a DEA agent, who was killed many years later by Herbie Pate, who had participated in the theft and whom I drove from the scene of the homicide," Casso wrote.

Finally the FBI confronted Casso about a disturbing story they had heard about his plan to kill one of the prosecutors he'd spent hours with since he agreed to help out the government. At first Casso denied everything. Then he suddenly remembered everything. It was possible that at one time before he came to his senses that in fact he wanted to kill the prosecutor Charles Rose. But he had his reasons, and in his opinion, they were good reasons.

In September 1991, after Casso had ordered the murder of his architect, Anthony Fava, a story appeared in the New York papers about why this may have occurred. The story quoted an unnamed law-enforcement source as stating that Fava had been having an affair with Casso's wife, Lillian. Casso was furious, and so was his wife. She called Casso's lawyer, Gerald Shargel, and asked if a retraction could be obtained. Shargel told her to forget about it, that the newspaper where it ran—*Newsday*—had a tiny circulation and hardly anybody saw the story anyway. Then some guy in prison in Lewisburg said he'd seen the story. This made the wife very angry. Then Casso heard that everybody in the entire City of New York had read the story. Something had to be done.

After this Casso's friend Avellino, the Golfer, told him his contact in law enforcement had told him Charles Rose the prosecutor had been very close to Fat Pete Chiodo and John Miller, a TV reporter. Casso—using the same deductive reasoning that had gotten the wrong Nicky Guido killed—concluded that the business about Lillian Casso and the architect Fava came from Fat Pete Chiodo to Charles Rose, prosecutor, to John Miller the TV reporter straight to *Newsday*.

The FBI report of this conversation notes that Casso employed a complex system of logic in evaluating this information: "Casso was angry with Chiodo and Rose for causing the item to appear in the paper. Casso stated he could understand why Chiodo wanted to get back at him, but expected Rose, a professional, not to have something personal like that appear in public, if indeed Chiodo did relate something like that to him."

That was all Casso needed. He claimed he asked Kaplan to find out from the cops where Rose lived. He claimed he involved only Kaplan and his longtime homicidal friend Georgie Neck in the plan to find the prosecutor because he trusted them more than anyone else. He claimed Kaplan came back with an address of an apartment building on Park Avenue South in Manhattan.

Georgie Neck, with a photo of Rose clipped from a paper, went to Park Avenue South and then to the courthouse in Brooklyn where Rose worked to try to follow him home. He never saw him. At one point Georgie had a contact with a telephone company. He sent him to Rose's Park Avenue South address to find a line on Rose, but that didn't work out either. Then Casso got arrested, and that was that.

Other informants in prison with Casso had already told the government some of this. The FBI and prosecutors Rose and O'Connell had spent hours with Casso, trying to get a full picture of his extensive criminal history, but by late 1995, it was clear divorce proceedings were in the works. He had been touted as the next Sammy Gravano, and he had yet to testify at a trial. Where was Gaspipe Casso? It was speculation—informed speculation—that he and the government were finished. He would never be used as a witness. All the murders he had committed and the lies he told the government made it impossible to use him in any credible way.

Hints about this began appearing in the *New York Daily News*. Word began to spread that the U.S. attorney was about to rip up Casso's 5K1.1 letter, the letter sent to the judge who would sentence Casso that would say what a great guy Casso had become and why he deserved to be set free to live among his fellow Americans.

May 1996

Burt Kaplan was tying up loose ends. He sat in the back-seat of a car registered to Garment City Warehouse being driven by a retiree from Sheepshead Bay, Brooklyn, named Willie. Willie was a nice guy who'd worked all his life and come out to Vegas to enjoy that final lap and landed a job as a gofer for Burt Kaplan, businessman. Burt made sure that Willie didn't know much more about Burt than that he sold ladies' dresses and put everything in somebody else's name. This was Vegas, so it was kind of expected.

Burt was on his way to meet Louie Eppolito. He needed Louie to pay back the loan on the house because Burt was shutting down his Vegas life and returning home to New York.

Burt Kaplan had done all right in Vegas. He had a nice place called Paradise Valley and sold a good number of ladies' dresses and, when he could, bales and bales of marijuana. He'd kept his nose clean. Sometimes he ran into other gangsters, but so far he hadn't run into the people who chase them. There was a guy from the Bonanno family and another guy from the Colombo family hanging around the Crazy Horse Saloon, a strip club notorious for gangsters. Burt tried to avoid notorious because there might be an unwanted entourage around but he was from Brooklyn and they were from Brooklyn and what could you do? Burt did not need the aggravation, but sometimes he couldn't help himself. He did the best he could, living a quiet life but knowing he could go to jail tomorrow. He couldn't determine his future by calling up the FBI and asking, "How's that thing going with your new friend Anthony Casso?" He had to live with uncertainty, and he could do that.

When the phone call came from one of his lawyers back

East saying the government had disqualified Anthony Casso from being a witness, those were the words Burt Kaplan needed to hear.

"I now felt that I had no more problems and that I was going to go home to my family," Kaplan said. "I told Louie that I was going back to New York."

Finally the government had come to its senses and realized it could not use the word of a madman like Anthony Casso. It was a bad idea from the start, like bringing King Kong to New York. Nothing but disaster could come of it. Burt couldn't know for sure whether the government believed anything that Casso had told him; all he knew was that more than a year had passed since Casso told them about Louie and Steve and, presumably, Burt Kaplan, and Burt and the two cops had not been arrested. That had to have some significance. When he got the word, he decided to close Garment City Warehouse and get as much of the house loan back from Louie as he could. Louie had promised thirty thousand dollars in cash today, with checks to follow. Louie was always promising.

Willie the driver pulled into a parking lot next to a bank, and Kaplan could see Lou waiting. He exited and returned a few minutes later with a fat white envelope in his hands. He could have taken the envelope, placed it in his ubiquitous briefcase, slipped quietly into the backseat, and said nothing on the drive home. But Burt couldn't help himself.

He held up the envelope.

"Do you know what's in here?" he asked Willie.

Willie shrugged.

Burt opened the envelope and riffled the stacks of hundred-dollar bills. Cash. Very Vegas. But Burt was through with Vegas. He was heading back to Brooklyn, where he was born and lived most of his life. His wife was there, in the same house on Eighty-fifth Street; his daughter still worked for the Legal Aid Society. He figured his connections to the garment industry were still intact. Anthony Casso had been sent back to the swamp from which he came. He was a pistol without bullets. Burt could once again get back to the life he used to be live.

September 9, 1996

Raining, thunderstorm, muggy, temperature headed into the eighties. Agent Eileen Dineen of the Drug Enforcement Agency and NYPD detective Thomas Limberg sat in an unmarked sedan outside a beige single-family at 2147 85th Street in Bensonhurst at about 6:30 A.M. They were staking out the house in hopes of finding a guy they'd been seeking for almost a year. When they noticed an aging white male wearing glasses peer out the window at them, the agent and the cop agreed that their search was over.

At 7:00 A.M. they stood on the steps of the house. In a recess in the bricks was a small security camera pointing straight at them. They knocked, and the door opened. There stood Eleanor Kaplan. Behind her stood their target, a small old man in glasses and pajamas. DEA agent Dineen handed an arrest warrant to the target with the heading *United States v. Burton Kaplan*.

Detective Limberg escorted Kaplan to his bedroom, where he began changing into khakis and a shirt. Limberg noticed there was a television monitor in the bedroom that had an image of the front stoop. The detective asked Kaplan if he wanted to make any statements. Kaplan said he wanted to call his lawyer. As he was thumbing through his little black phone book looking for the number, Limberg, who was naturally curious, glanced over Kaplan's shoulder. He noticed the name Frank Hot. He was a gangster who moved swag, and Limberg wanted to know why the gangster's telephone number might be in Burt Kaplan's little book. Limberg seized the book. Kaplan shrugged.

While Kaplan continued to get dressed, Limberg noticed the telephone numbers of numerous wiseguys. It was a veritable Cosa Nostra Yellow Pages, this book. There was Gerry Chilli of the Bonanno family. This would be helpful. The FBI had collected several tapes of Gerry stopping by Burt's Staten Island warehouse to pick up marijuana. On one tape Gerry described Kaplan as a "good Jew." There were other names in the little black book as well: a Colombo soldier, a Lucchese soldier, and a Gambino soldier—a nice Mafia cross section. There was even a boss in there, Vic Amuso. It was his inmate number in the Bureau of Prisons and his mailing address at the federal prison in Terre Haute, Indiana. It was an interesting collection of names for a guy in the business of dry goods.

There also was the number 917 616-0631 next to the name Marco. Next to that were two more numbers that had been blacked out. They were beeper and home phone numbers for Eppolito and Caracappa. Detective Limberg didn't know anything about that, and Burt Kaplan didn't bring it up as he was paraded out of the house in handcuffs past his friends and neighbors on Eighty-fifth Street.

On the way to the DEA building in Manhattan, the agents read Kaplan his Miranda rights, then immediately tried to rattle his nerves. They told Kaplan that Tommy Irish sent his regards. Tommy Irish was Burt's former business partner who almost made Burt file for Chapter 11. He also was a gangster and had recently decided to cooperate with the government. The cops mentioned him to see if Burt might get upset. Instead, Kaplan—who was used to this sort of thing—said he had no hard feelings against Tommy Irish and that Tommy did what he had to do. Kaplan explained to the agents and the detective that Tommy had been "out of the life" for a while and was working in construction, but was dragged back in. When told that nobody forced Tommy back in, Kaplan said Tommy was a man and that was his decision. Kaplan said that would not have occurred if Christy Tic had been around. He called Christy an "old-time wiseguy" who didn't try to hurt anyone. He admitted he knew Gas and Christy's son, Jumbo, and Fat Nicky DiCostanzo of the Lucchese family, but he was aware that just knowing guys like this isn't really a crime in the United States.

"If you know anything about me," Kaplan said, "then you know that ninety-five percent of what I do is legitimate."

Burt was taken to a room inside what looked like a factory on the far West Side of Manhattan, close to the Hudson River. There were no signs that this was a federal agency. They told Burt what they thought he had done. They said he was the CEO of a sophisticated marijuana distribution ring that sold thousands of pounds of marijuana each month. From a cursory read of the affidavit of the DEA agent on the case, the charge appeared to be based primarily on the word of one rat.

Even though the rat was referred to simply as CW, as in Co-operating Witness, Kaplan knew right away who it was: a lowlife hanger-on named Robert Molini.

As far as Burt could remember, he'd heard of Robert Molini but met him exactly never. The only thing Burt could recall about the guy was that he had convinced his own mother to carry drugs for him. This was the government's witness? There was a glimmer of hope here. Burt believed that like the heroin and passport matters that were thrown out in the past, he might walk away again.

And there was another surprise witness for the prosecution. Burt probably could have seen this coming, but when you're worrying about people like Anthony Casso ruining your life, you forget about all the other people who could do about the same thing. Monica Galpine—the now ex-wife of Tommy, the woman his wife had fired ten years ago. The woman who called his daughter "the princess." She was going to be coming to court to step back into the lives of Burt and Eleanor and Deborah, now as a government witness.

Burt sat in the room at DEA headquarters with what he believed was half the federal government when several men wearing New York City Police Department uniforms walked in. They did not look happy.

"We only came about the two dirty cops," one of them said. "You can go home tonight."

Kaplan said, "I want my lawyer."

September 13, 1996

Burt Kaplan stood in a magistrate's courtroom in down-town Brooklyn facing the prospect of spending at least the next twenty years in prison and knowing it was all about weight. In the federal system of criminal justice, if you sell one ounce of marijuana, you do five years. If you sell thousands of pounds, as it was alleged Burt Kaplan had done, you go to jail and maybe die there.

The Drug Enforcement Agency had made the case against Burt almost a year ago. It was a one-count criminal complaint, filed in U.S. District Court in Brooklyn and kept under seal since October 1995. It said that in 1991 and 1992, before Burt left for Vegas, he and several unidentified coconspirators sold truckloads of pot to dealers across America. All the time Burt was traveling back and forth from Las Vegas to New York in the past year he had been charged with a crime and he had never been noticed. And now here he was, standing in court, with everybody there because of him.

"Criminal cause for detention hearing, *United States versus Burton Kaplan*," said the judge's deputy. "Counsel, state your appearances for the record."

"Judith Lieb for the government."

"For the defendant, Judd Burstein."

In the back row of the spectator section of the tiny, cramped room was Burt's ninety-year-old mother, Tilly, and his daughter, Deborah. Here was the moment they had always feared. At ninety, Tilly needed this? And Deborah Kaplan, hardworking lawyer for the Legal Aid Society? The timing of Dad's arrest was not helpful, although she had to know this was coming. She was certainly aware that Dad had questionable friends, although he always made sure she was not involved in his business and would not know precisely what he did. That way she could stand up in court and talk about him just as a father and not have anything to say about all the rest. This she was prepared to do to get him home on bail.

Assistant U.S. Attorney Lieb, an intense young woman with black hair and a handy prosecutorial scowl that signified both disdain and outrage at the same time, thought bail was a bad idea. She made sure to tell Magistrate Judge Roanne Mann about all the bad things Burt had done since the time he was a teenager growing up in Brooklyn and the time he stole flashcubes. She said he sold "tens of thousands of pounds" of marijuana, and she accused him of being a millionaire as a result.

"We're talking in the neighborhood of fifteen million dollars," she said, "and that's only for that one year."

Surely Burt would flee to China if he was granted bail. She said Burt "took off" and became a fugitive in 1994 and only returned to New York recently "when he decided the heat was off." The more she talked to the judge, the more prosecutor Lieb with her multiple college degrees began to talk like an

Elmore Leonard character. Lieb then brought up the passport charge that was dropped by her office and noted that Kaplan had fled the city he grew up in not long after that matter had been put to rest. Why did he leave?

"There was a very significant development that occurred thereafter," the prosecutor earnestly explained. "That was publicity of the cooperation with the government of Anthony Casso."

There it was. For years, Burt Kaplan had avoided this. He had met hundreds of times with Anthony, conveyed messages that doomed men's lives, acted like Western Union conveying cash back and forth, and nobody had done anything about it. Or at least until that moment, that was what Burt had believed. Lieb said the evidence would show Burt was "very closely associated with Mr. Casso, who was the underboss of the Lucchese family and that Mr. Casso would have the goods [there was Elmore again] on Mr. Kaplan." Never before had Burt heard Casso referred to as Mr. Casso.

Burt was aware that his wife and daughter were in the courtroom. They both had met Anthony Casso many times. He was the nice man at Deborah's wedding with the envelope of money, and now they had to hear that he was really the underboss of a bunch of organized criminals and that their husband and father was "very closely associated" with him.

"As soon as newspaper articles appeared, Mr. Kaplan took off," Lieb said. "I'm not saying that he was not in and out of New York. He was in and out of New York, but I think he was living primarily out of New York. I understand that he was out of the country and he was really living a life where he didn't want to be found by law enforcement."

Under other circumstances, Burt might have laughed at that one. Out of the country? He was in Vegas. It didn't help that the prosecutor knew all about his alias. The agents found a Continental Airlines frequent-flier coupon in the name of Barry Mayers.

"The totality would indicate to the court that this isn't a man that can be trusted," declared Lieb, noting that because of the huge quantity of pot involved, Kaplan faced a mandatory minimum—emphasis on "minimum"—of twenty years in prison. He would turn sixty-three in a month.

"He'll find himself in a position where he would want to make himself scarce," Lieb said.

Burt's lawyer, Burstein, stepped forward and did what he could. He was a quiet, methodical man, a philosophy major in college. He called the case weak and attacked the credibility of the rat Molini, saying the government had already caught Molini in numerous lies. He ridiculed the idea that Burt had fled. He said Burt had testified in a deposition on Long Island in a civil case brought by Champion, and when the U.S. attorney in Newark had subpoenaed certain documents from Burt, he'd complied right away. Everybody knew where Burt was. Burstein even ridiculed the ghost in the courtroom, Anthony Casso.

"There's no concern about Mr. Casso," he said. "There never really should have been any concern because the government is never going to call him as a witness. He's just simply too unreliable."

Then he pointed to Deborah Kaplan in the back of the court.

"She is a respected member of the bar," Burstein said.

He pointed to the ninety-year-old mother and the two nephews, one a New York cop, the other retired from the department. He offered a twenty-million-dollar bond and said, "One could hardly find a defendant who has stronger roots in the community. He's lived in Brooklyn his entire life. He's been married to his wife for forty years. They lived in the same home for twenty years. He's had employment with the same company, Pisces Trading, for over ten years. These roots are strong as anyone could find for a criminal defendant. . . . He is a person extremely devoted to family."

Both sides were finished. It was Magistrate Judge Mann's turn to split the difference. He could go with the twenty-million-dollar bond, but Burt would have to remain inside his Eighty-fifth Street home wearing a special bracelet that would set off an alarm if he decided to walk to the corner bodega for a Milky Way bar.

For sixteen years, Kaplan had not been convicted of crimes. This allowed the judge to say that while the pending marijuana charges were serious, the bail package offered by the Kaplan family was significant and he would surely not abandon his family. The bail was set at twenty million dollars, and Burt Kaplan got to go home to Eighty-fifth Street. He now would get plenty of time to spend with his wife while he waited for his trial to begin.

Persons facing charges this serious have many options. They can plead guilty and hope this demonstration of acceptance of responsibility will be enough to reduce the amount of time they have to spend in the prison weight room. Or they can convince themselves that they have done nothing wrong and that this is an outrage that should be corrected. Or they can know in their hearts that they did what they did, but the government doesn't have enough on them to put them in jail, so it's time to fight like hell. Burt Kaplan embraced the latter view.

"He never took the position that he was innocent of this case," remembered Judd. "He had this view that I always found striking, which was even if I did it, this is America. They have to prove it. If they get me, it has to be fair."

1997

On the morning Deborah Kaplan took the witness stand in the criminal case known as *United States v. Burton Kaplan and Thomas Galpine*, she had much to lose. There she was in U.S. District Court in downtown Brooklyn, doing her very best to defend her drug-dealing father. She was hoping against hope that she might not have to spend the next twenty years making uncomfortable small talk with her father in Bureau of Prisons visiting rooms, but she was realistic. She had worked for years at the Legal Aid Society, defending indigents from ambitious prosecutors intent on furthering their careers. She knew all about how things worked in the system of criminal justice. Ninety-six percent of the cases brought by U.S. attorneys resulted in guilty pleas or convictions. Her father had refused to plead guilty, so here they were. And she had no reason to believe he should plead guilty. A family friend said Burt told Deborah flat-out that he was not guilty. She was very concerned about the charges but she had no way of knowing what, if anything, he had done, and he consistently insisted he was innocent.

So far things had not gone so well. After Burt was arrested, the prosecutors asked him to cooperate. During the trial, the prosecutors asked him to cooperate. Deborah's mother, Eleanor, had begged him to cooperate. Each time Burt refused without hesitation.

Now they were days into the trial, and the government was winning. They had paraded before the jury a cast of characters to produce a largely circumstantial case that Deborah's father was a major-league marijuana distributor. They claimed he'd been selling weed from Texas to New York for years. The main witness was Molini, who talked about huge quantities of pot. Four thousand pounds a month. The government had wheeled in a shopping cart with one of the bales, and everybody in the court could smell it.

Then came the audio portion of the trial. They played FBI tapes of Gerry Chilli and Stephen Lenehan stopping by the Staten Island warehouse to buy two pounds of marijuana. It was right there on tape—they walked in without marijuana and walked out with two pounds. Finally they had Monica Galpine take the stand and describe Burt Kaplan as a controlling oligarch who lurked behind the scenes but was aware of every facet of the organization. She also told everyone in the courtroom that Deborah was "spoiled."

Deborah Kaplan was there to set the record straight. She had won awards. She had been appointed as a Small Claims Court judge, a sinecure that was often a precursor to a job as a real judge. She had just finished two terms as president of the Brooklyn Women's Bar Association and belonged to numerous committees. Behind the scenes, she was in line to win a coveted job as principal counsel to the Honorable Juanita Bing Newton, deputy chief administrative judge for justice initiatives for the State of New York. And she was also the daughter of Burt Kaplan, marijuana dealer.

Sitting in the courtroom of U.S. District Court judge Carol Amon, Deborah was politely questioned by her father's lawyer Gerald Shargel. She knew him well. She was an intern in his office during law school. Gerry and Judd Burstein, the other lawyer in the courtroom on her father's side, had represented her father for years. They had brought her in as a defense witness to try to blow up the testimony of Monica Galpine, an embittered, disgruntled former employee who made frequent drunken midnight calls to the House of Kaplan. Deborah was there to set the record straight.

Under questioning by Shargel, Deborah was able to recite her many committee appointments. The judge cut her off when Shargel asked her about the awards. She moved on to the middle-of-the-night phone calls from the drunken Monica, the fraudulent claims of being beaten by her husband. She even brought up Monica calling her "the princess" and revealed that Monica had been upset about the dress she was supposed to wear to Deborah's wedding so many years ago. She then recollected blow by blow the day Monica threatened to get even when she was fired. Shargel then asked her opinion of Monica Galpine.

"I think that Monica's word cannot be trusted at all," Deborah Kaplan testified under oath. "She's not capable of telling the truth."

Prosecutor Lieb tried her best to rattle the witness, but Deborah wouldn't budge. She was used to this setting. This was her world. When it was over, Deborah Kaplan asked the judge if she could sit with her family, and the judge said fine. She stepped down from the witness stand, walked past her father, and stepped back outside the well of the court. This was her system, the system she had chosen as a career. She sat in the pew of the church of justice with her father's life in doubt and watched the system do its work.

January 9, 1998

In the courtroom of Judge Carol Amon, Burt Kaplan contemplated two key numbers: forty-eight thousand and twenty-seven. Forty-eight thousand was the number of pounds of marijuana that the federal government had decided Burton Kaplan and Thomas Galpine sold to willing consumers. Twenty-seven was the number of years in prison Judge Amon could impose on Burton Kaplan in his twilight years. It was Judgment Day for Burt Kaplan.

The jury had convicted in no time at all. The lawyers tried everything, but the jurors remembered that big bale of marijuana in the shopping cart sitting in the middle of the court and decided to participate in the war on drugs. Burt put the government's case to the test, and the government prevailed. It was as simple as that, except for one little factor that could have changed everything: Louis Eppolito and Stephen Caracappa.

First, the two NYPD chiefs had told him he could walk away from the marijuana charges if he gave up the cops. Then the prosecutors told his lawyers the same thing. Give up the cops, walk out the door. His wife, Eleanor, had urged him to take the offer before it disappeared forever.

"The issue of cooperating was brought up twice—once at the beginning of trial and once at the end," said Judd Burstein. "He was the last person I ever expected to become a cooperating witness. In his world, you don't become a government witness."

Burstein and Shargel had even tried to use the government's pressuring Burt to cooperate as a kind of defense. They themselves dragged the ghost of Anthony Casso into the courtroom, argued to the judge that the government was inflating its charges against Kaplan just to get him to cooperate and become a substitute for Casso. Prosecutor Lieb scoffed at what she called the "frame-up defense" offered by Shargel and even threatened to bring up what Casso had already told the FBI—that Burt Kaplan himself had participated in murders and obstruction of justice.

In the end it was posturing on both sides, and the secret of the two cops that Burt had held on to for all these years stayed a secret, at least technically. It seemed as if everyone on both sides of the case was aware that Burt had something to say, but no one was ready to open that door.

It was just like Louis Lepke, the old-time gangster electrocuted by the State of New York in 1944. At the end, there had been much speculation that Lepke was cooperating. The *Daily News* printed a story saying that before he died, Lepke had met with Manhattan district attorney Frank Hogan in his cell at Sing Sing. Lepke told Hogan about an unnamed man who was, as the *Daily News* put it, "in back of several crimes

[and] is a high political power." The *News* reported that the man in "high political power" was also a labor leader, but they didn't drop his name.

Because of this, a theatrical performance debuted in the hours before Lepke's execution. At 7:30 P.M. his wife, Betty, handed a statement to reporters covering her husband's execution. It read, "I am anxious to have it clearly understood that I did not offer to talk and give information in exchange for any promises of commutation of my death sentence. I did not ask for that. I insist that I am not guilty of the Rosen murder, that the witnesses against me lied and that I did not receive a fair trial." The statement went on to thank appeals judges who'd found fault with his trial and requested the appointment of a commission to reexamine the facts in the case of Rosen, the slain "Candyman of Brooklyn."

"If that examination does not show I am not guilty," Lepke's statement professed, "I am willing to go to the chair regardless of what information I have given or can give."

The Lepke way was the Kaplan way. He was the last of the old-time Jewish gangsters, and his last act was to make sure everybody knew he was not or never could be a rat.

The sentencing of Burt Kaplan began precisely at 9:30 A.M. Judd Burstein tried to get the judge to reduce the sentence from twenty-seven to twenty years, noting that Kaplan was sixty-four years old. Prosecutor Lieb reminded the court that forty-eight thousand meant twenty-seven.

Then it was Burt's turn.

"I keep being told all during this trial keep quiet, whatever you say is going to be held against you, don't even look at the liars that get on the witness stand, don't give them dirty looks because the jury is going to find fault with it," Burt said. "I sat here for two and a half weeks and listened to atrocities that are going on in the stand and even today Mr. Burstein made a beautiful appeal for me and what I'm going to say what might hurt me in your eyes and I apologize for that but I'm a man. I am sixty-four years old and I might go to jail for the rest of my life if I lost my appeal, and I want to give you my opinion of what went on at this trial and, if I may, I'll do that."

Judge Amon warned Burt to confine his comments to the

"judgment at hand," saying she would not be ruling that day on what was true or not true during the trial.

"What about the prosecutorial comments that were made during my trial that were not true?" Burt asked. "There is no way in a million years that I was involved in this thing. I waived it because I thought I did the right thing for my codefendant, who I love like my son."

Galpine sat next to him, waiting his turn. Kaplan claimed the forty-eight thousand pounds were made up by Bobby Molini, a man "I never met in my life."

"When he came on the witness stand, I thought he was the car salesman that sold Tommy or Monica the car," Burt said. "That is all I have to say, Judge."

Judge Amon asked if he wanted to say anything regarding the sentence that was about to be imposed. In his response to this, Burt seemed to be explaining to himself as much as to anyone else why he was standing there like this and how important it was that he make sure his past remained just that.

"I know you are not the jury," he said. "I lost that. I lost that, boob that I am for not taking the witness stand because I didn't want my past to come up."

He did what a thousand other defendants before him had done in that very courtroom—call the prosecution's witnesses liars, express regret that he should have taken the witness stand himself to clear his name. He knew this was folly. If he'd taken the stand and sworn an oath to tell the truth, prosecutor Lieb could have had the opportunity to begin questioning him about Anthony Casso and Louis Eppolito and Stephen Caracappa and then the whole thing—all those years of secrets—would have come spilling out into the courtroom of Judge Amon, right in front of his wife and daughter.

"This is a very very difficult moment for him and for his family," his attorney Shargel said. "He knows full well that he has the right to say whatever he wishes in connection with the sentence, almost without limit."

Burt sat down and listened to Tommy Galpine stand up and say nothing about whether he was a marijuana dealer but insist that he never hit his wife or kids. Then he sat down, and Judge Amon did what she was paid to do.

For Thomas Galpine, the right-hand man, that meant sixteen years in prison. For Burt Kaplan, that meant twenty-seven years in prison. With time off for good behavior in federal prison, that could mean Burt Kaplan might walk out of a jail cell and into the light of day when he was eighty-seven years old.

After the hearing, Kaplan and Galpine had a final word together, with the ghost of Louis Lepke presiding over their conversation. Kaplan remembered the conversation this way: "I told Tommy we're both men, we both gotta do what we gotta do. He said, 'I wouldn't think of doing anything else.'"

May 1998

The body of a young man lay between two parked cars in front of a strip club called Scarlett's on Staten Island. It was a bland stucco building with a giant sign that threw off a ghastly crimson light that made the body glow. The body lay on its side next to the open door of a sedan and was certainly not good for business. The strip club was closed for the night, with the yellow police tape everywhere and detectives placing those little plastic cones with numbers next to the bullet casings found on the street. Those little cones would tell the crime scene people precisely where the bullet casings fell, which would help identify where the shooters stood. There were quite a few little cones.

When Betty Hydell got the call, it was not a surprise, but it was a shock. This was her son, after all, Frankie Hydell. The cops told her not a lot, but she knew what she needed to know. He was dead. Somebody shot him. They did it because he was an informant, and somebody had let that little secret out. It was funny how all those secrets got out.

Betty Hydell was not one to run to cops. After her first son, Jimmy, had disappeared, the detectives had come by and asked certain questions and she had made a point not to mention that she'd seen two cops hours before Jimmy disappeared forever. When she had seen one of the cops, Louis Eppolito, on Sally Jessy Raphael, nearly six years ago, she had kept quiet. She had talked to FBI agents about her son a number of times, especially after she learned from the newspapers that

Anthony Casso had become an informant for a time. Even then, she said nothing about the cops. The reason she kept quiet was simple: her other son, Frankie.

"When I recognized them and realized they were detectives, who was I gonna go to?" Betty said. "I was afraid if I did go to anybody, they'd go after my other son."

Now he was gone, and Betty had no reason to stay silent. She says she got on the phone shortly after she identified Frankie's body, and she called FBI agent Dick Rudolph, the man who arrested Casso and who spent hours listening to his stories about Louis Eppolito and Stephen Caracappa.

Betty Hydell says she told FBI agent Rudolph all about seeing Eppolito and Caracappa the day Jimmy Hydell disappeared. She gave him a description—the fat guy with gold jewelry, the skinny guy in the black outfit. She told him about recognizing Eppolito on TV and then recognizing both in the book. She unburdened herself of her little secret.

"I called Agent Rudolph and told him about the detectives," she said. "I just wanted to say it and I said it."

April 17, 2001

On this day the Friends of Deborah Kaplan, Inc., filed incorporation papers with the State of New York. The Friends listed its place of business as the apartment of its treasurer on the Upper East Side of Manhattan. It was a neighborhood called the Silk Stocking District, dating back to a time when the Fifth Avenue millionaires called this their neighborhood. It had the highest concentration of wealth of any neighborhood in the entire city of eight million. The namesake beneficiary of the Friends was herself living within the Silk Stocking District in an eleventh-floor apartment building on East Fortieth Street. At night she had a sparkling view of the city that would be more familiar to Cole Porter than to Pete Hamill. It was Manhattan, a place bridge and tunnel people who live within the City of New York still call "the city." It was the perfect place to come and reinvent yourself.

The Friends of Deborah Kaplan, Inc., began raising money in earnest with the hope of winning a seat as a civil court judge in Manhattan. Its namesake had all the right credentials, although her journey was quite unique. When her father was convicted of selling thousands of pounds of marijuana to dealers across America, she landed a prestigious job as principal counsel to the deputy chief administrative judge for justice initiatives for the State of New York. When she won a promotion to chief management analyst for the court's drug treatment programs, her father was serving twenty-seven years in federal prison for selling narcotics. While her father sat in prison, U.S. representative Carolyn Maloney, a friend and supporter, praised her on the floor of the U.S. House for becoming president of the New York State Women's Bar Association. Deborah wrote a letter to the *New York Times* noting that women were far more likely than men to be drug offenders and criticizing the state's draconian drug laws. There was no mention of her father the drug dealer sitting in jail, of Anthony "Gaspipe" Casso, of Christy Tic Furnari, of Vic Amuso, or any of the rest. She knew them all, but they were part of the distant Brooklyn past, like the Dodgers. It was easy to see why Deborah Kaplan wanted nothing to do with the world she grew up in.

She chose Manhattan over her hometown of Brooklyn when she dove into the dimly lit pool of New York City politics. She worked as a judicial delegate for the New York County Democratic Party, a job that found her voting on which judges the party would endorse. Her former colleagues on that panel now had chosen her. She was aware that if she won the seat in civil court, she would likely be appointed to serve in criminal court because of her background as a Legal Aid attorney. She would likely preside over criminal cases similar to the ones her father once faced when he was a young man caught trying to sell stolen flashcubes.

In November she won a seat in civil court and, as expected, was appointed to serve in criminal court. She testified as an expert before a State Senate committee looking at redistricting congressional seats, and advocated on behalf of the same Representative Maloney who had praised her on the floor of the U.S. House. At the time her father had lost his appeal in the federal Second Circuit Court of Appeals. He had filed a new motion arguing that his lawyers, Burstein and Shargel, did a lousy job and that he deserved a new trial. This was his last hope. Her mother, Eleanor, would visit him every two weeks in rural Pennsylvania or West Virginia or wherever they put him.

Deborah, friends noted, rarely made the trip.

TWENTY-THREE

Dinner at Ferraro's, and Lou was back drinking. Forget the heart surgery and the doctors and all that. He ordered a martini straight up, very dry with an olive and a side of club soda. Then he spied the bartender using bottom-shelf booze.

"That's for me, hon?" he said. "That's not for me. The Tanqueray. That stuff, it stinks."

"Sorry about that," the bartender said.

"That's all right," he said. "I was watching."

He was in a good mood. Perhaps this was linked to the fact that he had actually received money from the king of promises, Steve Corso. So far he'd received fourteen thousand dollars, which was not the seventy-five thousand dollars he was supposed to get but was better than nothing, and how could he complain?

"That fourteen has to help a little bit," Corso said. "How was that?"

"It's good," he said. "I've managed all these years."

Eight days earlier, at two in the afternoon, Lou's son, Tony Eppolito, and Tony's friend Guido Bravetti roused themselves from bed to sit in Steve Corso's C.P.A. office, the one blessed by the priest. Agents with the FBI and the DEA sat in the room next door, watching a TV monitor. A camera was hidden behind Corso's desk, with an excellent view of Corso and Tony and Guido making idle chitchat. Corso expected Guido to show and had been a little shocked to see Tony, but there he was, and it was too late. Tony produced a foil packet of crystal meth and handed it to Corso, who then methodically counted out fourteen hundred dollar bills onto his desk, making sure not to block the camera. Corso asked about the Ecstasy, and Guido said not to worry, it would be arriving in a few days. Corso promised to call when the Hollywood guys arrived so Tony and Guido could show them around.

"Thank you, sir," Corso said. "Pleasure doing business."

When the two young men left, the phone on Corso's desk rang. The DEA agent in the next room told Corso to pick up the packet of drugs with a tissue paper and bring it to him.

This had occurred after the conversation in which Lou and Steve had said talk to Guido, but Lou Eppolito had no idea that his son had sold drugs to his financial savior in front of a video camera monitored by the federal government. All he knew was that he had fourteen thousand dollars more than he had the week before, and he was still willing to listen to Steve Corso and his stories. He'd even done a favor for his savior. The previous week Corso claimed he'd been at a restaurant in Manhattan when he noticed what he thought was an unmarked cop car sitting outside on the street. This was a little test devised by the DEA to see what Lou and Steve would do if asked to run a license plate. Lou told him he'd send the number to Caracappa.

"He knows the right way, the legal way," Lou said. "Maybe Monday we'll get it."

Lou claimed if it was an undercover law-enforcement car you wouldn't know it for sure but you would have a good idea. It would come back to somebody who didn't exist or to a leasing company. He appeared to be familiar with the need to be careful when running license plate checks.

"Guys, especially wiseguys, friends with cops, wiseguys will call you up and say, 'Who is this fucking plate?'" Lou said. "You run the plate, put in it in the computer, the FBI computer. You tell your friend, 'Oh, it's the FBI.' All of a sudden they walk over to the car the next day like jerkoffs and say, 'Hey, cops!' And then the cops say, 'Who blew our cover?' They come back and check the computer to see if anybody put in a request for a plate and it comes back as yes, then somebody comes and knocks on your door. Matter of fact, it didn't happen to me, but it could have happened to me."

He did not explain further, although it was clear from this statement that he did not have too much of a problem with the idea of running plates for wiseguys except for the issue of getting caught. As the Tanqueray martini slowly disappeared down Lou's gullet, his ability to distinguish between who was a good guy and who was a bad guy seemed to disappear with it.

The waiter showed up. Tonight it was osso buco for Corso, fettucine bolognese for Lou. Lou began talking warmly of John Gotti, the boss of the Gambino family who had died of cancer in a lonely hospital bed miles from his family two years previous. He claimed he grew up with Gotti and when he was a cop he consulted with him on a number of occasions at the Ravenite Social Club in Little Italy. He viewed him more as a popular culture icon, the Robin Hood man of the people that Gotti believed he was, rather than the sociopath who ordered people killed because they didn't jump when he offered up his ring to kiss.

"I used to go to him as a detective and I'd walk in the place and they'd say to me, 'Lou, am I in a tight place? Am I in a jam?' I said, 'No, I didn't hear nuthin' about you.' 'If you did, you'd let me know?' I said no. 'Fuck, did I ask you who killed so-and-so last week?' So that's what John liked about me. He had a pair of balls."

He told a story related to him by Gotti's criminal defense lawyer, Bruce Cutler, who also happened to be Lou's lawyer. He said Cutler had confided in him that on his deathbed, Gotti had revealed there were three people he admired the most.

"It's amazing how many people you know in this world, there's like three or four people in this world I've ever respected. One is my father, two is Neil Dellacroce, and three is Lou Eppolito."

"Wow," said Corso.

"Oh, the temperament," Lou said. "I'm not a gangster.

What the fuck is that? He says Gotti thought the world of me. He said Lou, he never came out of the war."

Now he was really opening up to Corso. All those dinners, all those martinis, all those stories of bravery and selfless sacrifice for the taxpayers of New York City that Corso had listened to were finally paying off. Lou Eppolito, the Mafia cop, was talking openly about his affection for his heroes in the world of villains. He worked his way through the five families of New York, starting with the Lucchese family. There was a nephew of a Lucchese captain who had kidnapped a little girl and he claimed he visited a social club to talk to the boss of the family, Tony Ducks Corallo, to find out where the guy was. As he told the story, a small jazz band in the corner began playing *The Godfather* theme.

"The guys say to me, There'll be ninety fucking cameras watching you go in that place. You're not going in there with a partner even though they know that's wrong. You're not signed out in the book so that means you are now automatically wrong."

He claimed he went to the club with the intent of confronting the capo with the offending nephew in front of Tony Ducks.

"I take out my shield. I tell the guy, 'Tell Tony I want to talk to him.' 'He don't talk to cops.' I said, 'I know, tell him I want him to listen.' He comes out. The guy comes right out. Tony comes out, says, 'What can I do for you?' I says, 'My family is Jimmy the Clam Eppolito,' and Tony Ducks says, 'What's your name? Eppolito? I know your Uncle Jimmy very well, I have a lot of respect for him.' I went like this, like I didn't ask you to talk."

"He's the boss," Corso said.

" 'The reason I'm putting you on the spot with the boss is, I want you to go out and find out where this kid is, give me a phone call, and I'll go get him. I give you my word I'll take him, I won't put him into a hospital, I'll put him into a jail. I said if he touches a fucking hair, I says this kid is three years old, if a barrette is missing, I'm going to throw him out the fucking window.' "

He claimed he got a call with an address, found the guy with the girl, and did not put the guy in the hospital but instead into a holding cell. When the district attorney asked him how he found the guy, he did what his father told him to do. He made up a story about how a neighbor called about a kid crying and he busted in and found her. Pure luck.

"So I lied," Lou said. "I made four good friends, including the boss of another family."

It did not matter that he lied to the district attorney and therefore the court about how he found the guy because the guy was a pedophile, and getting him off the streets was all that mattered. The New York City Police Department had rules that told all officers, detectives, and janitors the way to deal with wiseguys was either to stay away from them or arrest them when you could. The Lou Eppolito system for dealing with wiseguys was far more complex.

There was the catering hall owner who called up Lou because a made member of the Lucchese family had a big wedding there and then stiffed him on the bill. At first, Lou told the guy he couldn't help out.

"You gotta go through court, you gotta do the right thing," Lou said. "I do not collect from fucking wiseguys. If I was to do that, they'd put a fucking sign on me."

Then he noticed a beautiful girl at the catering hall and he said, "I'll see what I can do. Let me make a phone call." He claimed the Lucchese gangster suddenly paid when word got to him that Lou the cop was involved.

"The guy says thanks, he gave me two grand. I said no, I never take money. I don't do that. The quickest way to make a fucking problem is to take money. He says, 'What can I do to say thank you?' I says, 'You asked me for a favor, you got it.'" He said the pretty girl at the catering hall called him a day later, and that was his payment. He didn't need the two thousand dollars.

The Lou Eppolito system, as explained to Steve Corso, C.P.A., did not involve taking money from gangsters. It did, however, dictate that it was okay to look the other way. This lesson came in the form of yet another story, this one involving Todo Marino, a Gambino wiseguy whom Lou actually mentioned in his book *Mafia Cop*. In the book, however, this particular Todo Marino story never made it into print.

There was a party in the early eighties and Lou didn't like

somebody there and he decided to hitch a ride elsewhere and wound up at Todo's social club in Brooklyn late at night in the pouring rain. Todo told the bartender to give Lou what he wanted and then went to make a phone call. Lou was sipping his scotch and soda and chatting with the bartender when another gangster whose name he did not reveal showed up at the empty bar. The man was covered in blood.

"So me and the bartender are talking, this guy comes over," he said. " 'Fucking cocksucker,' he says. 'I should have shot him. I should have shot him.' Bartender says, 'What are you talking about?' He says, 'Anybody tells you, a knife in the back of the head they die instant? I must have stabbed this cocksucker a thousand times.' He said, 'I'm holding his mouth, I'm stabbing him in the fucking back, in the neck, in the head.' He says, 'Finally I strangled him to kill him. . . . It took me a half hour to wrap the prick up. I need a drink. He's in the trunk of the car outside.' "

Under normal circumstances this could have been a somewhat awkward moment—a full-time criminal has just admitted committing a heinous act and the evidence is in the trunk of a car a few feet away. Lou explained how he removed all awkwardness from the premises.

"I'm the law. I'm a fucking detective, I'm sitting in the car like this," he said. Todo lets the guy who just told the story that he told it to, as Lou put it, "a fucking detective in the homicide squad. Now what do we do? He knows who you are. He looked you right in the face when you're talking."

He said Todo came back out to the bar, clearly an unhappy man. "I can see he's seething. Seething. Todo comes around, he's sitting next to me. I can see he's nervous. The guy walks out and he looks at me. Todo says, 'Walker, I'll catch you later.' He says, 'I'll see you later, Mr. Marino.' The bartender says, 'Thanks, Louie. Thanks a lot. It could have been ugly.' I'm looking in the glass. He looks at Todo, he says, 'How many times you want me to apologize?' Todo's just sitting next to me, not saying a word. I'll be a son of a bitch, he touches my hand. I says, 'What's the matter?' He says, 'I'm sorry.' "

"For what?"

"For what happened."

"What happened?" Lou claimed he replied. "I'm deaf in my right ear. What happened?"

Under the Lou Eppolito system, it was none of his business. Shoeboxes of cash? No problem. Payments from gangsters in Florida under the table? What's the big deal? Forgetting all about a homicide? What else could you do? The guy in the trunk, whoever he was, probably deserved it. Lou believed the story that gangsters only kill other gangsters, not civilians, and anybody they kill knows what to expect from the life. Getting stabbed in the back and head and neck should not come as a big surprise to anybody who signs up for the program. There was no such thing as a sin of omission.

"It's not my business," Lou explained, "I don't give a fuck."

"But in the position you were in," Corso asked, "didn't you have to do that? I mean if you heard something."

"That's my father teaching me."

"Even as a cop, if you heard something that this guy got whacked and it was none of your business, you didn't hear it?" Corso asked.

"I didn't," Lou said. "Other guys would say I heard it. That's why I was always so respected by them."

"So respected," Corso said, "because, if you heard something that you didn't want to hear, you didn't hear it. If you saw something you didn't want to see, you didn't see it. It's no different than me, really."

Lou explained the Eppolito system in what he called "my laymen terms."

"Everything that you do personally, you do it to make a living. You don't do it to become judgmental," Lou said. "There's nobody in the fucking world I've ever met who can sit under a microscope. Not one person. A lot of people don't know this, I know it because I read all the time, but the pope was a Polish freedom fighter who killed thirty, forty people."

"Is that right?"

"He ambushed Germans. After the war was over, he became a priest and was ordained in '48. He was one of the biggest, toughest Poles to fight to free Poland. He has killed the book says as many as eight to ten people and he's killed them in hand-to-hand. After the war is over, he wants to get religious and he climbs up to the pope. Nobody can sit under a microscope. Nobody."

Lou's thinking was even the pope killed people. He had his reasons. So did Lou.

"When I do the movie, you want a part in it?" Lou asked.

"Nah," Corso said. "I'd rather not."

"You'd rather not. You could be a wiseguy."

"Nah. I'm behind the camera."

The dinner was over. Corso got a receipt for the check to submit to the FBI, and they waited outside for the valet with the rain coming down.

"This was pretty good," Corso said. "All right, sir. Very good."

"Check those tits over there," Lou said.

"It doesn't stop raining," Corso said. "It doesn't fucking stop raining. All right, boss. I'll call you Monday." The valet pulled up with Lou's car, and he got in and switched on the radio. It was Elvis, singing in that slow Elvis crescendo.

"I can't help falling in love with you," Elvis crooned as only Elvis could, and Lou Eppolito drove off into another perfect Las Vegas night.

TWENTY-FOUR

December 12, 2003

More than twenty years had passed since the day the people who govern first got word that Louis Eppolito was as corrupt as the day is long. That tape of a New York City detective negotiating a bribe for mug shots to help John Sciascia Jr. now sat in a dusty box in the basement of an office building in lower Manhattan. Sciascia himself was dead. So were Israel Greenwald, Jimmy Hydell, Nicky Guido, Otto Heidel, Anthony DiLapi, Eddie Lino, Bruno Facciola, Bobby Borriello, and Jimmy Bishop. Anthony Casso was alive but useless. Both Stephen Caracappa and Louis Eppolito had suffered public ridicule in the newspapers, but for all that they had accomplished in terms of subverting the system they were sworn to protect, they had escaped, unpunished. They lived the life of retired detectives in Las Vegas, accepted by their peers, coming and going as they pleased. Both men were allowed to carry guns. The idea that there might be some price to pay for all that sin back in New York seemed farfetched. The possibility of vengeance or retribution or penance seemed impossible. Eppolito and Caracappa, it seemed, got away with it.

Sometimes in this cruel and beautiful world, there is convergence.

Convergence is when evidence of bad behavior comes together by happenstance to prove guilt. The riddle gets answered. Convergence is when the stars align in such a way that a truth withheld becomes a truth revealed. Convergence is a symphony, not a song.

It usually starts out with something small and petty. Somewhere along the line a low-level hoodlum gets caught doing something stupid and needs a get-out-of-jail-free card. He becomes an informant and tells all. In the course of his confession, he reveals a secret long hidden. He says the right thing about the right guy to the right investigator, who connects that snippet of information to other snippets already gathered. This in turn provides the leverage to get another guy to cooperate, who says the right thing about the right guy at the right time. And so on, right up the ladder, until they're at the top and judgment day is at hand. Such was the case with the Mafia cops.

For years there were stories about NYPD cops and FBI agents working for the Mob. Mario Puzo put Mafia cops in *The Godfather*. Serpico talked about them in the 1970s. Usually they were involved in low-level stuff—tipping a local bookie to a pending raid, hinting about a possible bug installed in a social club. Most of it involved helping felons stay free.

In the New York City of the 1980s, rumors surfaced of more serious and pervasive bad behavior by cops in the employ of the Mob. The story was there were city cops or maybe federal agents or both who were killing people for the Mob. The rumors persisted and spread. These cops-as-criminals worked for a fee, sharing law-enforcement secrets, giving up names of informants, providing the address of a rival for a hit, and performing contract hits themselves when required. These were unbelievable rumors, the stuff of pulp fiction, but persistently circulating nonetheless. Again and again FBI agents and NYPD detectives heard this from informants on the street. This gangster had a mole in the Brooklyn DA's office. This guy had somebody in the bureau. This guy had a detective in the Sixty-second Precinct. And so on.

In the case of Caracappa and Eppolito, the convergence began years before, when Barclay Feranga started talking to

the FBI about a plumber buried under a toilet. This implicated
Pete Savino, who wreaked havoc on the Lucchese crime family, which in turn inspired Al D'Arco to call up the FBI.
D'Arco was the first to talk of Anthony "Gaspipe" Casso and
his "crystal ball," and in time Casso himself gave the FBI the
names of the two cops. Casso had gone off and imploded as a
witness, but he had put in motion something that could not be
stopped. He had put the names out there and, because of that,
it was tough for law enforcement paid by taxpaying citizens
to just walk away. Something had to be done.

Two weeks before Christmas 2003, in the offices of Brooklyn district attorney Charles Hynes, a group of investigators
from several agencies sat chatting with an older woman with
blond hair and sunglasses. She was the late Jimmy Hydell's
mother, Betty.

In the room were several investigators, including a retired
NYPD detective named Tommy Dades, who was now working for the Brooklyn DA; Billy Oldham, an investigator with
the Brooklyn U.S. attorney's office; and DEA special agent
Mark Manko. They were the team that had come together to
revive the case because they believed it was the right thing to
do. Dades had discovered Betty Hydell's story to the FBI back
in 1998, when her second son, Frankie, had been murdered.
Then and now she was remembering how on the day her son
Jimmy disappeared, she had seen and confronted two NYPD
cops she later figured out were Eppolito and Caracappa. She
told the story again about seeing Eppolito with Sally Jessy
Raphael and then buying the book *Mafia Cop*, and seeing
Caracappa.

"They know I saw them," Betty said. "From 1986 to 1992,
he had gotten away with everything. He had the nerve to go
on national television, knowing it was going to be on in New
York. He went on TV thinking he was going to get away with
everything. If I had not seen him, I would have never never
known. It was because of his ego going on TV that this case
comes to pass."

When the interview was over, Manko of the DEA was responsible for typing a report summarizing Betty's recollections. He took down what Betty had to say and concluded by
writing, "This is an ongoing investigation into the disappear-

ance and murder of Hydell." The file title Manko assigned to the case was "GALPINE, Thomas et al." This was a reference to Burt Kaplan's former top assistant, Burt's codefendant on the marijuana case who'd sworn allegiance to silence after the conviction five years earlier.

Betty Hydell was part of the convergence. She was there to corroborate what Casso had already said about his use of cops to kidnap her son Jimmy. The case against the cops was once again alive, this time using Casso's words without using Casso. The first stop in that journey was to visit an aging Jewish gangster who was serving a twenty-seven-year term in federal prison for selling thousands of pounds of top-quality marijuana.

August 11, 2004

Inmate 13103-053 sat in a room outside of the federal correctional institution in the remote coal town of Morganville, West Virginia, deep within the Appalachian woods and as far away as you could get from Bensonhurst and all it implied. Inmate 13103-053 was going to be seventy-one years old in October. He was sitting in the room with his lawyer, David Schoen, facing Assistant U.S. attorneys Mark Feldman and Robert Henoch, Special Agent Manko of the DEA, and investigator Joseph Ponzi of the Brooklyn district attorney's office. He had come to a crossroads.

Inmate 13103-053 had chronic eye problems and upper dentures. Recently he had been diagnosed with prostate cancer. His wife had begged him to have this meeting from the day he entered the federal prison system in 1998. She lived alone back in Brooklyn and would visit him twice a month, asking him again and again to reconsider the silence he had committed himself to. Then there was his daughter. Recently inmate 13103-053 had experienced certain pressures regarding his daughter.

She was now a state judge. While working in the top tiers of the state court system, she toiled for the Eleanor Roosevelt Democratic Club in Manhattan to win the endorsement of the Democratic Party. She had been elected and was now a prominent member of the community. And now she and her husband, a partner in a law firm, had adopted a little boy from Russia. She was his only child, and now for the first time inmate 13103-053 was a grandfather who knew that it was possible he would never get to see his grandchild outside the dismal confines of a prison visiting room.

He was presented with this dilemma: stand by the principles you have embraced since you were a child of the streets and forgo your family life. It was a dilemma that was breaking him.

In the past eight months, the prosecutors and detectives and agents had again started showing up with the usual request. They first appeared in 2003, and he told them to go away. They showed up again in early 2004 and asked again. At first he still held out hope for a new trial. He had lost his appeal but had filed a motion alleging that his lawyers did a lousy job and that there was evidence the prosecutors deliberately withheld to make the jury think he was a major-league marijuana dealer. Then it became clear: in these new visits, the prosecutors were now claiming they had new evidence about the cops and that they were going to charge the cops one way or the other. The implication was they were going to charge inmate 13103-053 as well. He was already serving twenty-seven years. Another indictment would mean death in a prison cell.

Burt's moment for redemption had arrived. His wife and daughter were both aware of the DEA's inquiries and let him know what he must do. A family friend said Burt's daughter, Deborah, had often encouraged her father to lead a law-abiding life and to cooperate with the government. Deborah was aware that after his appeal on the marijuana case failed, he was visited by DEA agents and asked to cooperate. She knew he had been asked to assist the government in the past and he had refused. He always told her he would not provide information about other people. Burt did not disclose to her the specific nature of the matter the DEA was seeking his assistance about except to tell her it involved law enforcement officers. She did not know Eppolito or Caracappa and Burt never mentioned their names to her. Deborah urged her father to cooperate with the DEA agents fully. She asked him to consider that not only was this the right thing to do but also to factor in his age, that he was suffering from prostate cancer and other ailments, and was now serving what amounted to a life sentence. Though he had never acknowledged guilt in the marijuana case or told his daughter what information he had that was important to the DEA, Deborah Kaplan made her feelings clear: her father should accept responsibility for his actions and cooperate. Why he ultimately decided to do so was a question only he could answer. It was not until he actually signed the cooperation agreement that Deborah Kaplan began to learn about the case involving her father and the former detectives.

He called his lawyer, Schoen, and said it was time. The lawyer called Assistant U.S. Attorney Henoch and said, "My guy will listen." There were no promises by either side as Henoch and all the rest sat in the room in the middle of nowhere, West Virginia. They prepared a form for him to sign called a proffer agreement, which began with the phrase, "With respect to the meeting of Burton Kaplan" and listed Feldman, Henoch, Ponzi, and Manko, misspelling his name Manco. The agreement stated in boldface "THIS IS NOT A COOPERATION AGREEMENT."

It was a little dance. Kaplan had to tell the truth, and if at the end of the day he decided not to cooperate, the prosecutors would forget that the proffer happened and not use it against him in an indictment. They could, however, use the information he provided to pursue leads in an investigation. Kaplan was taking a huge risk. He signed it.

"His demeanor was always the same," Henoch remembered. "He is a very straightforward guy who greatly values straight talk. The government did not promise they wouldn't indict him, but they did promise they won't mess with him. At the end of our pitch, we say, 'You gotta tell us something.' "

Kaplan began to talk in his usual monotone. The presentation lasted about ten minutes, maybe a bit longer. The story started off with Anthony Casso asking him if he could get his friends the cops to find and kill a gangster named Eddie Lino. He described meeting with Eppolito, getting him to agree to the request, obtaining the car and the guns for the cops, and listening to Casso complain that the cops were taking too long. He described the moment at New York Eye & Ear when Eppolito showed up and recounted the shooting for him as he sat there recovering from surgery on his retina. He had Eppolito saying, "Steve's the better shooter." Then he finished up with the guy with the baseball cap showing up at his doorstep with a box full of seventy thousand dollars in cash.

He hadn't yet signed a cooperation agreement with the government he so reviled, but he had opened the door, and it would no longer close. This was what everyone in that room had been waiting for—including Burt Kaplan—for a very long time. This was Burt's last chance to atone for so many sins. This was confession. This was penance. This was salvation for a man who had been trapped for too long in a rusty notion of "stand-up guys" and "rats" that was now more pervasive in movies than on the street.

"Stand-up is when someone has a problem, they take their punishment and go to jail, they don't give up anybody. They take responsibility for the crime," Kaplan said. "I was in jail nine straight years. I was on the lam two and a half years before that. In that period of time, I seen an awful lot of guys that I thought were stand-up guys go bad, turn and become informants. As I told Steve the night I left to go on the lam, I asked him if he could guarantee me that Louie would stand up and Steve said, 'Yeah, I could do that.' And after nine years, I felt that they were going to be indicted by the state on this case and I didn't think that they would stand up. I was tired of going to jail by myself. . . . My wife and my daughter had been asking me to cooperate from the first day, and I didn't do it. And my daughter adopted a boy from Russia, and he's two and a half years old now. I wanted someday to be able to spend some time with him. But I can't honestly say I did this for my family. I did it, in all honesty, because I felt that I was gonna be made the scapegoat in this case."

By October 2004, a few weeks before Steve Corso met Louie Eppolito in Las Vegas, Burton Kaplan began formal debriefing sessions with the federal prosecutor Henoch; DEA agents Manko and John Francolla; and Joe Campanella, an investigator with the Brooklyn U.S. attorney's office. The agreement could have a profound impact on Kaplan's ability to stretch his arthritic legs outside the confines of a prison yard. If he cooperated and testified and told the truth about everything, he would probably get out of jail. The government couldn't actually promise him that. They would just say they would recommend that and a federal judge would be the final arbiter, but in practical terms, when Kaplan chose to cooperate, he no longer had to worry about dying in prison.

The integrity of his testimony was criticial. Henoch arranged it so that the investigators would not ask Kaplan questions that might lead him in one direction or another. To increase their credibility, the memories had to be Kaplan's alone. Henoch's approach was to keep things simple and open, as in, "What did you do?"

In the first session, Kaplan said, "I think there's a murder you don't know about."

When they started listening to Kaplan, they already had a blueprint to work from—the words of Anthony Casso. Although he was no longer on their team, Casso had provided the FBI with the basic outline of the scheme with Kaplan and the cops, and they were now watching to see how much Kaplan could corroborate Casso. When Kaplan said he wanted to talk about a murder they didn't know about, it was clear he meant to say a murder Anthony Casso didn't know about.

His recollection of the mystery incident was both rich in detail and missing crucial facts. Kaplan did not know the name of the victim, although he claimed he once did. He called the victim a Hasidic jeweler and said he had no idea where the man was buried. He described the Treasury bill scheme with Herman and Kaplan's personal decision to have the jeweler killed without telling Casso. Much of the blame went to a dead man, Louie Eppolito's cousin Frankie Santora Jr.

Kaplan said Frankie Santora Jr. had arranged everything with the cops, but he was somewhat vague about the details of the actual killing. Frankie said he shot the Hasidic jeweler, and mentioned that the shooting occurred inside a garage in Brooklyn not far from Eppolito's precinct station house. He told the government that Frankie Jr. claimed he dumped the body "in the water," but Kaplan didn't necessarily believe that.

The investigators had to work their way back, using the information Kaplan had provided. They found Herman quickly enough and figured out Israel Greenwald was the victim Kaplan had mislabeled the "Hasidic jeweler." All they needed to do now was find Israel Greenwald's body in a garage in Brooklyn somewhere near Eppolito's old station house.

First investigator Campanella pulled the old homicide file on the still unsolved 1987 murder of Frankie Santora Jr. In the file he found Frankie Jr.'s old address book and an entry called "Pete's Towing." This was a shot in the dark, but they followed the line until they came upon Triple P Parking at 2232 Nostrand Avenue in Brooklyn. The current owner pointed them to a guy who sold it to him years ago, and two FBI agents were sent to the office of a city employee named Peter Franzone.

When Leah Greenwald received the letter from the FBI, she cried and laughed at the same time. It was so ridiculous she couldn't help herself. For eighteen years, she had lived with this kind of absurdity, which comes naturally when your husband disappears without a trace.

Leah Greenwald was a different woman from the part-time teacher she was the day her thirty-four-year-old husband, Israel, disappeared. She had raised two girls by herself, moving from house to house when she could not pay the rent, taking jobs that kept her away from her children, doing whatever was necessary to survive. First they left the brick colonial in Far Rockaway for a smaller house in Cedarhurst, Long Island. Then they left for an apartment in Brooklyn. Now they were in Queens. Income was always questionable. She was, technically, not a widow and thus unable to collect widow's benefits. Her daughters were not fatherless and thus ineligible for Social Security benefits. There was no life insurance policy to collect because, as far as the carrier was concerned, Israel Greenwald was still alive and hadn't paid his premiums in years.

More than this, she and her daughters were forced to live with questions she could not answer. What had happened? Where was her husband? In her search she had typed his full name—Israel Asher Greenwald—and his Social Security number into a person locator service on the Internet and come up with a post office box she had never known existed. When she asked the Postal Service to open the box, they said they would do it right away, as soon as she produced a death certificate.

The next best thing was a presumption of death declaration from a surrogate court. This she obtained in the summer of 2004. She took it to the Postal Service and they said that's not good enough, but a police officer can open it. She went to the local NYPD precinct and asked them for help. They said they would need a record of Greenwald's Missing Person Report, the one she'd filed days after he vanished. They put his name and other information into the NYPD computer, and nothing came up.

"As far as the New York City police were concerned, he was gone," Leah said. "Where did he go?"

Meanwhile, she had also requested all the information she could find from the FBI. She wrote a letter and asked for the entire file on the investigation into the disappearance of her husband, Israel Greenwald. And when she got their reply in the fall of 2004, that was when she decided to laugh and cry at the same time.

"The FBI wrote back and said we're very sorry, we can't help out, but we'd be happy to give you the file," Leah recalled. "Just have your husband sign the request."

TWENTY-FIVE

Las Vegas
March 3, 2005

Something seemed a little off about Lou. Corso was on time and at the right place, a high-priced ultrahip steak house called Boa at Caesar's overlooking the Strip with annoying Euro-hipster background drone and overly obsequious waiters who explain specials as if reciting the Magna Carta. Lou's daughter worked as a hostess here, which was why Lou would risk a heart attack and eat slabs of red meat in violation of his doctor's orders and common sense. But something wasn't right when Corso greeted Lou with an innocuous, "How are you?"

"All right," Lou replied, but in a monotone manner, unsmiling, terse. Not the usual garrulous Lou.

Andrea sat them at the bar and went away to do her job. Corso tried again.

"How you feeling?"

"I got a panic call from my son and I'm very, very fucking upset," Lou said. The "let me tell you a story" Lou had been secretly replaced with the "Don't fuck with me" Lou. He wasn't yelling. He wasn't throwing chairs. But Corso knew he had messed up.

"Don't call him anymore," Lou fumed. "You don't exist."

For the first time in a long time, Corso said nothing. Silence. Then he managed a whimpered "whatever," like a kid caught in a lie.

"Don't call him anymore," Lou said. "Okay? Don't call him anymore."

"Okay," Corso whined. "They were supposed to meet me."

"No," Lou said. "They're not meeting you."

"Why?"

"I told them not to."

"How come?"

"No more," Lou said. "It's an over situation. It's done. I don't want to go into it. I don't want to discuss any of it, or talk about it. Just do not reach for either of them. It's okay if the guys from California cancel out. It's fine with me. Do not worry about that. That's not going to have any bearing for me. I don't give a shit."

"Well, you seem upset."

"Right."

"Want to tell me about it?"

"No."

"Okay."

This was what is known in the inner circles of law enforcement as the dead end. Further inquiry might create suspicion, even in Lou Eppolito. It was clear what had happened. After the first drug sale at his office, Corso had tried twice to get back with Guido and Anthony to buy the Ecstasy he'd requested, but the meeting kept getting postponed. First Guido couldn't make it, then Corso had to cancel because a DEA agent had food poisoning. Anthony Eppolito must have told his father about the first drug sale, and this was why Lou was sitting in the bar at the high-priced steak house ready to murder Corso. Perhaps Corso thought at that moment of the fact that Lou carried a gun wherever he went. If so, he didn't mention it.

Corso decided it was time to change the subject.

"You were going to tell me about the license plate thing."

That was easy. Lou explained that Steve had checked the plate and it had come back to a plate that did not, technically speaking, exist. Lou would not say for sure that this meant the car was law enforcement, but there seemed to be no better explanation. It was an indicator. Sometimes cops used "unknown" to describe a plate to fool other cops.

"If I as a cop saw that plate behind me and I says, 'Who the fuck is this bum?' and I ran the plate and it says 'internal affairs, New York City Police Department,' then I say I'm in a fucking jam. They got me and I'm fucked. So now when I ran that plate and it says 'unknown,' well, is it the Police Department IAD? The FBI? Drug enforcement? Is it the terrorist task force? I don't know. But those plates aren't coming back to anything registered. If you went to a Police Department computer and said 'plate number,' it came back and said 'no hit,' which means you either got the wrong number or they're not telling you who that car is."

"Is there any way I can find out more specifics?" Corso asked. The inquiry was calming Lou down. He liked to be the guy who knew the most. Being that guy was distracting him from remembering his son selling drugs to the guy he was talking to.

"I mean you're saying it's some sort of cop car," Corso said.

"I'm saying it's gotta be some sort of car that does not want anybody to know what it is," Lou said.

"I knew it," Corso said.

The waiter appeared and gave a long presentation that indicated he'd attended several training sessions to get it just right. He called the restaurant a "great classic American steak house with some great classic American steak house stuff."

Lou asked why the filet mignon, the cut he almost always ordered, was called a Kobe filet mignon. Why wasn't it just filet mignon?

"The Kobe?" the waiter said. "It's a type of cow that's raised a certain way so that it's soft."

"In other words," Lou said, "they torture this fucking cow before they fucking kill it."

"Pretty much," the waiter said, deadpan. He was becoming part of the act. He went on and on, talking about the different cuts, and "some very nice vegetables, potatoes, and truffles."

"A little garlic in the potatoes is always going to hit the spot," he said, and he went away.

In a few moments, the waiter returned with Andrea

Eppolito, hostess. Corso ordered the most expensive item on the menu, the forty-year-aged bone-in filet.

"What do you suggest?" Lou asked his daughter.

"Well, you won't eat that. Try the bone-in filet."

In the background rap lyrics recited over "The Age of Aquarius" thumped quietly.

"I gave up soda, gave up cold cuts," Lou said. "Potato chips is good. One of them is about six times the amount I can have for the week. And the cheese is good. I can't stop."

Lou was ordering his trademark Tanqueray martini, very dry with an olive, when a blond woman who had been charged with murdering her drug-taking millionaire husband for his money but was later acquitted walked up to the table. Her name was Sandy Murphy. She was the subject of one of Lou's purported movies. She was important to Lou because if Sandy Murphy's life, as told to Lou Eppolito, was made into a movie, he would become a millionaire almost instantly, he believed.

"You ready to make your movie?" Lou asked.

"Who's going to play me?" Sandy asked.

"You know who I want to play you? Sandra Bullock."

"I know that I'm not a real feminine girl, but she's not either."

Corso sat in silence and listened while a woman who'd been accused of murder talked with a cop who allegedly worked for the Mob. He was in awe.

"She looks like you," Lou said. "I seen her in person."

"She doesn't have boobs."

"I know she's muscular," Lou said. "I seen her in person a couple of times. I gotta apologize because I never looked at your breasts. Lemme see." He laughed too loud. He then started talking about this deal and that deal and his coming trip to California and Warner Brothers and this and that and he was the old Lou, the guy with the killer pitch, the "when I was at Mangano's with Bobby DeNiro" Lou. All evil thoughts of his son doing drug deals with Steve Corso, C.P.A., were gone.

"What do you want the theme to be of the film?" Sandy asked.

"How you were treated after you were found guilty. How you endured four more years in jail for something you didn't do. The things you had to endure in that jail and you were not guilty."

"You say you want it to be an inspirational film that will inspire people?"

"No. I want it to show the degradation you had to go through. You see? Because without the people that were behind you, you were an expendable pawn."

All the bad feelings about Anthony's drug deal were gone. He was just warming up with his tales of derring-do in the NYPD, lecturing Sandy Murphy, who was from California, on the dangers of New York City in the 1970s. This ultimately degenerated into a discussion of "them" and "us."

The food arrived, the dinner was pleasant. There was more discussion of the pending movie company and all the money everybody was going to make. There was promise in the air again. If all went as planned, Lou Eppolito would officially become part of the movie-making machinery that lionized cops and crooks and made people happy for a little while on the weekends. He would become part of the big distraction. That was the plan that Steve Corso had presented in four months of filet mignons and Tanqueray martinis very dry. Lou Eppolito, Mafia cop, was finally going to make it.

"Wanna go to the bar?" Corso asked. "I'll meet you guys there."

Corso walked across the room, bathed in the lurid red-yellow light of Boa, the Euro-hipster music droning on. He walked into the bathroom and entered a stall. The FBI agents listening could hear him rustling around with his shirt as he removed the device. This was the moment Corso had been waiting for. He was finished. He wouldn't have to listen to Lou's stories about Todo and Gotti and all the rest anymore. He wouldn't have to discuss grooming practices with Stephen Caracappa. He might have to start paying for his own Pinot Noir, but that was okay. His job was done. He had infiltrated the House of Eppolito in a big way and left Lou with the impression that his world was about to change in a big way, which in its own fashion was true. He had presented what appeared to be a true story, and the ruse had worked. He could go home now and face the prospect of spending some time in prison, but not as much as he could have.

The line went dead. The final recorded conversation between Stephen Corso and Louis Eppolito lasted precisely two hours, twenty-five minutes, and eight seconds. The official end of all recorded conversations between Corso and his intended targets was logged in at 20:53:08 on March 3, 2006. The DEA, the FBI, and the U.S. attorney back in Brooklyn knew now what they had to do.

Outside of Boa in the neon glow of Sin City, the Strip was just warming up.

Las Vegas
March 9, 2005

The two men sat on the valet bench outside the restaurant in the Las Vegas Strip mall. The restaurant was Piero's Italian Cuisine, and the two men on the bench could have been mistaken for two guys who'd just finished a satisfying meal and were waiting for the kid in the white shirt and black pants to bring the Lexus around. This was not the case. The two men had no reservations at Piero's; they were waiting for something to happen. They'd been waiting for a long time.

One of the men was John Peluso, a veteran of the federal Drug Enforcement Agency. He'd been through the heroin years, the cocaine years, and the crack years, but on this night he had a different agenda. Several other men were waiting inside at the bar, including DEA agent Mark Manko. He also had been waiting a long time for this night.

It was dark, and a warm desert breeze blew in from the west when the SUV pulled into the lot.

Louie Eppolito emerged from the driver's side, Stephen Caracappa from the passenger door. Eppolito wore no jacket. He had on a black shirt, untucked, that hung away from his massive frame like a tent. His wavy hair and mustache had been dyed shiny black. Caracappa, as usual, wore a dark blue suit with white shirt and no tie. They walked toward Peluso sitting on the bench. Peluso pretended to be talking in argumentative tones to a girlfriend on his cell. As Eppolito and Caracappa approached, Eppolito glanced over at Peluso and laughed at the phone argument. Then he opened the door and stepped inside. As he did so, Peluso said, "I've got to eat soon" into the phone. On the other end was Manko at the bar, who unsheathed his .45 and began to walk toward the door.

Eppolito and Caracappa entered a long corridor that led to the hostess. Peluso came in behind them and said, "Louie Eppolito?"

Eppolito said nothing.

"DEA," Peluso said. "You're under arrest. Are you armed?"

Louie put his hands in the air and nodded. Peluso noticed that Caracappa didn't blink and put his hands up slower, then looked slowly behind him. From down the corridor came Manko and several other DEA and FBI agents holding their weapons in front of them. Peluso firmly but gently pushed Eppolito and Caracappa up against the wall, and a .45 with a round in the chamber was found in Louie's waistband. The agents confiscated the gun and cuffed both men behind their backs. One of the agents said to Eppolito, "It's been a long time coming."

"Yeah," Eppolito said. "I know."

The two detectives who'd led hundreds of handcuffed men they called perps and skels and mopes back in the glory days were themselves led out of the restaurant past all the diners who would never believe these were two of New York's Finest. They were placed in separate government sedans parked right outside the entrance, and the doors were shut.

In the car, Peluso in the front seat turned around and looked at Louie.

"You're sick," the agent said. "I know you had open-heart surgery."

"Please don't cuff me behind my back," Louie said.

"Help yourself," said the agent. "You're fifty-seven years old, you're sick, you don't need jail."

"I don't need nothing," Louie said. "I got a lawyer."

They made the eleven-o'clock news and were put in a local jail overnight. The next morning they were presented to a federal magistrate in Vegas and held pending extradition to that place where it all began so many years before. They had come far. They had weathered the storm and reinvented themselves in a city that had a hotel with a fake Empire State Building, a fake Brooklyn Bridge, a fake Statue of Liberty. That was what it was—they had moved to a place where they could believe they had escaped.

The wives showed up in court, Fran Eppolito and Monica Singleton. All of the Eppolitos were there except Anthony. He had his own problems. The DEA had arrested him that morning at the Silver Bear Way home of his parents, and picked up his friend Guido as well. Both were charged with selling crystal meth to Stephen Corso in his office on videotape.

Usually the flight from Vegas to New York takes about five hours. In this case, it took ten days. For ten days, Eppolito and Caracappa were kept away from all other prisoners while their nefarious deeds played out on television sets around the world. They were labeled the Mafia cops, after Lou's book, and their crimes were dubbed the worst case of corruption in the history of the New York City Police Department. Various investigators stepped forward to take credit for breaking a big case that was put together by a long string of investigators dating back to the mid-1980s. When cases like this occurred, things like this were inevitable.

In solitary, Louie said he got his first phone call six days after the arrest. He remembered the call well. Fran picked up and when he said hello, she immediately began crying and repeating, "Are you okay?"

"I'm okay."

"I want to know what's going on."

"Fran," Louie said, "I have to ask you a question. Did any of this hit the newspapers?"

"Are you out of your mind?" Fran hollered into the receiver. "You are bigger than the pope. I got letters coming in from Kuwait, London, England, Mexico, with your picture in the paper. It's all over the world."

"What am I being charged with?"

"Are you kidding me? Twelve murders, fifteen murders, kidnapping. I'm sick."

"I'll face it as it comes," Louie said.

"Bruce says you have a hundred thousand dollars by Friday, he'll take the case."

April 21, 2005

The sky above U.S. District Court in downtown Brooklyn was scrubbed clean of fault. Porcelain blue, not a cloud in sight. Perfect in every way. Daffodils and crocuses poked through in the park across the street like tourists, out of place. Somewhere children played in the mild spring breeze, their voices carrying through the air like a sad song. At the federal court in Brooklyn, April is the cruelest month when the sky is blue and the sound of life progressing floats on the breeze. If you are forced to be inside this court on such a day, your life is anything but progressing.

The courthouse was under construction, so visitors had to enter a jerry-rigged security checkpoint, but everybody who spent time here for a living knew the drill. Remove the cell phone, the BlackBerry, the pens, the change, the belt with the metal buckle. File through, collect your belongings, check the phone, enter the theater. That's what U.S. District Court was. Schadenfreude, gratuitous titillation, cheap thrills—this courtroom had it all. This was where John Gotti the gangster had finally been sent off to die in prison, a broken megalomaniac. Here was where the FBI busted open a nest of Nazis in the infamous "House on Ninety-second Street" case. Here the Lufthansa heist played itself out, kicking off the writing career of gangster wannabe Henry Hill. And here, on this perfect day, came the dog-and-pony show known by the media shorthand "Mafia cops."

In the raggedy park across from the courthouse, the TV vans had set up shop, parking on the sidewalk and lifting their absurd live-shot antennae to the skies. A tangle of microphones had been taped together across the street from the courthouse entrance, convenient for defense attorneys and other experts to hold forth. The lights, the cameras, the set were prepared. All that was needed was the two main characters: Louis Eppolito and his buddy for life, Stephen Caracappa.

They had arrived hours earlier, shuttled in through a back garage in a black SUV with tinted windows, front-cuffed and shackled at the ankles like all prisoners at the federal detention center on the Brooklyn waterfront. This was where they were being kept, the Mafia cops, isolated from the general population of run-of-the-mill murderers because they once were cops, a long time ago. Now, of course, their reputations were soiled by indictment and implication, accused of acts far more heinous than most of their fellow inmates. In the prison they were kept in twenty-three-hour lockdown, allowed out only one hour a day to exercise in a windowless room. Sometimes they were given their hour at 5:00 A.M. The room itself was freezing. After that, going to court was a vacation. They were driven into an underground garage and escorted up a special elevator to a holding cell to sit and wait.

The courtroom of Judge Jack Weinstein sat on the sixth floor, a soulless place made even more so by the lack of windows, the polished oak walls, and the high ceilings with glaring white lights designed explicitly to highlight every frailty in existence on the human face.

Most of the spectators were lawyers and law-enforcement agents and officers assigned to the case. The U.S. attorney's office was well represented, the Federal Bureau of Investigation, the Drug Enforcement Administration, the Brooklyn district attorney, the New York City Police Department—everybody who had even a bit part to play in this Broadway production was there. The press assembled, placed in the jury box, a fitting gesture in that so far the Mafia cops case had exclusively played itself out on TV and in the papers. They read the morning papers and tried to calculate whether they'd have time for lunch and file by deadline. All the big-city columnists showed up. There were little handwritten labels taped to the spectator rows, such as "U.S. Attorney" and "Defense Attorneys" and "Press" and "Family Members."

In that section, the front row directly behind the seats where the defendants would be placed, sat a fortysomething white woman with a Staten Island mane of black hair, pale features, and a tan pantsuit with a plunging neckline to show off her cleavage. She'd flown in from Vegas, where she helped run a restaurant. She looked very Vegas, which means she fit right in in Brooklyn. She was surrounded by an entourage whose members frequently patted her on the back and said, "Don't worry, Andrea." She was, after all, there under tough circumstances. Seeing your father arraigned on multiple charges of murder isn't something that happens to everyone.

She appeared to be aware that others were looking at her. She whispered to a friend and pointed out Jimmy Breslin in the audience. She was certainly there for her father, but it was clear she would need to stand before a camera before the day was done. Perhaps she had known this day would come. Perhaps she'd been waiting for this very moment when she would step forward and be seen by millions of people all at once. That was one of the things that made this country great. You could face adversity, your loved one could be on trial for his life, and you could face the possibility of fame both instant and notorious. She was clearly ready for her close-up.

The buzz was that this was the real deal. This was one of those cases that transcend the usual sludge that flows through courtrooms across America. This had it all—cops gone bad; a psychotic Mafia hit man; an old-school criminal who'd finally turned informant. The amount of melodrama within one story made your head spin. That was why all those TV cameras waited outside. That was why Breslin and all the rest were here. They knew that this was going to be big, and now was the time to get a piece of it.

Judge Weinstein entered the courtroom ten minutes before the scheduled noontime appearance of the Mafia cops. He had other business to attend to, a pretrial conference scheduled weeks earlier. The anonymous defendant who was unlucky enough to have his case heard just before the Mafia cops was a big man in a suit without a tie, and he looked truly bewildered at the presence of all these people in the courtroom.

Judge Weinstein did not wear a black robe but a tan suit and sat not at the bench elevated above all but ringside at a table, a few feet across from the defendant whose life he could change forever. The judge greeted the defendant by name, and lawyers for the government and the defendant talked about schedules and discovery and the usual claptrap of criminal justice. Throughout the proceeding, the press in the jury box went back to sleep, perusing the movie times and searching for their bylines. They could have been at a bus station.

Inside the well of the court, Assistant U.S. Attorney Robert Henoch and an assistant stacked red and tan binders on the table as Judge Weinstein headed up to the bench. The prosecutors were both young and earnest, with careers in the balance. They knew what this case could mean to them. The prosecutor who brought down John Gotti was now a federal judge sitting in this very courthouse. Anything was possible. They would have little to say today. Much of what the government had to say had already been said when the two cops were indicted a month earlier. This was to be merely an arraignment, where the judge asks the defendants how they wish to plead and asks them if they understand the charges filed against them. This was not the government's day. This was the first day for the other side—the lawyers for the Mafia cops—to step up to the plate.

Bruce Cutler and Eddie Hayes were famous lawyers in a city of lawyers. They knew it. Everybody knew it. The balding, ursine Cutler had helped defend John Gotti and cultivated a tough-guy persona that was made for TV. He was famous for throwing indictments in trash cans and trashing informants on the witness stand, but he hadn't had a big media case for quite some time. Hayes was a street kid from Queens who became famous as the inspiration for the defense attorney in Tom Wolfe's *The Bonfire of the Vanities* back in 1987. But that was nearly twenty years ago. Now he mostly represented the rich and famous and wore suits that cost more than the judge's law clerk made in a month.

At 11:55 A.M., a side door opened and in walked Caracappa. He was as pale as a cadaver. The skin on his face was tight on his skull. His black eyes seemed to jump around on their own, scanning the crowd and sizing up the situation. He looked like he was going to puke. He wore a tan short-sleeved jumpsuit with blue canvas laceless sneakers.

Then came Eppolito. He was enormous, barely stuffed into his tan prison jumpsuit. He seemed far more relaxed, as if he knew better than to be worried. He greeted his lawyer, Cutler, warmly, and waved to his daughter, Andrea.

The proceeding was over in a minute. Both men were asked if they'd seen the indictment, and both said yes, and then they were sent back to the holding cell and prison, and the expectation in the courtroom evaporated like the air out of a balloon.

Outside of court in the beautiful spring sunshine, Andrea Eppolito strode up to the bank of microphones like a hostess ready to check the reservation book, brushing back her mane of black hair in the breeze. She was a natural in front of the lenses. She said she would not answer questions, but she did want to show her support for her father and his friend.

"I love them very very much," she declared as the shutters whirred and clicked. "My father loved being a cop. He was so proud of all the things he did while working for the city. He protected women, he protected children, he worked with the elderly. We are so proud of him for absolutely everything. My dad made a vow to protect this city, and now it's time for someone to protect him. I'm very very confident that when this is over, he'll be coming home."

Though she said she wouldn't answer any questions, she did answer a reporter who shouted out, "How's your dad doing?"

"My father is very very strong," she said. "My father is not a man who's weak. He's doing very very well and we all love him and will support him." She then thanked the assembled rabble and then headed off across the park with the press scrum in tow like moths following a flame.

TWENTY-SIX

It was archaeology. The DEA agents and U.S. prosecutor Henoch worked their way through wedding photographs, cataloging names. Eleanor Kaplan had dredged them up from the house in Bensonhurst, and they were beginning to fade. The bride and groom were about to celebrate their twentieth anniversary. They looked like a thousand other photographs—men and women in black tie and dressing gowns, smiling at the camera, immersed in the celebration. The DEA agents and prosecutor Henoch knew what they were looking for, and they found it. The photograph showed Anthony "Gaspipe" Casso and his wife, standing next to Burt Kaplan and his wife. Another photo had Gas and Vic at the wedding, while another put Frankie Santora Jr. there. Burt Kaplan and all his gangster pals. Corroboration.

By the time the indictment was unsealed, Henoch and the team of investigators had collected an impressive amount of evidence to back up the words of Burt Kaplan. They even found Las Vegas phone books from 1995 with Louie's name in them, just like Burt said. They had tracked down anybody in Vegas who could remember seeing Burt with Louie and Steve, and they found the driver, Willie, who witnessed Burt taking an envelope of cash from Louie. They tracked down business partners out there who remembered Louie—prominent people who wanted nothing to do with this mess.

They found Frankie Santora Jr.'s daughter, Tammy, and she remembered Burt and Frankie meeting at their house in Bensonhurst. They found a tape of Louie Eppolito on Sally Jessy Raphael, just like Betty Hydell said.

They still had a long way to go. Burt was just the hub of the wheel. They needed to see if the spokes would hold up as well.

For weeks on end, Kaplan sat in a windowless room with Henoch and Manko and a rotating cast of agents. Kaplan was supposed to tell them every bad thing he had ever done, back to the flashcubes in the early 1960s. He even had to explain why he'd been put into solitary in federal prison a few months before prosecutor Henoch showed up. An inmate tried to shake him down, and so he arranged to pay another inmate to give the guy a severe beating. The feds needed to know everything.

It helped that he was telling them things they did not know. Besides revealing the Greenwald homicide, Kaplan mentioned Caracappa making a request for Christy Tic's prison records, which they were able to find. He mentioned dumping the body for the corrupt cop up in Connecticut. He told them to look in the phone books they'd confiscated from him in 1996 and they'd find the cops' telephone numbers next to the name Marco.

He even brought up a wild story Casso knew nothing about involving yet another scheme with Greenwald's former business partner Herman. This time Herman—the guy he said helped launder the Treasury bills in 1986—was supposed to get rid of some stolen checks, but the scheme fell apart, and Kaplan believed Herman was going to cooperate. Once again Burt got information on where Herman worked and lived and asked Eppolito and Caracappa to kidnap and kill Herman. Kaplan said this time when the cops pulled him over, Herman noticed a man sitting in a van watching the interchange. Herman figured out what was happening and pushed his way past Eppolito. He went running down the street waving his arms and screaming, "They're trying to kill me! They're trying to kill me!" According to Kaplan, Eppolito told him they had to abort their mission but that they had invented a good cover story. Eppolito told him he rented a van and made a point of going to the local precinct to tell them he was using the van in the filming of a movie. This way they would leave him alone.

Burt took the agents on a little road show of his life. They went to Vanderbilt Avenue, where he grew up, and Eighty-fifth Street in Bensonhurst, where he met with Casso and Lou at the kitchen table. They went to all the spots where he'd met with Lou and Steve. They drove out to Staten Island to the cemetery where Caracappa's child was buried. Kaplan said he'd met with Steve many times there. They drove up and down the Long Island Expressway looking for the right rest stop where Kaplan met with Eppolito, but Kaplan couldn't remember the correct stop. They drove to Caracappa's old address in Manhattan, where Kaplan remembered the cop and his girlfriend had cats. They got the super of the building to remember the cats, although he didn't remember the cats' names.

Much of what Kaplan told them could be tested by returning to the original record generated during Anthony Casso's brief tenure as a government witness. They pulled everything that was discovered during the original investigation of the two cops and found that much of what Kaplan said in 2005 matched what Casso told the FBI in 1994. That included Kaplan's recollections regarding the murders of Eddie Lino, Nicky Guido, Otto Heidel, Bobby Borriello, and Anthony Di-Lapi, the attempted murder of Domenic Costa, and the kidnapping of Jimmy Hydell. Both seemed to tell more or less the same stories about these crimes.

The investigators also found that years ago when Casso began cooperating, the FBI had collected printouts of the NYPD computer requests completed by Caracappa and Eppolito. It was about two inches thick and tough to read, but from this they could look for ways to back up Burt's seventy-one-year-old memory.

From the reams of printouts, they created a hand-scribbled blueprint. On one side was a list of Mob homicide victims with their dates of birth that included people named by Burt: Bruno Facciola, Jimmy Bishop, Pete Savino, Bobby Borriello, and two different Nicky Guidos. On the other side was the date when Caracappa or Eppolito requested the information from the NYPD's computer about these individuals. Nearly all of the requests came from Caracappa. Henoch scribbled "Date of Run" and circled it at the top. In a separate column, they created a "Date of Homicide" list.

In this manner, one name jumped off the page: Nicky Guido. They found the November 11, 1986, computer run for the Nicky Guido who was a phone installer, not a gangster. That Nicky Guido was murdered about a month later, on Christmas Day.

Other dates also looked interesting. Caracappa had run a criminal check on Romuel Piecyk, who was not a criminal. The investigators learned that he had done this at the same time Gotti's lawyer, Bruce Cutler, was looking for the hapless refrigerator repairman, who'd been beaten by Gotti to get him to testify in favor of Gotti's bail request. This would be difficult for Caracappa to explain because Piecyk was not under any criminal investigation and he would have no business looking up the name.

They also found that Caracappa's request on Pete Savino was entered at about the time rumors were circulating that Savino was an FBI cooperator.

Other computer runs offered no help. The request for Bruno Facciola's information came years before his death, as did the requests for Bobby Borriello and Jimmy Bishop.

The team even checked out the name Louis Tuzzio, who happened to be the son of the cop who was charged with leaking the secret license plate check to Anthony Casso so many years before. Tuzzio's son had been killed by the Bonanno crime family in an unrelated matter in 1990, and Caracappa had made a computer check on him ten years earlier.

They got some help from Burt's longtime associate Tommy Galpine. Days after the cops were arrested in Vegas, prosecutors in Brooklyn pulled Galpine out of a prison camp in Duluth, Minnesota, and flew him to Brooklyn. At first he refused to cooperate. He was forty-nine and due to get out of jail in 2011. But his two boys were growing up, and he'd been sitting in federal prison for nearly a decade. He talked with a lawyer and changed his mind.

He first met with the DEA, the FBI, and Henoch in April 2005, months after Burt had begun cooperating and long after the arrest of Caracappa and Eppolito. He had seen the arrest on the prison TV and decided then that Burt was cooperating. He had expected to hear from the FBI.

He could not identify Caracappa, but he remembered Louie well. There was the strange journey to St. Maarten to hand Louie cash in an envelope. Galpine also remembered dropping off cars that looked just like unmarked cop cars for Anthony Casso. He remembered that Casso once complained to him that the law-enforcement information Kaplan provided was too late to be any good. He remembered Frankie Santora Jr., although he didn't remember his full name. He remembered eating dinner at a Chinese restaurant in Brooklyn and seeing Eppolito's photograph on the wall. He told his wife, Monica, "That's one of Burt's cops." He remembered talking to Eppolito about opening up a Korean massage parlor, which was another way of saying he was going to open up a brothel, on Thirty-second Street in Manhattan. He remembered Eppolito giving him advice on how to avoid police detection, such as put paper on the windows so nobody can see inside and realize that a Korean massage parlor wasn't really a massage parlor.

Mostly they relied on a seventy-one-year-old man who was a memory machine. Burt Kaplan could recall details going back to the early 1970s, and was pretty good with names and dates. When he began to recall the events of his seven-year conspiracy with Anthony Casso and the cops, he was able to remember small things that made the stories seem right. Plus much of what he said—although not all—corroborated what Casso had already told the FBI. Repeatedly Henoch, Manko, and Campanella met with Kaplan, going through each criminal act one by one.

It was a sea of information, and Henoch tried to organize it by creating what he called his matrix. This was a list of the "overt acts" charged against both cops—each case of murder, each case of kidnapping, each case of obstruction of justice, each case of bribery. For each act, he created a list of witnesses and relevant evidence necessary to prove each act. Act by act, they went to work, starting with the surprise murder victim, Israel Greenwald. They had not put him in the original indictment because they did not have enough information yet to back up Burt. Mostly, they needed to find Israel Greenwald.

When two FBI agents first approached Pete Franzone in March 2005, they said they were looking into the murder of Frankie Santora Jr. This was almost true. Frankie Jr. was dead eighteen years. That was forever ago. Pete told them flat out to go away. He had a wife and a kid and wasn't interested and had nothing of interest to offer. Frankie Jr. was dead, and that was all they needed to know. Pete was out of the tow business and working for the city and was hoping to retire soon with his pension intact. The secrets he'd been carrying around for all these years needed to stay that way. When they asked him if he knew Louie Eppolito, he denied it.

"I was afraid because I didn't know if they were working for Louie Eppolito," Franzone said.

The second time the FBI visited, Franzone had a better idea about what this was all about because Eppolito and Caracappa had been all over the news as the Mafia cops. This time he admitted to the FBI that he knew Louie Eppolito, but so what? He admitted that Louie rented a parking space but claimed he knew nothing else about the guy except that he was a cop. He didn't know anything about any Mafia.

Then he got a subpoena to testify before a grand jury in downtown Brooklyn. He got out the Yellow Pages and looked under Attorneys. In the letter A, he found Alan Abramson and called him up. He explained that it was true he knew Louie Eppolito and had received a piece of paper from the government, and Alan told him to get down to the U.S. Attorney right away. Franzone did not mention to his new lawyer the incident in the garage.

In the next few weeks the FBI began to press down upon Pete Franzone's world. They told him they believed his wife had been in contact with Frankie Santora Jr.'s wife recently, but he denied this. At the end of this meeting, he began to think that maybe they were going to arrest him, so he called his lawyer, Abramson, and this time he told him everything he'd been living with all these years. When he started talking to the lawyer, he realized he would now have to tell all this to his wife.

When he met with the prosecutors, he started by describing February 10, 1986. He told them everything he could remember.

He described Eppolito sitting in the car outside the garage and the thin, dark-haired man in the trench coat who'd accompanied Santora and the Jewish man inside the garage. He described only what he'd seen and nothing more. After all these years, he was back in that garage in the waning light of a cold winter's evening.

Stepping into the garage, Franzone was confronted with a choice between fear and death. There in the dirt lay the man in a dark suit with the Jewish skullcap. The man was slumped over, in a fetal position, lying on the cracked concrete in the empty garage. Pete Franzone had some parking tickets. As a kid he once bought himself a cowboy hat at Coney Island with money he had reason to believe was stolen. Mostly Pete stayed away from the problems of the neighborhood. He was now viewing the corpse of a man murdered in his garage by Frankie and the man in the trench coat, with Louie the cop keeping watch outside. He was now officially an accessory after the fact. He figured that Frankie brought him in to see this precisely to keep him quiet.

Frankie Jr. shut the garage door and said, "You're going to help me dig this hole, and if you tell anybody, I'll kill you and your fucking family." Then Frankie Jr. walked outside the garage with the body on the dirt floor, and Frankie a minute later pulled into the lot with a white Cadillac. He parked in front of the garage with the man and cracked open the door. They unloaded steel shovels, bags of cement and lye, and jugs of clear liquid that smelled terrible. They closed the garage door, and Frankie Jr. handed the shovel to Franzone.

"The layer of cement was all broken up. We dug five feet, Frankie and I. It was almost over my head because I'm five feet, four inches tall. It was like daylight when I went in. I was afraid he'd dig deep enough to put me in there."

While he was digging, Franzone told the FBI he watched Frankie Jr. go through the pockets of the dead Jewish man. He saw him remove certain papers and a little black book. He noticed the dead man had a nice, expensive watch that Frankie did not take.

When the hole was finished, it was circular and deep. Franzone had to be pulled out. Then they pushed the man inside, and he landed in a fetal position on his front. Frankie had brought along cartons of lye and bags of cement. Frankie Jr. dumped the lye inside the hole on top of the man and told Franzone to get some water. The two men began mixing cement, then poured some on top of the man in the hole. They filled in the rest with dirt.

He was sure it was Eppolito because he remembered for a while around that time, Eppolito had paid him $150 a month to park a red Chrysler that looked just like an unmarked car at the lot for several months. He said Eppolito told him, "You don't have to put my name in the book." He remembered asking Eppolito for a favor, seeing if he could do something about a gangster named Bruno from Canarsie, who was shaking down a man who owed Franzone money. He remembered that Eppolito said he'd see what he could do and then he remembered that one day Bruno from Canarsie wasn't around anymore to bother his friend. He didn't know the man's name was Bruno Facciola and that he'd been murdered after Eppolito whispered to Kaplan that Facciola was a rat.

He described living in fear of Frankie Jr. and Louie Eppolito almost all the time, making sure to attend the sweet sixteen birthday of Frankie's daughter, Tamy, so Frankie Jr. wouldn't think he was turning into a rat. At the party, Franzone remembered seeing Louie Eppolito with the man in the trench coat from the day Franzone had to bury the man in the garage.

Two weeks after he helped bury the Jewish man in the dirt inside his garage, Pete Franzone's son was born. Frankie Jr., who had threatened to kill Franzone and his entire family, showed up with a nice bag of clothes for the baby. Pete Franzone figured they were stolen. He thanked Frankie. As soon as Frankie went away, Pete took all the baby clothes and threw them in the trash. Nevertheless, when Frankie Jr. died, he felt relief but the fear continued. He made sure to show up at Frankie's funeral "to show that I was going to keep my secret."

Then Franzone offered the FBI another surprise that neither Anthony Casso nor Burt Kaplan knew anything about. Franzone told them about the guy who was wrapped in the white tarp with the fancy knots. He didn't know the guy's name or even what happened to him. All he could really remember was the tarp and the knots.

The investigators once again were confronted with a problem: how to find a body. They decided that the ornate method of wrapping might be a way to find the guy Franzone was talking about. They requested all the crime scene photos from about December 1986 through March 1987 and began looking for a tarp wrapped in ropes.

This was how they discovered Pasquale Varriale. His was an open homicide case dating back to the predawn hours of Valentine's Day 1987. That was when Sixty-third Precinct cops got a call that a body wrapped in a tarp was lying between parked cars on Coleman Street near Avenue U, half a mile from the Nostrand Avenue garage. They tracked down the cops who found the body. One of them, Sylvia Cantwell, remembered there was a church across the street and that it was quiet.

To the team prosecuting the Mafia cops, Franzone was a major coup. He did not know Burt Kaplan, had never met the man. He had no criminal record. He was just a guy who owned the wrong garage and had lived with a secret for most of his life. On March 29, 2005, twenty days after the arrest of Eppolito and Caracappa, Franzone finished with the questions and signed a proffer agreement to help in any way. Although he had assisted in the disposal of two murder victims, he would not be prosecuted. Instead, he promised to help the team do what Leah Greenwald had been doing for nearly twenty years: find Israel Greenwald.

April 1, 2005

The FBI backhoe chipped away at the dirt inside Bay 4 at Pete Franzone's old garage on Nostrand Avenue in Brooklyn. This was the second day of digging inside the garage. They had tried the first bay and found nothing but dirt.

It was the same with the second bay, and now they were on the third bay. Franzone's memory of digging a hole for a body was precise, although his recollection of where specifically he did this was a little vague. Suddenly the backhoe appeared to hit something solid.

The crowd inside the garage came alive. Most were Emergency Services Unit cops from the NYPD or FBI agents. This was their second day digging, and they were ready to find something, anything. They had started digging by hand and graduated to the backhoe after the first day. When the backhoe hit whatever it hit, a middle-aged thin man with longish blond hair who did not look like a cop came forward and peered into the hole. He was Bradley Adams, a forensic anthropologist from the city's office of the medical examiner. His specialty was bones.

It was odd what the backhoe had hit. In the other two bays, they had gone down five feet and found nothing but dirt and a sewer line. Here several feet down was a big mass of concrete. It could be nothing, or it could be everything. They went to work chipping it out.

When they were back to dirt they resumed the dig by hand, and soon found yet another intriguing anomaly: clumps of white powder. How would white powder get four feet underground in a garage in Brooklyn? The theory was that it was lye, but Adams didn't know for sure.

"It wasn't something we had seen in the other areas," Adams recalled.

The dig slowed and became more precise. The agents and cops working the shovels now watched the dirt for signs. And then there it was—a small square of black fabric, nearly five feet below the surface of the garage floor. They dug a little more and found more black fabric.

"We felt within the fabric. I felt a shoulder blade," Adams said. "At this point it was very clear we had found what we were looking for."

When they finished and removed the body from the hole, they found what appeared to be some fabric on the top of the skull that could have been a yarmulke. There was a black scarf knotted around the neck and plastic ligature around each wrist. The shoes had plastic liners to protect from snow, and there was a Shop Rite plastic bag over the head. There appeared to be at least one gunshot wound at the top of the skull, with the bullet entering from behind. On what remained of the right wrist there was an expensive Rolex. Inside, near the left chest between the white shirt and suit jacket, there was a wallet. Inside the wallet was a large collection of credit cards and ID cards with a name that was clearly visible:

Israel Greenwald.

April 1, 2005

Leah Greenwald had finished her work for the day as an elementary school teacher and was walking up the sidewalk toward her apartment in Queens. She lived alone now. Her daughters were all grown. They'd both graduated from high school and college and gotten married and lived their own lives. In some ways the life she once had with her husband and little girls was a fuzzy memory from long ago. In other ways it was something she carried around like a weight.

The night before, she had seen on the TV news that the FBI was digging for a body at a garage in Brooklyn. There were pictures of the garage and a yellow backhoe, but the announcer had said they were looking for a Hasidic jeweler. Her husband was Orthodox, not Hasidic. She changed the channel.

As she approached the entry to her apartment building, she noticed a man and a woman standing nearby, moving toward her. The woman had brown hair and glasses and was holding up a gold badge. She said she was Geraldine Hart of the FBI. The man said he was Mark Manko of the Drug Enforcement Agency. She didn't know about the drug agency, but she did know about the FBI. They had just sent her that crazy letter asking for her husband's signature.

"I've been hoping you'd come by," Leah said, and the agent, Hart, looked startled. Leah invited them in and went to a drawer to show Agent Hart the crazy letter from the FBI. Agent Hart shook her head. Then she looked into Leah Greenwald's eyes.

"We think we found your husband's body," she said. "I

can't give you more information. We have to do some tests, but we're ninety-nine percent sure that it's him."

For twenty years Leah Greenwald had waited to hear these words. For twenty years she had no husband but could not be a widow. For twenty years her daughters, Michal and Yael, had to explain what happened to their father without knowing what happened. For twenty years the mother and daughters lived with Israel Greenwald's ghost, every day and every night, never knowing when he might come home. Most people were bound to traditional dates—birthdays and wedding anniversaries. Leah and Michal and Yeal were bound to another date—February 10, 1986, the day their view of what life was supposed to be changed forever. Now they had another date—April 1, 2005, the day Israel Greenwald returned.

"I was very very happy," Leah said. "The sadness came later."

Creating a narrative that a jury will understand about events that occurred when many were just children was no simple task. All of the murders occurred more than a dozen years ago. Some of the bad behavior dated back to the 1970s. Memories had faded. Witnesses had died. Evidence was lost. In most criminal investigations, the need for speed was crucial. Here it didn't exist. It was like trying to figure out how a dinosaur walked while scraping dirt off a fossilized femur.

Working within Prosecutor Henoch's matrix, the investigators started at the beginning, digging Eppolito and Caracappa's NYPD applications out of the department's dusty archives. Then they found Arthur Hearns, the former NYPD sergeant who had recommended twenty-six years ago that Stephen Caracappa be rejected as a recruit. They visited Hearns in upstate New York and showed him pages from his report, and he remembered.

They discovered a report from Maria Provenzano telling the DEA many years ago about the time in the late seventies when Detective Eppolito demanded money to help her find her brother's killer in Vegas. Then they found Maria Provenzano, who was married and living under a new name. She remembered the incident well and was happy to chat.

They sent investigator Campanella up to the state's Orga-

nized Crime Task Force in White Plains to see what they had
on Caracappa and Eppolito, and they found the investigation
of Eppolito selling mug shots to Sciascia Jr. in 1979. When
they checked with the state's attorney general, they couldn't
find the tape of Eppolito and Sciascia Jr., but they did find the
transcript and the property-of-the-NYPD mug shots Eppolito
stole for a fee. They found Sciascia Jr.'s lawyer and the
Brooklyn district attorney who had the case, and he agreed to
testify. They realized that the attorney from the long-defunct
special prosecutor's office, Edward McLaughlin, was now a
sitting state Supreme Court justice in Manhattan. He didn't
remember the case.

They tracked down check cashing store owner Joseph Ingrassia, who corroborated the story Gravano told about paying
Eppolito five thousand dollars in 1982 to drop his investigation
into the Fiala murder. They learned that in 1986 a detective in
the Sixty-third Precinct had interviewed a Mob associate
named Brigante, who looked just like the guy Peter Mitchell
saw dumping the body of Virginia Robertson by the highway.

Sometimes they were too late. When they started looking
at the 1991 murder of Anthony DiLapi, they could not find the
letter Caracappa allegedly wrote to DiLapi's parole officer requesting work and home address information that Kaplan had
mentioned. The Los Angeles authorities didn't keep records
like that going back that far. They did find correspondence between Caracappa and the LAPD discussing DiLapi that included address information.

Regarding Eddie Lino, they dredged up records from New
York Eye & Ear Hospital confirming that Kaplan was there
for eye surgery the day of the Lino homicide. The records
showed he had his operation the day before Kaplan said Louie
showed up bedside to describe the hit. They had less luck with
a witness named Michael, who'd been just lucky enough to
pull up behind the cops seconds after they shot Lino. About
fifteen minutes after the shooting he told the cops he'd seen a
small, skinny man jump into the back passenger door of a car
that looked like an unmarked police car that sped away. Now
he was refusing to testify because he was afraid.

Nothing was deemed insignificant. They examined Eppolito and Caracappa's vacation days and discovered that

Caracappa (although not Eppolito) had taken off the Monday, February 10, 1986, that Greenwald was murdered on Nostrand Avenue.

They examined the question of Louis Tuzzio, the scooter cop from Brooklyn who'd been suspended for pulling the license plate of an undercover police vehicle for Anthony Casso. They were able to confirm that Tuzzio knew and had contact with Eppolito, but they weren't able to determine why Tuzzio remained on the force after he was caught.

And they even connected Eppolito and Caracappa to yet another dead gangster. His name was Russell Mauro, a soldier in the Bonanno crime family. In May 1991 Mauro's body was found in the trunk of a blue Lincoln Town Car parked on a Queens street. The body was stuffed inside a green plastic garbage bag. Investigators looking into the homicide found Mauro's address book, and on the "E" page they found a beeper number next to the following entry: LOUIE EPP. The day after the Mauro homicide, Caracappa—who was not assigned to the Bonanno crime family—made a request to see the homicide records on Mauro.

What they could not figure out was how this could have gone on for so long. The New York City Police Department had been warned again and again about these two. Their names were in state organized-crime investigation files going back to the 1970s. Eppolito had stolen NYPD property from his precinct and nobody seemed to notice. Caracappa had regularly accessed the NYPD computer with its highly classified system as if he were tapping into an ATM, and nobody seemed to care. People came forward to complain, but nothing was done. They could solve murders that were years old, but they could not solve this particular mystery of governmental failure on a monumental scale.

The 1988 memo from Pat Harnett, former commander of the Major Case Squad, said it all. He'd rebuffed an inquiry into "Misuse of Informants." Seventeen years later, Harnett, now chief of police in Hartford, couldn't recall a thing: "I don't remember any issues back in those days questioning the integrity of anyone in the organized crime unit." It was like it never happened.

• • •

At first the FBI would not tell the Greenwalds much of anything. They had taken DNA samples from Leah and Yael to try to make a match with DNA taken from the skeleton in the ground. It would not be for another month that the FBI would confirm the DNA match. In the meantime, Leah and her daughters knew right away it was he.

During a trip to Brooklyn, Leah even dared to visit the spot where Israel had been buried. When she got to the decrepit garage a few blocks from Brooklyn College on a busy street surrounded by thousands of people, she realized with a start that for a time after they had been forced to leave Far Rockaway, they had lived about two blocks from this very garage. At times she had parked her car behind the very garage where her husband lay. This was her life now. Everything had significance. She would tell anyone who asked that a few nights before the visit from the FBI agent Hart and DEA agent Manko, she had a dream. In the dream she saw her husband and he told her, "I'm coming home."

The long-delayed funeral of Israel Greenwald took place in May 2005 on a Saturday in the synagogue near the Far Rockaway home they owned when they were a family as one. Dozens of friends from those many years ago showed up to pay their respects. Then they flew his body to Israel and buried him twenty years after his death in a town called Petrach Tikvah, next to the burial plot of a child who had recently died. The tombstone read in Hebrew:

Israel Asher Greenwald
    May he be remembered as son, husband, brother, and father.
    Devoted to and loved by his parents and family,
    A learned person who loved the Torah.
    A charitable and kind man, a true friend.
    Born September 2, 1951, murdered by the hands of evil people in New York on February 10, 1986, when he was thirty-four.
    Left behind him a widow and two daughters.
    His burial place was discovered by the grace of God and he was privileged to arrive to be buried in Israel.
    May his soul be remembered forever.

• • •

The day Eppolito and Caracappa were arrested at Piero's in Las Vegas, a team of FBI and DEA agents raided both of their houses and carted out boxes of material. In Eppolito's house there were twelve boxes filled with everything imaginable. Most of it was the junk of life—phone bills, canceled checks, a Men's Wearhouse credit card. They could read this stuff and learn how much he paid for an air conditioner, how often he cleaned his pool, an inventory of all his Home Depot purchases. The boxes were filled with the quotidian and the banal, revealing nothing about a man who needed to be anything but ordinary. They weren't looking for that. They were looking for the secrets.

In any house, there are bound to be secrets. In Louie Eppolito's twelve boxes, there were plenty.

Some secrets were predictable. It was clear Louie had carefully collected and preserved the proof that long ago he had once had a brief moment of fame. There was a video he'd saved of his appearance on Joan Rivers' TV show, another of an interview with Las Vegas Channel 5, and another marked "ABC Eyewitness News/NBC David Letterman." There also was evidence of his first failed marriage: a court order requiring Louie to make child support payments to his first wife, Theresa, for his estranged son, Lou Jr.

Some secrets were just strange. They found several grotesque crime scene photos, including one of a dead baby in a garbage can. Perhaps he kept this photo as some sort of inspiration. Perhaps he showed it only to special friends. They found lots of guns—all the guns Corso had seen, including the machine guns and the revolver with "Sept. 11th" carved into the handle. There were lots of photos of snakes. Louie liked snakes. He considered himself to be an expert on the subject. The photos showed Louie with snakes, Andrea with snakes, Fran with snakes. They found one photo of Louie with a group of guys labeled "EPPOLITO & A COLOMBO FAMILY CLIMBER."

Some of the material was relevant to the investigation of Eppolito's deal with Casso. There were all the clips of the newspaper stories revealing Casso's allegations back in 1994, and there were documents related to the time-share Eppolito bought into in St. Maarten—the one Galpine said he'd visited to drop off cash from Burt Kaplan.

Then they found secrets that were a little more on the serious side. What they discovered in Eppolito's Las Vegas palace was that all of the bad things they believed the two detectives had committed in their years on the force did not begin after Frankie Santora Jr. had a conversation with Burt Kaplan at Allenwood. The corruption had begun much earlier—almost from the start.

Inside Louie Eppolito's office the DEA found two complete and original folders of homicide cases he'd been involved in that had been stolen from the offices of the New York City Police Department. They wondered why this might be.

The first involved a very unlucky guy named Nick Scibetta. Nick was the brother of Salvatore Gravano's wife, Debra. When Scibetta was twenty-two years old, Gravano killed him for reasons that were never made clear. This was in 1978, long before Gravano became a major figure in organized crime. After Scibetta was reported missing and presumed murdered, Detective Eppolito began asking questions in the neighborhood about Scibetta. Investigators learned that when Eppolito learned that Scibetta was Gravano's brother-in-law, he stopped asking questions and dropped the case. Scibetta's murder remained unsolved until 1991, when Gravano admitted to it as part of his deal with the government. Now here was Scibetta's file, sitting in Las Vegas.

This raised questions about how Eppolito was able to simply take the file, which was contained in a manila folder and included NYPD reports, photos, Scibetta's dental records (important for identifying a corpse), correspondence, and newspaper clippings. Why did Eppolito have it, and how did he get it out of the NYPD without anybody noticing? The department supposedly had strict rules prohibiting the removal of internal police documents such as this.

Then there was another manila folder, this one marked Virginia Robertson. This was another case Lou worked on back in November 1986, the sad young woman whose body had been dumped by the side of the highway. Now sitting in a file in Las Vegas was the original NYPD homicide folder, including NYPD lab analysis reports, motor vehicle runs, steno notebooks, crime scene photos, property clerk invoices for evidence, notes, mug shot photos of Barry Gibbs, and a *Canarsie Digest* newspaper with an article about the death of Virginia.

When he learned of the file, DEA Supervisor Peluso remembered wondering why—of all the collars Eppolito had made or took credit for—this one was sitting in a file in his home. Like the Scibetta file, this one implicitly raised certain questions. Two DEA agents were assigned to figure it out, and they started by taking the case apart piece by piece.

A close look at the case made it clear that the defendant, Barry Gibbs, was convicted mostly due to a single witness identification. The witness claimed to have seen Gibbs pull up in a car and dump the body of Virginia Robertson on the side of the road, sprinkle some beer cans around her body, then coldly drive back onto the highway. There was none of the usual corroborative evidence—fingerprints, hair samples, skin under the fingernails, etc. This was a one-witness case, and Gibbs—a drug-ingesting loser who couldn't remember where he was half the time—was the perfect collar.

The first thing the DEA decided to do was knock on the door of that witness. His name was common, so it would be tough to find him, but that was the job. Within a week, they thought they had the right guy. He was a thin black man in his forties who worked as a clerk on Wall Street, and his name was Peter Mitchell.

July 2005

The July Fourth weekend was approaching, and Peter Mitchell had decided to take the day off from his job on Wall Street. He walked down the street to the corner bodega to pick up a pack of Newport 100s and was heading back toward his house when he noticed what he thought was an unmarked cop car parked on his Brooklyn street. It had the long antenna in the back that said "Government," and he immediately slowed his pace.

As he approached the stoop of his apartment building, two

white men who looked like cops turned and faced him. Peter said, "What do you want?"

"We're looking for Peter Mitchell," said one of them, showing a badge that read Drug Enforcement Agency. The other guy showed a badge that said FBI. Not NYPD, not private investigators for Barry Gibbs. These were feds.

Peter thought for a moment about walking away. What could they do, arrest him? For what? For keeping secrets? Maybe they could. Maybe he had broken the law when he lied on the witness stand. Maybe they couldn't know what it was like to live with that kind of secret all these years. He remembered his dream the night before. In the dream he was fighting with Barry Gibbs and Louis Eppolito and the dead woman and he woke up in a cold sweat. He thought about how many years had passed since he had first seen the body of Virginia Robertson dumped on the roadside. He thought about the white-haired man who looked like the guy in *The Godfather*. He thought about Detective Louis Eppolito.

"Yeah," he said. "You got him."

In Mitchell's living room the agents explained why they were there, but they really didn't say too much about what they expected from him. They just said they wanted to talk about what they called "the Belt Parkway incident." Could he help them in any way?

He could have kept lying. He could have said, "Barry Gibbs was the guy I saw." He could have said, "I don't even remember any of it." It was so long ago. He could have said a lot of things, and if he said he'd made it all up, that he'd lied on the witness stand, that the cop scared him into doing it, he'd have to live with that.

Peter Mitchell said, "That cop coerced me."

"Do you remember his name?" one of the agents asked, deadpan but leaning forward.

"Vittorio," Mitchell said, then he corrected himself. "No. Eppolito."

Mitchell swears the two cops jumped off the sofa. They said he should know the statute of limitations to prosecute Eppolito for obstruction of justice had run out but that they wanted to know everything.

"Do I need to get a lawyer?" Mitchell asked.

A week later Mitchell came to the office of the U.S. attorney in downtown Brooklyn, and they gave him a lawyer, Fred Cohn. They sat down in a room, and Peter Mitchell unburdened his soul for a little while, doing the best he could to recreate the events of nearly twenty years ago. He told them all about the guy with the white hair from *The Godfather* and about Eppolito telling him that Gibbs did it and he needed to put the guy in jail. He even recalled missing Gibbs in a mug shot array, and Eppolito surreptitiously showed him a Polaroid so he could nail the ID in the lineup. It was good to tell the truth, but it did not make the fear go away. It was a different fear. Before he had believed Eppolito could summon any form of law enforcement to believe Eppolito's version of events. "Who are they gonna believe: the drifter or the hero cop?" Mitchell would say. Now Eppolito was in prison facing trial. Mitchell's only fear was that he might get acquitted and then track him down and shoot him dead.

"I felt relief, but the other part of me was getting ready to go on the run," he said. "The Mob cops? For real. They kind of assured me that this was all good. I said, 'So? You gotta protect me.'"

A few days later the Brooklyn district attorney asked him to come for a little visit. By now they had been pushed out of the case by the feds, primarily because they had leaked the fact that the cops were arrested at about the same time as the arrests were going down in Vegas. This had enraged the feds, who had long ago taken control of what had been a loose case based on much supposition. When Mitchell sat down and told his story to the DA, he said their response was, "You're confused."

Nevertheless, the next day Peter Mitchell was on his way to work when he picked up a free newspaper handed out at subways and saw the smiling face of Barry Gibbs on the cover.

The story said Gibbs was a free man. The Brooklyn district attorney had asked a judge to void his conviction and release him from prison after eighteen years based on the newly released testimony. An unnamed witness had come forward to say he'd been forced to testify against Gibbs by Louis Eppolito. In the story, the reporter quoted Gibbs calling the unnamed witness a hero, but Mitchell didn't really feel like a hero. If the story had been written at the time Barry Gibbs went away to prison for a crime he did not commit, the reporter probably would have called Detective Eppolito a hero cop and maybe mentioned he was the eleventh-most-decorated cop in NYPD history.

Now the reporter just called Eppolito a Mafia cop.

TWENTY-SEVEN

It was the Ides of March. Up on the witness stand sat Burt Kaplan, recounting his life and times in front of the judge and the jury and the two defendants, Louis Eppolito and Stephen Caracappa. The courtroom was packed. Burt Kaplan was a big draw.

For months, he had been billed as the prosecution's star witness, and he had suddenly shown up the day before for a few hours at the end of the day. Today was his first full day and the word was out, so the court was full of people who sought to witness the debut of the latest Mafia informant. Deborah Kaplan was not there, nor was Burt's wife, Eleanor, or anyone else from the Kaplan family. There were defense attorneys who had nothing to do with the case and spectators who merely enjoyed the theater and spectacle. As the prosecutor Henoch worked his way through Kaplan's memory, Caracappa almost never reacted in any way. Eppolito couldn't help himself. Again and again he would shake his head in disgust, as if Burt's performance was preposterous and not something he must have expected for most of his retirement years.

On the stand, Kaplan looked like a tiny seventy-two-year-old man in a too-big blue suit with too-big owl-eye glasses that made his head seem smaller. He was nearly bald, with a silver fringe at the edges. His Brooklyn accent had not faded, and he recalled events from years ago in a resigned monotone, like an accountant going through the books. He said things like, "Stand up is what I used to be," and "I liked Steve. I still like Steve." He often said nice things about Caracappa. He never said nice things about Eppolito.

Now Henoch the prosecutor was bringing out photographs and putting them on an audiovisual device. He started with Frankie Santora Jr. smiling in a tuxedo with a group of people at Deborah Kaplan's 1985 wedding. The photo was more than twenty years old, but it did the trick. Frankie truly looked the part.

Henoch: "Were there various members and associates of yours from organized crime at that wedding as well?"

"Yes."

"Were various legitimate businessmen at that wedding as well?

"Yes."

One by one Henoch produced the photographs. There was Burt and Anthony Casso holding hands. There was Anthony with Christy Tic and Vic Amuso, with everybody smiling and nobody in jail. Burt was not asked to review any photographs that included Manhattan Civil Court Judge Deborah Kaplan.

Then there were no more photographs and it was back to the murders. First Israel Greenwald, then the attempt on Casso's life. When he recalled Anthony Casso telling him how he did not put Jimmy Hydell's body in the street so his mother could collect the life insurance, Burt's voice wavered just a bit and he needed a drink of water. He finished the day in dramatic fashion, recounting how Louie described the Eddie Lino shooting during his bedside visit with Burt at the New York Eye & Ear Hospital. The jury leaned forward, listening to every word.

May 16, 2006

The newspapers all ran the wedding photographs in garish display. Whatever belief Judge Deborah Kaplan held that only a handful of people knew her father was a gangster must have evaporated. There at the judge's wedding was the Lucchese killer, Casso, holding hands with her beloved drug-dealing father. There was a busload of these guys, all leering at the camera and looking like they owned the world.

On this day Kaplan was back in the witness stand, and now it was the defense attorney's turn. Caracappa's lawyer, Eddie Hayes, was the point man for both defendants. He and his private investigators, Dave Giordano and Jack Ryan spent months preparing for this, trying to learn everything about Burt Kaplan. Hayes spent quite some time getting Burt to admit he'd laundered two hundred thousand dollars for Anthony Casso through a real-estate deal, but Hayes had another plan in the works. He wanted to let the jurors know all about the relationship between Burt Kaplan and his daughter the judge. He figured it would rattle the guy. He did his best.

He asked Burt if he paid for his daughter's law school.

"I paid part of her way through law school," Burt corrected.

"And you adore your daughter, isn't that right?"

"I love her more than death."

Hayes went right after the wedding photos. How was it that a woman who was now a judge had half the Lucchese crime family at her wedding?

"Didn't you think when you invited table after table full of gangsters to this wedding, which I assume you paid for, that that might down the road be very embarrassing for your daughter?

"I'll tell you the truth, counselor," Burt replied, his voice rising ever so slightly. "At the time of my daughter's wedding, I didn't know what she was going to do down the road, other than become a lawyer. She might have become a criminal defense lawyer, because she clerked for Gerry Shargel."

"She might have become a criminal defense lawyer," Hayes said. "So you wanted to cover it either way? In other words, if she became a criminal defense lawyer, you wanted to make sure that she could go with your side of the family, with all these gangsters at your wedding and, if not, you wanted to make sure she could go on the other side, where the cops were?"

"I had no thoughts in my mind that my daughter would go and take the type of job that she has today," Kaplan said. "I felt she would be a criminal defense lawyer, just one side."

After the trial ended for the day, the press horde immediately started calling up the chambers of Manhattan Civil Court Judge Deborah Kaplan and reciting the exchange between Hayes and her father that seemed to imply he invited gangsters to her wedding to introduce her to future clients. She was not amused. This was the second time she had been forced to confront her family in public. The first time, she had worked out a terse but telling statement with the spokesman for the state courts. The statement was released to those in the media who sought an explanation for the unexplainable.

"I am deeply saddened to learn of the conduct attributed to my father," Deborah Kaplan said in her statement when it was first revealed that she was his daughter. "This is a painful time for me and my family and we ask that our privacy be respected."

There were many interesting aspects to this statement. First, it implied that Deborah Kaplan had no clue about any of this until the day her father testified in court. While it was likely she had no clue that he was involved in murders, it was doubtful that she had no clue he was involved with gangsters like Anthony Casso.

But after her father appeared in court and testified and her wedding photos had appeared in the newspapers, the judge had had enough. All the choices her father had made were now on display in all their lurid glory. The world now knew that Deborah Kaplan's father chose to sell counterfeit designer clothing and quaaludes and marijuana. He chose to associate with gangsters and help them kill. He chose to pay the two detectives to subvert the system she had dedicated her life to. He chose to transport the name of informants from the detectives to a killer, knowing exactly what the killer would do. He chose to stand in that Toys "R" Us parking lot with Jimmy Hydell in the trunk of a car. And finally, he chose to end the life of Israel Greenwald all by himself without any help from his gangster friend, Anthony Casso.

In her statement after her father testified in court that he invited gangsters to her wedding as potential future clients, she was simply furious.

"I am very offended that my father thought he could help my career by inviting criminals to my wedding," she stated. "My career from the beginning was as a lawyer for Legal Aid, representing indigent people. My father's actions continue to be very painful to my family."

Burt Kaplan did not read those words in the newspapers the next day. He wasn't allowed to look at the newspapers. He was kept away from the narrative he was creating as reported by the press. He was supposed to be insulated from outside influences. He was kept away from the words of his only daughter, the little girl he "loved more than death." He had come all this way and had finally made the correct choice, and in the end, he was quite alone.

April 6, 2006

Shortly before 9:00 A.M. Louie Eppolito rolled into the U.S. District Courthouse in downtown Brooklyn, his hefty bulk filling up a green-gray suit with sunflower yellow shirt and tie. He had no topcoat to ward off the forty-two-degree chill. The sky above was scrubbed blue, clouds scudding by in the brisk spring breeze. To ward off the sunshine and any optimism it implied, Lou's wife, Fran, and his daughters, Andrea and Deanna, all wore black, like widows in mourning.

It was a Thursday, day two of jury deliberations in the world-famous Mafia cop trial. The end of the road was in sight. There had been three and a half weeks of testimony. The government paraded through the fourth-floor windowless courtroom of Judge Jack Weinstein no fewer than thirty-five witnesses, with Burt Kaplan the star and all the rest appearing in supporting roles. They dropped into evidence a blizzard of photographs, 140 in all, including the sweet sixteen party of a gangster's daughter. Jurors had watched a videotape of a guy pulling a wiretap off a telephone pole and read a request for a vacation day from Stephen Caracappa. They had perused a grisly autopsy report discussing two holes in the skull of Israel Greenwald, and wondered at the significance of a 1994 Las Vegas phone book with Louie Eppolito's name right there in print.

The defense put on two witnesses and a boxful of Louie's police commendations, including an award from a synagogue in Brooklyn. The prosecution took three weeks. The defense took three hours.

The jury had begun deliberating at 9:55 A.M. on the previous day and spent all day in the small room behind the courtroom methodically working their way through the indictment. Several times they'd requested bits of specific testimony and evidence. They adjourned at 5:30 P.M., and were set to begin again this morning. On his way toward the courtroom, Louie seemed strangely ebullient, almost hyper. He told reporters, "I feel great." His wife and daughters said nothing.

The jury began deliberating at 9:30 A.M. Fifteen minutes later they requested New York Eye & Ear Hospital records of Burt Kaplan. This would indicate that they were examining the death of Eddie Lino, which was the last murder in the conspiracy count of the indictment. This implied they were moving faster than anticipated.

At 10:45 A.M. the jury requested evidence relating to the unsuccessful attempt to murder Herman, the Hasidic jeweler involved in Kaplan's unsuccessful stolen-check scheme. This was the last of the bad acts in the conspiracy in Brooklyn. That left only the final counts in the indictment, the money laundering and a drug deal in Vegas.

At noon, Judge Weinstein announced that the jury would be going to lunch at 12:30 P.M. and that he'd be heading over to nearby Brooklyn Law School to give a speech on the death penalty. He intended to return at 2:15 P.M. Louie and his family left the building for their usual lunch across the park at a diner. Caracappa and his brother, Domenic, kept to themselves in the cafeteria of the courthouse. Everybody settled in for a long lunch.

At 2:00 P.M., fifteen minutes ahead of schedule, Judge Weinstein suddenly showed up bounding into court, moving at a quick pace to take his spot on the bench. He was a judge who did things for himself. He picked up the phone on his deputy's desk and said loud enough for the entire courtroom to hear, "Ellen, have the people come down here immediately."

Somehow the air in the room seemed to shift. Defense lawyers and prosecutors and reporters who had joked during downtime now stopped smiling. The sensation of being in the moment was powerful. All verdicts are a strange combination of theater and reality, a ceremony of tension that builds to a resolution few can predict. It is a strange combination of the predictable and the unpredictable, and the revelation of a jury's decision almost always comes down like a bomb on a house. As the seats were all taken, the temperature in the room seemed to rise. It was filling up with ghosts.

There were eight ghosts in all: Israel Greenwald, Jimmy Hydell, Nicholas Guido, Pasquale Varriale, John "Otto" Heidel, Anthony Dilapi, Bruno Facciola, Eddie Lino. Most were plain gangsters, but they had rights, too. Jimmy Hydell was a tough kid. Pasquale Varriale was a street thug. John "Otto" Heidel was a safecracker. Anthony Dilapi was a thief. Bruno Facciola was a loan shark. Eddie Lino was a heroin-dealing killer. Israel Greenwald was not as bad, but a criminal just the same. The only ghost present without fault was Nicky Guido, poor Nicky Guido, the son who lived with his mother and committed no crime save having the wrong name. A courtroom full of ghosts.

Lou Eppolito lumbered into the room, fear evident in his tiny eyes. Gone was the bravado, the cockiness of a man who had convinced himself he'd done nothing wrong his entire life. This was it. He was followed by his daughters, Andrea and Deanna, and his wife, Fran, who took seats in the row directly behind him. They were his chorus, his backup team. They, too, had convinced themselves that this jury would surely see the truth and that tonight they would celebrate with champagne and a dose of bitterness at all those who had done them wrong. That had always been their expectation, but maybe they weren't so sure. Andrea fingered the rosary beads around her neck, Deanna kissed the cross around hers. Fran stared straight ahead, as if she could not bear to think about where she sat and why.

Louie slumped back in his chair at the defense table, his head tilted back, trying as hard as he could to look relaxed. Instead he looked like a good candidate for a heart attack, his face puffy, his eyes darting back and forth. Now he seemed to keep his eyes focused on the door through which the jury would enter. Surely he understood that in a few moments, everything would be different.

Steve Caracappa took his seat at the far end of the defense table, as far from Louie as he could get. His brother, Domenic, sat right behind him in the well, looking as if he was about to vomit. Steve's face was, as always, phlegmatic, a mask. He seemed at the edge of furious. Throughout the trial, he had kept to himself, barely interacting with his former partner and lifelong friend. Slowly he had come to immerse himself in anger. An hour earlier he had railed about the press's bizarre habit of taking fresh photographs each morning as he and Eppolito entered the courthouse. "It's humiliating," Steve spat. Now he sat with his elbows on the table in front of him, glaring at the same door Louie could not take his eyes off of.

In the spectator section the family members assembled. That's what they were always called—the family members. They were the reminder that real people had been murdered. Most had deliberately avoided the trial, not wishing to spend too much time in the same room with men they believed had killed their loved ones. A few had decided that this would be a moment worth experiencing. There had been a terrible price paid, but now there might be something offered in return. The families of two of the eight murder victims had shown up. Each had different expectations about what they would get out of this. The options were many: revenge, closure, a sense of justice, a measure of peace. They all needed to be here, even if they could not precisely explain why.

In the fourth row back, directly behind Louie and Steve, were the wife and two daughters of Israel Greenwald, the jeweler whose body was found in that cold, dark hole inside the Brooklyn garage. Leah Greenwald wore white, a color not associated with mourning. Perhaps she was past grief. Next to her sat the daughters, Yael and Michal. Both were proof that a terrible thing had happened. They had lived for twenty years without him, knowing nothing of his fate until recently, when these two cops had suddenly showed up in their lives. Now they knew all about what had happened to their father, information they would have to live with the rest of their lives. They sat in a courtroom in Brooklyn, waiting to see how they would feel in a few moments. They sat in silence, their arms around their mother, waiting.

Two rows behind the two cops sat Liz Hydell, sister of Jimmy in the trunk. She had chosen to wear black. During the trial she had shown up a few times. At one point she'd been sitting in a booth at the diner across from the court when Eppolito strutted by with his family. She'd looked right at him and said, "I hope you enjoy frying slowly." He'd turned pale but said nothing. Now she sat right behind him, waiting.

"I want absolute silence when the verdict comes in," Judge Weinstein said.

Andrea Eppolito made the sign of the cross.

The jurors entered grim-faced, none looking at either cop. One by one they stood in front of their assigned chairs until all had entered; then they sat down as one. The judge asked the forewoman, juror seventy-eight, a forty-year-old black woman named Sarah Cherry, to stand. She faced the judge's deputy, June Lowe. She did not look at the cops or the families or anyone else who'd packed themselves in to see how a group of twelve citizens felt about two men who'd been accused of some of the worst acts of betrayal in the City of New York's history. The deputy took out the twelve-page verdict sheet, a list of the crimes attributed to both men, presented one by one. She began to read:

"The defendants have been charged with racketeering conspiracy. You have already been instructed on the law as it pertains to racketeering conspiracy. Do you find the defendants agreed to participate in the conduct of the affairs of an enterprise? Defendant Eppolito."

In a voice barely audible, the forewoman unleashed the ghosts.

"Yes," she said.

For more than twenty years this had gone on. Maybe it started the year Eppolito and Caracappa first joined the force, way back in 1969, in a different time and a different New York. Who really knew when it began? Lou undoubtedly was the one who started it, probably doing little favors for his gangster cousin Frankie Jr., then dragging his partner, Steve, in a little later. Turning the truth upside down. Flipping all assumptions on their ear. You see the cop? That's not a cop. That's a criminal. A pretty good one, too. One who knows how to get around and can do pretty much anything he wants whenever he wants and no one will ever know. Years of secrets, of hiding what was really going on. Now it was all spilling out, right there in that courtroom in front of all those people.

Eppolito barely flinched. Behind him, his daughters appeared confused. They clearly hadn't heard what the forewoman had said. Then the deputy asked, "Defendant Caracappa?" The forewoman said "yes" again, this time a little louder, and the message began to dawn on the family Eppolito.

One by one the judge's deputy went through the list of alleged crimes, asking the forewoman if they were proved or unproved. Each time, in a tiny voice that cut like a razor, the forewoman said, "proved."

"Proved," said the forewoman, and Lou completely stopped moving. He was looking at the forewoman, but not really. His eyes saw nothing. He certainly did not look over at his partner, Caracappa, who was now glaring with open hostility at the jury. There had been a moment of shock for him, but it had quickly transformed into fury. Eppolito and Caracappa, united for eternity, watching the waves crashing in.

"Proved," said the forewoman, and Andrea Eppolito, Daddy's little girl, the one who would never give up on her hero father, began to shake her head ever so slightly back and forth. Her eyes quickly teared up, but she did not break. This was shock that was quickly replaced by rage. Her sister, Deanna, clutched the cross that hung around her neck. Their mother, Fran, seemed to be somewhere else. She stared straight ahead at her husband, a man she had known almost her entire adult life. They'd met when she was nineteen, and now here they were, nearly forty years later, and only now was she seeing what this man was really all about. There he sat, just a few feet away, revealed for all the world to see.

"Proved," said the forewoman, and in the back rows, Leah Greenwald nodded her head. Her daughters rested their heads on her shoulders. They appeared to be settling back, allowing the moment to wash them clean. It was like a door had opened and light had entered a very dark room. They did not smile, but that was unnecessary.

"Proved," said the forewoman, and Liz Hydell allowed herself a tiny half smile, almost a smirk. She kept her eyes on Eppolito. For some reason, she felt he was to blame. She had never spoken of Caracappa at all. She looked at him as she sat one row directly behind his daughters and surrendered to that little smile.

Seventy times the forewoman said "proved." Then the deputy asked if the jury had found that the conspiracy had ended before March 9, 2000, the date that would trigger the statute of limitations and make the whole thing come crashing down. "No," she said. The rest seemed superfluous, the money laundering, the drug deal in Vegas. Who really cared about that? Not the ghosts.

But Lou did care. This was the count where his son Anthony was caught on videotape selling crystal meth to the sleaziest accountant in America, Steve Corso. The guy who tried to date his daughter. That was his son in that video. He had pulled his own family into this mess. When the forewoman said "guilty" on the drug count, Eppolito flinched for the first time. His son Anthony sat a few feet away, staring at his feet.

Then it was over. When the jury was polled, each member answered with a firm "guilty" without hesitation. The secret Lou and Steve had carried with them for twenty years was no more. This jury had taken a mere ten hours to reach this decision on fifteen counts and two defendants. The judge ordered that bail for both cops be revoked immediately, and a U.S. marshal stepped forward to begin the new journies of Louis Eppolito and Stephen Caracappa.

Caracappa was immaculate in his stoicism. He did not shed a tear. He carefully removed his tie and belt and handed them to the marshal. He said, "Don't worry, Fran" to Louie's shell-shocked wife, then hugged his distraught brother, Domenic, who appeared to be crying. Caracappa's lawyer, Edward Hayes, was clearly crying. Caracappa gave him a kiss on the cheek, a quick hug, and Hayes said, "It'll be okay." As Caracappa was led away, he did not acknowledge his partner.

The marshal approached Eppolito. He handed over his tie and belt, his wedding ring, and a garish gold chain. Andrea had abandoned her tears and was now putting herself back together with mortar made of anger. "It's not over, Daddy," she blurted. On the defense table lay Louie Eppolito's life, what he for years had pointed to as proof that he was really a hero, never a criminal. It was proof that he was once a decorated detective second grade in the New York City Police Department. He was New York's Finest, or as he put it in his book of fiction, *Mafia Cop*, "one of NYPD's worthiest cops." He had carried the proof to court in a box and presented it to the jury as his only defense: two framed medals of valor, a battered wooden plaque displaying the gold shield of the detective, and a pile of paper commendations and awards, including accolades from a Brooklyn synagogue.

As Louie was led away, his family gathered up the plaques and the medals and the commendations he had collected while he was a member of the New York City Police Department. The eleventh-most-decorated cop in NYPD history. There they were, being put back into a box. One by one, they went back in the box. Once they were displayed on the wall of Louie's palace in Las Vegas, next to the photo of Louie with Robert DeNiro and Louie with Boom Boom Mancini. Once they served a purpose. Louie could look at them and remember with a smile those glory days. He could recall the heroics, the days of selfless service to the public of New York. He could tell himself he was once a fearless warrior defending the defenseless and putting the bad guys behind bars. They were real, these plaques and medals and commendations, weren't they? They meant something. They were proof, evidence.

Wasn't the story he had told himself all those years true?

"All of a sudden I'm sitting there saying to myself, 'No, no. Not happening. They're believing these lowlife vultures. There was nothing but reasonable doubt.'"

Louie Eppolito was sitting inside the Metropolitan Detention Center in his old hometown of Brooklyn remembering the moment he heard that first "proved." A few weeks before, he and his partner, Caracappa, had been sitting in that courtroom listening to that word over and over. Now Louie was an inmate and a felon. He had been convicted of some of the worst crimes imaginable. Now he was living in the same cell twenty-three hours a day with his partner, Caracappa. The Bureau of Prisons had done that. They were allowed one hour per day for exercise, and only Caracappa took advantage of his time out of the cell. Louie stayed in the cell all the time.

"This hasn't sunk in yet," Louie said. "When they started saying 'proved,' I was saying to myself, 'How could this be? Did they hear what was said? What were they listening to for these weeks?' "

His wife, Fran, had flown back to Vegas, distraught. Since the case began, she had been indicted on tax charges. They were worried that the federal government would come and take their home on Silver Bear Way, and that Fran and Caesar the dog would be out on the street. They also needed money for everything. Anthony, Lou's younger son, was still headed for trial on the drug deal with Corso. That cost money, too.

"I got bent over here like you wouldn't believe," he was saying. "What they did to me I don't think they would do to a black man in Little Rock, Arkansas, in 1963."

The best way to explain how Louie Eppolito saw things after the verdict was that he was the victim. This was done *to* him. He had done absolutely nothing wrong, except be born to a Gambino gangster. A sweeping conspiracy had occurred. Anthony Casso, sitting in one prison in Colorado, communicated secretly with Burton Kaplan, sitting in another prison in Pennsylvania to bring him down. "I thought it was a very-well-thought-out plan. It was a perfect frame. There's no more perfect a frame than this. It's so obvious that he and Kaplan had spoke about this. I was the most perfect scapegoat in history. Nobody was better than I was. I had that thing in 1984. It left a stigma that I was connected to the Mob. It was a perfect stigma."

"When this happened to me I said, 'Nah, if the federal government calls me in, I would be able to tell them everything about this case. If they had gone through the case one by one, I would have a hundred percent been able to show them that this was wrong. I thought that they knew it was bullshit. They were being fed a story from a guy who was looking to get out of jail. We're sitting here, we did not do this. I was willing to by polygraphed. For me to hear that I got up in the morning and kidnapped somebody and bring them to their death, I would rather be tried with treason than hear that.'"

In Louie's world, there was an explanation for everything.

Nicky Guido: There was no evidence that the computer check his partner, Caracappa, ran on the wrong Nicky Guido was ever passed on to Casso.

Jimmy Hydell: Jimmy Hydell's mother, Betty, saw another pair of detectives, his brother-in-law and his partner, sitting outside her house that day.

Eddie Lino: Casso said during a *60 Minutes* interview that Steve ran alongside the car shooting Eddie Lino, but witnesses at the scene saw a skinny, small guy jump into a car.

Israel Greenwald: Israel Greenwald? Never heard of him.

Barry Gibbs: Peter Mitchell, the eyewitness central to the conviction of Barry Gibbs? Never spoke with him. He said he took the NYPD file on Gibbs home "to write that story. Many many people in Hollywood had heard that story. To take this white cop to work this case? I broke my ass on that case. I worked very hard. At no time did I speak to Peter Mitchell."

He blamed the lawyers, Bruce Cutler and Eddie Hayes, especially Cutler. Louie claimed the bombastic Cutler spent more time waving his arms around and telling the jury about his eating habits and movie preferences than in defending Eppolito from life in prison. During his summation, Cutler had gone on and on about *The Bridge on the River Kwai* and Crazy Horse and the fact that he'd lost weight during the trial. His defense had consisted of not a whole lot. The high point was his red-faced eruption when he claimed Al D'Arco had suddenly remembered Anthony Casso's "crystal ball" was a couple of cops—something D'Arco had never mentioned before. The low point was when Cutler put Lou's police commendations before the jury as evidence.

"I felt we didn't do enough to show our innocence. I should have never been arrested in the first place. . . . I don't know. They're very competent lawyers. I just don't know what they were thinking. I wanted to take the stand. I begged them. I said put me up there. This is my life I'm fighting for.

We were abandoned by the lawyers. I think they felt it was a weak case and they didn't have to go into it head over heels."

The day of the verdict, the judge set a date for sentencing. Lou was aware that under the rules of federal court, he would probably hear from the judge that he would have to spend the rest of his life in prison. That was bad, but he believed he had been wrongly convicted and that he would win on appeal. What truly disturbed him about sentence day was the fact that he'd have to stand there in front of all the families of those he'd been convicted of killing and explain himself.

"I'm going to have to stand there and have people look at me and say, 'You killed my father.' 'You killed my son.' I didn't kill anybody. What am I supposed to do? They'll say, 'You don't have remorse.' These people do not have closure in this case. This case is not over."

June 5, 2006

The two detectives sat in suits in the courtroom of Judge Jack Weinstein, alone. Their families were nowhere in sight. Caracappa's brother, Domenic, was gone. Eppolito's wife and sons and daughters were gone. They had new lawyers, but it was over. They had been convicted by a jury of their peers. They would get their chance to speak, but in truth, this was a forum for the aggrieved. They were facing their day of judgment in a room surrounded by ghosts.

Again the courtroom was full of ghosts. The story of Louis Eppolito and Stephen Caracappa was mostly a ghost story, with men murdered in basements, in cars, in lonely garages. All of these men had families who became part of the ghost story without consent. Today they sat in rows of stiff wooden benches. In the back row, Leah Greenwald sat with her daughters, Yael and Michal. There was Danielle Lino, daughter of Eddie, sitting by herself. There was Jimmy Hydell's sister Liz, and his mother, Betty. There was a woman named Tina Morris, the daughter of Otto Heidel. None of these people knew each other. None had much in common. Their only link was the sudden and unexpected deaths of their sons, fathers, and brothers, caused in some manner by Detectives Eppolito and Caracappa. They were waiting their turn to speak and then to take home some form of justice.

Leah Greenwald presented the power of the victim. She had written out remarks and read in a faltering voice on the edge of collapse. Sitting just a few feet away from the judge, she held the statement and her hand trembled. She began by addressing the two cops directly without actually looking at them: "Mr. Eppolito and Mr. Caracappa."

"We were a happy family with our two beautiful and cheerful little daughters. We lived in a nice house on a quiet block surrounded by good friends and neighbors. Our door was always open to everyone," she said. "We didn't even have a death certificate, a grave to go to, for over nineteen years."

Her daughter Michal did not hesitate to look the cops in the eye. She faced them directly. It was the first time she spoke to them. Caracappa seemed to look away. Eppolito looked right back, presenting a face of concern, as if he understood exactly how she felt because he, too, was a victim.

"You did all this for what, thirty thousand dollars?" she said, not bothering to conceal her fury. "Thirty thousand dollars? That's what my father's life was worth to you?"

Otto Heidel's daughter, Tina Morris, wore sunglasses and did not bring a written statement. She was comfortable with the power of guilt but uncomfortable in front of a roomful of strangers. "I hope you two can live with yourselves the rest of your lives," she said, before hurrying off the witness stand.

Betty Hydell performed her role as the eyewitness, displaying not a hint of vulnerability. She confronted the men and pointed a finger at them. "I wasn't going to speak today but I read in the papers you had no remorse because you say you didn't do it. I saw you two that day. I was closer to you than I am today. You deny it. I just wish you stay in jail the rest of your life and you die in jail alone, the way my son died."

Danielle Lino took it one step farther. She had a sense of bitter joy. She reveled in the two detectives' fear, offering fire and brimstone, eye-for-an-eye language that tilted the balance from sadness to hatred.

"Louis Eppolito and Stephen Caracappa, I'm so happy that you have been found guilty," she said. "It is our sincere hope that you will spend the rest of your life rotting in jail. We are hopeful that you will spend eternity burning in hell."

Now it was the cops' turn. Detective Caracappa demurred, letting his new lawyer, Dan Noble, say a few words in his defense. Then it was Louis Eppolito's turn. He stood up, wearing his suit and a knotted tie, presented as a respectable, taxpaying citizen, a decorated cop, a hero in his own mind. This was his first chance to explain himself, and he seemed a little excited.

"I've been a police officer for twenty-two years. I know the feelings of every single family here," he said. He started by facing the judge, then turned to face the families sitting in the courtroom. "I would invite the Greenbergs, the Linos, the Hydells, let met tell you the rest of my story. I was not allowed to do that. I could prove to them I never hurt anybody. Never."

Suddenly a man in the third row stood up. He was a large man, wearing a black-and-white Hawaiian shirt, untucked, with round jazz sunglasses and a scraggly, unshaven face. He was pointing a finger at Eppolito and yelling as loud as he could:

"You remember me? You remember what you did?"

It was Barry Gibbs, the man Eppolito had put in jail for a crime he did not commit. He had been sitting quietly, waiting for his moment.

"I had a family, too. You remember that?"

The crowd burst into applause, and Judge Weinstein told the man to sit down or he would be removed from the courtroom. Barry Gibbs would not be stopped. He kept shouting "Eighteen years!" and "You remember!" as court officers escorted him out the door.

Decorum restored, Eppolito continued his speech, begging the families to believe his version of events and not the three weeks of trial testimony and evidence presented by the federal government.

"I can hold my head up high," he said. "I have never done any of this."

Throughout this performance, Assistant U.S. Attorney Robert Henoch could be seen slowly shaking his head from side to side in abject disbelief. It was difficult to listen to, this speech. It was so separate from reality that at one point Eppolito denied ever meeting Peter Mitchell, the eyewitness against Barry Gibbs, even though there was a mountain of paper and testimony that he, in fact, spent quite a bit of time with Peter Mitchell. Henoch waited until it was over; then it was his turn.

He talked about the United States as it was meant to be. He said there were no death squads here. Here the police were not a weapon wielded by the powerful. Here the color of law was used to protect the citizenry. The color of law is a powerful thing, and when you turn that principle on its head, then the United States is no longer the United States.

"They lied under the color of law. They kidnapped under the color of law. They killed under the color of law," he said. "They did everything they could to make sure this day wouldn't come."

At 3:25 P.M. Judge Weinstein explained the situation. Because the detectives had decided the lawyers they'd paid had done such a lousy job that they received an unfair trial, the judge was going to do something a bit unusual. He was going to tell the cops what sentence he was going to impose, but not formally impose it until the question of legal representation was resolved. There was also a pending question about the nature of the conspiracy. Had there been one conspiracy—killing people for the mob in the 1980s and early 1990s and then selling drugs in 2005—or had their been two: the killing and then the drugs later. If they were separate, that was a problem. The statue of limitations required that the government bring a racketeering case in which a crime had actually occurred in the last five years. Weinstein reserved on that one as well. Since almost everyone who had spent even a few weeks in courtrooms believed that the question of lousy lawyers was going nowhere, whatever Judge Weinstein decided to do about that other statute of limitation question would more likely than not determine where Louis Eppolito and Stephen Caracappa spent the rest of their lives. For now, he kept it simple.

"A heavy sentence is required to promote respect of the law. A heavy sentence is required to deter the conduct by any person who might be in the position of these defendants."

Life. Without parole. For the moment, the ghosts could go home.

After the funeral of her father, Israel Greenwald, Michal went back and found her diaries from when she was twelve years old. She looked for the passage she knew she had written back then to try to re-create the day her father disappeared: February 10, 1986. She was nine years old then, almost ten. She had written it down when she was twelve—just two years after the event—so she would not forget the small details that make a memory easier to carry. She was now twenty-nine years old and she had dug up the diary and found the passage.

In the diary, she wrote that she remembered standing in the doorway in her school uniform on a winter morning. The sun was out, the yellow school bus would soon arrive. Her lunch was packed, her homework finished. It was just a Monday. She remembered her father bounding down the stairs on his way out the door to work. She remembered that he stopped at the door to say good-bye and suddenly gave her a strong hug. She remembered his blue Cadillac pulling away. She remembered that when he didn't come home that night, her mother told her he probably had car problems. She remembered waking up the next morning and realizing her father was gone. This is what she wrote:

"I had no doubt in my mind that he would come back. Every movie I had seen up until then always ended happy. I knew this would be no different."

EPILOGUE

July 25, 2006

In the brightly lit courtroom of Judge Jack Weinstein, the movie was not over. The Mafia Cops sat at the defendants' table, wearing business suits that implied freedom. They were ready to walk. The judge sat at his deputy's desk, not on the bench, at eye level with Eppolito and Caracappa. They looked at him and saw a judge who had given them hope. The jury verdict, even the sentence, had not been the end of the movie. Judge Weinstein had intervened and turned the predictable on its head. The Mafia Cops were convinced that in a few moments, they would be strolling out the door, free to shop at Wal-Mart and pretend that they were normal, tax-paying citizens just like everybody else. They waited for the judge to set them free.

A month earlier, Judge Weinstein had authored an amazing decision. It was not foolish, impulsive, or rash. It was well-reasoned and made a lot of sense, and it turned everyone's world upside down. The judge was known to be a hardworking, reasonable man, renowned for his understanding of the technical aspects of the law. He was one of the few people on this planet who truly understood the rules of evidence that determined what a jury was allowed to consider when rendering its decision. In the case of Eppolito and Caracappa, he knew both the law and the facts better than most, and he had nevertheless chosen to do the thing that he had done.

On June 30, on a Friday just before the July Fourth weekend, with everyone heading out the door for sun and sand, Judge Weinstein had changed the channel. Everyone else was on the channel that said the Mafia Cops were going to prison for the rest of their lives, but Judge Weinstein knew different.

He had tossed the case. He threw it out.

He said that two men convicted by a jury of their peers of crimes most heinous were not guilty. Sort of. What he actually said was this: Both Eppolito and Caracappa were profligate men who had kidnappend and killed and subverted the system they had sworn to protect, without remorse. In return, the system had failed them. He believed that the law was more important than a single case, no matter how terrible. He had issued a decision that said there were actually two separate conspiracies, and that one of them—the one that really counted—had happened too long ago.

Judge Weinstein decided that the United States government had made a grand mistake in charging the two cops with a single conspiracy that started in 1986 with the murder of Israel Greenwald and ended in 2005 with the conspiracy to sell narcotics in Las Vegas. The government had told the jury, and the jury had agreed that this was all one conspiracy, but Judge Weinstein saw it differently. He saw two conspiracies: the murder and mayhem in Brooklyn from 1986 through 1992, when Caracappa retired from the force, and the single drug sale in Vegas in 2005—two separate conspiracies.

"Once Anthony Casso and Burton Kaplan had both been arrested, once the two defendants had both retired from the police force and reestablished themselves on the opposite side of the country," the judge wrote, "the conspiracy that began in New York in the 1980s had come to a definite close."

Judge Weinstein had decided that the first conspiracy had ended at the latest with Kaplan's arrest in 1996, many years before the statute of limitations on racketeering conspiracy kicked in. The statute said it was not fair to charge a defendant with a conspiracy that ended more than five years before the charges. Witnesses were dead. Documents were missing. Defending against such old charges is too difficult. The law was clear: The same conspiracy had to be going on within five years of the arrest or the case was no good.

On June 30, 2006, Judge Weinstein tossed out the mob murder conspiracy, and ordered a new trial on the drug conspiracy, which fell within the five-year cutoff. Betty Hydell said, "I never heard of anything so stupid." Leah Greenwald broke into tears and said, "In our minds they are guilty and we want them to be in jail." The front page of the *New York Daily News* proclaimed, GETTING AWAY WITH MURDER.

When the announcement found its way inside the Metropolitan Detention Center in Brooklyn, Eppolito was ecstatic. On the phone from prison, he was effusive in his praise of Weinstein. "He stood up like a man, and he went right for the law. I don't think I would have gotten the opportunity with another judge," Eppolito said, paying the judge the highest possible compliment. On the phone he was preparing himself to walk out of prison and fly back to Vegas and his pool and Caesar the dog. He was preparing to restore the image he had created of himself over those many years. "We won on the statute of limitations. I got a wife and kids—they look at me like I'm a god. Now they have to look at me like I'm a murderer? A multiple murderer?" Convicted by a jury and sitting in a federal prison with his partner, Caracappa, in the same cell, Eppolito had figured it all out. He had convinced himself that it was all a masterful conspiracy cooked up not just by Anthony Casso and Burt Kaplan, but also by the FBI and the New York City police department, too. "I found it," he said, declaring his independence from reality. "There are things here, when I get out, your head's going to spin around. There was always somebody behind this case pulling the strings of the marionettes. They conspired, and there's a reason for it and I know it, but I can't say it because I can't prove it."

Now in the courtroom sitting in front of the judge, this was Eppolito's last best hope. It was a sunny day in July. Eppolito was ready for some good news for a change.

The judge took the bench and appeared to listen intently to all the arguments. He even furrowed his brow at one point.

In the well of the court sat DEA Agent Mark Manko, a man who had spent two and a half years of his life on this single case. Two rows behind him sat his DEA supervisor, John Peluso, and Joe Ponzi of the Brooklyn District Attorney's office. All of them had spent countless hours pursuing these two corrupt cops, believing that the system would work in the end. A few weeks earlier Peluso had sat in a diner and discussed this system and how he still believed in it, though this case had made him wonder if it was worth it. He saw the two cops in terms that implied there were larger questions here than the simple question of why two men would do such a thing. He wanted to know why, after all that had occurred, no one had asked the New York City Police Department how they had allowed this to happen.

As he and the team collected the documents from the dusty homicide files in the NYPD's Major Case Squad, the personnel files, the state Organized Crime Task Force files, the Brooklyn District Attorney's office files, they had come to realize just how many opportunities the NYPD had over the years to make this stop before it started. It was remarkable, really.

The warning not to hire Caracappa.

The gangster background of Eppolito.

The memo about "Misuse of Informants" in Major Case so many years ago, and the commander's brush-off response.

Caracappa's computer queries with no explanations.

The audiotape of Eppolito arranging a bribe to help a gangster's son.

The fact that Caracappa was kicked off the task force.

Informants—many informants—warning the FBI and DEA and even the NYPD that Eppolito was a dirty cop.

Wiretaps that went dead once Caracappa learned of them.

The files and evidence Eppolito took with him when he retired.

The letter to the prison officials about Christy Tic.

And on and on and on.

"I want to know how this happened," Peluso said that day in the diner. "I want to know where they were. Where were the supervisors? Didn't anyone ask questions? Didn't anyone care?"

Was it a kind of institutional narcissism? Was the fear of bad publicity that powerful? Or was it simply a matter of, "We know best how to take care of our own"? Perhaps in the mid-1980s the supervisors and commanders thought they had seen the finish line in the race against the Mafia in New York and they decided it was okay to cut corners here and there. By then, there was a heavy reliance on informants to get the job done, and maybe this had colored the picture. Perhaps they had come to believe that it was better not to look too closely at the unholy alliances as long as there was a big press conference at the end of the day. Maybe the system had broken down.

And now here Peluso sat again, wondering if the system was ever going to work right. He had been there when the evidence was collected, he had been there when it was presented to the jury, and he had been there when the jury forewoman kept saying "proved" again and again. And yet here they all were, waiting to see if the Mafia Cops would walk. Manko and Peluso and Ponzi didn't glare or cringe or blanch. They also didn't smile. They waited along with everyone else, watching the demeanor of the always-confident Judge Weinstein.

The lawyers for Caracappa and Eppolito told the judge their clients should be released on bail right away. They were not a threat to the community. They were not flight risks. They were no longer convicted of multiple murders. Now they were just two cops charged with a minor league drug conspiracy charge, with Eppolito also facing a minor league money-laundering charges for the money he allegedly got from Steve Corso for the bogus FBI movie deal. Attorney Daniel Nobel called the drug case "enormously weak" against Caracappa, and he had a point. Caracappa said four words of support for Eppolito's son's pal, Guido, when Corso asked about drugs. That was about it for him. Eppolito's lawyer, Joseph Bondy, questioned the validity of bringing the case in state court if the federal drug case failed.

"Now having run the gauntlet of this prosecution, there is simply no good reason for him to be detained," Bondy said.

Eppolito leaned forward hopefully, his eyes pleading. Caracappa sat with his chin on his hands, expecting the worst.

Assistant U.S. Attorney Daniel Wenner did his routine. He said the government had appealed the judge's ruling and if

Weinstein's decision was upheld, they planned on bringing the drug conspiracy charges that could result in a sentence of forty years in prison. If that didn't work out, they planned on bringing murder charges in state court, where there was no statute of limitations problem. There were plenty of murders to work with, including some that met the tougher standards of state court that required witnesses to corroborate the testimony of coconspirators like Burt Kaplan. There were many options left. The idea that the two Mafia Cops were off the hook was laughable. The two cops still faced the possibility of dying in a cell.

The judge nodded, then sat back and began to speak.

"Since the indictment has in effect been dismissed, resting on that ground may raise serious constitutional issues," he said.

For a moment, Eppolito seemed to rise out of his seat. These were the words he had waited more than a year to hear. The United States Constitution was about to set him free.

"The court now denies bail," said the judge.

Eppolito sank back into his suit. Caracappa didn't move a muscle. He almost seemed pleased, as if he had been expecting this and it confirmed in his mind everything he had always suspected.

The judge explained how it was going to be. The narcotics crime the two faced was "serious" and could lead to forty years in prison. The weight of the evidence was "not insubstantial." This was something he'd said before when the statute of limitations issue had come up before. Before, during, and after the verdict he'd said it again and again—the evidence was "overwhelming" that Eppolito and Caracappa had conspired with Burt Kaplan and Anthony Casso to commit atrocity after atrocity. In his decision throwing out the case, he had opened by stating, "The evidence presented at trial overwhelmingly established the defendants' participation in a large number of heinous and violent crimes, including eight murders. While serving as New York City police detectives, the defendants used their badges not in service of the public, but in aid of organized crime. They kidnapped, murdered, and assisted kidnapers and murderers, all the while sworn to protect the public against such crimes."

Now he was saying it to their faces.

"The defendants are dangerous criminals with no degree of credibility," Judge Weinstein said. He denied everything. No bail. No escape. No walking out the door in clean pressed suits, able to mix in with the general population of civilians who pay taxes and expect the police to do their jobs. They were headed back to prison to watch and wait and see what the system they had mocked for so long would do to them.

Eppolito seemed to slump forward. On all his days in court, he had appeared confident. Even after the verdict, he kept his back upright, holding his own. He had always been so sure of himself. He was the Mafia Cop, a self-created man who existed in both worlds—the world of chaos and the world of order. If anybody could beat the system, it was Louis Eppolito. He was always ready for another fight. Now somehow, that Louis Eppolito seemed to have disappeared. Now Eppolito sat still while others moved about, trying not to glance over at his wife, Fran, who looked like she had just swallowed floor cleaner. He somehow seemed pale and even sad, sitting there all by himself in the brightly lit courtroom of the judge who had given so much and then taken it all away.

"Marshals," said the judge, "remove the prisoners. This hearing is at an end."

Greg B. Smith is the author of *Made Men: The True Rise-and-Fall Story of a New Jersey Mob Family*. He is an award-winning investigative reporter at the *New York Daily News* and has covered crime and the courts for more than twenty years. His work has been published in *Penthouse*, the *Boston Globe*, the *San Francisco Examiner* and the *Seattle Post-Intelligencer*. He lives with his wife and two boys in Brooklyn, New York.

THROUGH THE FLAMES
CAME THE MOORISH PHYSICIAN'S VISION:

"Your destiny, O woman, is to journey through darkness
towards the sun, like our mother, the Earth.
But the night is dark and the sun is far away.
In order to reach it—for you will reach it—
you will need more courage than has hitherto
been demanded of you.
I see many trials, and blood—much blood.
The dead line your path as the altars of fire
line the mountain roads of Persia.
Lovers too . . . but still you move on and on.
You might almost be queen,
but you will have to give up everything
if you wish to find real happiness . . ."